D1613162

The Great Powers and the Polish Question 1941-1945

The Great Powers
and the Polish Question
1941-45

A Documentary Study in Cold War Origins

edited by

Antony Polonsky

Published by the London School of Economics
and Political Science

Distributed by Orbis Books (London) Ltd.,
66 Kenway Road, London SW5 0RD

© Antony Polonsky 1976

First published 1976 by The London
School of Economics and Political
Science, Houghton Street, London
WC2A 2AE. Distributed by Orbis Books
(London) Ltd., 66 Kenway Road,
London SW5 0RD

ISBN 0 85328 046 0

Cover design by Philip Clucas

Produced by D.P.Press Ltd., Sevenoaks;
printed in Great Britain by Anchor Press
Ltd., and bound by William Brendon Ltd.,
both of Tiptree, Essex.

For my grandmother, to whom I owe more than I can ever repay.

CONTENTS

LIST OF MAPS

INTRODUCTION

'Marshal Stalin said that the Prime Minister had stated that Poland was for His Majesty's Government a question of honour. He understood that point of view. For Russia, Poland was both a question of honour, and also a question of security.'

> 2nd Plenary meeting of the Yalta Conference,
> 6 February 1945

In July 1945, Sir Archibald Clark-Kerr, the British Ambassador in Moscow, wrote to Eden describing the Polish question as 'the greatest single source of friction between the Soviet Union and her Western Allies.'[1] Churchill himself later affirmed that 'Poland. . . was to prove the first of the great causes which led to the breakdown of the Grand Alliance.'[2] In the West, it has been argued that Britain and the United States made great concessions to the Soviets both on the question of the post-war frontiers of Poland and on the composition of the Polish government. These concessions were exploited by the Soviets to impose on the unwilling Polish people a government dominated by Communists and entirely subservient to the Soviet Union. Soviet and revisionist historians have argued, for their part, that the Soviet frontier demands were reasonable both on grounds of security and in the light of the ethnic composition of the territories concerned. The Soviets made repeated attempts to come to terms with the Polish government in London, attempts which were frustrated by the anti-Soviet beliefs of the leaders of this government and their unrealistic views on the Polish Eastern frontier. The settlement reached at the Yalta and Potsdam conferences, was, in Soviet and revisionist eyes, an honest compromise on the part of the Soviet Union.

In this collection, I have tried to make it possible for the student to make up his own mind on this question. I have attempted to let the documents speak for themselves and have endeavoured in this introduction to outline the points of dispute rather than make any final judgement. The documents themselves are drawn from a variety of sources: the published American documents (*Foreign Relations of the United States*), the State Department files and the files of President Roosevelt; the Public Record Office in London, the two volume *Documents on Polish-Soviet Relations* edited by the Sikorski Institute (1961, 1967); the two volumes of Stalin's correspondence with Churchill, Attlee, Roosevelt and Truman and Vol. VII (January 1939 – December 1943) of *Dokumenty i Materiały do historii stosunków Polsko-Radzieckich* (Documents on Polish-Soviet Relations, Warsaw 1973). In addition, I have consulted the Soviet protocols of the Teheran, Yalta and

Potsdam conference in the English translation of Robert Beitzell (Mississippi, 1970). I have reproduced the documents as they stand and have made no attempt to correct or alter the punctuation and spelling, in particular the spelling of proper and place names.

I have dealt above all with the way the Great Powers handled the Polish question and have introduced material on internal Polish politics only where this seemed relevant to my general theme. The great gap in the source material lies in the making of Soviet policy. We know a great deal about how British and American policy was made and what factors affected the decisions of these two governments. But while the actions of the Soviet Government can be charted, much less is known about how that policy was made, what factors dominated its evolution and to what extent different views were expressed within the Soviet government. This makes any conclusion on the nature of Soviet policy inevitably much more tentative than similar judgements on British and American policy.

Transcripts of Crown-copyright records in the Public Record Office appear by permission of the Controllor of HM Stationery Office. I must in addition thank the Director of the Historical Office, Bureau of Public Affairs, Washington D.C., for allowing me to use maps from *Foreign Relations of the United States*. I am also grateful to Miss Janet Astley of the Map room, L.S.E. Geography Department for drawing the map facing page 15. I should further like to express my appreciation to the London School of Economics and Political Science which made possible the publication of this volume, to Dr. Jan Ciechanowski for reading and commenting on the typescript, to the archivists at the Public Record Office, London, the National Archive in Washington and the F.D. Roosevelt Library in Hyde Park, N.Y., as well as to Mr. Marian Mikołajczyk who made available to me the papers of his father. Finally, I owe a special debt to my wife, without whose help and support this work could never have been completed.

1. FROM 1939 TO THE INVASION OF THE
SOVIET UNION

Poland within the frontiers established by the treaties of Versailles and
Riga was a multinational state. In the census of 1931, only 68.9% of the
population gave Polish as their mother-tongue, 13.9% gave Ukrainian or
Ruthenian, 3.1% gave Byelorussian (another 2.2% stated they spoke the
'local' language, which meant in practice Byelorussian), 8.6% gave Yiddish
or Hebrew and 2.3% gave German. These figures were the product of a fair
amount of administrative pressure and almost certainly overstate the strength
of the Polish element. Moreover, while the Jews and Germans were
minorities dispersed over Poland as a whole, the Ukrainians and Byelorussians
were concentrated in eastern Poland where they constituted a majority of the
population. By 1939, all these minorities were seriously alienated from the
state. The Ukrainians and Byelorussians were predominantly peasants and
they resented the failure to introduce a land reform which would have
limited the rights of the Polish landlords in Eastern Poland and also the rather
half-hearted government schemes for introducing Polish colonists into these
areas. The attempt by the Polish authorities to reach a *modus vivendi* with
the predominantly nationalist and anti-soviet Ukrainians in East Galicia had
broken down by 1938 in the face of the growing dynamism of Nazi Germany.
Though the German support for Hungary's suppression of the sub-carpatho-
Ruthenian republic in March 1939 caused a certain revival of pro-Polish
sentiment, this, as events were to show, was not to prove lasting. The
Byelorussians proved more responsive to Polonization and by the late 1930's
nationalist and communist organizations were rather weaker here than they
had been in the late '20's. Indeed, it should be stressed that in both the
Ukrainian and Byelorussian areas, the desire for incorporation in the Soviet
Union was not shared by more than a minority of the population. Pro-Soviet
feelings had been drastically undermined by collectivization and by Stalin's
crushing of nationalist deviationists in the Soviet Ukraine and Soviet
Byelorussia. The German minority bitterly resented Polish attempts to
undermine the effects of 130 years of German rule in western Poland, and
many gave at least tacit support to German revisionist demands. The loyalty
of the Jews, who were particularly numerous in eastern Poland, was undermined by growing anti-semitism, especially after 1935.

These minority problems inevitably affected Polish foreign policy. Until
about 1932, the basis of this policy had been above all the alliance with
France and the defence of the Treaty of Versailles which would it was hoped,
keep Germany in check and prevent her from satisfying her demands for the
revision of the Polish western frontier. The Soviet Union was regarded with

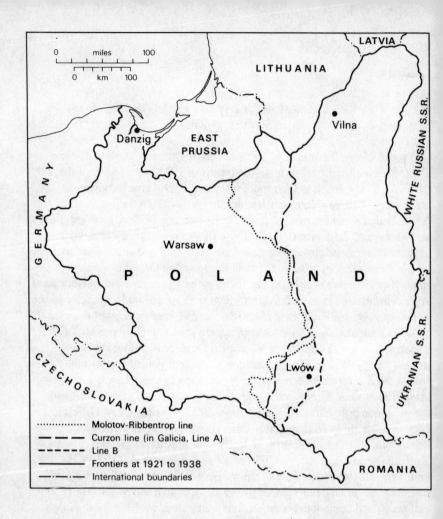

<!-- Map legend -->
.... Molotov-Ribbentrop line
– – – Curzon line (in Galicia, Line A)
- - - Line B
——— Frontiers at 1921 to 1938
–·–·– International boundaries

FRONTIERS OF POLAND

fear and suspicion, particularly after Piłsudski returned to power in May 1926, but it was believed that Polish military strength would limit Soviet ambitions. With the increasing influence of Józef Beck, who had been made Secretary of State in the Foreign Ministry in December 1930 and Foreign Minister in November 1932, this policy began to change. Both Beck and Piłsudski increasingly doubted the willingness and ability of France to maintain the Versailles system in eastern Europe. As a result, they sought an accommodation with Nazi Germany, which took the form of a German-Polish Non-Aggression Agreement concluded in January 1934. They did not take seriously the change in Soviet policy provoked by the Japanese invasion of Manchuria and by Hitler's coming to power, and refused to cooperate with the French plans for an 'Eastern Locarno' in 1934. After Piłsudski's death in May 1935, Beck took this policy still further. Although ostensibly his object was to achieve a 'balance' relation with her two powerful neighbours (a Non-Aggression Agreement had been concluded with the Soviet Union in January 1932), in practice he aligned his policy with Germany, though he rejected German proposals for an anti-Soviet alliance both before and after Pisudski's death. The parallel nature of Polish and German policy was particularly evident in 1936 and during the Czech crisis of 1938.

Following the Munich agreement, the Germans put pressure on the Poles to conclude an alliance and make some territorial concessions. The Polish government refused to accede to these terms and in March 1939 secured a guarantee of Poland's territorial integrity from Great Britain, which was converted into an Agreement for Mutual Assistance in August of that year (No. 1). Attempts to induce the Soviet Union to enter the anti-Nazi coalition failed, and the Germans were able in late August to conclude a Non-Aggression Treaty with the Soviets, which, in a secret protocol, made provision for the partition of Poland (Nos. 2, 3). This secret protocol allowed the Soviets to annex the Ukrainian and Byelorussian areas of Poland as well as some territory in which Poles were in a majority. Vilna and the area around it were to be given to Lithuania. The German attack followed shortly afterwards, on 31 August, and in the face of Polish military unpreparedness and the total lack of assistance from Britain and France, the Poles were soon in a militarily hopeless position. The Soviets then denounced their Non-Aggression Treaty on 17 September and invaded Poland, claiming that they were acting to defend 'their blood brothers, the Ukrainians and Byelorussians' (no. 4). After the defeat of Poland, a new line of demarcation between the Germans and the Soviets was established. This transferred some Polish territory west of the Bug River to Germany, in return for Germany's recognizing that Lithuania lay within the Soviet sphere of influence (No. 6). It was also agreed that no residual Polish state would be established. Subsequently, the areas annexed by the Soviets were incorporated into the Byelorussian and Ukrainian Soviet Republics (No. 9). In July 1940, the Soviets also incorporated Lithuania, Latvia and Estonia, as well as Bessarabia and Northern Bukovina.

These territorial changes were to dominate the Polish question throughout the war. The Soviets regarded the incorporation of these areas as the result of the will of the people there, and were not prepared to abandon the overwhelming part of their territorial acquisitions of 1939 and 1940. The annexation of these regions strengthened the strategic position of the Soviet Union and the Soviets may also have felt that only by the incorporation of all Ukrainian territory in the Soviet Union could they prevent Ukrainian nationalism from being exploited for anti-Soviet purposes. The Poles, for their part, regarded the Soviet annexations as entirely illegal and saw the majorities in the plebicites which had accompanied them as the produce of force and fraud. They bitterly resented the Soviet 'stab in the back' during the German invasion of Poland and regarded themselves as being at war with the Soviet Union. This did not prevent the Polish leaders from expressing more moderate views in private. After the Polish defeat, a new Polish government had been formed in France under General Sikorski which represented, for the most part, the democratic opposition to the semi-authoritarian regime which had ruled in Poland until 1939. On his visit to London in November 1939, Sikorski himself expressed the view that if Poland was unable to recover the territory she had lost to Russia, she should be compensated at the expense of Germany (No. 10). Similar views were expressed by Władysław Kulski, Counsellor at the Polish Embassy in London, in a memorandum which he submitted on 10 October 1939 and in conversation with Roger Makins, Head of the F.O. Central Department on 18 February 1940 (No. 10, note 1).

The British position on this problem was somewhat unclear. The British had criticized Poland after the First World War for extending its frontier eastwards beyond the areas in which Poles constituted a majority of the population. In October 1920, for instance, Sir Percy Loraine had told Prince Eustachy Sapieha, the Polish Minister in London, that in the opinion of the British government, the Riga frontier lay 'considerably further east than was desirable or prudent'.[3] Throughout the interwar period, the problem of the minorities in Poland had been very much in the public eye, and the view was widespread in the United Kingdom that Poland within her 1921 frontiers was not viable. The official Foreign Office position was that the British government hoped that the Poles would be able to reconcile their minorities, particularly the Ukrainians and Byelorussians, to Polish rule. Polish successes in this respect were recognized, but so, too, were Polish failures. The report on the deterioration of Polish-Ukrainian relations submitted to the Foreign Office by Chatham House in December 1937 received a sympathetic hearing there.[4] In July 1939, both Sir Howard Kennard, U.K. Ambassador in Warsaw, and Sir Reginald Leeper, Head of the Foreign Office Political Intelligence Department, expressed agreement with Kenneth de Courcy, First Secretary in the Warsaw embassy, who had written that the Ukrainians 'will take sides with anyone who offers them something. The Poles have offered them nothing.'[5]

Before the outbreak of the war, the British were seeking an alliance with the Soviet Union, and, accordingly, the secret protocol to the Anglo-Polish agreement of August 1939 stipulated that it was directed only against Germany (No. 1). British reaction to the Soviet Union's invasion of Eastern Poland was also somewhat equivocal. The statement made on 18 September, while condemning the Soviet attack, also affirmed that 'the full implication of these events is not yet apparent' (no. 5). Halifax's speech in the House of Lords on 26 October 1939 (No. 7) even seemed to excuse the Soviet annexations on the grounds that the new Soviet-German frontier approximated to the Curzon Line (which, in fact, was not really the case). This occasioned an interchange of letters between Zaleski, the Polish Foriegn Minister, and Halifax, in the course of which the British Foreign Secretary stressed that Germany was the main enemy (No. 8).

However, though the British were not prepared to commit themselves to the reconstitution of Poland within her 1921 frontiers, they were also not particularly eager to recognize Soviet annexations. British policy was outlined by Churchill in the House of Commons on 5 September 1940, following the 2nd Vienna Award which partitioned Transylvania. On this occasion, he stated that the British would not recognize any territorial changes during the war 'unless they take place with the free consent and goodwill of the parties concerned' (No. 12). At the same time, the view was widely held in the Foreign Office that the Poles would have to make large-scale concessions in the east, as can be seen by the letter from Sir William Strang, Assistant Under-Secretary of the Foreign Office, to Kennard on 16 March 1940 (No. 11).

This issue first became a question of practical politics in October 1940, as a result of British attempts to reach an accommodation with the Soviet Union. In order to induce the Soviets to pursue a policy of more benevolent neutrality towards the United Kingdom, the British were prepared to recognize de facto but not de jure Soviet 'control' of Estonia, Latvia, Lithuania, Bessarabia, Northern Bukovina and eastern Poland. When Cripps presented these proposals on 22 October, however, he offered the Soviets de facto recognition of Soviet 'sovereignty' which would have committed the British much more deeply. He was accordingly instructed by the Foreign Office to correct this mistake and also not to refer to Poland as 'the former Polish state'. In the event, the Soviets decided not to pursue these negotiations and the proposals lapsed. However, rumours about them leaked to the press and led Zaleski to write to Halifax, protesting against the acceptance of Soviet claims to eastern Poland. In his reply Halifax pointed out that what involved was de facto control and not sovereignty of these areas and assured the Poles that they would be consulted before any decision affecting their interests was taken (No. 14). Though the negotiations had proved abortive, the U.K. continued to hope for a change in Soviet policy and, to facilitate this, strong pressure was put on the Poles to moderate their more extreme anti-soviet statements.

2. FROM JUNE 1941 TO THE BREACH IN POLISH-SOVIET RELATIONS, 1945

Hitler's invasion of the Soviet Union enabled the British, acting as mediators, to achieve a temporary alleviation of Polish-Soviet hostility. The negotiations which led to the conclusion of the Polish-Soviet agreement of 30 July (No. 17) were, however, to prove protracted and difficult. There were a number of points at issue between the two governments, including Soviet recognition of the Polish government in London, the liberation of Polish prisoners in the Soviet Union and the proposed establishment there of a Polish army, but the key problem proved to be the Polish-Soviet frontier. Ivan Maisky, Soviet ambassador to the U.K., made the Soviet position clear in a conversation he had with Eden on July 4 (No. 16). The Soviets, he affirmed, were prepared to establish an independent national Polish state within its ethnographic limits, and were accordingly prepared to return to Poland some towns and districts seized in 1939.

For the Polish side, Sikorski told Bevin on 3 June that the Poles wanted the Soviets to declare their agreements of August and September 1939 no longer valid, thereby tacitly reaffirming the Riga frontier. In return, he claimed, the Poles would be prepared to compromise on their eastern frontier provided they were compensated in the west at German expense (No. 15). However, he had great difficulty in persuading his cabinet colleagues to accept this moderate line and was compelled to assume in his talks with Maisky and Eden on 11 July the more uncompromising position suggested by his Foreign Minister, Zaleski. What the Poles now wanted was an explicit recognition either from the Soviets or from the British of the validity of the Riga frontier. The furthest the Soviets were prepared to go was a statement that the Soviet-German treaties were no longer valid. The British, in order to win Polish support for the treaty, were willing on 18 July to offer the Poles a reaffirmation of their stated policy of refusing to recognize the territorial changes which had taken place in Poland since 1939 (No. 18). Under strong British pressure, Sikorski accepted this assurance, although, as Eden made clear in his statement in the House of Commons, it was not to be construed as involving 'any guarantee of frontiers' (No. 19).

The agreement was finally signed on 30 July (No. 17). According to its terms, the Soviets renounced their treaties of August and September 1939 with Nazi Germany, and provision was made for the reestablishment of diplomatic relations between Poland and the Soviet Union and the creation of a Polish army on Soviet territory. An amnesty was proclaimed for Poles detained in the Soviet Union. The signing was accompanied by the agreed exchange of notes between the British and Polish governments (No. 18) and by Eden's explanation of this exchange in parliament (No. 19).

The conclusion of the agreement was strongly opposed by the more anti-Soviet of the Poles, and three members of the cabinet resigned, General

Sosnkowski, Minister of War, the Foreign Minister, Zaleski, and Marian Seyda, Minister of Justice. One of the leaders of the opposition was the Polish ambassador in Washington, Jan Ciechanowski, who vainly sought American support to block the agreement (No. 20). The critics of the agreement argued that since the Soviet Union was likely to be defeated, or at least gravely weakened, there was no point in allowing Poland's claim to the eastern territories to be called into question. Most of them hoped (and in this their views were shared by many in the Polish government) that events would follow the same course as during the First World War:— Germany would first defeat Russia and then in turn be defeated by the western powers.

Indeed, in spite of the conclusion of the agreement, and also of a military agreement on 14 August (No. 22), the two sides remained very far apart. This can be seen in General Sikorski's radio broadcast of 31 July, in which he affirmed that the agreement 'does not permit even of the suggestion that the 1939 frontiers of the Polish state could ever be in question,' and in the Soviet reply in the leading articles in *Pravda* and *Izvestia* of 3 August (No. 22).

The signing of the agreement left the Poles in a highly nervous mood. They felt that with the entry of the Soviet Union into the war, their importance in the anti-Nazi alliance had greatly diminished, and feared, above all, British willingness to make concessions on the Polish eastern border. Their uneasiness also manifested itself in apprehensions that article 2 of the Atlantic Charter, which laid down that territorial changes should be in accord with the 'freely expressed wishes of the peoples concerned' would be used to deprive them of territorial gains at German expense, which they had demanded as early as November 1940.[6] These fears were first expressed by Count Raczyński, the Polish Ambassador in London to Eden on 18 August 1941 (No. 23), and repeated in his letter to the British Foreign Secretary on 25 August, when he asked the British to make a gloss on the Atlantic Charter to meet Polish doubts. Eden refused to do this at meetings on 29 August and 15 September, and suggested that the Poles make clear their objections to the wording of article 2 at the Inter-Allied Meeting to be held in London on 24 September. This was accordingly done by the Poles (No. 23, note 3).

Moreover, the course of Polish-Soviet relations did not run particularly smoothly, in spite of the agreement. Although an amnesty was proclaimed on 12 August, the Poles complained that large numbers of their nationals were not being released, and that, in particular, 8,000 of the 9,000 officers who had been taken prisoner in 1939 had not been freed. The failure to fulfil the terms of the amnesty was repeatedly raised by the Poles and also by the British, who submitted an *aide-memoire* on this subject to the Soviets on 3 November (No. 25). The Soviets merely replied that all Polish prisoners had been released.

The formation of the Polish army in the Soviet Union also ran into difficulties. This was not surprising, considering the vagueness of the Polish-Soviet Military Agreement of the 14 August which had laid down that while this army was to be 'part of the armed forces of the sovereign Republic of Poland,' it was to be 'subordinated operationally to the High Command of the U.S.S.R.' Polish units were not to be moved to the front until they were ready, and were to operate in groups not smaller than divisions and 'in accordance with the operational plans of the High Command of the U.S.S.R.' Inevitably, given the desperate military situation of the U.S.S.R., both Poles Soviets began to think that this Polish force could play a large role in developments in the Soviet Union if the military position deteriorated. The precedent of the Czech Legion in 1918 could not have been far from the thoughts of either side. Sikorski, indeed, in his instructions of 1 September to Gen. Anders, Commander of the Polish forces, specifically excluded using Polish troops on the Soviet western front (No. 24) and on 19 September even told Averell Harriman, who was about to visit the Soviet Union to discuss American military supplies, that in the event of a Soviet defeat 'the Polish Army might become the leading element ' (No. 24, note 1). The Soviets, too, became increasingly unwilling to supply the Polish forces, though following British and Polish intercessions (Nos. 25, 26), Stalin told Stanisław Kot, Polish Ambassador to Soviet Union, that there was no limit to the size of the Polish army which could be created in the Soviet Union.

A major factor in continuing tension was clearly the unsettled state of the Polish-Soviet border. On 10 November, the Poles submitted a note to the Soviets complaining that Polish citizens in the Soviet Union of non-Polish nationality (Ukrainians, Byelorussians and Jews) were being conscripted into the Red Army (No. 27). The Soviets replied that they had made a major concession in recognizing as Polish citizens Poles from eastern Poland since 'the frontier is not yet settled.' An inconclusive exchange of notes on this subject followed (No. 27, note 1).

It was in order to settle these problems that Sikorski paid a visit to the Soviet Union in early December 1941. His talks there did achieve a temporary improvement in relations, and a Declaration of Friendship and Mutual Assistance was signed on 4 December (No. 29). In the course of his meetings with Stalin (No. 30), Sikorski, to the chagrin of Gen. MacFarlane, Head of the British Military Mission in Kuibyshev, abandoned the British and Polish plan of withdrawing the Polish army in the Soviet Union to Persia, where it could be more easily supplied. Stalin, in return, agreed that this army could be concentrated in Uzbekistan and could be expanded to 5–7 divisions. It was also to remain together as an army rather than have its divisions separately deployed. Stalin further assured Sikorski the release of the Poles would be fully carried out. In addition, he suggested that the two sides come to an informal agreement on the Polish-Soviet frontier, and, according to Sikorski, who was prone to exaggeration, assured the Polish leader that 'Lwów should again become part of Poland' (No. 30, note 4). Poland was also to annex east Prussia. Sikorski refused to discuss the problem, and has since been strongly criticized for this, on the grounds that he could at this time by concession of the frontier question, have assured the future of his government. In fact, though by now convinced that the Soviet Union would not be defeated, Sikorski was also sure that it would be gravely weakened by the war. The dominant powers in the post-war world would be the United Kingdom and, above all, the United States. A close alliance with the Soviet Union was thus, in his view, quite unnecessary.

This improvement in relations did not prove lasting. One source of tension was the plan for a Polish-Czechoslovak confederation, which the Soviet Union came increasingly to feel was imbued with an anti-Soviet character. Proposals for a union of this type had first been made public in the Polish-Czechoslovak Declaration of 11 November 1940 (No. 13). Several coordinating committees were established, and a measure of agreement was reached on a common foreign policy, in spite of differences of attitude towards Hungary and, above all, the Soviet Union (No. 26). Nevertheless, the position of the two sides remained distant, quite apart from the unresolved frontier dispute between them over the Teschen (Cieszyń) district. To the Czechs, the 'establishment of European equilibrium' in Beneš' phrase, required close cooperation between the Soviet Union and the proposed confederation (No. 26, note 1). The Poles, for their part, as Raczyński made clear in his interview with the *Sunday Times* on 11 January (No. 32, notes 1, 2), thought that Russia could not compensate for the weakening of France, because 'though sufficiently tough and persevering in defence, she is less able to take action outside her own borders.' This role could only be taken by a central European bloc, created around a Polish-Czech confederation. A component part of this bloc was to be an independent Lithuania. This interview was strongly attacked by Bogomolov, Soviet Ambassador to the Polish government, in a note to the Poles on 23 January (No. 32).

Another source of Soviet irritation was Polish hostility to the proposed Anglo-Soviet Treaty. A treaty, which would guarantee to the Soviet Union its 1941 frontiers with the exception of the Polish-Soviet border, which was to be settled by direct negotiations between the two states concerned, was first proposed by Stalin during Eden's visit to Russia in December 1941.[7] Eden, on his return to London, failed to persuade Churchill to accept Stalin's suggestion. The Prime Minister criticized the view that, if victorious, the Soviets would anyway establish these frontiers on the grounds that it underestimated the probable strength of the U.S.A. and the British Empire.[8] Eden reiterated his views to the War Cabinet on 28 January[9] and by March 1942 Churchill, under the influence of British defeats in the Far East and the stalemate in the western desert, came round to the view of his Foreign Secretary.[10]

Sikorski first objected to the proposed treaty in a conversation with Eden on 19 January when he stressed the Polish interest in an independent Lithuania, and argued that 'the Soviet Union might not be in such a strong position in, say, six months time as they were today.'[11] He developed these

arguments in conversation with Eden on 3 March (No. 33), and also in a
letter to Eden on 9 March and a conversation with Churchill on 11 March. On
the latter two occasions he emphasized the Polish interest not only in the
Baltic States but also in the Rumanian claim to Bessarabia and Northern
Bukovina.[12]

He also tried to enlist American support for his views during his trip to
the United States during the second half of March, and he found a
sympathetic hearing, since State Department policy, as outlined to him by
Welles, was against dealing with territorial questions in Europe until the end
of the war (No. 34). The State Department also shared the Polish suspicion
of Soviet motives and felt that the proposed treaty would merely
stimulate further Soviet demands. In spite of the American and Polish
objections, Eden nevertheless decided to push on with the proposed treaty,
cabling Halifax on 26 March 1942 that 'I cannot take the risk of keeping
Anglo-Russian relations in a state of suspended animation any longer.'[13] He
was particularly concerned about the possibility of the Soviets concluding a
separate peace with the Germans.

The Poles now reaffirmed their reservations on the treaty in notes on 27
March and 13 April and in Sikorski's conversation with Eden on 16 April.[14]
The British stated their position in Eden's letter to Raczyński of 17 April
(No. 36). It rejected the Polish contention that the recognition of Soviet
claims to the Baltic States, Bessarabia and Northern Bukovina infringed the
Anglo-Polish Agreement of August 1939. The Poles were conceded to have a
case in respect of Vilna. This letter was followed by a further exchange of
views (No. 36, notes 1, 2) in which the British tried to reassure the Poles.

In the event, American objections, which were made clear by the U.S.
Ambassador, Winant, to Eden on 24 May[15] and Soviet intransigence during
the negotiations in London in late May, led the British to abandon their
original conception of the treaty. On 23 May, a new treaty which provided
for a post-war alliance against Germany and omitted all mention of frontier
claims was proposed to the Soviets and accepted by them on the 26th
(No. 37). This was welcomed by the Poles as a great triumph (No. 37, note 2)
but as Bogomolov told Ripka, the Czech Foreign Minister, on 24 July, the
Soviets had noted how the Poles had allied themselves with 'circles in
England who are not sympathetic to the Anglo-Soviet treaty.'[16]

One casualty of the deterioration of Polish-Soviet relations was the Polish
army in the Soviet Union. During their talks in December 1941, Stalin had
agreed with Sikorski that 30,000 Polish troops should be allowed to leave
the Soviet Union (No. 30, para. 6). On 25 March, the Soviets unexpectedly
gave permission for 40,000 troops to be evacuated to Iran, pleading
difficulties of supply. It was certainly true that the U.K. was experiencing
severe difficulty in providing equipment for the Polish troops because of
the war in the Far East (No. 35, note 2). By April, some 31,000 soldiers and
12,000 dependents had left the Soviet Union for Iran. On 14 May, Stalin

refused to allow any further recruitments of Poles, even for transfer out of the Soviet Union, and on 16 June, the Poles were informed that no more evacuations could take place. Two weeks later Stalin asked the British if they would also take the three divisions remaining in the Soviet Union and, by the end of August, they too had left for Iran, numbering altogether some 44,000 soldiers with 26,000 dependents. Biddle, the U.S. Ambassador to the Polish government, attributed this development to the growing Soviet suspicion of Polish behaviour (No. 35), while Eden concluded later that the agreement of July 1941 had probably attempted too much and could not convert enemies into allies over-night (No. 35, note 3).

Plans for Polish-Czechoslovak confederation also ran into difficulties. Already on 18 May 1942, the Czechoslovak State Council had passed a resolution criticizing the Polish demands for an independent Lithuania, and affirming that Czechoslovak policy 'cannot overlook a circumstance which the Soviet Union regards as fundamentally essential to its state policy and security' (no. 38). Both Molotov and Bogomolov now put pressure on the Czechs to choose between the Poles and the Soviets (No. 39, No. 39 note 1) and on 12 September Beneš told Bogomolov that the Czechs were not prepared to pursue the confederation 'in the face of direct Soviet opposition' (No. 39, note 1). Beneš indeed decided to seek a simple treaty with the Poles rather than the more ambitious plans for a confederation (No. 40). When putting this new policy to Raczyński on 23 November he stated, however, that this could only be concluded if Polish-Soviet relations improved and the Teschen question were settled (No. 40, note 1). This effectively killed the idea of a confederation. Its failure has been ascribed to the 'first Soviet veto.'[17] This is hardly correct. No Soviet veto was required, for when faced with a choice between the Soviets and the Poles, there was no question what the Czechs and above all, Beneš, would decide (No. 65).

From now on, Polish-Soviet relations deteriorated steadily. Conflict was first caused by Soviet claims that the extensive network of delegates which had been established under the auspices of the Polish embassy to deal with the welfare of Polish deportees (No. 30, para. 15) had been exploited for purposes of espionage. In July, the Soviets had accordingly closed these offices in a number of towns. Subsequently a sizeable proportion of the delegates were arrested and charged with espionage. The Soviets seemed to respond to Polish, British and American representation on behalf of these men (No. 40). Nevertheless, on 19 October, Henryk Sokolnicki, Polish Minister Plenipoteniary to the U.S.S.R., informed Standley, the U.S. Ambassador that 'of the 109 Polish relief workers still under arrest, 15 have been found not guilty and are being released, 78 have been found guilty of offences serious enough to warrant immediate deportation and 16 have been found guilty of such serious crimes that they have been turned over to the courts for prosecution.'[18]

Matters took an even more serious turn early in 1943. On 16 January, the

Soviets informed the Polish Embassy in the U.S.S.R. that they were withdrawing the 'privilege' whereby people of Polish origin from eastern Poland
were regarded as Polish citizens (No. 43). This new harder line was probably
occasioned by General Sikorski's visit to the U.S.A. and by his attempts to
obtain American support for Polish territorial ambitions in the East (No. 42).
What the Soviets were trying to do was, it seems, to put pressure on the
Poles to compel them to accept the Curzon Line. The Poles responded to the
Soviet note on 26 January, and also appealed to Eden and Churchill to protest
against Soviet behaviour, which they feared would otherwise be followed by
additional unilateral actions at Polish expense. Further exchanges merely
emphasized the gulf dividing the two sides (No. 43, note 1). In this situation,
Sikorski told Eden on 22 January that he was contemplating a new trip to
the Soviet Union and was willing to discuss the Polish-Soviet frontier. Eden
told him that in his view neither the U.K. nor the U.S.A. could support 'any
particular frontier' (No. 44).

A certain relaxation of tension followed a meeting between Tadeusz
Romer, Polish Ambassador to the U.S.S.R. and Stalin on 26 February
(No. 45, note 1), but a further exchange of notes, in which the rival claims
to the disputed territories were set out, soon embittered the atmosphere
(Ibid). Certain members of the Polish embassy in the U.S.S.R. were even
moved to ask Sir Archibald Clark-Kerr, U.K. Ambassador, to intercede with
Romer and persuade him to discuss the frontier question with the Soviets
(No. 45). The Foreign Office instructed him that this was not advisable and
that the border should be settled by direct negotiations between the two sides,
(No. 45, note 2). At the same time, Maisky again informed Eden that the
Soviets wanted the Curzon Line as the Polish eastern frontier (No. 46).

Sikorski's belief that the U.S. was prepared to support Polish claims in the
east was fundamentally misconceived. It is true that the official U.S. position
still upheld the view that no territorial committments should be made before
the peace conference. But already on 9 December 1942, Ray Atherton, Acting
Chief of the European Affairs Division of the State Department, had argued
in a memorandum that the Riga frontier should not be reestablished (No. 42,
note 3). In conversation with Eden on 16 March 1943 Roosevelt claimed that
if the Poles were compensated in the West, they 'would gain rather than lose
by agreeing to the Curzon Line' (no. 47). He also argued that the Big Three
should agree on a solution of the Polish problem, which they would then
impose on the Poles. These statements led Sir Orme Sargent, Deputy
Undersecretary in the Foreign Office, to advocate the adoption of such a
policy in a memorandum of 15 April (No. 49, note 1). There was a certain
amount of support for his views in the Foreign Office but the course he
advocated was rejected by Eden on 26 April. What primarily worried the
British, as Cadogan made clear in a minute for Churchill on 31 March, was
that the Poles would break off relations with the Soviets (No. 42). He
suggested that Churchill intervene with Stalin, requesting him, in the

interest of allied unity, to adopt a friendlier line towards the Poles, and also to allow certain groups of Poles to leave the Soviet Union.

3.   FROM APRIL 1943 TO THE TEHERAN CONFERENCE

In the event, it was the Soviets who broke off relations with the Poles. There seems today little doubt that the 4,000 bodies discovered by the Germans in a mass grave near Katyn in Byelorussia were murdered by the Soviets in April or May 1940.[19] They formed part of a group of approximately 15,000 prisoners-of-war, mostly officers, non-commissioned officers and reservists, who had been held at the three camps of Starobielsk, Kozielsk and Ostashkovo, which were known to have been wound up in April 1940. The Poles had pressed the Soviets repeatedly after July 1941 to reveal the whereabouts of these men and had received a series of evasive answers. If the men *had* been killed by the Germans, nothing would have easier than to make this public. There were many close personal and family ties between these men and the Polish government and army in the west, and the news of the mass grave created an almost uncontrollable wave of anger and despair in Polish circles. In these circumstances, the Polish reaction, though understandable, lent itself to exploitation by the Russians. This was particularly true of the Polish government's appeal to the International Red Cross to investigate the German accusations (No. 50) and the statement by General Kukiel, Minister of National Defence, which, with considerable circumstantial evidence, implied that the Soviets were responsible (No. 50, note 2). These actions gave the Soviets the opportunity to accuse the Poles of collaboration with the Nazis, who had also proposed a Red Cross investigation, and provided them with a pretext for breaking off relations with the Polish Government on 25 April (Nos. 51, 53). The Soviet campaign against the Polish government was certainly carefully orchestrated, and their seems some truth in the argument of Biddle, the U.S. Ambassador to the Polish government, that it had been prepared as early as the despatch of the Soviet note on 16 January (No. 43). The Soviet objective, in his view, was the advancement of 'Russian post-war "security-frontier" aspirations in the "middle-zone" ' (No. 60, note 1). The frontier question was certainly not far from Soviet thoughts throughout this controversy. Molotov, in his note announcing the breach of relations even accused the Poles of undertaking 'this hostile campaign against the Soviet Union . . . for the purpose of wresting from it territorial concessions at the expense of Soviet Ukraine, Soviet Byelorussia and Soviet Lithuania' (No. 53).

In this tense situation, the British attempted to restrain both sides. They put pressure on Sikorski to withdraw his appeal to the Red Cross and to curb the more anti-Soviet elements in the Polish press. At the same time, Churchill appealed to Stalin not to break off relations and to allow certain categories of

Poles to leave the Soviet Union (No. 52). The Soviets exploited this uneasy response very successfully. While denying rumours that they were intending to establish a rival Polish government in Moscow, they allowed the pro-Communist Union of Polish Patriots, which had been functioning in Moscow since early 1942, to set up a Polish Division to fight on the eastern front. They also stressed that they could not contemplate re-establishing relations with the Polish government in London until it had been radically reorganized and the 'pro-Hitler elements' within it removed. As a concession, Stalin stated that he was prepared to allow 'Polish citizens' to leave the Soviet Union (Nos. 54, 55, 56, 58).

Eden broached with Sikorski on 7 May the question of a reconstitution of his government. Sikorski agreed to consider establishing a smaller 'war-council' within his cabinet, but retracted his views following a violent attack on the Poles by Vyshinsky on the same day (No. 56, note 2). The British came to the conclusion that further pressure on the Poles could well lead to Sikorski's fall and Churchill accordingly wrote to Stalin on 12 May that while 'the Polish Government was susceptible of improvement,' changes in it should not appear to be the result of foreign pressure and could only be achieved slowly (No. 57). The Americans were even more opposed to putting pressure on Sikorski to remodel his government. Welles wrote to Biddle on 16 June that 'it would be unfortunate for a precedent to be established under which the government of one United Nation could successfully force changes in the composition of another government of the United Nations' (No. 60).

Indeed the only major changes in the composition of the Polish government which occurred in 1943 further complicated the resolution of the problem. These took place after the tragic death of General Sikorski in an air crash, almost certainly accidental, off Gibraltar on 5 July 1943. Sikorski was probably the only individual with sufficient stature to persuade the Poles in the emigration to accept major concessions in order to achieve some sort of *modus vivendi* with the Soviets. He was replaced as Prime Minister by Stanislaw Mikołajczyk, a shrewd and able Peasant Party politician but one who inevitably could not command the respect which Sikorski had enjoyed. Mikołajczyk realized the weakness of his own position in the emigration and tried vainly to curb the powers of the army and consolidate his control over the London-directed underground in Poland before accepting office (No. 62, note 3). He was also unable to prevent the appointment of General Sosnkowski as commander-in-chief, an office which had large powers under the 1935 constitution, which was still, with some modification, in force, and the holder of which was the designated successor of the President. Sosnkowski had resigned from the government in protest against the conclusion of the Polish-Soviet agreement in July 1941, and his personality was anathema to the Soviets, as Bogomolov made clear to Harrison of the Central Department on 8 July. This was not however realized by the British who gave Mikołajczyk little support in his attempts to curb the power of the army and prevent Sosnkowski becoming commander-in-chief. Eden, for instance, saw no reason to oppose Sosnkowski's appointment, arguing that '. . . If the Russians want to make trouble for the Poles they will do so whoever is appointed Commander-in-Chief' (No. 62, note 4).

Neither the British nor the Americans were very sure how to deal with the Polish-Soviet breach. According to Beneš, Roosevelt, whose position on this question was studiously vague, told him in early June that he regarded the Curzon Line as 'an equitable solution to the Polish-Soviet frontier problem.' He also asked Beneš to intercede with Stalin on this basis (No. 59). The British were thinking along similar lines, and on 22 June, G. H. Wilson of the Foreign Office Central Department submitted a memorandum on 'Russia's Western Border' in which he argued, much on the line of Sargent's earlier memorandum (No. 49, note 1) that an improvement in Polish Soviet relations would only prove lasting if agreement on the Polish eastern frontier were reached. He favoured a border based on the Curzon Line, with Poland receiving Lwów and also being compensated at German expense in the west (No. 61, notes 1, 2). The minutes on this memorandum showed that this policy now commanded considerably more support than in April. Eden for intance, expressed approval for letting the Soviets know that the U.K. favoured the Curzon Line, excluding Lwów as the Polish-Soviet frontier (No. 61).

The official position of the two western allies was much less yielding. It was decided to undertake a joint approach to the Soviets, but considerable delay was incurred before this could be done because of the difficulty of harmonizing the British and American positions. The British wanted a simple approach confined to the issue of the evacuation of Poles from the Soviet Union. To raise larger issues would, the Foreign Office claimed, inevitably lead to a discussion of the question of frontiers, which was not regarded as desirable. While strongly agreeing that the border problem should not be raised, the Americans felt that no progress could be made without discussing broader issues, in particular the definition of Polish citizenship. Both sides also agreed that the time was not yet ripe to bring pressure on the Poles to reconstruct their government (No. 63, note 1).

The joint approach was finally made at a meeting with Stalin and Molotov on 11 August. Clerk Kerr in an introductory statement stressed the importance of an improvement of Polish-Soviet relations for the solidarity of the anti-Hitler coalition (No. 63, note 2). The British note requested the Soviets to allow certain groups of Poles to leave the Soviet Union, including 'Polish nationals from Western Poland whose nationality is not in doubt' (No. 63, doc. 1). The U.S. *aide-memoire* suggested that the Soviets permit relief and welfare work for the Poles to be carried out by Soviet organizations. A compromise was proposed on the citizenship question whereby 'racial Poles' from eastern Poland would be recognized as Polish citizens and 'non-racial Poles' would be permitted to opt for Polish or Soviet citizenship. The emigration of certain categories of Poles from the Soviet Union was also requested (No. 63, doc. 2). In addition, the U.S. Ambassador made a statement affirming American opposition to discussing frontier questions at this stage of the war (No. 63, doc. 3).

The Soviet response was not encouraging. Stalin and Molotov listened to the British and American expositions 'in complete silence', and refused to be drawn into discussion (No. 63, note 2). The Soviet reply came only on 27 September in the form of identical notes to the U.K. and U.S. embassies in the Soviet Union, and it was chilly in the extreme (No. 70). It argued that relations had been broken off because of the hostile policy of the Polish government, and its attempt 'to use the German fascist provocation concerning the Polish officers killed by the Hitlerites in the Smolensk District for the purpose of wringing from the Soviet Union territorial concessions at the expense of the interests of the Soviet Ukraine, Soviet Byelorussia and Soviet Lithuania.' Molotov claimed that Soviet agencies were providing relief for the Poles, and that the Polish welfare organization had been closed down because of the espionage activities of some of its members. He reaffirmed the Soviet position on the citizenship question but conceded that people who were non-residents of 'western Ukraine' and 'western Byelorussia' but who found themselves in these areas in September 1939 could leave the Soviet Union.

The failure of this approach stimulated the British to move towards the policy advocated in the Wilson memorandum (No. 61, notes 1, 2). At the Quebec conference in late August, Eden discussed the problems of the Soviet western frontier with both Harry Hopkins and Cordell Hull. He told Hopkins that the forthcoming meeting of Foreign Ministers in Moscow would not be able to make any progress unless some advance was made towards meeting Soviet demands in their western border. Hopkins replied that Roosevelt agreed with the British position on this question and that 'he [Hopkins] had said as much to Molotov and Litvinov also', but that he was reluctant to authorize Welles to act on this position (No. 64). Roosevelt, as ever ambiguous, was indeed to tell Welles and Hull on 5 October, that the new Polish-Soviet border should be 'somewhat to the east of the Curzon Line' (No. 72). Eden submitted to Hull a memorandum arguing in favour of joint action by the U.K. and U.S. to accept the Curzon Line as the Polish-Soviet frontier and also to recognize the other western frontiers of the U.S.S.R. as they had been before German invasion in 1941. This, it was argued would induce the Soviet Union to be more cooperative on other questions, above all the coordination of military planning and the handling of the German question. The proposed agreement on frontiers was to be informal and the Poles would need to be persuaded of its desirability (No. 67). In discussion, Hull claimed that 'considerable concessions' were being demanded, and that these should be made dependent on the Soviets 'falling in with out ideas on the general post-war plan' (No. 66).

Eden made his first approach to the Poles on 9 September. On this occasion Mikołajczyk objected to the proposed frontier settlement on the grounds that the Poles could not abandon Vilna. He argued that no government-in-exile could make major territorial concessions and claimed that the issue was not fundamentally one of frontiers, but was concerned with 'the survival of Poland as an independent state' (no. 69). The issue came before the war cabinet on 7 October when Eden presented two memoranda, one on the Soviet western border and a second on relations between the London-directed underground and the Soviets. The first set out the case, on similar lines to that presented to Hull at Quebec (No. 67), for meeting Soviet demands on their western frontier, while pressing the Polish claim to Lwów. In return, it was hoped that the Soviets would resume relations with the Polish government and prove cooperative over the difficult problems of the Polish underground, the Poles in the Soviet Union and Soviet support for the Union of Polish Patriots (No. 71). The dangers of a clash between the underground and the advancing Red Army were stressed in the second memorandum (No. 71, note 2). During the cabinet dicusssion, the Prime Minister argued that while the Poles 'could not be forced' to accept the proposed agreement, the British should strongly urge them to do so (No. 71, note 5). Eden however had been unable on 6 October to persuade the Poles to allow him to discuss the frontier question at Moscow (No. 73) and informed the cabinet that he would not, therefore, raise this issue.

As a result, no progress was made at Moscow on the Polish problem. The question was discussed on 29 October, when both Hull and Eden stressed to Molotov the importance for the allied cause of the reestablishment of Soviet Polish relations. Molotov replied that what was needed was a Polish government 'with friendly intentions towards the Soviet Union'. He expressed strong suspicion of General Sosnkowski, and when asked for the Soviet view on whether arms should be supplied by the British to the Polish underground replied that arms should only be given into safe hands. 'Were there any safe hands in Poland?' (No. 79).

British pressure on the Poles was stepped up after Eden's return from Moscow. Though the Poles still adopted an inflexible position in public, in private they proved much more accommodating. On 17 November, for instance, Raczyński told Eden that while a government-in-exile could not make territorial concessions, if 'Poland's friends were to tell the Government that they must accept such and such a settlement in order to safeguard the future of Poland, this would create a new situation' (No. 75, note 1). Similar statements had been made by Raczyński to Orme Sargent on 12 November and by Romer to Richard Law, Minister of State at the Foreign Office, on 17 November (No. 75, note 1). Eden therefore told the war cabinet on 17 November that the Polish government 'might . . . welcome the imposition of a settlement by the British and United States Governments' (No. 75). On 22 November, Mikołajczyk himself informed Eden that the Poles would welcome

the British taking up with the Soviets all aspects of the Polish problem,
including the border dispute (No. 76).

British policy was summed up in a memorandum, drawn up by Orme
Sargent, which Eden presented to the war cabinet on 22 November (No. 77).
This again proposed the Curzon Line as the Polish eastern frontier, with
Lwów remaining in Poland. The Poles were to receive compensation in the
west, in the form of Danzig, East Prussia and the Opole district of Silesia. In
return the Soviets were to re-establish diplomatic relations with the Poles and
make arrangements to allow the Polish Government to return to Poland and
'be associated with the Administration of the country as soon as military
necessities permit'. The Poles were to be encouraged to join the proposed
Soviet-Czechoslovak treaty. Sargent argued that the Soviets would not be
justified in demanding changes in the Polish government or in calling for the
entry of members of the Union of Polish Patriots into the Polish cabinet. Eden
opposed the memorandum's advocacy of British participation in the proposed
tripartite treaty on the grounds that this was 'an engagement in an area where
our influence cannot be great' (No. 77, note 1).

It has sometimes been argued that the Polish question was settled at the
Teheran conference, but in fact no clear agreement was reached there.
Churchill did inform Stalin on 28 November that he favoured moving Poland
westward in order to give the Russians the western frontier they wanted
(No. 78, doc. 1). Roosevelt made similar remarks in a private conversation with
Stalin on 1 December, while also informing him that he could make no public
statements on this question, since he would need the votes of 'six to seven
million Americans of Polish extraction' (No. 78, doc. 2). The Soviets claimed
during the Moscow talks of October 1944 that Roosevelt had committed
himself to the Curzon Line, leaving Lwów to Poland. This was denied at that
time by Harriman (No. 78, doc. 2, note 1). Though the truth of the matter
cannot yet be known, the Soviets were convinced that such statements had
been made, and, as Eden was latter to comment, 'Roosevelt's remarks were
hardly calculated to restrain the Russians.'[20]

At the more detailed discussion of the question on 1 December, the
differences between the two sides were clear. Agreement was reached that the
Curzon Line should be the Polish eastern frontier, and Churchill asserted that
'he was not prepared to make a great squawk about Lwów' (No. 78, doc. 3).
The Poles were to be compensated in the west 'up to the line of the Oder'.
Churchill then proposed a formula whereby the frontiers of the Polish state
would be agreed on and the Poles pressed to accept. He clearly envisaged that,
in return for securing the agreement of the Poles to the proposed frontiers, the
Soviets would re-establish relations with the Polish government in London.
Stalin did state that he was prepared to accept Churchill's formula, provided
the Soviet Union received Königsberg, which meant also half of East Prussia.
But he had also made it clear earlier in discussion that 'he was by no means
sure that the Polish government-in-exile was ever likely to be the kind of

government it ought to be.'

4. FROM THE TEHERAN CONFERENCE TO THE FALL OF MIKOLAJCZYK (NOVEMBER 1944).

The sort of settlement the Soviets wanted from the Poles became clearer with the signing of the Soviet-Czechoslovak treaty on 12 December 1943. This contained a protocol making provision for 'some third country which borders on the U.S.S.R. and the Czechoslovak Republic and which forms the object of German aggression in the present war' to accede to the treaty if it so desired (No. 79). This could only mean Poland, as was made clear in speeches by Beneš and Ripka after the signing of the treaty (No. 79, note 2). Zinchenko, Counsellor at the Soviet Embassy in London, asked Wilson of the Central Department on 22 December whether he thought the Poles would accede to the treaty.[21] He also made it clear 'speaking personally and unofficially' that the Soviets would like the Poles to approach them directly and that this would enable all major problems between them to be solved. The frontier question 'could wait until the end of the war' though the position of Sosnkowski might cause difficulties. Zinchenko was particularly insistent that 'for reasons of prestige', the Soviets did not want intermediaries, since 'the relations between the Soviet Union and one of its neighbours was of direct interest only to the two countries concerned'.

Churchill left Teheran eager to settle matters, cabling from Marrakesh, where he was convalescing, to Eden on 20 December that he should 'open the Polish frontiers' question with the Poles' (No. 80). The Foreign Secretary did not have much success in winning over Raczyński and Mikołajczyk, with whom he discussed the issue on 17, 20 and 24 December (No. 81, also note 1). He was able to induce the Poles to produce an *aide-memoire* stressing the Polish desire for co-operation between the London controlled underground (A.K.) and Soviet partisans in Poland, which was intended to answer the Soviet accusations at Teheran that the A.K. was killing members of pro-Soviet underground groupings (No. 81, note 3). The chances of a settlement were further diminished by an exchange of polemics between the Polish and Soviet governments, sparked off by a Polish government statement issued when the Red Army crossed the 1921 frontier of Poland (No. 82 and note 3). The Foreign Office exercised strong pressure on the Poles to moderate the tone of their notes of 5 and 14 January, and was disappointed by the harsh tone of the Soviet rejoinder of 17 January.

This exchange of notes had several consequences. It seems to have led the Soviets to adopt a harsher line towards the Poles. As Gusev, Soviet Ambassador to the U.K., told Eden on 17 January, the Soviets 'had offered the Curzon Line and the Poles had not accepted' (No. 82, note 3). Accordingly, they now began to demand the reorganization of the Polish government and the elimination from it of elements 'hostile to the Soviet Union' (No. 83, note 3). Encouragement of the pro-Soviet forces in Poland was also stepped up. On 22 January, a 'Polish National Council', representing the various groupings of the pro-Soviet underground, was established. Soon afterwards, this body made contact with the Union of Polish Patriots.

The Poles also became aware that a purely negative stance was no longer possible and in the last sentence of their note of 14 January they requested the British and American Governments to mediate between them and the Soviets (No. 82, note 3). Cordell Hull thus instructed Harriman on 15 January to approach the Soviets and 'ask them to give the most favourable consideration to the Polish offer to discuss outstanding questions' (No. 83). The Soviet response was chilly. Molotov replied to Hull on 23 January that conditions 'were not yet ripe for mediation' since the Polish government had rejected the Curzon Line. A 'radical improvement' of the composition of the Polish government was required (No. 83, note 3). This the Americans were not prepared to consider (No. 83, note 3).

Churchill came back from Morocco convinced that a more drastic approach was required. As a result, he put increased pressure on the Poles to compromise, informing the war cabinet on 25 January that if the London government did not prove more yielding, there was a real danger that the Soviets would establish their own puppet authority in Warsaw (No. 84). He also wrote to Stalin on 1 February informing him of his efforts to induce the Poles to accept a settlement (No. 85). In his reply, Stalin stated that the Polish government should be reorganized and should accept the Curzon Line (No. 86). Two weeks of intense negotiation followed (No. 87, note 1), as a result of which Churchill was able to persuade the Poles to agree to what was essentially a *de facto* acceptance of the Curzon Line, the final settlement of frontiers being left for the peace conference. In addition, new orders were to be given to the A.K. in accordance with which local underground commanders were to disclose their identity to Soviet commanders when the Red Army entered a district, and seek to coordinate activity against the Germans. The Polish government also undertook to 'include among themselves none but persons fully determined to cooperate with the Soviet Union.'

These proposals were outlined in a letter from Churchill to Stalin on 20 February (No. 87), and were rejected by him in a conversation with Clark-Kerr on 28 February (No. 88), and in a letter to Churchill on 3 March (No. 89). A number of reasons can be adduced for the Soviets' adoption of this position. The understanding proposed was vague, and given Stalin's deep distrust of the Polish government he must have feared that it would attempt to evade the terms agreed on. In addition, he may have wished to make clear to the Polish government that it would have to accept a subordinate position in relation to the Soviet Union. The demands for an explicit acceptance of the Curzon Line and for an immediate reconstruction of the government can be considered as indications of this desire. Stalin also probably resented British mediation, since, as Zinchenko had made clear, the Soviets would have preferred to deal directly with the Poles. Finally he did not believe in the sincerity of the British commitment to the proposed terms. As he told Mikołajczyk on 27 July 1945, 'Churchill did not trust us, and in consequence we could not fully trust him either.'[22]

An acrimonious exchange of letters followed (Nos. 90, 91), which led the British to decide to abandon their attempted mediation. Churchill indeed wrote to Eden on 1 April that the correct course would be 'to relapse into a moody silence so far as Stalin is concerned' (No. 92, note 2). The visit that Mikołajczyk had been wanting to make to the U.S.A. should also now be encouraged to show the Soviets that the Poles 'were not entirely without friends' (No. 90, note 1). At the same time, in a memorandum of 27 March, Roberts argued that it was not in the British or Polish interest 'to quarrel with Russia over Poland' and claimed that 'there is nothing inconsistent with British interests in the existence of . . . a Poland under strong Soviet influence, provided there is some reality of independence and the Russians behave themselves in Poland' (No. 92).

Mikołajczyk remained convinced that the strength of the A.K. would induce the Soviets to become more yielding. This was a fundamental misconception since Soviet alarm and suspicion was far more likely to be aroused by the existence of a powerful non-communist underground in Poland. Mikołajczyk greatly exaggerated the significance of the cooperation in April between an A.K. commander in Volhynia and the Red Army (No. 94). This more hopeful news also persuaded Churchill not to send the stiff reply drafted by the war cabinet to Stalin's message of 23 March (No. 93). However, by the beginning of May it was clear that Mikołajczyk's expectations were not being fulfilled (No. 95).

Nevertheless, there were other signs that the Soviets were prepared to adopt a more conciliatory approach. The visit to the Soviet Union in late April and May of Professor Oskar Lange of Chicago University and the Reverend Stanisław Orlemański, both Poles known for their opposition to the government-in-exile, shed some light on Stalin's views (No. 96, note 1). While 'quietly confident' that events were moving in his favour in Poland, Stalin told Lange that 'the door to an understanding' with the London government 'is never closed'. He argued that Poland should be compensated at German expense 'as far as Stettin' and that he had no intention of interfering in Polish domestic affairs, though he would try to exert his influence over foreign policy. He seemed to Lange not yet to have made up his mind as to whether or not Lwów should be given to Poland (No. 97).

The Soviets also made a direct approach to the Polish government through their ambassador Lebedev. The first moves were made before Mikołajczyk's visit to the United States in mid-June, a visit which brought him little more than a signed photograph of the President (No. 98). Roosevelt did urge Mikołajczyk to make changes in his government and gave some support to Polish territorial aspirations, declaring that he did not favour the Curzon

Line and would intervene 'at the appropriate time' to obtain Lwów,
Drohobycz and Tarnopol for Poland. He further hoped Stalin would not
insist on his claim to Königsberg (No. 98, note 3). He told Mikołajczyk that
he did not believe that Stalin wished to 'Sovietize' Poland, and urged him to go
to Moscow to discuss Polish problems directly with Stalin. He himself wrote
to Stalin to this effect. The Russian leader replied that he found it 'hard to
express an opinion' on such a visit since Mikołajczyk had not advanced at all
to meet Soviet requirements (No. 98, note 4).

Mikołajczyk resumed the talks with Lebedev on his return from
Washington. He was now convinced that the Soviets had been driven to the
conclusion that the pro-Soviet groupings in Poland were too weak to form a
government, and that they would have to reach an understanding with the
London government (No. 100). He thus did not prove particularly yielding,
telling Lebedev on 20 June that the Poles wanted an immediate resumption of
diplomatic relations, the establishment of a common military plan between
the A.K. and the Red Army and administrative cooperation between the
Polish government and the advancing Soviet military authorities. Frontier
questions were to be postponed until the end of the war. He subsequently
told Lebedev that a provisional demarcation line to the east of the Curzon
Line should be established. Lebedev rejected these terms on 23 June,
demanding the resignation of President Raczkiewcz and of Sosnkowski, Kot
and Kukiel, a reorganization of the government, and condemnation of its
'mistake' over Katyn and the acceptance of the Curzon Line (No. 99).
Eden commented on the failure of these negotiations, 'They opened their
mouths too wide and Russia has turned tough' (No. 99, note 4).

The failure of these talks was followed by increased Soviet pressure
on the Poles. Representatives of the Polish National Committee came to
Moscow for talks with the Soviet government and Union of Polish Patriots
in late June and early July and also met the British and American
Ambassadors (No. 100). By late July, the Red Army was approaching the
Curzon Line and on 23 July Stalin wrote to Churchill that since it was not
the Soviet intention to set up their own administration in Poland, he was
allowing the Polish Committee of National Liberation (P.C.N.L.),
established on 21 July by the Polish National Committee, to set up such an
administration. This was not to be considered a Polish government, but
might later become 'the core of a Provisional Polish Government made up of
democratic forces' (No. 101). On 25 July the Soviets recognized the
P.C.N.L. as 'the only lawful temporary organization of executive power' in
Poland (No. 101, note 3). Their policy was, in effect, to demand the
creation of a new Polish government based on the P.C.N.L. and 'democratic
elements' in the London government. Stalin had replied in his letter of 23
July to Churchill's request that he meet Mikołajczyk in Moscow by stating
that he would 'certainly not refuse to see him' but that Mikołajczyk should
rather approach the P.C.N.L. which was 'favourably disposed towards him'

(No. 101).

The British felt their position was being steadily eroded by the c events. They put pressure on Mikołajczyk not to cancel his proposed Moscow, Churchill writing to Stalin on 26 July, 'I am sure M. Mikołaj most anxious to help a general fusion of all Poles on the lines on which you and I and the President are, I believe, agreed' (No. 101, note 3). This was a significant retreat from the position he had adopted earlier in the year.

The Polish Prime Minister spent a week in Moscow between 4 and 10 August (No. 102). A good personal relationship was established between Stalin and Mikołajczyk, who was, 'at least partically convinced' that it was not the Soviet leader's intention to communize Poland, though he remained suspicious of the P.C.N.L. Stalin again demanded the Curzon Line and promised compensation in the west including Stettin and Breslau. He counselled Mikołajczyk to seek an agreement with the P.C.N.L. Mikołajczyk's talks with the committee, though cordial, did not produce any significant results. The P.C.N.L. demanded the abrogation of the 1935 constitution and the establishment of a new government in which they should have fourteen out of eighteen members. Agreement was reached that both sides should abstain from public recriminations and Mikołajczyk decided to return to London where he would endeavour to replace President Raczkiewicz by some person more acceptable to Moscow. This would, he hoped, enable him to renew talks so that he and some of his associates could go to Warsaw when it was taken and reach agreement with the P.C.N.L. on a new cabinet. His objective was 'to join all factions at this time in a government which will have a legal basis and which can hold the country together until such time as a truly free general election can be held . . .' (No. 102, doc. 2).

Mikołajczyk's task was greatly complicated by the outbreak of the Warsaw uprising on 31 July.[23] This took place primarily on the orders of the A.K. command in Poland, which had made use of the division in the Polish government in London between Mikołajczyk and Sosnkowski to establish its own policy for the underground. Their policy rested on a brutally simple strategy. Without previously informing the Russians, the A.K. would stage an uprising in Warsaw and seize power as the Germans were retreating. This would make it possible to establish a London-oriented authority in Warsaw. The Soviets would then be faced with a choice; either to compromise with the London authorities or to crush the Warsaw government and risk alienating western opinion. The plan was a gamble and it failed disastrously. The A.K. could only have been successful if its uprising had been followed quickly by the Soviet capture of Warsaw. Yet even as the plan was being set in motion, it became clear that the Germans had repulsed the Soviet thrust and that the Red Army would not be able to take Warsaw for at least two weeks.

Mikołajczyk himself had not opposed the decision to call for the uprising, since he too had hoped that its success would strengthen his hand in his negotiations with the Soviets and the P.C.N.L. But the failure of the Germans o retreat and the long martyrdom of Warsaw, with the accusations it brought of deliberate Soviet bad faith, gravely imperilled his position. Indeed, on 5 September he even told Eden that he might be compelled to resign (No. 107 and note 3).

Soviet policy on the uprising went through several phases. The Soviets were not at first hostile to the revolt, though they belittled its significance and on 9 August Stalin told Mikołajczyk that he would drop arms to the underground forces in Warsaw (No. 102). As the political implications became more obvious, Soviet attitudes hardened, and the rising was bitterly denounced in a Tass communiqué on 12 August (No. 103), and in a letter from Stalin to Churchill on 16 August replying to a request for Soviet aid for the insurgents (Nos. 104, 105). The Soviets even refused to allow U.S. aircraft to undertake missions to aid the Poles in Warsaw and then land on Soviet Airfields (No. 106). This led to several fruitless interventions by the British and American Ambassadors (No. 106, note 2, No. 107 and note 2), and induced Harriman to conclude that the Soviet action was dictated by 'ruthless political considerations' (No. 106, note 2). A joint letter from Roosevelt and Churchill was despatched to Stalin on 20 August (No. 108) and also received a dusty answer (No. 109). British and American responses now diverged. The Americans, and Roosevelt in particular, were unwilling to take a strong line on the question of aid to Warsaw for fear this would endanger their shuttle-bombing arrangement with the U.S.S.R. The President therefore refused to sign another joint message to Stalin (No. 109, note 1). The British were much exercised by the problem, and a stiff note was sent from the cabinet to Stalin on 4 September (No. 110). This was successful in causing the Soviets to modify their policy (No. 111) and allow a substantial supply flight to Warsaw on 18 September. Permission for a second large drop was refused, and the Warsaw insurgents finally surrendered on 4 October.

The success of British pressure led Churchill to make another attempt at a solution. Under strong British influence, President Raczkiewicz thus finally relieved General Sosnkowski of his post on 28 September (No. 111, note 1). Eden and Churchill were also able to persuade Stalin to invite Mikołajczyk to the talks they were having with him in Moscow in the second week of October. The British were well aware of the weakness of their position. As Roberts pointed out in a memorandum on 4 October, all the Soviets had to do to achieve their objectives was to delay a settlement (No. 112, doc. 1, note 1). They thus exercised all their persuasive powers in Moscow to induce the Poles to reach agreement before the situation deteriorated still further (No. 112). They were able to convince Mikołajczyk to accept the Curzon Line as the Polish-Soviet frontier, provided that Lwów remained in Poland. This was not acceptable to Stalin. The Poles then agreed to the Curzon Line without Lwów, but as a 'line of demarcation' which was also refused by Stalin. As a result, Mikołajczyk decided to return to London to persuade his followers to accept the Soviet terms. Stalin had also told Churchill on 18 October that Mikołajczyk, as Prime Minister, could have 50% of the portfolios in a reconstructed government for his supporters, though he 'rapidly corrected himself to a worse figure' (No. 112, doc. 2, note 5).

Mikołajczyk found the task of convincing his cabinet to accept the Soviet terms much more difficult than he had anticipated. In order to win over the waverers, he addressed three questions to the British government on 31 October, to obtain firm guarantees that Poland would receive the promised compensation in the west at German expense, even if the U.S. government proved lukewarm on this question. The British replied in a reasonably reassuring way on 3 November (No. 113), but this failed to satisfy the Polish cabinet, which voted on the same day to reject Mikołajczyk's policy. Mikołajczyk hesitated to inform the British of this (he had been subjected to a blistering attack by Churchill on 2 November) (No. 113, note 3) and, in a further attempt to convince his cabinet, sought assurances on a number of points from the United States (No. 114, note 3). Roosevelt replied on 17 November (No. 114). Though his answers were 'less non-committal and unhelpful' than the Poles had feared (No. 114, note 4), it was becoming obvious that Mikolajczyk had only minority support for his views. Accordingly, he resigned on 24 November explaining his reasons to Harriman (No. 115). After some difficulty, a less compromising government was formed on 19 November under the veteran socialist Tomasz Arciszewski.

5. FROM DECEMBER 1944 TO THE POTSDAM CONFERENCE

Mikołajczyk's resignation left the British effectively without a policy. In spite of Churchill's hopes that Arciszewski's government would prove short-lived, it was soon too firmly established to be dislodged. Churchill rejected Clark-Kerr's advice that recognition of the new government would mean 'a head-on collision with Stalin', though he kept official contacts to a minimum (No. 116, note 2). On 3 December he wrote to Stalin explaining that the decision to recognize the new government did not constitute a change of policy, and that he hoped Mikołajczyk would shortly return to power (No. 116). Stalin replied on 18 December that Mikołajczyk was now 'incapable of helping a Polish settlement', since he had countenanced anti-Soviet terrorism. The P.C.N.L., on the contrary, was making 'substantial progress in consolidating its national democratic organizations on Polish soil' (No. 117).

With Roosevelt's re-election, the U.S. was now prepared to play a larger role in the settlement of the Polish question. The statement issued by Stettinius, the new American Secretary of State, on 18 December was, however, studiously vague, stressing only that while the U.S. favoured postponing the settlement of frontier questions to the end of the war, it would support a negotiated agreement between the Soviets and the Poles. No clear reference was made to the compensation of Poland, at German expense, for her losses in the East (No. 118

and note 1). In his reply to Roosevelt's letter sending him this statement, Stalin argued that events dictated that he should shortly recognize the P.C.N.L. as a provisional Polish government, because the Soviet Union had a greater stake than any other country in a 'pro-Ally and democratic Poland' since that state 'borders on the Soviet Union' (No. 119). The Soviets duly announced on 31 December the transformation of the P.C.N.L. into a provisional government (No. 119, note 1).

British policy was set out in a memorandum written for the Yalta conference on 27 January by Christopher Warner, head of the Northern Department. Already earlier in January the Foreign Office had rejected a proposal by Cripps for a conference in London to establish a 'more representative' Polish government in London on the grounds that it was probably more sensible 'to try to "penetrate" the Lublin Government by arranging for Mikołajczyk and other political leaders and groups who want to work for a Polish-Russian entente to go to Lublin while the Lublin people are still prepared to welcome them' (No. 120, note 7). Warner's memorandum argued that the principal British objectives should be the eventual securing of free elections in Poland and an agreement with the Soviets to establish an interim regime in Poland which would avert 'the danger of civil war'. These were to be achieved by the entry of representatives of the three centre and left-wing parties of the emigration into the Lublin government, and various methods were proposed for achieving this aim (No. 120).

Both the British and the Americans were also becoming uneasy about the scale of compensation in the west which the Soviets envisaged for Poland. These doubts had first been expressed in July 1944, when the P.C.N.L. manifesto was issued,[24] and were reiterated in Roberts' memorandum of 4 October 1944 (No. 112, doc. 4, note 1). They grew stronger after the fall of Mikołajczyk which removed one of the main reasons for this policy: the need to make Soviet terms acceptable to the Polish premier. Thus Clark-Kerr expressed strong misgivings following an article by Stefan Jędrychowski, representative in Moscow of the P.C.N.L., which claimed for Poland a frontier on the Oder and western Neisse.[25] Clark-Kerr's unease was shared by Eden and the Foreign Office and also by Harriman.[26] On 2 January, Eden informed the war cabinet that he was 'disturbed at the extent to which the Poles were opening their mouths'.[27] He expressed similar views to the cabinet on 23 January.[28] British unease was clearly articulated in the memorandum submitted by Eden to the war cabinet on 26 January and in the discussion which followed (No. 121 and note 1).

British and American policies were co-ordinated before the Yalta conference at a meeting between Stettinius and Eden in Malta on 1 February. The two Foreign Ministers agreed that 'the time has probably gone by for a "fusion" of London and Lublin, and the only remedy we can see is the creation of a *new* interim Government in Poland, pledged to the holding of free elections, as soon as conditions permit.' This was to include representatives from the Lublin (now

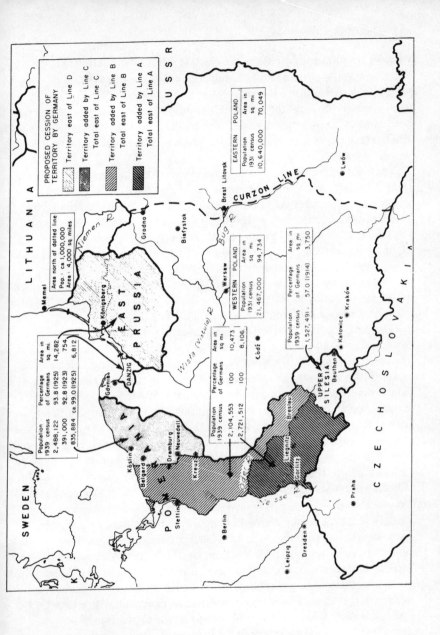

PROPOSED CESSION OF
TERRITORY BY GERMANY

	Territory east of Line D
	Total east of Line C
	Territory added by Line C
	Total east of Line C
	Territory added by Line B
	Total east of Line B
	Territory added by Line A
	Total east of Line A

EASTERN POLAND

	Area in sq mi
Population (1931 census) 10,640,000	70,049

Area north of dotted line
Pop. ca 1,000,000
Area : 4,000 sq miles

WESTERN POLAND

	Area in sq mi
Population (1931 census) 21,467,000	94,734

	Percentage of Germans	Area in sq mi
Population (1939 census) 1,527,491	57.0 (1914)	3,750

Population 1939 census	Percentage of Germans	Area in sq mi
2,104,553	100	10,473
2,721,512	100	8,106

Population 1939 census	Percentage of Germans	Area in sq mi
2,488,122	93.8 (1925)	14,282
391,000	92.8 (1923)	754
835,884	ca 99.0 (1925)	6,812

CURZON LINE

Warsaw) government, from Poles in Poland and from Poles abroad. Members of the new Polish government in London should not be suggested, but Mikołajczyk, Grabski and Romer should certainly be included. The British were prepared to accept the Curzon Line without Lwów as the Polish eastern border, while the Americans wished to press the Soviets to give Lwów to Poland. It was agreed to oppose a Polish western frontier on the Oder and western Neisse (No. 122).

The Polish question played a prominent part in the discussions at Yalta (Nos. 123–30). Agreement was soon reached that the Curzon Line 'with adjustments in some regions of 5–8 km. in favour of Poland' should be the Polish eastern frontier. Lwów was finally assigned to the Soviet Union (Nos. 124, 125). On the western frontier no unity was attained, but a compromise was accepted that Poland should receive substantial accessions of territory in the north and west and that the new Provisional Government of National Unity which was to be established be consulted about 'the extent of the accessions'. The final settlement of the western frontier was to take place at the peace conference (Nos. 124, 125, 126, 130).

The central point of difficulty was the composition of the Polish government. As had been agreed at Malta, the British and Americans wanted the creation of an entirely new government, to be composed of members of the Provisional government, democratic Poles in Poland and Poles abroad, and which would be pledged to hold free elections (Nos. 125, 126). The Soviets, for their part, wanted it to be made clear that the Provisional government was to be the core of the new administration (No. 124). The final agreement was a not very precise compromise between these two positions. It read: 'A new situation has been created in Poland as a result of her complete liberation by the Red Army. This calls for the establishment of a Provisional Polish Government which can be more broadly based than was possible before the recent liberation of western Poland. The Provisional Government which is now functioning in Poland should therefore be reorganized on a broader democratic basis with the inclusion of democratic leaders from Poland itself and from Poles abroad... M. Molotov, Mr. Harriman and Mr. A. Clark-Kerr are authorized as a Commission to consult in the first instance in Moscow with members of the present Provisional Government and with other democratic leaders from within Poland and from abroad, with a view to the reorganization of the present Government on the above lines.' The new government was to be pledged to the holding of free elections (No. 130).

It has often been asked whether Stalin in accepting this formula intended to do more than allow the western powers to save face in Poland. Churchill, for his part, certainly believed that Stalin would implement the terms of the agreement in a sense acceptable to the West (No. 131). At the same time, the Soviet promise to hold elections as soon as possible was to prove very flexible, while the Soviet commitment to free elections also raises some doubts. Stalin's views on free elections were probably accurately summed up by Walter

Ulbricht's statement at this time. 'It's quite clear — it's got to look democratic but we must have everything in our control.'[29] Moreover, Stalin's claim that he could not contact members of the Provisional Government in Poland so that they could be brought to Yalta for discussions was certainly disingenuous (No. 124, note 1) and suggests that he realized that the composition of the new government was likely to cause serious difficulties. This was particularly true in relation to Mikolajczyk, whose entry into the new government was regarded as crucial by the western powers. Yet in the course of the Yalta discussions, both Stalin and Molotov had stated that he was 'unacceptable' to the Warsaw Poles (No. 123, note 1, No. 125, note 3). It may be that having created this government which was still very weak, Stalin was somewhat tied down by the commitments he had undertaken to it.

In fact, it proved much more difficult to establish the new government than the western powers had anticipated. The Foreign Office instructions to Clark-Kerr of 18 February laid down that he was to ensure that this government contained 'adequate representation of different non-Lublin sections of opinion' (No. 132), while Churchill told the war cabinet on 21 February that the 'acid test' of Soviet sincerity would be whether Mikolajczyk would be allowed to return to Poland (No. 132, note 2). These views were also broadly shared by the U.S. (No. 132, note 3). However, it soon became evident that Molotov, perhaps under the pressure of the Warsaw Poles, was unwilling to allow Mikolajczyk to enter the new government (No. 133, note 2).

The dispute soon widened in scope. The British became convinced that the Soviets intended to use democratic phraseology to cover the creation of a new government 'which would merely be the present one dressed up to look more acceptable to the ignorant' (No. 133). They were also extremely upset by the Soviet refusal to allow Allied observers into Poland (No. 133 and note 3). The United States, though more unwilling to believe in Soviet bad faith, also came increasingly to share the British view. These misgivings were expressed in identical notes submitted by Harriman and Clark-Kerr to Molotov on 19 March (No. 134), in Roosevelt's letter to Stalin of 1 April (No. 136), and in the joint letter of Truman and Churchill to Stalin on 18 April (No. 138).

The Soviets, for their part, came to the conclusion that the western powers were departing from the terms of the Yalta agreement in their attempt to create an entirely new government, and stressed that the Provisional government was to be the 'core' of the reconstituted administration. Molotov even claimed, with little justification, that the relevant paragraph of the Yalta should read: '. . . . to consult in Moscow, in the first instance with members of the present Provisional Government, and with Polish democratic leaders from within Poland and abroad' (Nos. 135, 137), in the sense that there was to be prior discussion with members of the Provisional Government. The Soviets also probably resented the concerted action of the Western powers. Stalin now argued that the 'Yugoslav precedent' should be followed in settling the Polish question, which would have meant giving the non-Warsaw Poles virtually no power (No. 137). He wrote to Churchill that 'Poland borders on the Soviet Union, which cannot be said about Great Britain or the U.S.A.' (No. 140). He went on to stress that 'We cannot acquiesce in the attempts that are being made to involve in the forming of a future Polish Government people who, to quote you, "are not fundamentally anti-Russian" or to bar from participation only those who, in your view are "extreme people unfriendly to Russia"[30] . . . We insist, and shall continue to insist, that only people who have demonstrated by their deeds their friendly attitude to the Soviet Union . . . should be consulted on the formation of a future Polish Government' (No. 141).

The Soviets were not really prepared to break with the west on this question, particularly since Britain and the United States had in effect already conceded all points of substance. In the joint note of 18 April, for instance, Truman and Churchill had stated, 'We have never denied that among the three elements from which the new Provisional Government of National Unity is to be formed, the representatives of the present Warsaw government will play, unquestionably, a prominent part' (No. 138). Already in his letter of 7 April, Stalin had informed Churchill that he was prepared 'to use [his] influence with the Provisional Polish Government to make them withdraw their objection to Mikołajczyk' provided he made a declaration accepting the Yalta decisions on Poland, which he duly did (No. 137, note 1). The original Soviet decision not to send Molotov to the San Francisco conference was also abandoned (No. 136, and note 4).

A settlement was delayed by a number of factors. Firstly, Truman, new and inexperienced, was determined that the Soviets should not think him weak, and accordingly told Molotov during his visit to the U.S.A. 'in words of one syllable' of his displeasure at Soviet conduct (No. 139, note 1). He also sent a strong note to Stalin on 23 April (No. 139). Little progress was made on this question in talks in Washington and San Francisco (No. 139, note 1, No. 142, note 1), and matters were further delayed when Molotov told Harriman on 4 May that fifteen prominent members of the London-controlled underground as well as Gen. Okulicki, last commander of the A.K. had been arrested by the Soviets (No. 141). The fifteen men had disappeared early in April, and rumours had circulated widely that the Soviets were negotiating directly with them in order to present the western powers with the *fait accompli* of a reorganized Polish government on Soviet terms. It seems more likely that these rumours were a Soviet ruse to enable them to arrest the leaders of the underground and destroy its organization. From 4 April, the British and American Ambassadors in Moscow had been asking for information about the missing men, and had received a series of evasive answers.

Churchill was now determined to postpone any further discussion of the

Polish question until the forthcoming meeting of the Big Three (No. 141, note 1) and thus rejected a rather elaborate plan to settle the problem proposed by the State Department to the British at San Francisco (No. 142). Truman, however, decided to make one final attempt at a settlement and sent Harry Hopkins to Moscow at the end of May. Hopkins was able to break the deadlock on terms with which the Americans, and, to a lesser extent the British, were satisfied (Nos. 143, 144). After some hesitation, Mikołajczyk left for Moscow on 16 June with the socialist Stańczyk. In spite of the simultaneous trial of the sixteen Poles, some of whom received severe sentences on 21 June (No. 144, note 2), the negotiations were cordial and relatively easy. On the 21st, the Poles reached agreement and Mikołajczyk and his supporters were allotted six cabinet posts out of twenty. Mikołajczyk became Deputy Prime Minister and Minister of Agriculture. Bierut became chairman and Witos and Grabski members of a seven-man presidium of the Polish National Council, which was to be regarded as the sovereign body of the Polish state.

Harriman regarded this settlement as satisfactory though he felt that better terms could have been obtained if Stańczyk had proved less yielding. He expressed unease at the continued existence of an independent Ministry of Internal Security under the communist Stanisław Radkiewiz and commented, 'The manner in which this Ministry is administered is the crux of whether Poland will have her independence, whether reasonable personal freedom will be permitted and whether reasonably free elections can be held' (No. 145). Churchill was also content, though he expressed strong disquiet at the sentences on Okulicki and his associates (No. 145, note 4).

At Potsdam, the two outstanding issues were settled. Agreement was soon reached on the winding up of the Polish government-in-exile. The Polish western border occasioned more difficulty. This issue was first discussed at the fifth plenary session on 21 July, when the Soviets proposed a frontier on the Oder and western Neisse.[31] On this occasion, both Truman and Churchill made it clear that there was a close connection between the settlement of the Polish western frontier and the question of reparations. Truman claimed that, while he was perfectly willing to discuss the Polish western frontier, a final settlement would have to await the peace conference. (In fact, the briefing paper on 'Suggested U.S. policy regarding Poland' prepared for the conference proposed a Polish western frontier including Danzig, southern East Prussia, Upper Silesia and land in German Pomerania to give Poland additional sea coast.[32] The U.K. position, outlined in an *aide memoire* submitted to the Americans on 13 July was roughly similar.[33]) However, Truman argued that the territories involved could not be treated from the point of view of reparations, as having been detached from Germany, since the division into occupation zones was based on the 1937 frontiers. Stalin argued for the Oder-western Neisse line, but agreed to leave the question in suspense. This the western powers were unwilling to do, and it was therefore

BALTIC SEA

Köslin
(Koszalin)

Danzig
(Gdańsk)

FREE CITY
OF
DANZIG

EAST
PRUSSIA

Swinemünde
(Świnoujście)

Stettin
(Szczecin)

Bydgoszcz
(Bromberg)

Vistula (Wisła)

Frankfurt

Poznań
(Posen)

POLAND

Fürstenberg

Crossen
(Krosno Odrzańskie)

Oder (Odra)

Sagan (Żagań)

GERMANY

Łódź
(Łódź)

Görlitz

Liegnitz
(Legnica)

Lauban
(Lubań)

Breslau
(Wrocław)

Oder (Odra)

Zittau

Brieg
(Brzeg)

Oppeln
(Opole)

CZECHOSLOVAKIA

Glatz
(Kłodzko)

Glatzer Neisse

Nysa Kłodzka

Neisse
(Nysa)

Lausitzer Neisse / Nysa Łużycka

Queis (Kwisa)

Bobr (Bóbr)

Prague
(Praha)

Ratibor
(Racibórz)

Katowice
(Kattowitz)

Ostrava

**CONSIDERATION OF THE WESTERN FRONTIER OF POLAND
AT THE BERLIN CONFERENCE**

——·—·—·—— 1937 International Boundaries

●●●●● Western Limit of Polish Administration Pending the
Final Determination of Poland's Western Frontier
at the Peace Settlement

decided to hear the views of the Polish delegation as was provided for in the Yalta agreement.[34] The Poles, including Mikołajczyk, also argued strongly for the Oder-western Neisse line.[35]

No progress was made at the eighth and ninth plenary meetings on 24 July.[36] At the ninth meeting, Churchill claimed that the Poles could not be allowed to become a fifth occupying power without arrangements being made for spreading the food produced in Germany equally over the whole German population and without agreement being reached on a reparations plan or a definition of booty. If this occurred, it would 'undoubtedly mark a breakdown of the conference'. He further proposed a bargain whereby supplies from the Ruhr for the Russian zone and for Poland were to be bartered for food from these areas. This was in fact Churchill's last statement at the conference, since he was overwhelmingly defeated in the U.K. elections and resigned on 29 July.

Truman and Byrnes, his new Secretary of State, tried to break the deadlock in a meeting on 29 July. Byrnes now proposed U.S. acceptance of a frontier on the Oder-eastern Neisse line, in return for Soviet acceptance of a reparations plan in accordance with which each power would take reparations from its own zone but the Soviets would receive 25% of the total equipment available as reparations from the Rhur (No. 147). This was an advance on his proposal of 23 July for an agreement according to which each ally was to take reparations from its own zone of occupation.[37]

The proposal was sufficiently attractive to Stalin for him to propose that evening to the Poles that they accept the line of the Quiess (Kwisa) River to which they agreed.[38] On 30 July, however, at the Foreign Ministers' meeting, Byrnes accepted the Oder-western Neisse line and clarified his earlier scheme.[40] The Soviets were now to receive 25% of the industrial capital equipment of the Ruhr not necessary for the peacetime economy in exchange for food and raw materials and a further 15% without exchange. The acceptance of this proposal was linked with agreement on the admission of states to the United Nations, and the Polish western frontier. The question was finally settled at the eleventh plenary meeting of the conference on 31 July (No. 148). On this occasion, as in his talks with the members of the Polish delegation, Bevin, the new British Foreign Secretary, tried to obtain assurances on the holding of free elections and the withdrawal of Soviet troops from Poland (No. 148 and note 5). The communiqué of the conference embodied the agreements on the winding up of the government-in-exile and on the provisional settlement of the Polish western frontier. The final delimitation of this frontier was to await the peace conference which, as is well known, never took place (No. 149).

The Polish question, which had been the subject of so much bitter controversy, was thus finally resolved by an agreed settlement. This settlement did not, however, prove lasting. The elections to which the new government was pledged both at Yalta and Potsdam were only finally held in

January 1947, and then proved far from free. By October 1947, Mikołajczyk himself decided that his own position was untenable and that his personal safety was in jeopardy, and fled to the west. In 1948 and 1949 even the more nationalist and independent-minded communists, of whom the most important was Władysław Gomułka, were purged from the government. Close Soviet control of all aspects of Polish life was established and only began to break down after the death of Stalin in 1953.

The question is often asked whether this development was inevitable from the start, or whether the settlement reached in June and July 1945 was rather a casualty of the deterioration of east-west relations, particularly from 1947 on. British policy was certainly based on the assumption that Soviet objectives were limited, and that if Soviet frontier demands were satisfied, the Polish government-in-exile would be able to return to Poland. This policy was first set out in Sargent's memorandum of 15 April 1943 and adopted as British policy later in the year. The agreement at the Teheran conference was very vague, however, and the British attempts to mediate foundered on the Soviet distrust of the Poles, with whom anyway they wanted to deal directly, and the Polish refusal to agree to a clear-cut acceptance of the Curzon Line. After this, British policy followed a consistent course of attempting to amalgamate the pro-western and pro-Soviet groupings, lowering the terms as the latter became ever more firmly established.

U.S. policy is more difficult to describe, both because, at least until October 1944, the Americans were far less involved in Polish affairs and because of the deviousness of Roosevelt, perhaps dictated by his concern for the Polish-American vote in the 1944 elections. The Polish belief that the U.S. would give more support to Polish territorial aspirations was fundamentally misplaced, and played a role in the Polish failure to reach agreement with the Soviets during 1944. Had Mikołajczyk's critics been aware of the true nature of the U.S. position, some of them might have been less prepared to push their opposition to the lengths they did. These groups were, however, for the most part convinced that a Soviet-American clash was inevitable and that Poland was more likely to obtain American support in a subsequent war if they adopted a more intransigent line. Under these conditions, it seems doubtful whether they could under any circumstances have been brought to support Mikołajczyk's position. Certainly after Yalta, the Americans were more willing than the British to accommodate the Soviets over Poland.

The Soviet position was also consistent from July 1941. They demanded the Curzon Line for a number of reasons. They feared that Ukrainian and Byelorussian minorities in Poland could be used to foment anti-Soviet nationalism in the Soviet Union, while the abrogation of the decrees of November 1939 incorporating these areas would have called into question the legitimacy of the Soviet system. There were, in addition, important strategic advantages in the possession of Vilna and Lwów. The Soviets also wanted a 'friendly' government in Poland, and, given Stalin's extremely narrow definition of friendship, this made the chances of a compromise acceptable to the west rather small. One might speculate that, both in general terms and in relation to Poland, the Soviets had a maximum and a minimum policy. As Maisky told Eden on 31 August 1943, there were two possible ways of trying to organize Europe after the war. On the one hand, a general system of security would be established, in which case the Soviets should be granted a say in the regulation of all parts of the continent. Alternatively 'we could agree each to have a sphere of interest, the Russians in the East and ourselves and the Americans in the West . . . if [this plan] were adopted, we should be at liberty to exclude the Russians from French affairs, the Mediterranean and so forth, and the Russians would claim similar freedom in the East' (No. 68); In relation to Poland, if Soviets objectives could be achieved by a compromise with the Polish government-in-exile, this should be welcomed. But if not, Soviet security requirements would have to come first with the inevitable risk of a clash with the west. Indeed, having allowed the creation of the P.C.N.L., the Soviet to some extent found their freedom of manoeuvre limited by the need to protect the interests of their protegés.

The fundamental problem was that western expectations of the Soviet Union were unrealistic. Given the nature of the Soviet system, it was very unlikely that Soviet behaviour in the countries adjoining the U.S.S.R. would ultimately prove acceptable to western statesmen. The western powers thought if a sphere of influence in nineteenth century terms: a country's foreign policy would be determined by the great power concerned, but it would retain a fair degree of internal autonomy. Mikołajczyk held a similar position (No. 149). However, given the strength of anti-Soviet views in a country like Poland, the extent of this freedom of manoeuvre was bound to be small. If a more satisfactory solution of the German problem had been achieved and if relations between the Soviet Union and the western powers had not deteriorated drastically, particularly from 1947, the extent of this freedom would have been greater than was in fact the case. Nevertheless, it was fundamentally unlikely it could have been very great in any circumstances. As Churchill repeatedly told Mikołajczyk, the western powers were not prepared to go to war with the Soviet Union over Poland. The essential fact was that control of Poland was seen as vital by the Soviet Union, as it was not by Great Britain or the United States.

FOOTNOTES

1. F. O. 371. N8674/165/38.
2. W. Churchill, *The Second World War*, (London, 1948–54), VI, p. 332.
3. Quoted in H. J. Elcock, 'Britain and the Russo-Polish Frontier 1919–21', *Historical Journal*, Vol. 12, no. 1, 1969, p. 150.

4. F.O. 371. C8603/24/18.
5. F.O. 371. C9802/327/55.
6. F.O. 371. C14/14/62.
7. W.M.(42) 1.4 C.A.
8. F.O. 371. N 8,9/5/38.
9. W.P. (42)48.
10. W. Churchill, *The Second World War,* IV, p. 293.
11. F.O. 371. C794/19/55.
12. D.O.P.S.R.I., Nos. 189, 191.
13. F.O. 371. C3353/19/55.
14. F.O. 371. C4077/19/55; D.O.P.S.R.I., Nos. 196, 202.
15. F.O. 371. N3717/5/38.
16. F.O. 371. C7636/151/12.
17. E. Taborsky, 'A Polish-Czechoslovak Confederation: A Story of the First Soviet Veto.' *Journal of Central European Affairs,* January 1950.
18. F.R.U.S. 1942, III, p. 195.
19. The best account of this problem is that of J. K. Zawodny, *Death in the Forest. The Story of the Katyn Forest Massacre,* (London 1971).
20. A. Eden, *The Reckoning* (London, 1965), p. 428.
21. F.O. 371. C15378/258/55.
22. F.R.U.S. Potsdam, II, No. 1388.
23. A comprehensive account of the causes of the rising is provided in J. Ciechanowski, *The Warsaw Uprising of 1944*, (Cambridge, 1974).
24. F.O. 371. C10529/8/55. On this occasion Roberts wrote that he found the committee's claim to a frontier on the Oder and western Neisse 'frankly alarming'.
25. F.O. 371. C17671/8/55.
26. F.R.U.S. 1944, III, pp. 1347–9.
27. W.M.(45) 1.6.C.A.
28. W.M.(45) 7.4.C.A.
29. W. Leonhard, *Child of Revolution* (London, 1957), p. 303.
30. Phrases used in Churchill's letter to Stalin of 28 April. See No. 140, Note 2.
31. F.O. 371.U6197/3628/70, pp. 148–53; F.R.U.S. Potsdam, II, pp. 208–21; Soviet protocols pp. 199–208.
32. F.R.U.S. Potsdam, II, Nos. 483, 510.
33. Ibid., No. 518.
34. F.O. 371. U6197/3628/70, pp. 165–9; F.R.U.S. Potsdam, II, pp. 247–52, 261–4, Soviet protocols pp. 211–8.
35. F.O. 371. U6197/3628/70, pp. 195–9; F.R.U.S. Potsdam, II, pp. 337–6.
36. F.O. 371. U6197/3628/70, pp. 201–2, 211–3; F.R.U.S. Potsdam, II, pp. 367, 382–91; Soviet protocols, pp. 236–41, 248–52.
37. F.R.U.S. Potsdam, II, pp. 274, 297.
38. Ibid., p. 1539.
40. F.O. 371. U6197/3628/70; F.R.U.S. Potsdam, II, pp. 484–92, 500–1.

LIST OF PRINCIPAL CHARACTERS

Anders, Władysław, Lt. General,-C.-in-C., Polish Army in the USSR 1941–2; in the Middle East 1942–4; and Italy 1944–5.

Attlee, Clement R., – Deputy British Prime Minister 1942–5; Prime Minister 1945–51.

Beneš, Eduard – President of exiled Czech Government in London 1941–5; President in Prague 1945–8.

Bevin, Ernest – Minister of Labour 1940–5; Foreign Secretary 1945–51.

Bogomolov, Alexander Y. – Soviet Ambassador to Allied Governments in London 1941–3.

Butler, Richard Austin – Parliamentary Under-Secretary of State at the Foreign Office 1938–41; Minister of Education 1941–5.

Butler, Neville Montagu – Minister at the Foreign Office 1941–4; Assistant Under Secretary of State 1944.

Bullitt, William – Former American Ambassador to France and the Soviet Union; influential adviser to President Roosevelt.

Byrnes, James F. – Director of Office of War Mobilisation, U.S.A., 1943–5; Secretary of State, July 1945 – January 1947.

Cadogan, Sir Alexander – Permanent Under Secretary of State in the Foreign Office, January 1938 – February 1946.

Churchill, Sir Winston S. – British Prime Minister and Minister of Defence, May 1940 – July 1945.

Ciechanowski, Jan – Polish Ambassador in Washington, 1941–5.

Clark-Kerr, Sir Archibald – British Ambassador in Moscow, February 1942–1946.

Cripps, Sir R. Stafford – British Ambassador in Moscow, 1940–2; Minister of Aircraft Production, 1942–5.

Dormer, Sir Cecil – British Ambassador to the Polish Government in exile, May 1941 – February 1943.

Eden, Anthony (Lord Avon) – British Foreign Secretary, December 1940 – July 1945.

Grew, Joseph C. – Acting U.S. Secretary of State, 1945.

Gromyko, Andrei – Soviet Ambassador in Washington, 1943–6.

Gusev, Feodor T. – Soviet Ambassador in London, 1943–6.

Halifax, Viscount Edward – British Foreign Secretary, 1938–40; Ambassador in Washington, 1941–6.

Harriman, W. Averell – American Ambassador in Moscow, 1943–6.

Harvey, Oliver – Private Secretary to Eden, 1941–3; Acting Assistant Under Secretary of State for Foreign Affairs, 1945–6.

Hopkins, Harry – Special Adviser and Assistant to President Roosevelt.

49

Hull, Cordell — American Secretary of State, 1933—44.

Kennard, Sir Edward — British Ambassador in Warsaw since January 1935; continued as Ambassador to the Polish Government in exile until May 1941.

Kot, Stanisław — Polish Ambassador to the Soviet Union, 1941—2; Minister of Information, 1943—4.

Law, Richard — Parliamentary Under-Secretary of State, Foreign Office, 1941—3; Minister of State, 1943—5.

Leahy, Admiral William D. — Chief of Staff to the President of the United States, 1942—9.

Lebedev, Victor — Soviet Ambassador to the Allied Government in London, 1943—5.

Lockhart, Sir Bruce — British Representative with the Provisional Czechoslovak Government in London, 1940—1; Deputy Under-Secretary of State for Foreign Affairs and Director-General of the Political Warfare Exec. July 1941—1945.

Makins, Roger — Head of the Central Department in the Foreign Office, 1941—2; Assistant to the Minister Resident at Allied Force Headquarters, Mediterranean Command, January 1943 — September 1944.

Maisky, Ivan — Soviet Ambassador in London, 1932—43; Assistant People's Commissar for Foreign Affairs, 1943—6.

Masaryk, Jan — Czech Foreign Minister, 1941—8.

Mikołajczyk, Stanislaw — Vice-Chairman of the Polish National Council, 1939—41; Deputy Prime Minister and Minister of Interior, 1941—3; Prime Minister, 1943—4; Deputy Prime Minister, 1945—7.

Molotov, Vycheslav — Chairman of Council of People's Commissars, 1930—41 People's Commissar for Foreign Affairs, 1939—46; Foreign Minister of Soviet Government, 1946—9; Deputy Chairman of Council of Ministers of USSR, 1941—57.

Nichols, Philip — British Ambassador to the Czech Provisional Government in London, October 1941—1945.

O'Malley, Sir Owen — British Ambassador to the Polish Government-in-exile, February 1943 — July 1945.

Raczyński, Count Edward — Polish Ambassador in London, 1934—45; Acting Foreign Minister in Sikorski's Cabinet, August 1941 — July 1943.

Raczkiewicz, Władysław, President of the Polish Republic, 1939—47.

Rettinger, Joseph — Private Secretary to General Sikorski, 1941—3; Counsellor in the Polish Embassy in London, 1943—5.

Roberts, Frank — Acting First Secretary in the Foreign Office, December 1940 Chargé d'Affairs to the Czech Provisional Government in London, July — October 1941; Head of Central Department, 1943—5; British Change d'Affairs in Moscow, 1945.

Romer, Tadeusz — Polish Ambassador to the Soviet Union, 1942—3; Foreign Minister, 1943—4.

Roosevelt, Franklin D. — President of the United States, 1932—45.

Sargent, Sir Orme — Deputy Under-Secretary of State for Foreign Affairs, 1939—46.

Savery, Frank — Consul-General in the British Embassy in Warsaw, 1939; Attached to the Embassy to the Polish Government-in-exile and given local rank of a Counsellor, November 1939.

Sikorski, General Władysław — Prime Minister of the Polish Government-in-exile and C.-in-C. of the Polish Army, September 1939 — July 1943.

Sosnkowski, Kazimierz — Polish Minister of War, 1939—41; C.-in-C. of the Polish Army, July 1943 — September 1944.

Stalin, Joseph V. — Chairman of the Council of Ministers, USSR.

Stettinius, Edward, American Under-Secretary of State, 1943—4; Secretary of State, November 1944 — June 1945.

Strang, Sir William — Assistant Under-Secretary of State for Foreign Affairs, 1939—43; British Representative on European Advisory Commission, 1943—5.

Truman, Harry S. — President of the United States, 1945—53.

Vyshinsky, Andrei — Soviet Vice-Commissar for Foreign Affairs, 1940—9.

Warner, Christopher — Head of the Northern Department of the Foreign Office, 1942—5.

Welles, Sumner — American Under-Secretary of State, 1937—43.

Winant, John — American Ambassador in London, 1941—6; American Representative on European Advisory Commission, 1943—7.

ABBREVIATIONS

A.K.	—	Armia Krajowa (The London-directed under-ground)
C.A.B.	—	War Cabinet Minutes and Conclusions
D.G.F.P.	—	*Documents on German Foreign Policy 1918– 1945*
D.O.P.S.R.	—	*Documents on Polish-Soviet Relations 1939– 1945*, 2 vols. (London 1961, 1967)
Dokumenty i Materiały	—	*Dokumenty i Materiały do historii stosunków polsko-radzieckich tvii* (Warsaw 1973)
F.O.	—	Foreign Office
F.O. 371	—	Foreign Office: General Correspondence
F.R.U.S.	—	*Foreign Relations of the United States*
G.H.S.I.	—	General Sikorski Historical Institute
H.C. Deb.	—	House of Commons Debates
Prem.	—	Prime Minister's Office. Operational Papers
S.D.	—	State Department Papers, National Archive, Washington
Stalin Correspondence	—	*Correspondence between the Chairman of the Council of Ministers of the U.S.S.R. and the Presidents of the U.S.A. and the Prime Ministers of Great Britain during the Great Patriotic War* (2 vols, Moscow 1957)
Soviet Protocols	—	*Tehran, Yalta, Potsdam. The Soviet Protocols* ed. by R. Beitzell (Mississippi, 1971)
W.M.	—	War Cabinet Conclusions
W.P.	—	War Cabinet Papers

LIST OF DOCUMENTS

CHAPTER ONE

FROM 1939 TO THE GERMAN INVASION OF THE SOVIET UNION

No. 1

Anglo-Polish Agreement of Mutual Assistance and the Secret Protocol
LONDON, 25 August 1939
H.M.S.O., Cmd 6616, Poland No. 1 (1945)

Article 1

Should one of the Contracting Parties become engaged in hostilities with a European Power in consequence of aggression by the latter against that Contracting Party, the other Contracting Party will at once give the Contracting Party engaged in hostilities all the support and assistance in its power.

Article 2

(1)   The provisions of Article 1 will also apply in the event of any action by a European Power which clearly threatened, directly or indirectly, the independence of one of the Contracting Parties, and was of such a nature that the Party in question considered it vital to resist it with its armed forces.

(2)   Should one of the Contracting Parties become engaged in hostilities with a European Power in consequence of action by that Power which threatened the independence or neutrality of another European State in such a way as to constitute a clear menace to the security of that Contracting Party, the provisions of Article 1 will apply, without prejudice, however, to the rights of the other European State concerned.

Article 3

Should a European Power attempt to undermine the independence of one of the Contracting Parties by processes of economic penetration or in any other way, the Contracting Parties will support each other in resistance to such attempts. Should the European Power concerned thereupon embark on hostilities against one of the Contracting Parties, the provisions of Article 1 will apply.

Article 4

The methods of apply the undertakings of mutual assistance provided for by the present Agreement are established between the competent naval, military and air authorities of the Contracting Parties.

Article 5

Without prejudice to the foregoing undertakings of the Contracting Parties to give each other mutual support and assistance immediately on the outbreak of hostilities, they will exchange complete and speedy information concerning any development which might threaten their independence and, in particular, concerning any development which threatened to call the same undertakings into operation.

Article 6

(1)   The Contracting Parties will communicate to each other the terms of any undertakings of assistance against aggression which they have already given or may in future give to other States.

(2)   Should either of the Contracting Parties intend to give such an undertaking after the coming into force of the present Agreement, the other Contracting Party shall, in order to ensure the proper functioning of the Agreement, be informed thereof.

(3)   Any new undertaking which the Contracting Parties may enter into in future shall neither limit their obligations under the present Agreement nor indirectly create new obligations between the Contracting Party not participating in these undertakings and the third State concerned.

Article 7

Should the Contracting Parties be engaged in hostilities in consequence of the application of the present Agreement, they will not conclude an armistice or treaty of peace except by mutual agreement.

Article 8

(1)   The present Agreement shall remain in force for a period of five years.

(2)   Unless denounced six months before the expiry of this period it shall continue in force, each Contracting Party having thereafter the right to denounce it at any time by giving six months' notice to that effect.

(3)   The present Agreement shall come into force on signature.

In faith whereof the above-named Plenipotentiaries have signed the present Agreement and have affixed thereto their seals.

Done in English in duplicate, at London, the 25th August, 1939. A Polish text shall subsequently be agreed upon between the Contracting Parties and both texts will then be authentic.

(L.S.) Edward Raczyński
(L.S.) Halifax

PROTOCOL

The Polish Government and the Government of the United Kingdom of Great Britain and Northern Ireland are agreed upon the following interpretation of the Agreement of Mutual Assistance signed this day as alone authentic and binding.

1. (a) By the expression 'a European Power' employed in the Agreement is to be understood Germany.

(b) In the event of action within the meaning of Article 1 or 2 of the Agreement by a European Power other than Germany, the Contracting Parties will consult together on the measures to be taken in common.

2. (a) The two Governments will from time to time determine by mutual agreement the hypothetical cases of action by Germany coming within the ambit of Article 2 of the Agreement.

(b) Until such time as the two Governments have agreed to modify the following provisions of this paragraph, they will consider: that the case contemplated by paragraph (1) of Article 2 of the Agreement is that of the Free City of Danzig; and that the cases contemplated by paragraph (2) of Article 2 are Belgium, Holland, Lithuania.

(c) Latvia and Estonia shall be regarded by the two Governments as included in the list of countries contemplated by paragraph (2) of Article 2 from the moment that an undertaking of mutual assistance between the United Kingdom and a third State covering those two countries enters into force.

(d) As regards Roumania, the Government of the United Kingdom refers to the guarantee which it has given to that country; and the Polish Government refers to the reciprocal undertakings of the Roumano-Polish alliance which Poland has never regarded as incompatible with her traditional friendship for Hungary.

3. The undertakings mentioned in Article 6 of the Agreement, should they be entered into by one of the Contracting Parties with a third State, would of necessity be so framed that their execution should at no time prejudice either the sovereignty or territorial inviolability of the other Contracting Party.

4. The present protocol constitutes an integral part of the Agreement signed this day, the scope of which it does not exceed.

In faith whereof the undersigned, being duly authorized, have signed the present Protocol.

Done in English in duplicate, at London, the 25th August, 1939. A Polish text will subsequently be agreed upon between the Contracting Parties and both texts will then be authentic.

(signed) Edward Raczyński
(signed) Halifax

No. 2

Treaty of Non-Aggression between Germany and the U.S.S.R.
MOSCOW, 23 August 1939
D.G.F.P., VII, No. 228

The Government of the German Reich and the Government of the Union of Soviet Socialist Republics, desirous of strengthening the cause of peace between Germany and the USSR, and proceeding from the fundamental provisions of the Treaty of Neutrality, which was concluded between Germany and the USSR in April 1926, have reached the following agreement:

Article 1

The two Contracting Parties undertake to refrain from any act of violence, any aggressive action and any attack on each other either severally or jointly with other Powers.

Article II

Should one of the Contracting Parties become the object of belligerent action by a third Power, the other Contracting Party shall in no manner lend its support to this third Power.

Article III

The Government of the two Contracting Parties will in future maintain continual contact with one another for the purpose of consultation in order to exchange information on problems affecting their common interests.

Article IV

Neither of the two Contracting Parties will join any grouping of Powers whatsoever which is aimed directly or indirectly at the other Party.

Article V

Should disputes or conflicts arise between the Contracting Parties over questions of one kind or another, both Parties will settle these disputes or conflicts exclusively by means of a friendly exchange of views or if necessary by the appointment of arbitration commissions.

Article VI

The present Treaty shall be concluded for a period of ten years with the proviso that, in so far as one of the Contracting Parties does not denounce it one year before the expiry of this period, the validity of this Treaty shall be deemed to be automatically prolonged for another five years.

Article VII

The present treaty shall be ratified within the shortest possible time. The instruments of ratification will be exchanged in Berlin. The treaty shall enter into force immediately upon signature.

Done in duplicate in the German and Russian languages. Moscow, August 23, 1939.

For the Government
of the German Reich:
   v. Ribbentrop

With full power of the
Government of the USSR:
   V. Molotov

No. 3

Secret Additional Protocol to the Treaty of Non-Aggression between Germany and the U.S.S.R.
MOSCOW, 23 August 1939
D.G.F.P., VII, No. 229

On the occasion of the signature of the Non-Aggression Treaty between the German Reich and the Union of Soviet Socialist Replublics, the under-signed plenipotentiaries of the two Parties discussed in strictly confidential conversations the question of the delimitation of their respective spheres of interest in Eastern Europe. These conversations led to the following results

1. In the event of a territorial and political transformation in the territories belonging to the Baltic States (Finland, Estonia, Latvia, Lithuania), the northern frontier of Lithuania shall represent the frontier of the spheres of interest both of Germany and the USSR. In this connection the interest of Lithuania in the Vilna territory is recognized by both Parties.

2. In the event of a territorial and political transformation of the territories belonging to the Polish State, the spheres of interest of both Germany and the USSR shall be bounded approximately by the line of the rivers Narew, Vistula, and San.

The question whether the interest of both Parties make the maintenance of an independent Polish State appear desirable and how the frontiers of this State should be drawn can be definitely determined only in the course of further political developments.

In any case both Governments will resolve this question by means of a friendly understanding.

3. With regard to South-Eastern Europe, the Soviet side emphasizes its interest in Bessarabia. The German side declares complete political désintéressement in these territories.

4. This Protocol will be treated by both parties as strictly secret.

Moscow, August 23, 1939

For the Government of
the German Reich:
   v. Ribbentrop

With full power of the
Government of the USSR:
   V. Molotov

No. 4

Note of the Soviet Government to the Polish Embassy in Warsaw
MOSCOW, 17 September 1939
D.O.P.S.R., I, No. 43 (Translated)

The Polish-German war has revealed the internal bankruptcy of the Polish state. After ten days of military operations, Poland has lost all its industrial areas and cultural centres. Warsaw, as the capital of Poland, no longer exists. The Polish government has collapsed and shows no sign of life. This indicates that the Polish state and government have, in effect, ceased to exist. In view of this state of affairs, the treaties concluded between Poland and the Soviet Union have no validity. Abandoned to its fate and deserted by its leaders, Poland has become a fertile field for all sorts of acts and surprises which could become a danger to the U.S.S.R. This is why, having preserved its neutrality until the present, the Soviet government can no longer remain neutral in the face of these facts.

Neither can the Soviet government remain indifferent when its Ukrainian and Byelorussian blood-brothers, inhabiting Polish territory, abandoned to their fate, are left without defence.

Taking this situation into consideration, the Soviet government has given instructions to the Supreme Command of the Red Army to order its troops to cross the frontier and take under their protection the lives and property of the population of the western Ukraine and western Byelorussia.

At the same time, the Soviet government intends to do everything it can to deliver the Polish people from the disastrous war into which it has been plunged by its senseless rulers and to give them the possibility of living a peaceful life.

No. 5

Statement by the British Ministry of Information
LONDON, 18 September 1939
'The Times', 19 September 1939

The British Government have considered the situation created by the attack upon Poland ordered by the Soviet Government. This attack made upon Great Britain's ally at a moment when she is prostrate in face of over-whelming forces brought against her by Germany cannot in the view of His Majesty's Government be justified by the arguments put forward by the Soviet Government. The full implication of these events is not yet apparent, but His Majesty's Government take the opportunity of stating that nothing that has occurred can make any difference to the determination of His Majesty's Government with the full support of the country, to fulfil their obligations to Poland and to prosecute the war with all energy until their objectives have been achieved.

No. 6

The German Ambassador to the U.S.S.R. to the Ministry for Foreign Affairs:
Telegram
MOSCOW, 25 September 1939
D.G.F.P., VIII, No. 131

Stalin and Molotov asked me to come to the Kremlin at 8 p.m. today.
Stalin stated the following: In the final settlement of the Polish question anything that in the future might create friction between Germany and the Soviet
Union must be avoided. From this point of view, he considered it wrong to
leave an independent residual Poland. He proposed the following: From the
territory to the east of the demarcation line, all the Province of Lublin and
that portion of the Province of Warsaw which extends to the Bug should be
added to our share. In return, we should waive our claim to Lithuania.[1]

Stalin designated this suggestion as a subject for the forthcoming negotiations
with the Reich Foreign Minister and added that, if we consented, the Soviet
Union would immediately take up the solution of the problem of the Baltic
countries in accordance with the Protocol of August 23,[2] and expected in this
matter the unstinting support of the German Government. Stalin expressly
indicated Estonia, Latvia and Lithuania, but did not mention Finland.

I replied to Stalin that I would report to my government.

Schulenberg

1. This new demarcation line was brought into operation by a secret additional protocol
to the German-Soviet Boundary and Friendship Treaty of September 28, 3939 (D.G.F.P.,
VIII, No. 159).
2. See above, No. 3.

No. 7

Extract from a speech in the House of Lords by Lord Halifax
LONDON, 28 October 1939
H. of L. Debates Vol. 114, cols. 1565-6

It is quite true, of course . . . that it makes no difference to the Poles
whether they are invaded from East or West, and nobody who has any information as to what is now going on in the several parts of Poland can feel any
other than a sense of the complete and utter tragedy of the suffering and
want which . . . is going to grow much worse this winter and of which even
today we have the most distressful reports. The last thing I would wish to do
in this matter is to defend the action of the Soviet Government at the particular
time at which they took it. But it is right to remember two things: Firstly, that
they would never have taken that action if the German Government had not
started it and set the example that they did set when they invaded Poland
without any declaration of war. In the second place, it is perhaps, as a matter
of historical interest, worth recalling that the action of the Soviet Government

has been to advance the Russian boundary to what was substantially the boundary recommended at the time of the Versailles Conference by the noble Marquess, who used to lead the House, Lord Curzon, and who was then Foreign Secretary.[1]

1. This speech led to a letter of protest from the Polish Foreign Minister, August Zaleski to Halifax on 27 October 1939. Halifax's statement about the Curzon Line would, he claimed, 'be seized upon both by German and Soviet propagandists as a definite indication of the line of future British policy in the matter of a future Russian Western boundary' (F.O. 371. C17490/1321/55).

No. 8

The British Foreign Secretary to the Polish Minister of Foreign Affairs: Letter
1 November 1939
F.O. 371. C17490/1321/55

. . . I should like first of all to assure you that my speech of the 26th October did not represent any new departure in the policy of His Majesty's Government. As you will remember, the attitude of His Majesty's Government towards Soviet action against Poland was stated by the Prime Minister in the House of Commons on the 20th September, when he said that, in the view of His Majesty's Goverment, the attack by the Soviet Government upon Poland (a country with whom they had a non-aggression pact) at a moment when Poland was prostrated in the face of overwhelming forces brought against her by Germany, could not be justified by the arguments put forward. This remains the view of His Majesty's Government and, when I stated on the 26th October that the last thing I wished to do was to defend the action of the Soviet Government at the particular time at which they took it, I had in mind precisely the point put by the Prime Minister on the 20th September. My intention was to make clear not only that the action of the Soviet Government was in itself incapable of justification, but that it was made all the more reprehensible by reason of the fact that it was so timed as to constitute a stab in the back at a moment when Poland was already the victim of an over-whelming attack by Germany. You will appreciate that this passage in my speech on the 26th October was not a formal and prepared statement on behalf of His Majesty's Government, but was an impromptu reply to an intervention in the debate. My thought was not therefore fully developed. I need hardly assure you that I should much regret if my words led to misunder-standing in any quarter.

I have read with interest your remarks about the effect of the advance of Soviet rule in Eastern Europe. We are, of course, fully alive to those dangers, but, as we agreed at our last meeting in London, we must concentrate our united forces against Germany, the country responsible for the war, and therefore for the resulting intervention of the Soviet Government. This does not, however, imply that we are prepared in any way to extenuate Soviet action, and it was far from my intention to do so. . .

F.O. 371. C17490/1321/55

No. 9

Decree of the Supreme Council of the U.S.S.R.
MOSCOW, 1 November 1939
D.O.P.S.R., I, No. 67

The Supreme Council of the Union of Soviet Socialist Republics having heard the report of the Authorized Committee of the National Assembly of Western Ukraine has decided as follows:

1. To comply with the petition of the National Assembly of Western Ukraine to incorporate it in the Union of Soviet Socialist Republics and to unite it with the Ukrainian Soviet Socialist Republic.[1]

2. To instruct the Presidium of the Supreme Council to fix a date for the election of representatives of Western Ukraine to the Supreme Council of the USSR.

3. To propose to the Supreme Council of the Ukrainian Soviet Socialist Republic the admission of Western Ukraine to the Ukrainian SSR.

4. To instruct the Supreme Soviet of the Ukrainian SSR to submit to the Supreme Soviet of the USSR for examination a plan for the demarcation of boundaries between the provinces and districts on the borders of the Ukrainian Soviet Socialist Republic and the Byelorussian Soviet Socialist Republic.

> Chairman of the Presidium of the Supreme
> Counfil of the USSR:
> M. Kalinin
> Secretary of the Presidium of the Supreme
> Council of the USSR;
> A. Gorkin

1. A similar decree 'to comply with the petition of the National Assembly of Western Byelorussia to incorporate Western Byelorussia into the U.S.S.R.' was issued on 2 November 1939 (D.O.P.S.R., I, No. 68).

No. 10

Rex Leeper (Political Intelligence Department) Foreign Office to Sir William Strang, Assistant Under-Secretary of State for Foreign Affairs: Letter (Extract)
25 November 1939
F.O. 371. C19288/27/55

. . . Sikorski's view[1] is that it will not be possible to have any hard and fast ideas about Poland's future until the end of the war. Although he will not a admit officially any difference between the two invaders of Poland, he does realise perfectly well that the reconstruction of Poland in her pre-war frontiers is very problematic. If it proves impossible to recover from Russia what has been lost, he aims at finding compensation elsewhere which would at the same time increase Poland's security. In this connection his mind is turning towards East Prussia as the means for finding such compensation, and it appears that he is being encouraged by the French Government. He is therefore toying with the idea of the demilitarisation of East Prussia under some international control with Poland in a special position of responsibility. This idea at present seems to be pretty vague but no doubt we shall hear more of it in the future.

1. This had been expressed to Leeper by Stefan Litauer, President of the Foreign Press Association in London who had spoken to Sikorski during his visit to London in November 1939. Similar views were voiced by Władysław Kulski, Counsellor at the Polish Embassy, to Roger Makins, head of the F.O. Central Department on 18 February 1941 (F.O.371. C1611/6/12).

No. 11

From Sir William Strang, Assistant to the Undersecretary of State for Foreign Affairs, to Sir Howard Kennard, British Ambassador to the Polish Government-in-exile: Letter (Extract)
LONDON, 16 March 1940
F.O. 371. C1762/116/55

8. You may also be interested in the following views put forward by a member of the Foreign Office who has had considerable experience of these problems, since they illustrate another impression left by Savery's memorandum:[1]
‘. . .d. If the Soviet regime is standing at the end
“of the war there is little likelihood of the Poles
“themselves being able to recover any of the districts
“now in Soviet occupation nor of the Allies being
“willing or able to force the Russians out of these.
“If, on the other hand, the Soviet regime has collapsed
“anything may happen and speculation is really useless.’[2]

1. In a letter to Strang on 29 January 1940 (C1794/116/55), Kennard had enclosed a Memorandum by Frank Savery, Consul-General at the British Embassy in Warsaw until 1939 who had been attached to the Embassy to the Polish Government-in-exile and given the rank of Counsellor in November 1939. Savery had felt, in Kennard's words that it wa
‘. . . desirable to consider the question whether, in the interests of her future well-being as a well ordered State, she [Poland] may not have to sacrifice almost one third of her territory and relinquish approximately all that is east of the Curzon Line in order (a) to get rid of the running sore of bad relations with at least one irreconcila minority and (b) to settle, if possible, once and for all accounts with Russia.’
2. In a letter to Strang on 2 May 1941, Kennard himself expressed the view that ‘no matter whether we win a decisive victory or not, Poland will have to accept certain major sacrifices, especially on her eastern frontiers. . . ’ (F.O. 371. C4598/4598/55).

No. 12

Statement made by Mr. Churchill in the House of Commons
LONDON, 5 September 1940
H. of C. Debates, Vol. 365, col. 40

. . . We have not at any time adopted, since the war broke out, the line that
nothing could be changed in the territorial structure of various countries. On
the other hand, we do not propose to recognize any territorial changes which
take place during the war, unless they take place with the free consent and
good will of the parties concerned.

No. 13

Polish-Czechoslovak Declaration
LONDON, 11 November 1940
F.O. 371. C11838/8531/12

The Polish Government and the Provisional Czechoslovak Government have
decided to issue the following declaration:—

I.

Imbued with an inflexible faith that the heroic struggle now being waged
by Great Britain, together with her Allies, against German tyranny will end in
the final defeat of the forces of evil and destruction.

Animated by the profound conviction that the future order of the world
must be based on the co-operation of all elements which recognise the
principle of freedom and justice, as constituting the moral foundation of all
our common civilisation.

The two Governments consider it imperative to declare solemnly that
Poland and Czechoslovakia, closing once and for all the period of past
recriminations and disputes, and taking into consideration the community of
their fundamental interest, are determined, on the conclusion of this war, to
enter as independent and sovereign States into a closer political and economic
association, which would become the basis of a new order in Central Europe,
and a guarantee of its stability. Moreover, both Governments express the hope
that in this co-operation, based on respect for the freedom of nations, the
principles of democracy and the dignity of man, they will also be joined by
other countries in that part of the European continent. The two Governments
are resolved already now to co-operate closely for the defence of their
common interests and for the preparation of the future association of the
two countries.

II.

The two Governments stigmatise the cynical farce which the leaders of
Nazi Germany are endeavouring to stage by proclaiming themselves the
builders of a new European Order. The hypocrisy of these assertions is most

clearly revealed in the light of German endeavours aiming at the destruction of our two ancient nations, which have contributed their important share to the common treasure of human civilisation. The violence and cruelty to which our two nations are being subjected, the expulsions of the native populations from large areas of its secular homelands, the banishing of hundreds of thousands of men and women to the interior of Germany as forced labour, mass executions and deportations to concentration camps, the plundering of public and private property, the extermination of the intellectual class and of all manifestations of cultural life, the spoliation of the treasures of science and art and the persecution of all religious beliefs, are unparalleled in all human history. They offer a striking example of the spirit and methods of the German New Order.

The two Governments address this burning appeal to all free people immune from the German terror, that in the measure of their strength they should help the nations allied in the struggle for the freedom of all nations and the deliverance of the world from its present monstrous nightmare.

No. 14

The British Foreign Secretary to Count August Zaleski, Polish Minister of Foreign Affairs: Letter
LONDON, 27 November 1940
D.O.P.S.R., I, No. 80

When I saw you on the 18th November[1] I promised to let you have some account of our policy towards the Soviet Union, with particular reference to the proposals for an understanding, which, as I told you, we recently made to the Soviet Government.

These proposals included an offer on the part of His Majesty's Government to recognize, on a temporary basis pending a general settlement of all such outstanding questions at the end of the war, Soviet de facto control of the areas which have been occupied by the Red Army since the beginning of the war. The question of sovereignty would of course remain unaffected by such recognition.

In this connection, I would draw your attention to the Prime Minister's declaration of the 5th September last that: 'We don't propose to recognize any territorial changes which take place during the war unless they take place with the free consent and goodwill of the parties concerned', and to my own statement to this effect of the same date. Our proposal to the Soviet Government in no way invalidates or weakens this principle to which we are fully resolved to adhere.

In general our proposals to the Soviet Government were only tentative, and you may rest assured that it was our intention to approach the Polish Government before any agreement affecting Polish interests was reached. In the course of the conversations which we have been conducting with the

Soviet Government with the object of effecting some improvement in Anglo-Soviet relations, it had, however, become quite clear that, so long as we refused to admit that the Soviet authorities were in fact in control of the areas occupied by the Red Army since the beginning of the war at the expense of other countries, it would, for purely practical reasons, be difficult to find any basis for discussion. In actual fact the existence of British interests in certain of the areas in question had already made it necessary for us to treat with the Soviet Government and local authorities on the assumption that they were in control of these areas, and our proposals therefore only implies the acknowledgement on our part of a state of affairs which already existed in fact.

As I have already pointed out, however the proposals made by us to the Soviet Government only contemplated a temporary arrangement, based on an existing state of affairs, which we cannot deny or ignore if we are to protect British interests in the territories concerned. But, in our view, the definite settlement of the future of the territories concerned, which have of course in no way been prejudiced by our proposals, can only be effected at the end of the war. As it would clearly be impossible to exclude the Soviet Government from such a settlement, our offer to consult them about it may be regarded as a necessary consequence of our refusal to recognize enforced territorial changes which take place during the war.[2]

1. At a meeting with Halifax on November 18, 1940 (F.O. 371. C12548/7177/55), Zaleski had complained that the proposals for an Anglo-Soviet agreement which had been reported in the press directly affected Poland's interests. In particular, he objected to the proposal for the *de facto* incorporation of the Baltic States, claiming that if this applied to Lithuania, it must involve the annexation of Polish territory, since Lithuania had no common frontier with the Soviet Union. In addition, he stated, 'Poland was the only Power among the Allies who was in a state of war with the Soviet Union.'
2. In his reply to this letter on 14 December 1940. (D.O.P.S.R.I, No. 81) Zaleski argued that the Treaty of Riga was a negotiated settlement between the Soviet Union and Poland and had been accepted by both sides. In addition, he claimed that article 2, para. b. of the secret protocol attached to the Anglo-Soviet treaty (see above No. 1) recognized that the independence of Lithuania lay 'within the vital interests of Poland'. This argument was not accepted by the British, although they agreed that the Poles had a stronger case in relation to Vilna, which had been Polish territory.

CHAPTER TWO

FROM JULY 1941 TO THE BREAK IN RELATIONS (APRIL 1943)

No. 15

Conversation between Ernest Bevin, Secretary of State for Labour and
General Sikorski (Extracts)
LONDON, 3 July 1941
F.O. 371. C7458/3226/55

. . . Soviet-Polish relations: General Sikorski said that what the Polish
Government would like the Soviet Government to do would be to declare as
null and void the German-Soviet Treaty of non-aggression of August, 1939,
and the German-Soviet friendship and frontier Agreement of September, 1939,
which partitioned Poland between Germany and the Soviet Union. He was
glad to note that the Soviet Government now appeared to be adopting a more
favourable attitude towards Poland. . .

Mr. Bevin asked what the Polish Government proposed to do for the Soviet
Government in return, especially as regards the frontiers of Eastern Europe,
e.g. the Lithuanian-Polish frontier and the Polish-Soviet frontier.

General Sikorski replied that the Polish Government, without surrendering
their claim to the pre-war frontiers, admitted that these frontiers might be a
matter for discussion. In any event, the Polish Government proposed to give a
wide measure of authonomy to the non-Polish populations who would be
included within the Polish frontiers. . .

General Sikorski then outlined as follows the various suggestions which the
Polish Government would wish to submit to the Soviet Government at an
appropriate time, possibly through the good offices of His Majesty's
Government, either in London or in Moscow. He promised to have an aide-
mémoire on the subject communicated to the Foreign Office. He did not ask
for immediate action, and indeed had told Sir Stafford Cripps (to whom he
had spoken on the subject) that he preferred to wait a week or two until
Sir S. Cripps could see whether the moment was propitious or not.

The Polish suggestions were as follows:—

(1) that Polish prisoners of war and deportees should be released;

(2) that these prisoners or war and deportees should be recognized by the
Soviet Government as Polish citizens;

(3) that the Soviet Government should recognise the right of the Polish
Government to protect them. (Poland was willing to spend her gold reserve
for the benefit of these Polish citizens in the Soviet Union);

(4) that the Soviet Government should receive, as a Polish representative, one of the persons on the list given by General Sikorski to Sir Stafford Cripps;

(5) that the Polish Red Cross should be allowed to work in the Soviet Union;

(6) that the Polish army should be created in Russia;

(7) that the Soviet Government should cease anti-Polish propaganda;

(8) Poland, for her part, would be willing to come to some compromise arrangement about the Soviet-Polish frontier after the war. Poland would seek compensation at Germany's expense to the westward.[1]

---

1. Sikorski had considerable difficulty in persuading his cabinet to accept the relatively moderate line he outlined in this conversation. The note which the Polish Foreign Minister, August Zaleski, submitted to the British Foreign Office on 7 July (D.O.P.S.R. I, No. 92) was much more unyielding in tone, demanding a Soviet abrogation of the agreements with Germany of 23 August and 28 September 1939 and a clearer recognition of the frontier established by the Treaty of Riga of March 1921. The memorandum Zaleski submitted to the Foreign Office on 8 July (D.O.P.S.R.I, No. 93) stressed Polish interest not only in the territories occupied by the Soviet Union in September 1939, but also in the independence of the Baltic States and in the Soviet renunciation of Bessarabia and Bukovina.

No. 16

The British Foreign Secretary, Anthony Eden, to the Ambassador in Moscow, Sir Stafford Cripps: Telegram (Extract)
LONDON, 4 July 1941
F.R.U.S. 1941, I, pp. 239–40

The Soviet Ambassador[1] asked to see me this afternoon, when he said that he had brought me a message from his Government. The Soviet Government had been considering their relations with Poland, Czechoslovakia and Yugoslavia. They had taken the decision to give facilities to all three States to form national committees in the U.S.S.R. These committees would have facilities to form national military forces, Polish, Czechoslovak and Yugoslav. The Soviet Government undertook to supply arms and equipment to these forces. It followed as a result of this that all Polish prisoners of war in Russian hands would be handed over to the Polish National Committee. Their number was nothing like as large as General Sikorski had told me; there were only 20,000.[2] These forces, would fight with the Russian armies against the German aggressor.

2. With regard to Poland, Soviet policy was to favour the establishment of

---

1. Ivan Maisky.
2. On 24 June 1941, Eden had told Maisky that General Sikorski had asserted that these prisoners numbered 'as many as 300,000'. (F.O. 371. C7016/3226/55). According to *Krasnaya Zviezda* of 17 September 1940, there were in Soviet captivity 181,000 soldiers, as well as 12 generals, 58 colonels, 72 lieutenant-colonels and 9,227 officers of other ranks.

an independent national Polish State. The boundaries of this State would correspond with ethnographical Poland. From this it might follow that certain districts and towns occupied by Russia in 1939 might be returned to Poland. The form of internal government to be set in Poland was, in the view of the Soviet Government, entirely a matter for the Poles themselves. If General Sikorski and his Government found these statements of policy acceptable, the Soviet Government were prepared to make a treaty with him to form a common front against German aggression. . .

4. . . . I pressed him further for some definition of what he meant by ethnographical Poland, and the Ambassador said that he felt that there would be no great difficulty in defining frontiers on this basis provided that there was goodwill on both sides.

No. 17

The Soviet Polish Agreement
LONDON, 30 July 1941
D.O.P.S.R.I, No. 106

The Government of the Union of Soviet Socialist Republics recognises the Soviet-German Treaties of 1939 as to territorial changes in Poland as having lost their validity. The Polish Government declares that Poland is not bound by any agreement with any third Power which is directed against the Union of Soviet Socialist Republics.

2. Diplomatic relations will be restored between the two Governments upon the signing of this agreement and an immediate exchange of ambassadors will be arranged.

3. The two Governments mutually agree to render one another aid and support of all kinds in the present war against Hitlerite Germany.

4. The Government of the Union of Soviet Socialist Republics expresses its consent to the formation on the territory of the Union of Soviet Socialist Republics of a Polish army under a commander appointed by the Polish Government in agreement with the Soviet Government, the Polish army on the territory of the Union of Soviet Socialist Republics being subordinate in an operational sense to the supreme command of the Union of Soviet Socialist Republics, upon which the Polish army will be represented. All details as to command, organisation and employment of this force will be settled in a subsequent agreement.

5. This agreement will come into force immediately upon signature and without ratification.

Protocol

The Soviet Government grants an amnesty to all Polish citizens now detained on Soviet territory, either as prisoners of war or on other sufficient grounds, as from the resumption of diplomatic relations.

Secret Protocol

The various claims of a public as of a private nature will be considered in the subsequent negotiations between the two Governments.

No. 18

Exchange of Notes between the British Foreign Secretary and General Sikorski[1]
LONDON, 30 July 1941
F.O. 371. C8958/3226/55

After the signature of the agreement, the Secretary of State handed General Sikorski a note in the following terms:—

On the occasion of the signature of the Polish-Soviet Agreement of to-day's date I desire to take the opportunity of informing you that, in conformity with the provisions of the Agreement of Mutual Assistance between the United Kingdom and Poland of the 25th August, 1939, His Majesty's Government in the United Kingdom have entered into no undertaking towards the Union of Soviet Socialist Republics which affects the relations between that country and Poland. I also desire to assure you that His Majesty's Government do not recognize any territorial changes which have been effected in Poland since August 1939.[2]

General Sikorski handed him a reply in the following terms:—

The Polish Government take note of your Excellency's letter dated the 30th July, 1941, and desire to express sincere satisfaction at the statement that His Majesty's Government in the United Kingdom do not recognise any territorial changes which have been effected in Poland since August 1939. This corresponds with the view of the Polish Government, who, as they have previously informed His Majesty's Government, have never recognised any territorial changes effected in Poland since the outbreak of the present war.

1. This note had been suggested by the British on 18 July in order to obtain Polish acquiescence to the Agreement (F.O. 371. C8602/3226/55). When Maisky learnt of the proposed exchange of notes, he told Cadogan on 27 July that the final sentence seemed to imply a 'guarantee of the former Soviet-Polish frontier', which his government 'would not like' (F.O. 371. C8480/3226/55).
2. The Poles claimed that the last sentence of the Note had been weakened in relation to what had been offered them on 18 July by the inclusion of the final phrase 'unless they take place with the free consent and goodwill of the parties concerned.'

No. 19

Statement made in the House of Commons by Anthony Eden (Extracts)
LONDON, 30 July 1941
H. of C. Debates, vol. 373, cols. 1052–4

... I want to say a word in connexion with the note which I handed to General
Sikorski. It is stated in paragraph 1 of the Soviet-Polish Agreement that the
Soviet Government recognise the Soviet-German Treaties of 1939 concerning
territorial changes in Poland as having lost their validity. The attitude of His
Majesty's Government in these matters was stated in general terms by my
right hon. friend the Prime Minister in the House of Commons on the 5th
September, 1940, when he said that His Majesty's Government did not
propose to recognise any territorial changes which took place during the war,
unless they took place with the free consent and goodwill of the parties
concerned.[1] This holds good with the territorial changes which have been
effected in Poland since August 1939, and I informed the Polish
Government accordingly in my official note. As to the future frontiers of
Poland, as of other European countries, I would draw attention to what
my right hon. friend said in the speech to which I have referred. I am sure
the House will agree with me that both parties are to be warmly con-
gratulated on the signature of this agreement. This is an historic event.
It will lay a firm foundation for future collaboration between the two
countries in the war against the common enemy. It will, therefore, be a
valuable contribution to the Allied cause, and will be warmly welcomed in
all friendly countries, and not least, I feel sure, by public opinion throughout
the British Empire.

1. See above, Document No. 12. This phrase was included in Eden's statement to
mollify the Poles.

No. 20

Lord Halifax to Anthony Eden: Telegram
WASHINGTON, 30 July 1941
F.O. 371. C8567/3226/55

... He [Welles] told me that he had already made it plain to the Polish
Ambassador here and to the U.S. Ambassador in London that the United
States government would be glad to see agreement reached between the
Poles and the Soviet but that they thought that any necessary detailed
discussions should take place in London, where they had already been in
progress.[1]

1. This was in reply to a telegram from Eden on 29 July, in which he informed
Halifax that Sikorski was concerned that the Polish ambassador in Washington, Jan
Ciechanowski, was stirring up opposition in American government circles to the
Polish-Soviet agreement (F.O. 371. C8498/3226/55).

No. 21

Leading article in Izvestia of 3 August 1941 (Extracts)

... thus it is clear that there is not and cannot be any analogy, between 1795 [the third partition of Poland] and 1939.[1]

Is it not obvious that the entry of the Soviet armies into the eastern provinces of Poland in 1939 took place in conditions when, as V. M. Molotov accurately stated in his speech of 17 September 1939,[2] Poland had become the scene for all kinds of chance happenings and unexpected occurrences which could threaten the Soviet Union?

Is it not well-known that these provinces are inhabited in the overwhelming majority of Ukrainians and Byelorussians to whom the U.S.S.R. felt bound — and justly bound — by solemn obligation to extend its aid when they were threatened by the danger of German occupation? ...

In the light of recent events and the treacherous attack of Hitlerite Germany on the U.S.S.R., it is particularly clear how correctly the Soviet government acted in Autumn 1939, in not giving German fascism western Ukraine and western Byelorussia, which German fascism would not have neglected to turn into a jumping off point for its invasion of the Soviet Union. ...

In the Polish-Soviet agreement of 30 July 1941, the Soviet government has recognized that the clauses of the 1939 agreement [with Germany] regarding territorial changes in Poland have lost their force. This shows that 'territorial changes' are not eternal, and also that the borders envisaged by these 'changes' are not immutable. For instance we do not regard as immutable the borders established between Poland and the Soviet Union by the Treaty of Riga of 1921 and we do not share the position that 'no-one can take the view that the borders of the 1939 frontiers of the Polish state can be questioned'[3] as General Sikorski stated in his speech. It was not without reason that the British government refused to guarantee the borders of Poland as they existed in 1939 before the outbreak of war between Germany and Poland.

The problems of the future Soviet Polish border — this is a task for the future. There is no doubt that with statesmanship and good will on both sides these problems will be solved in the same way as the problems which have recently been settled.

1. As had been claimed by Gen. Sikorski in his speech of 31 July 1941 (D.O. P.S.R.1, No. 109).
2. For this speech, see D.O. P.S.R. 1, No. 46. See also no. 4.
3. Sikorski had said ... 'But it [the agreement] does not permit even of the suggestion that the 1939 frontiers of the Polish State could ever be in question.'

No. 22

Polish-Soviet Military Agreement
MOSCOW, 14 August 1941
D.O.P.S. R.I, No. 112

1. The military agreement derives naturally from the political agreement of July 30, 1941.

2. A Polish army will be organized in the shortest possible time on the territory of the USSR, wherefore:

   a) it will form part of the armed forces of the sovereign Republic of Poland,

   b) the soldiers of this army will take the oath of allegiance to the Republic of Poland,

   c) it will be destined with the Armed Forces of the USSR and other Allied States for the common fight against Germany,

   d) after the end of the war, it will return to Poland,

   e) during the entire period of common operations, it will be subordinated operationally to the High Command of the USSR. In respect of organization and personnel it will remain under the authority of the Commander-in-Chief of the Polish Armed Forces, who will co-ordinate the orders and regulations concerning organization and personnel with the High Command of the USSR through the Commander of the Polish Army on the territory of the USSR.

3. The Commander of the Polish Army on the territory of the USSR will be appointed by the Commander-in-Chief of the Polish Armed Forces; the candidate for this appointment to be approved by the Government of the USSR.

4. The Polish Army on the territory of the USSR will consist of units of land forces only. Their strength and number will depend on manpower, equipment and supplies available.

5. Conscripts and volunteers, having previously served in the Polish Air Force and Navy, will be sent to Great Britain to complement the establishments of the respective Polish services already existing there.

6. The formation of Polish units will be carried out in localities indicated by the High Command of the USSR. Officers and other ranks will be called from among Polish citizens on the territory of the USSR by conscription and voluntary enlistment. Draft boards will be established with the participation of USSR authorities in localities indicated by them.

7. Polish units will be moved to the front only after they are fully ready for action. In principle they will operate in groups not smaller than divisions and will be used in accordance with the operational plans of the High Command of the USSR.

8. All soldiers of the Polish Army on the territory of the USSR will be subject to Polish military laws and decrees.

Polish military courts will be established in the units for dealing with military offences and crimes against the establishment, the safety, the routine or the discipline of the Polish Army.

For crimes against the State, soldiers of the Polish Army on the territory of the USSR will be answerable to the military courts of the USSR.

9. The organization and war equipment of the Polish units will as far as possible correspond to the standards established for the Polish Army in Great Britain.

The colours and insignia of the various services and military ranks will correspond exactly to those established for the Polish Army in Great Britain.

10. The pay, rations, maintenance and other material problems will be in accordance with regulations of the USSR.

11. The sick and wounded soldiers of the Polish Army will receive treatment in hospitals and sanatoria on an equal basis with the soldiers of the USSR and be entitled to pensions and allowances.

12. Armament, equipment, uniforms, motor transport, etc. will be provided as far as possible by

a) the Government of the USSR from their own resources,

b) the Polish Government from supplies granted on the basis of the Lend-Lease Act (an Act to promote the defence of the United States, approved March 11, 1941).

In this case, the Government of the USSR will extend all possible transportation facilities.

13. Expenditures connected with the organization, equipment and maintenance of the Polish Army on the territory of the USSR will be met from credits provided by the Government of the USSR, to be refunded by the Polish Government after the end of the war.

This problem will be dealt with in a separate financial agreement.

14. Liaison will be established by

1) a Polish Military Mission attached to the High Command of the USSR,

2) a Soviet Military Mission attached to the Polish High Command in London.

Liaison officers attached to other commands will be apointed by mutual agreement.

15. All matters and details not covered by this agreement will be settled directly between the High Command of the Polish Army on the territory of the USSR and the corresponding authorities of the USSR.

16. This agreement is made in two copies, in the Polish and Russian languages, both texts are equally valid.

Plenipotentiary of the Polish High Command.	Plenipotentiary of the High Command of the USSR.
Szyszko-Bohusz, Brigadier-General.	A. Vassilevsky, Major-General.

No. 23

Anthony Eden to Sir Cecil Dormer: Dispatch
LONDON, 18 August 1941
F.O. 371. C9279/3226/55

THE Polish Ambassador[1] called on me this afternoon, on General Sikorski's
instructions, to speak of the difficulties which the Polish Goverment were
encountering as a result of the conclusion of the Polish-Soviet Agreement and
of other recent events.

2. He said that as it was likely that he would himself shortly be charged
with the conduct of Poland's foreign relations,[2] it might be useful if he were
to describe to me the background as he saw it. Polish opinion, both here and
in Poland, had undoubtedly been disturbed by the conclusions of the Polish-
Soviet Agreement. The entry of Soviet Russia into the war was certainly
regarded by Poles generally as a good thing, not only because it would mean a
heavy drain upon German resources, but also because it would weaken the
Soviet Union. But it was realised that the fact that the Soviet Union was now
an active ally would be bound to throw Poland and Polish interests rather
into the background. There was also a general feeling, to put it bluntly, that
the conclusion of the Polish-Soviet Agreement had weakened rather than
strengthened the Polish position *vis-à-vis* the Soviet Union as regards their
Eastern frontiers. On top of this had come the Anglo-American 8-point
declaration, which, by its insistence on the principle of self-determination,
would disappoint Polish hopes as regards their western frontier also. Danzig
was undoubtedly a German town, but it was for economic reasons essential
to Poland, and so long as the Germans were in East Prussia, Poland's Western
frontier was, from a military point of view, almost indefensible. The morale
of the Polish population was still firm and unbroken, but there were now, for
the first time, signs that German propaganda was taking a dangerous turn
and adopting a line which might perhaps have some appeal in Poland —
namely, that under the allied dispensation Poland would be a miserable
enclave at the mercy of the Russians.

3. The Ambassador therefore suggested, though he did not wish to press
the point for the present, that His Majesty's Government might make some
public statement, or at any rate some communication to the Polish
Goverment, to the effect that it was not their intention to insist on a rigid
application of the principle of self-determination, to the exclusion of other
considerations such as economics and defence. In all honesty, however, he
felt bound to say that the 8-point declaration had caused misgivings in
Polish opinion.[3]

4. I told Count Raczynski that I was always glad to hear anything he had
to tell me about the views of the Polish Government. I thought it most unlikely that the Prime Minister and President Roosevelt had had the Polish
frontiers in mind when they drafted the 8-point declaration. It would be very

difficult for His Majesty's Government to put any gloss upon that declaration in the sense desired by the Polish Government, except possibly in the most general terms; but I should be quite ready to explore the question further with the Ambassador. . .

1. Count Edward Raczyński.
2. Raczyński became Acting Foreign Minister in August 1941.
3. In a letter to Eden on 25 August 1941, Raczyński suggested that the British government make a gloss on article 2 of the Atlantic Charter accepting the Polish right to territorial expansion at German expense (F.O. 371. C9653/5996/55). On 29 August, Eden told Sikorski and Raczyński that he could not comply with this request, which would, in any event, require American agreement (F.O. 371. C9959/5996/55). Eden reiterated this view on 15 September, when he also suggested that the Poles make plain their objections to the wording of article two at the Inter-Allied meeting to be held in London on 24 September. This the Poles accordingly did (F.O. 371. C10382, 10607/14/62).

No. 24

General Sikorski's instructions to Lt.-General Anders, Commander of the Polish Forces in the Soviet Union (Extract)
LONDON, 1 September 1941
D.O.P.S.R.I, No. 120

. . .I attach the greatest importance to our troops being used for military operations as a whole, obviously under your command. This is indispensable both from the point of view of our prestige, and of operational considerations which do not allow any breaking up of the Polish troops which would lead to sheer waste of their effort. I am absolutely unrelenting on this point since the French campaign, when, owing to jealousy, meanness and envy our divisions were scattered during the training period, and it could not be remedied in June 1940. I think that the Soviet Command will appreciate this principle, and the advantages of its being put into effect. I advise you, however, to be both firm and vigilant in this question of paramount importance for the Polish Army.

I expect from you, General, the same firmness and independence from Soviet military factors in relation to personal and organizational matters. The troops commanded by you depend on the Soviet High Command in what concerns military operations only. Their dependence is explicitly defined in the Military Agreement. In order to emphasize this point and also to help you, I intend to come over there some day and to spend some time among your troops.

I do not overlook the problems of operations and of the use in fighting line of the troops put under your command *after they have attained full combat readiness*. As regards this question, I wish in the first place that the troops may be used in a way enabling them to fulfil single-handed a task which would be important from the point of view of the whole war, and secondly that they may operate as closely as possible with our British Allies.

I am writing these words in full agreement with Prime Minister Churchill.

As it appears from General Szyszko-Bohusz's first report, you are completely free to put forward proposals relating to this question. In fact, it was decided in the conversation with Yevstigneyev on 7th August that the Polish Military Mission 'will produce plans concerning the possible course of action to be taken by the Polish military units when they come into action'.

One of the most vital issues for our enemy is to take hold of the oil-fields, and all his operations aim at this. The defence of the oil-fields becomes therefore a very important and self-sufficient task. I consider it to be so important that it deserves to be assigned to our troops in the USSR.

The most appropriate target for the operations of our troops is, in my view, in the direction of the Caucasus and Iran, where, beside operating in a sector of considerable strategic importance, they would have the opportunity of stretching a hand to our British Allies and of fighting side by side with them as well as with the Russian ally.

I ask you therefore to do everything possible to obtain the assignment of the Polish troops in the USSR for this target, so that, in due time, they may be entrusted with a task of their own.

I consider the use of our troops on the Russian western front as undersirable as they would be diluted there, broken up and playing a secondary role. These harmful consequences would by no means be compensated for by their possibility of reaching Poland at an earlier date. . .[1]

---

1. Sikorski expressed similar views to Averell Harriman, who was heading a United States Mission on supplies to the Soviet Union on 19 September. (D.O.P.S.R.I, No. 124). He also told Harriman that in the event of a Soviet defeat, 'the Polish Army might become the leading element, a factor that could dominate the situation and group around them all forces still capable of resistance.'

No. 25

The British Ambassador to the U.S.S.R., Sir Stafford Cripps to Andrei Vyshynsky, Deputy Commissar for Foreign Affairs: Aide-Memoire
KUIBYSHEV, 3 November 1941
D.O.P.S.R.I, No. 138

His Majesty's Government have been much concerned at information they have recently been receiving from the Polish Government about the difficulties that have arisen over the implementation of the terms of the Agreement of July 30th, 1941, and of the subsequent Military Agreement between the Polish and the Soviet Governments.

The Prime Minister and Mr. Eden have discussed this matter fully with General Sikorski and the Polish Government in London, and they are all in agreement about the desirability of General Sikorski's visiting the USSR.

His Majesty's Government feel some responsibility in the matter owing to the part which they played in assisting the Polish and Soviet Governments to arrive at an agreement in the first instance. In particular, the Soviet Government will recollect that the actual clause about the amnesty for Polish citizens was settled in Moscow between M. Stalin and the British Ambassador.

As a result of conversations which have taken place in London between the British and Polish Governments, and in view of the declaration made by M. Molotov to the Polish Ambassador at Kuibyshev a few days ago to the effect that the Soviet Government were unable to supply the Polish forces with either arms or food in adequate quantities, it has been suggested that it would be best if these forces were to be moved down to the South where they could be equipped by the British authorities and would be more accessible from British sources of supply.

There is a further question, about which His Majesty's Government are much concerned, relating to the amnesty already mentioned above, for which they feel, as already stated, a measure of responsibility. They understand that there are still many thousands of Polish citizens, including many of military age and fit for military service, in prisons, concentration camps and forced labour camps, particularly in the extreme North of the USSR. They do not understand why these persons have not yet been released, as agreed some three months ago and as laid down in the Ukase of the Supreme Council of the USSR of August 8th which was subsequently published.[1] It would seem to them that the immediate release of these Polish citizens is imperative if good relations between the Polish and Soviet Governments are to continue. The Soviet Government would no doubt at the same time make whatever arrangements were necessary for these Polish citizens to receive the necessaries of life either by providing them with free work at adequate wages or else by making them the necessary allowances in money or kind.

His Majesty's Government feel impelled to draw the attention of the Soviet Government to the above-mentioned matters since they are most anxious to do all they can to assist in preserving the good relations that exist between the Soviet and Polish Governments.

His Majesty's Government would urge the Soviet Government to give its decision in principle upon the above points at the earliest possible moment, so that it may then be possible for General Sikorski to visit the USSR at an early date.[2]

1 . This should be 'Ukase of August 12th'.
2. In a telegram to Stanisław Kot, the Polish Ambassador to the Soviet Union on 28 October, Sikorski made the release of all detainees and the concentration of the Polish army at a point where it could be supplied by the British from Iran conditions on whose satisfaction his proposed visit to the U.S.S.R. depended (D.O.P.S.R.I, No. 134).

No. 26

Statement made at the meeting of the Polish-Czechoslovak Co-ordinating
Committee by Hubert Ripka, Czechoslovak Foreign Secretary (Extract)
LONDON, 4 November 1941
F.O. 371. C13252/6/12

. . . I. It was clear to us from the beginning that it would be necessary for
the foreign policy of our Governments to be coordinated at least in the
most important problems. . . We were aware that we should certainly
easily come to agreement on a common policy towards Germany. We had
however to consider how to agree on our policy towards Russia and
indeed also towards Hungary; it was in these directions that the
orientations of our policies was divergent or at any rate not in conformity.
But in this respect the events of the war have helped us considerably. . .
Thus. . . there came about in this essential matter [policy towards Russia] a
great rapprochement between Polish policy and Czechoslovak policy
which . . . uninterruptedly supports the view of the need for political
collaboration between Western Europe and Central-Eastern Europe and
the Soviet Union on the other hand.[1] Finally in view of the fact that
Hungary is the military ally of Germany and is fighting by her side against
the ally of Great Britain, Poland and Czechoslovakia, our policy towards
Hungary has also reached greater conformity.

II. . .[frontier problems] We consider it necessary that each party
should behave with loyal respect for the claims of the other party and
should not undertake anything that would be to the disadvantage of the
attitude and claim of the other party.

III. As far as the frontier between Poland and Czechoslovakia is concerned . . . we are in agreement in the principle that we shall exert all our
efforts to come to agreement . . . among ourselves through direct and
cordial negotiations. . .

1. On 10 November at Aberdeen University, Beneš had argued that 'the active
participation of Soviet Russia in the establishment of European equilibrium must, of
course, find expression first of all in an agreement between the Soviets and the
Czechoslovak-Polish Confederation' (F.O. 371 C13398/216/12).

No. 27

The Polish Embassy in Kiubyshev, to the People's Commissariat for
Foreign Affairs: Note
KUIBYSHEV, 10 November 1941
D.O.P.S.R.I, No. 143

                                          Transl. from Polish: Pol.-Sov.R., No. 56
According to information received, the War Commissar for Kazakhstan at
Alma-Ata, General Shcherbakov, issued orders that all Polish citizens de-

ported by the Soviet Authorities from occupied Polish territory and possessing documents issued to them by these authorities, endorsed to the effect that they are of Ukrainian, White Ruthenian or Jewish origin, are to be enrolled in the Red Army if they meet the age and fitness requirements.

After an intervention by the interested parties and by a representative of this Embassy, General Shcherbakov declared that he was acting on instructions from the Central Authorities, who are alleged to have directed him to treat as citizens of the USSR all citizens of the Republic of Poland of other than Polish origin possessing Soviet passports. . .

This same discrimination between Polish citizens according to origin or race, devoid of any impartial basis and contrary to the provisions of the Polish-Soviet Agreement of July 30, 1941, is being practised by the military authorities in Alma-Ata, who also explain to the Polish citizens reporting to them to settle various formalities connected with their enlistment in the Polish Army in the Union of Soviet Socialist Republics, that they are acting on instructions from the Central Authorities. Only Polish citizens of Polish originaare given permits to travel to centres where the Polish Army is being organized, while Polish citizens of Ukrainian and Jewish origin are, it seems, categorically refused permits by the aforementioned authorities.

The Polish Embassy has the honour to request the People's Commissariat for Foreign Affairs to cause instructions to be given to the War Commissar in Kazakhstan to apply impartially to all Polish citizens residing in the area under his authority, the principles resulting from the Polish-Soviet Agreement of July 30, 1941, and the Polish-Soviet Military Agreement of August 14, 1941, which guarantee the right to serve in the Polish Army in the USSR to every Polish citizen who is capable of bearing arms.[1]

. The Soviet government replied on 1 December claiming that all citizens of 'Western Ukraine' and 'Western Byelorussia' had acquired Soviet citizenship and that the Soviet readiness to recognize as Polish citizens 'persons of Polish nationality' in these areas was a sign of the good will of the Soviet government, since the Polish-Soviet frontier is not yet settled'. (D.O.P.S.R.I, No. 157). The Polish reply of 9 December reaffirmed the view that Polish law did not distinguish nationality in deciding questions of citizenship (D.O.P.S.R.I, No. 163). The Soviets upheld their position in a further note of 5 January 1942 (D.O.P.S.R.I, No. 167). This question was also raised by General Sikorski in his conversation with Stalin on 1 December (D.O.P.S.R.I, No. 160).

No. 28

Sir Stafford Cripps to Foreign Office: Telegram (Extract)
KUIBYSHEV, 17 November 1941
F.O. 371. C12812/3226/55

Polish Ambassador returned from Moscow last night and reports a very satisfactory and sympathetic reception by Stalin.[1]

2. So far as two main points are concerned result was as follows:—

(a) Military forces. Stalin agreed that there was no limit to the number that Poland could raise up to five, six, seven or more divisions. Russia would keep to their original promise to arm the divisions. On the question of food Stalin said that it was difficult as he had to find food for this country and millions of his own troops, but it might become easier a little later on. He alluded to the order which had been sent by the staff to General Anders as to limitation of numbers to thirty thousand, and said that it should never have been issued and that he would see to it. He offered to allocate a district in Uzbekistan for the assembly of military personnel and also of civilians but the Ambassador asked him to wait until the arrival of Sikorski before doing so.

(b) Civilians. Stalin stated categorically that *amnesty* was without exception and that he could not understand why there were any Poles still not released. He rang up the Ogpu headquarters immediately and asked if this was so, and then promised to see to the matter himself.

3. Discussion lasted over two hours and they talked of relations between the two countries generally. Stalin said that he wished to do all he could to improve these, and that he had no idea of interfering in any way with the internal affairs of Poland. He expressed a keen desire to see Sikorski. Molotov was present and as usual bringing up points which Stalin brushed aside.

4. Ambassador saw Molotov alone next day[2] but found him petty-minded about a lot of detailed points which they discussed and the atmosphere was not nearly so sympathetic and helpful as it had been with Stalin. Stalin had told the Ambassador to go to him personally if he got into any difficulties. . .

1. This conversation took place on 14 November. For a more detailed account, see D.O.P.S.R.I, No. 149.
2. This conversation is described in D.O.P.S.R.I, No. 151.

No. 29

Declaration of Friendship and Mutual Assistance
MOSCOW, 4 December 1941
D.O.P.S.R.I, No. 161

The Government of the Polish Republic and the Government of the Union of Soviet Socialist Republics, animated by the spirit of friendly understanding and fighting collaboration, declare:

1. German Hitlerite imperialism is the worst enemy of mankind — no compromise with it is possible.

Both States together with Great Britain and other Allies, supported by the United States of America, will wage war until complete victory and final destruction of the German invaders.

2. Implementing the Treaty concluded on July 30, 1941,[1] both Govern-
1. See above No. 17.

ments will render each other during the war full military assistance, and troops of the Republic of Poland located on the territory of the Soviet Union will wage war against the German brigands shoulder to shoulder with Soviet troops.

In peace-time their mutual relations will be based on good neighbourly collaboration, friendship and reciprocal honest fulfilment of the obligations they have taken upon themselves.

3. After a victorious war and the appropriate punishment of the Hitlerite criminals, it will be the aim of the Allied States to ensure a durable and just peace. This can be achieved only through a new organization of international relations on the basis of unification of the democratic countries in a durable alliance. Respect for international law backed by the collective armed force of the Allied States must form the decisive factor in the creation of such an organization. Only under this condition can a Europe destroyed by German barbarism be restored and a guarantee be created that the disaster caused by the Hitlerites will never be repeated.

For the Government of the	By authority of the
Republic of Poland	Government of the Soviet Union
Sikorski	Stalin

No. 30

Sir Stafford Cripps to Anthony Eden: Telegram (Extract)
KUIBYSHEV, 6 December 1941
F.O. 371. C13550/3226/55

I saw General Sikorski this morning and he gave me account of his talks with Stalin which he asked me to let you have as soon as possible.[1] He was good enough to state that my estimate of Stalin's views which I had given him before he went to Moscow was accurate and better than any other he had received here.

2. His talks were completely successful from the point of view of changing the atmospheric relations between the two countries to one of trust and collaboration. At times they were difficult and required a good deal of insistence on the part of the General. When he first mentioned the question of the withdrawal of Polish forces to some country outside Russia, Stalin interpreted this as a conspiracy between the United States, Poland and ourselves and told the General that all the world would laugh at him (Stalin) if such a thing were to happen. Thereupon the General asked him for his alternative suggestions (as to which see below).

3. Stalin made a very friendly speech about Poland at the dinner and the General is certain that Stalin has, as he stated, accepted the idea of a strong and independent Poland after the war. Stalin stated that he approved

---

. Sikorski was in the Soviet Union from 3 to 12 December. For the Polish record of his conversations with Stalin see D.O.P.S.R.I, Nos. 159–60.

every word of the broadcast speech which the General gave.[2] He saw it and said this before it was broadcast. The Declaration that was signed was almost unaltered in form from that proposed by the Poles.

4. Stalin was most insistent as to the release of all the Poles and said that it would certainly be carried through completely. He was so furious about the lack of provision for Polish troops which was explained to him in detail by General Anders that the Poles had to intervene between him and the Soviet officers to moderate his anger. He stated to his Quarter-Master General that you could not feed troops with regulations and ukazes. Those Russian officers who had sympathy to Poland before stated after the meetings that they were delighted with the outcome and that things would now be quite different.

5. The nett result of the talks is that according to Stalin's suggestions all Poles both civilian and military are to be concentrated in Uzbekistan mostly between Tashkend and the Persian border though some possibly east of Tashkend. Russians say that they can feed them but that they will have to rely largely on us and the United States for arms. Sikorski has seen the latest telegrams and realizes that this will be a long job but hopes by May next there will be a chance of their being armed. He hopes the food situation will be all right and as far as I can gather is not relying on us for any help in this direction. (Nevertheless demands may well be made later on if the Russians are unable to live up to their promises). I drew his attention to the difficulties and specifically asked if he had had in mind the latest telegrams as to the capacity of Persian routes. (I had of course communicated to him before his departure for Moscow the substance of War Office telegram 53,861 M.O.I. of November 24th). He assured me that he had. He said he considered it was essential to the future of Soviet-Polish relations that this offer of Stalin's should be accepted, and that he should not press for the Poles to be moved out of Russia.[3]

6. Stalin agreed to 30,000 Poles being sent out. The extra 5,000 is I gather to cover airmen and naval ratings whom Sikorski had overlooked in his former estimate. Sikorski now says that he wants only 9,000 in the Middle East and the rest in England. Stalin has consented to 5 to 7 divisions being raised in this country and they will remain together as an army.

7. At my suggestion Sikorski asked Stalin to appoint two of his advisers to visit camps with him and this seemed to please Stalin and he has appointed General Panfilov and Vyshinski to go.

8. General Sikorski will go back and see Stalin on Friday December 12th.

2. For this speech, D.O.P.S.R.I, No. 162.
3. This decision was very unwelcome to Gen. Macfarlane, Head of the British Military Mission in Kuibyshev who cabled the Chiefs of Staff on 6 December asking whether they approved this abandonment of the plan to concentrate the Polish forces outside Russia, where problems of supply would be easier (F.O. 371. C10728/3226/55).

12. The General was impressed by the attention Stalin was paying to the military rather than to the civilian members of his entourage. He is convinced there is no danger of the régime falling at the present time.

13. The General told me that there had been some immediate improvement as regards the treatment of Poles. For instance at Tashkend where there had been an order for expulsion of Poles from this area, this has now been withdrawn and Poles are being allowed into the town which was not the case before.

14. He fully realises that there are still going to be many practical difficulties especially as regards those Poles who are in the far north but he thinks that a genuine effort will be made to solve these though he also realises that some of the local authorities will prove recalcitrant even after receiving instructions from Moscow.

15. Permission has been given for Polish Embassy here to send representatives to the various districts with quite wide powers to investigate condition of the Poles and do what they can to help them. . .

17. During the dinner Stalin started to talk about the eastern frontiers of Poland but the General told him he could not discuss the question as if he came back from Russia having altered the frontier "all the world would laugh at him". Stalin accepted the position very good humouredly and said that he was sure that there would be no difficulties that could not be overcome at the peace conference but that he hoped that even before that time they would come to an understanding.[4] Stalin was very violent in his language against Hitler whom he called a mad man and a rabbit apeing a lion. He said however that Hitler had some good men around him on the military side.

18. I asked General Sikorski if he had any clue as to Stalin's feelings towards His Majesty's Government and he told me most confidentially that he was certain from what had been said that Stalin profoundly distrusted the British Government. This he thought was partly due to failure to concert military plans. He thought that type of approach made at recent conference had not helped and that it was necessary to abjure pleasant and laudatory phrases and grasp the realities of the relationships and discuss the difficulties frankly if they were to be overcome.

19. He said that he tried to explain how much help we had given in many ways and how difficult it was in practice for us to do anything about a second front. He avoided all reference to north Persia and the Caucasus as he saw it was much too dangerous a subject to get on to. He explained too, that we were all out as regards production but that America was a long way behind and that the Russians should do their utmost to stir up America to greater efforts.

4. Sikorski told Eden on 18 January that on this occasion Stalin had stated that 'Lwow should again become part of Poland' and that Poland should annex East Prussia (F.O. 371. C794/19/55).

20. He instanced as a case of distrust the suggestion made by Stalin that we wanted to get Polish troops to Singapore to fight for us which naturally he denied, pointing out that we had plenty of our own there with the Poles. The General made quite clear to Stalin his own complete loyalty to Great Britain and after that no more was suggested on the subject.

No. 31

Polish-Czechoslovak Declaration
LONDON, 19 January 1942
F.O. 371. C897/151/12

IN execution of the declaration of the Governments of Poland and Czechoslovakia of the 11th November, 1940, whereby both Governments decided that after the war Poland and Czechoslovakia shall form a Confederation of States in that area of Europe with which the vital interests of the two countries are bound, the Governments of Poland and Czechoslovakia conducted uninterrupted negotiations on the subject of the method of bringing the above declaration to fruition. Both Governments reached agreement with regard to a number of principles of the projected Confederation, which were detailed in the following declaration adopted during the current week:—

The Governments of Poland and Czechoslovakia have agreed on the following points with regard to the future Confederation of Poland and Czechoslovakia:—

1. The two Governments desire that the Polish-Czechoslovak Confederation should embrace other States of the European area with which the vital interests of Poland and Czechoslovakia are linked up.

2. The purpose of the Confederation is to assure common policy with regard to:—

    (a)   Foreign affairs.
    (b)   Defence.
    (c)   Economic and financial matters.
    (d)   Social questions.
    (e)   Transport, posts and telegraphs.

3. The Confederation will have a common General Staff, whose task it will be to prepare the means of defence, while in the event of war a unified supreme command will be appointed.

4. The Confederation will co-ordinate the policy of foreign trade and customs tariffs of the States forming the Confederation, with the view to the conclusion of a customs union.

5. The Confederation will have an agreed monetary policy. Autonomous banks of issue of the States forming the Confederation will be maintained. It will be their task to assure that the parity established between the various national currencies shall be permanently maintained.

6. The development and administration of railway, road, water and air transport, as also of the telecommunication services, will be carried out according to a common plan. An identical tariff for postal and telecommunication services will be binding on all territories of the Confederation.

The States in possession of sea and inland harbours will take into consideration the economic interests of the Confederation as a whole. Moreover, the States forming the Confederation will mutually support the interests of the sea and inland harbours of the States forming the Confederation.

7. The Confederation will co-ordinate the financial policies of the States forming the Confederation, especially with regard to taxation.

8. Co-ordination will also be applied in the realm of social policy of the various States of the Confederation.

9. The Confederation will assure co-operation among its members in educational and cultural matters.

10. Questions of nationality will remain within the competence of the individual States forming the Confederation. The passenger traffic between the various States included in the Confederation will take place without any restrictions — in particular, without passports and visas. The question of the free domicile and of the right to exercise any gainful occupation of the citizens of the individual States forming the Confederation over the whole territory of the Confederation will be regulated.

11. The question of the mutual recognition by the States forming the Confederation of school and professional diplomas, of documents and sentences of courts, as well as the question of mutual legal aid, in particular in the execution of court sentences, will be regulated.

12. The Constitutions of the individual States included in the Confederation will guarantee to the citizens of these States the following rights:—

(a) Freedom of conscience.
(b) Personal freedom.
(c) Freedomsof learning.
(d) Freedom of the spoken and written word.
(e) Freedom of assembly and association.
(f) Equality of all citizens before the law.
(g) Free admission of all citizens to the performance of all State functions.
(h) The independence of the courts of law.
(i) The control of government by representative national bodies elected by means of free elections.

13. Both Governments have agreed that, in order to ensure the common policy with regard to the above-mentioned spheres, the establishment of common organs of the Confederation will be necessary.

14. The States included in the Confederation will jointly defray the costs of its maintenance.

For the Czechoslovak Government:
                    HUBERT RIPKA.[1]

For the Polish Government:
                    EDWARD RACZYNSKI.

1. This declaration was never countersigned by Beneš, who told Mikołajczyk on 13 November 1943 that it 'entered into too many details' (D.O.P.S.R. II, No. 48).

No. 32

Alexander Bogomolov, Ambassador to the Polish Government-in-Exile to The Polish Government: Note
LONDON, 23 January 1942
D.O.P.S.R. I, No. 175 (translated)

The interview of Mr. Raczyński, acting Polish Foreign Minister, published in the *Sunday Times* of 11 November 1942 contains several statements which are not compatible with the interests of friendly relations between the Soviet Union and the Polish Republic. These statements express views which deny a positive role to the Soviet Union in the solution of European problems, which does not accord with the spirit of the agreement between the U.S.S.R. and Poland, as expressed in the declaration of friendship and mutual assistance between the government of the U.S.S.R. and that of the Polish republic.[1]

In particular, the Soviet government draws attention to the fact that Mr. Raczyński, when speaking of the guarantee of the independence of certain states, including the Baltic states, and when describing the situation of these states in relation to the war of 1939, also speaks of their defeat and capitulation. This distorts the real course of events in the Baltic, which culminated in the formation of the Soviet Socialist Lithuanian Republic, the Soviet Socialist Latvian Republic and the Soviet Socialist Estonian Republic and their voluntary entry into the Soviet Union.

When discussing next the proposed Polish-Czech confederation and describing it as a union attractive to other states, Mr. Raczyński includes Lithuania among these states, ignoring the fact that the Soviet Socialist Lithuanian Republic is a part of the Soviet Union.[2]

1. In the interview, Raczyński had stated that Russia could not compensate for the weakening of France because, though she was 'sufficiently tough and persevering in defence, she is less able to take action outside her own borders.' This role could only be taken by a central European bloc, created around the Polish-Czechoslovak confederation.
2. Raczyński had stated that the Polish-Czechoslovak Confederation would 'become a centre of attraction for other nations occupying the strip of Europe from north to south — , from Lithuania through Poland and Czechoslovakia to Hungary and the Balkan group of states" ' (*Sunday Times* 11 January 1942). This position was re-affirmed by the Polish National Council which on 17 March 1942 passed a resolution in favour of the cooperation of an independent Lithuania with the nations of Central Europe.

The Soviet government feels it necessary to declare concerning Mr. Raczyński's interview, that several statements in this interview cannot but produce an unfavourable impression on public opinion in the U.S.S.R. and cannot contribute to the development of friendly relations between the U.S.S.R. and Poland.[3]

3. Gen. Sikorski replied to this note on 30 January (D.O.P.S.R.I, No. 178). He claimed that the Polish-Soviet Agreement did not involve the renunciation of Polish territory occupied by the Soviet Union in 1939 and it also did not mean that a member of the Polish cabinet could express his views on Lithuania. He also suggested an end to discussions which could lead to friction between the Soviet Union and Poland. This proposal was accepted by the Soviet government on 28 February 1942 (D.O.P.S.R.I, No. 186) while maintaining the position expounded in its Note of 23 January.

No. 33

Conversation between Anthony Eden and General Sikorski (Extracts)
LONDON, 3 March 1942
F.O. 371. C2488/19/55

Proposed Anglo-Soviet Treaty

General Sikorski said that . . . he hoped H.M. Government would not be in a hurry to decide anything with the Russians. The Russians would be in a much weaker position to negotiate two or three months hence, when the German spring offensive had been launched.

The Secretary of State gave General Sikorski a brief outline of the position for his secret and personal information. He emphasised that he was telling the General more than he had as yet told the Russians.

He assured the General that nothing had so far been signed with the Russians. Further, nothing would be signed with the Russians concerning Poland without consulting the Poles. H.M. Government were at present in consultation with the United States about the answer to be returned by H.M. Government to the Russian proposal. Mr. Winant had gone back to Washington with a paper from H.M. Government in order to discuss the matter with the President. The U.S. Government might either acquiesce in the signature by H.M. Government of the proposed agreement, or they might agree to associate themselves with it. In the latter event, it might be possible to bring the Russians to accept less than they had originally requested. An important point, from the point of view of Poland, was that the treaty would give H.M. Government a right, recognised by the Russians, to interest themselves in European frontiers. In the absence of such a treaty, the Russians might well say that the question of Soviet-Polish frontiers was of concern only to the Soviet and Polish Governments and was nothing to do with H.M. Government. If the treaty was signed, the Soviet Government could not use this argument, and the Poles might think it an advantage that H.M. Government might have a word to say when the time came. He recalled that Stalin had been in favour of the acquisition of East Prussia by Poland, a proposal which the Secretary of State himself also favoured.

The General said that, as he had already explained, he had thought it essential not to be drawn into conversations about frontiers with Stalin. He could, however, say, for the Secretary of State's personal and secret information, that if Poland were to acquire East Prussia, it might well be that Poland could make concessions to the Soviet Government in regard to Poland's easter frontiers. But no concession could be made about either Vilna or Lwów. During their conversations in Moscow, Stalin had seemed to have moderate ideas about this frontier, particularly as regards Lwów. . .

No. 34

Conversation between United States Acting Secretary of State, Sumner Welles and General Sikorski (Extract)

WASHINGTON, 25 March 1942
F.R.U.S. 1942, III, p. 130

I told General Sikorski[1] . . . in order that there might be no misunderstanding between our two Governments, that I had better crystallize the position of this Government with regard to this general subject.

I stated that the views of the President, as already communicated to the British Government, were as follows:

1. The United States will approve no secret treaty during the course of the present world war.

2. The President believes that all questions involving definitive boundaries and territorial readjustments in Europe should be determined only after the war is won.

3. The policy of the United States is clearly set forth in the principles enunciated in the Atlantic Charter.

4. This Government will, however, be glad to receive the views of the other United Nations as to their feelings with regard to the national interests of their own peoples in order that it may give full consideration to these problems and be in a position to determine its own views, after such consideration, when the time comes for these questions to be finally settled.[2]

I asked if the views as thus set forth were in accord with the views of the Polish Government. General Sikorski replied that his Government was completely in accord with the statements I had made to him covering the views of the United States. . .

1. Sikorski had expressed his objections to the proposed Anglo-Soviet treaty to Roosevelt on 24 March (D.O.P.S.R.I, No. 194) and to Welles on this occasion. During this talk, he also presented to Welles a very detailed memorandum outlining Polish objections. This was also submitted to the British (D.O.P.S.R.I, No. 196).
2. Roosevelt had also spoken to the Soviet Ambassador to the United States, Litvinov, to this effect (F.O. 371. N1364/6/38). The Soviet Government had replied that it considered Roosevelt's statements to be of an 'informative nature' (F.O. 371. N1526/5/38

No. 35

The Ambassador to the Polish Government-in-exile, Anthony Biddle to
Cordell Hull: Telegram
LONDON, 30 March 1942
F.R.U.S. 1942, III, pp. 133–5

Referring to my despatch Polish series No. 89, of December 12, 1941,[1]
wherein I reported the substance of General Sikorski's arrangement with
M. Stalin for the evacuation of about 25,000 Polish troops for service partly
in the Middle East, partly in Britain, I have the honor herein to report the
following information and observations imparted to me both by the Acting
Chief of Polish Military Intelligence, and by the Polish Foreign Office
Specialist on Russian affairs:

They said that the Russian military authorities had issued orders for the
evacuation into Iran of about 40,000 Polish troops, now in the area just east
of Kuibyshev, to commence on March 25. According to latest information,
this movement was already under way. These instructions had been, for the
Polish military authorities in Russia, as well as for the Polish authorities here,
a source of surprise. The only explanation given by the Russian authorities
was the shortage of food and arms; that the Russians were finding it
difficult to feed these troops, and impossible to find sufficient arms and
equipment for them.[2] My informants said that in absence of further
clarification, they were able only to speculate as [to] the real motive behind
this move. On the face of it, they were inclined to feel that it did not presage
well for Polish-Russian relations. It seemed to them that, on the one hand,
the Russians no longer wished to have so many Polish troops concentrated in
one area in Russia, and, on the other hand, they wanted to eliminate any
pretext for Polish insistence that, in event the Russians forced their way into
Polish territory, these and perhaps additional Polish forces accompany the
Russian forces.[3]

Since it had become known to the Polish community in the Kuibyshev
area that these troops were to be moved into Iran, there had been somewhat
of a rush on part of the hitherto unenrolled Poles, to join up [with] the
forces. (It was therefore difficult at this moment to estimate the present total
beyond the original 40,000). Strangely enough moreover, this rush to enlist,
was apparently being permitted by the Russian authorities. Moreover, it was
estimated that about 10,000 Polish civilians, mostly women and children,
were to be permitted to accompany the troops into Iran. In this connection,
however, the British military authorities in Russia had objected to the
evacuation of this civilian element into Iran on grounds of lack of food and
accommodations. Consequently the Polish Government authorities here were
about to make a formal and urgent request of the British Government that
it permit these civilians to enter Iran. In presenting their case, the Polish
authorities would point out that although living conditions in Iran might be

uncertain and poor at best, they would undoubtedly be an improvement over the hardships these civilians had been and were now enduring in Russia.

In connection with the foregoing, and in particular with my informant's interpretation of the Russian authorities' instruction to evacuate the presently assembled Polish forces, the following observations may be of interest: it may be recalled that in previous writings I pointed out *(a)* that in initiating steps to bring about a declaration of post-war principles on part of the Allied Governments established here, General Sikorski was risking Russian suspicion and ire, which in turn might conceivably work to the disadvantage of whatever arrangements he had previously made with M. Stalin; *(b)* that I had discerned accumulating irritation on part of Russian diplomatic quarters here over the public utterances of certain Polish authorities; for example, Foreign Minister Raczynski's statement to effect that Poland regarded Lithuania as historically lying within her sphere of interest; statement by the Polish press organs here regarding Poland's insistence on the *status quo ante* as regards the Polish-Russian frontier. Only recently the Russian Ambassador to the Polish Government told me that Moscow had long been annoyed by the Polish Government's frequently published contention that there were between 1,500,000 and 2,000,000 Polish men, women and children in Russia. Moreover, Moscow was equally annoyed that the British press should continue to publish these figures. They were erroneous. Indeed, there were probably no more than 300,000 racial Poles in Russia. He could not understand why the British press had allowed itself to become the instrument of the policy of Polish propagandists.

Since my above-described talk with the Russian Ambassador the Polish National Council, on March 17, adopted a formal resolution stating in effect that despite Lithuania's unjustified pretensions to the essentially Polish city of Vilno, the Polish National Council, in the name of the entire Polish nation, wished for the Lithuanian nation, the swiftest possible return to the road of progress of its Christian western culture, in cooperation with the nations of central Europe, after it had been liberated from the German occupation and had recovered complete independence.[4]

The publication of this resolution, coming as it did at the time of General Sikorski's visit to Washington, served to augment Russian annoyance which his visit had already aroused. In mentioning the foregoing points, I feel that they call for consideration in searching for whatever motive there might be behind the Russian authorities' having ordered the evacuation of the Polish forces from the Kuibyshev area into Iran.

1. Not printed, but see above, Nos. 28, 30.
2. This was partly due to the difficulties which the war in the Far East was causing the British. Already on 20 February, the Secretary of State for War had recommended that the transfer of supplies to the Polish forces in Russia should be postponed for the present 'other than maintenance of such items of clothing etc., that have already been sent and are in good supply' (F.O. 371. C1861/19/55). This drastic suggestion was not implemented though problems of transportation considerably impeded the supply of equipment.

3. By the end of August altogether some 44,000 soldiers with 26,000 dependents had left for Iran. The responsibility for the departure of the Polish troops from the Soviet Union became the subject of an acrimonious controversy after the break of relations between Poland and the Soviets. On 6 May 1943, Vyshinsky claimed that 'notwithstanding the repeated assurances of the Polish Command as to their determination to send their units into action as soon as possible, the actual date of despatch of these units to the front was continually postponed.' This had led the Soviet government to decide that they should leave the Soviet Union. (D.O.P.S.R.II, No. 7). The Poles replied to these allegations on 7 May (D.O.P.S.R.II, No. 8). In a memorandum submitted to the War Cabinet on 10 May (W.P.(43)198), Eden concluded, 'the most that can be said is that the matter is not so simple as either M. Vyshinsky's statement or the Polish reply would suggest. It was not simply a question, as M. Vyshinsky says, of the Polish Government refusing to allow the Polish forces to be used against the Germans and the Eastern front, still less is it true, as has been suggested in some Soviet quarters, that the Polish troops themselves were unwilling to fight in Russia. On the other hand, it is not fair, as the Polish statement suggests, that the whole responsibility for the removal of the Polish troops from the U.S.S.R. should be attributed to the Soviet Government. The truth of the matter was perhaps that General Sikorski's agreements of 1941 with Premier Stalin attempted too much. Events showed that it was not possible for enemies to become fully cooperating allies overnight, especially at a time of such serious strain and stringency as obtained in Soviet Russia in 1942.'

4. See above, No. 32, note 2.

No. 36

Anthony Eden to Count Raczyński: Note
LONDON, 17 April 1942
D.O.P.S.R.I, No. 208

IN his note of the 27th March M. Kulski enclosed a strictly confidential memorandum giving the views of the Polish Government on Eastern European problems, with particular reference to the contemplated negotiations for an Anglo-Soviet Treaty. The note which your Excellency left with me on the 13th April expressly confirmed the contents of this memorandum.[1]

2. These documents have been studied with the greatest care and attention. His Majesty's Government observe that the memorandum gives the reasons for which the Polish Government consider that the negotiations for a political agreement between His Majesty's Government and the Soviet Government at the present juncture are inopportune. The grounds of the Polish Government's criticism are, broadly speaking, threefold: —

1. General Sikorski and Raczyński had outlined their objections to the proposed treaty to Eden on 16 April 1942 (F.O. 371. C4077/19/55). For the Polish note of 27 March, see D.O.P.S.R.I, No. 196; for that of 13 April, D.O.P.S.R.I, No. 202. Both stressed the Polish interest in Lithuania and Bukovina. Sikorski also set out his objections in a letter to Eden (D.O.P.S.R.I, No. 204). Eden replied to this on 21 April (D.O.P.S.R.I, No. 210). On this occasion, in order to reassure the Polish Prime Minister, he did affirm '. . . as I said to Count Raczyński, His Majesty's Government do not propose to conclude any agreement affecting or compromising the territorial status of the Polish Republic and it is their intention in any agreement which may be concluded to safeguard the assurance given to you on the occasion of the Polish-Soviet Agreement last July.'

    (i) That the contemplated agreement will be detrimental to the general
       war policy of the Allies;

   (ii) That it will affect Polish vital interests; and

  (iii) That it will constitute an infringement of the spirit, if not of the letter,
       of the Anglo-Polish Agreement of the 25th August, 1939.

3. I wish at the outset to make it clear that the object of the proposed
negotiations is not, as stated in your note of the 13th April, the conclusion
of a political agreement dealing with the post-war status of the Continent of
Europe, but an agreement for Anglo-Soviet collaboration during and after
the war, which will take into account, on the one hand, the desire of the
Soviet Government for the security of certain of the Soviet frontiers, and,
on the other, the interests of the United Nations.

4. The first point, namely, whether the contemplated agreement is
detrimental to the general war policy of the Allies, may well be one on which
opinions differ. His Majesty's Government, for their part, do not share the
opinion which the Polish Government have formed. They have naturally
taken into full account the interests of all the United Nations in reaching
their decision to open negotiations with the Soviet Government, and they
would not have embarked on such a course without the firmest conviction
of its necessity. Your Excellency will not wish me to enter into an elaborate
exposition of the policy of His Majesty's Government, but I can assure you
that any agreement which may now be concluded with the Soviet Government will not modify the intention of His Majesty's Government to regard
their policy for the post-war settlement in Europe as based upon the
principles of the Atlantic Charter, which have already been accepted by the
Soviet Government. Secondly, until the war situation is clearer than it is at
the present time. His Majesty's Government intend to abide by the
principles set out in the Prime Minister's statement of the 5th September,
1940. But Hist Majesty's Government consider that it is in the general
interest of the Allied cause, both for the successful prosecution of the war
and also for the elaboration of a satisfactory post-war settlement, that the
relationship between the Soviet Union and the Western Powers should be
strengthened and placed on a firmer basis of mutual confidence than has
existed in the past. This objective cannot be achieved by denying to the
Soviet Union a position commensurate with the major part which it is at
present playing in the war, and with the influence which its victorious armies
will inevitably win for it in the period of reconstruction.

5. In the second place, the Polish Government consider that the proposed
agreement will affect their vital interests. His Majesty's Government do not
presume to assess the vital interests of an ally, but they observe that at the
outset of their memorandum of the 27th March, the Polish Government
affirm that good neighbourly relations and friendship between Poland
and the Soviet Union are the indispensable conditions of a lasting peace. His
Majesty's Government welcome this declaration, which applies equally to

the relations between the Soviet Union and the United Kingdom. It is the principal object of the negotiations now impending to place Anglo-Soviet relations on a firm basis of confidence, and His Majesty's Government consider that this objective is as much in the interests of Poland as in their own. The policy of His Majesty's Government towards Poland is governed by the Anglo-Polish Agreement of the 25 August, 1939. This policy has been confirmed and strengthened by the experiences of the last two and a half years, during which Polish and British forces have fought side by side, on land, on sea, and in the air, and the Polish people have steadfastly refused, in spite of manifold sufferings, to collaborate in any way with the forces of occupation. His Majesty's Government would not, therefore, be likely to contemplate entering into an agreement with a third party which would injure the interests of so loyal an ally. The Polish Government will appreciate that any Anglo-Soviet agreement will establish the right of His Majesty's Government to interest themselves generally in the future settlement of Europe, and it could not longer be claimed that any question affecting Polish-Soviet frontiers, for example, is not the concern of His Majesty's Government. In any case, His Majesty's Government do not propose to conclude any agreement affecting or compromising the territorial status of the Polish Republic.

6. In this connexion the Polish memorandum of the 27th March referred to the position of Lithuania and Bukovina in relation to Polish security. In regard to Lithuania, reference was made in particular to the Secret Protocol attached to the Anglo-Polish Agreement of the 25th August, 1939, and to the observations contained in your Excellency's note of the 30th December, 1941. In the latter document your Excellency quoted article 2 *(b)* of the Secret Protocol as recognising implicitly the vital importance of Lithuania to the security of Poland. Your Excellency will, however, recollect that article 1 *(a)* of the Secret Protocol provided that "by the expression 'European Power' employed in the agreement is to be understood Germany". Any implicit recognition by His Majesty's Government of the vital importance of Lithuania to the security of Poland could therefore only apply to the possibility of a threat from Germany, just as the reference in article 2 *(b)* of the Secret Protocol to the importance of Belgium and the Netherlands to British security could only be held applicable to a case of aggression by Germany. Article 2 *(b)* of the Secret Protocol could therefore only become operative in the event of Poland becoming involved in war with Germany consequent on action by Germany threatening the independence of Lithuania, and it was not, in fact, suggested that this provision could be invoked by Poland when Lithuania was incorporated into the Soviet Union in 1940.

7. The position is different in regard to Vilna and any other territory within the frontiers of Poland on the 25th August, 1939. The Polish Government have already been assured that His Majesty's Government do not

recognise any territorial changes effected in Poland since August 1939, and it is intended to safeguard this assurance in any agreement which may be concluded with the Soviet Government.

8. As regards Bukovina, the Polish memorandum of the 27th March admits that the question of this territory has never been raised in any negotiations between His Majesty's Government and the Polish Government. The memorandum refers, however, to the British guarantee which Roumania had received at the time of the conclusion of the Anglo-Polish Agreement of the 25 August, 1939. I need not enter into the circumstances in which the Roumanian Government decided to dispense with the guarantee of His Majesty's Government, and eventually to place the full resources of Roumania, including the armed forces of the country, at the disposal of Germany. But His Majesty's Government, who have since declared war on Roumania, cannot regard themselves as in any way bound in regard to future territorial arrangements by an earlier guarantee rejected by the Roumanian Government.

9. His Majesty's Government therefore conclude that their aim in the forthcoming negotiations with the Soviet Government will not conflict in any respect with the obligations which they have assumed to the Republic of Poland. But, as the Polish memorandum suggests, the questions at issue extend beyond the terms of any written documents, and His Majesty's Government intend to uphold the interests of their Polish Ally, as of their other Allies, to the fullest extent of which they are capable. For this purpose they will accept their full share of responsibility for the establishment and maintenance of peace in Europe after the war. But in order to fulfil this task and to prevent the re-emergence of the threat of aggression by Germany, collaboration and agreement with the Soviet Government will be required. It is with the object of placing this collaboration on a firm and enduring footing that His Majesty's Government have undertaken their present negotiations.[2]

2. Raczyński replied to this note on 21 April, reaffirming the Polish position (D.O.P.S.R.I, No. 209). When he handed his note to Cadogan, he stressed the apprehension which the proposed treaty was causing to Poles all over the world (F.O. 371. C4305/19/55). The British position was reaffirmed in a stormy interview between Sikorski and Churchill on 26 April (D.O.P.S.R.I, No. 211) and in a note from Eden to Raczyński on 6 May (D.O.P.S.R.I, No. 217). In this Note, Eden also affirmed 'I trust that the above explanation, coupled with the statements of His Majesty's Government set out in earlier correspondence, will convince the Polish Government that, in any negotiations with the Soviet Government, His Majesty's Government intend fully to safeguard the position of their Polish allies, and do not contemplate any action inconsistent with the provisions of the Anglo-Polish Agreement of 1939 or of the Secret Protocol annexed to it.'

No. 37

Anglo-Soviet Treaty (Extracts)[1]
26 May 1942
F.O. 371. N3129/3059/38

PART I.

Article I. — In virtue of the alliance established between them the High
Contracting Parties mutually undertake to afford one another military and
other assistance and support of all kinds in the war against Germany and all
those States which are associated with her in acts of aggression in Europe.

Article II. — The High Contracting Parties undertake not to enter into any
negotiations with the Hitlerite Government or any other Government in
Germany that does not clearly renounce all aggressive intentions, and not to
negotiate or conclude except by mutual consent any armistice or peace
treaty with Germany or any other State associated with her in acts of
aggression in Europe.

PART II.

Article III. — The High Contracting Parties declare their desire to associate
themselves with other like-minded States in adopting proposals for common
action to preserve peace and resist aggression.

They agree that, pending the adoption of such proposals.

(1) They will take all the measures in their power to render impossible a
repetition of aggression and violation of the peace by Germany or any of the
States associated with her in acts of aggression in Europe.

(2) Should, nevertheless, one of the High Contracting Parties become
involved in hostilities with Germany or any of the States mentioned in (1)
above in consequence of an attack by that State against that Party, the other
High Contracting Party will at once give to the Contracting Party so involved
in hostilities all the military and other support and assistance in his power.

Article IV. — The High Contracting Parties agree to work together in close
and friendly collaboration after the re-establishment of peace for the
organisation of security and economic prosperity in Europe. They will take
into account the interest of the United Nations in these objects, and they will
act in accordance with the two principles of not seeking territorial aggrandise-
ment for themselves and of non-interference in the internal affairs of other
peoples.

Article V. — The High Contracting Parties agree to render one another all
possible economic assistance after the war.

Article VI. — Each High Contracting Party undertakes not to conclude any
alliance and not to take part in any coalition directed against the other High
Contracting Party. . .[2]

1. Eden had first presented this treaty to the War Cabinet on May 12 as an alternative
should the negotiations be deadlocked (F.O. 371. N2498/5/38). It avoids all mention of
territorial guarantees. The British introduced the new draft to the negotiations on 23 May.
2. The Poles were very satisfied with the revised treaty. On 8 June, Sikorski told Eden
that the agreement 'would . . . be well received in Polish circles, and he was ready to do
·· · ·   · ·· · ·   · ·   · ·· ·   · ·· its merits in the world at large' (F.O. 371. C3814/19/55).

No. 38

Resolution of the Czechoslovak State Council (Extracts)[1]
LONDON, 18 May 1942
F.O. 371. C6731/151/12

... Czechoslovak policy, fully comprehending the vital interests of the
Polish nation at the same time respects the vital needs of the Soviet Union
and therefore cannot overlook a circumstance which the Soviet Union regards
as fundamentally essential to its State policy and security.[2] ... The
Czechoslovak government recognizes no annexations which took place
after Munich whether in the Teschen area or in Northern Slovakia, and ... it
insists upon the continuity of our pre-Munich territory. We hope that this
point of view will find favour also with the British and American Governments.

1. This resolution was provoked by the Polish National Council's resolution of 17
March calling for the 'complete independence of Lithuania.' See above, No. 32, note 2.
2. In the debate in the Czechoslovak State Council, Ripka stated, 'Any military or
political association [with Poland] is possible only if Polish policy is clearly and un-
mistakeably pervaded by the spirit of friendship for her eastern neighbour, Soviet
Russia...'
3. In response, the Polish National Council passed a resolution on 6 June 1942 to the
effect that '... the National Council hereby declare that the tendency towards
confederation with Czechoslovakia and other nations in Central Europe does not in
any way affect the main duty of the Polish Government which is to defend the
territorial integrity of the Polish State...'

No. 39

Anthony Eden to Sir Cecil Dormer: Dispatch
LONDON, 8 June 1942
F.O. 371. C5813/151/12

During my luncheon with General Sikorski to-day I asked him about his
relations with the Czechs. As I expected the General said that Dr. Beneš had
been behaving badly. He had apparently assumed that His Majesty's
Government were abandoning the Poles in their Treaty with the Russians
and had adjusted his attitude to the Poles accordingly. He had shown signs
of backing out of the proposed Polish-Czech confederation, and the General
had found it necessary, at a recent luncheon, to tell Dr. Beneš in no uncertain
terms what he thought of him. Though Dr. Beneš professed to be as strongly
anti-Communist as General Sikorski himself, he was under Communist
influence and seemed to be adjusting his policy away from Poland towards
the Soviet Union.

2. I told the General that His Majesty's Government were still in favour of a
Polish-Czech confederation and, indeed, of the extension of the confederation
principle to other parts of Central and South-Eastern Europe. They had,
indeed, included an article in this sense in the first draft of the Anglo-Soviet
Treaty. In order to facilitate negotiations, they had not included this article

in the second draft, but this did not mean that the Russians were necessarily opposed to the idea of confederation. M. Molotov had told him that the Soviet Government were favourable in principle to the idea; but that they had some doubts as to the application of it, since they had received indications that the confederation at present in contemplation were directed against the Soviet Union. If we had included an article about confederations in the Treaty we should, of course, have made it clear that the confederations we contemplated were directed against Germany. We hoped, therefore, that the Poles and the Czechs would pursue their negotiations.

Minute of Foreign Office (20 June 1942)

We have now, however, learnt that in a conversation with Molotov on the 9/6/42 . . . Dr. Beneš went very far in arriving at a Soviet-Czechoslovak agreement at the expense of the Poles. The salient points are that:—

a) Molotov recognised the pre-Munich frontiers of Czechoslovakia, which involves the recognition of Teschen as part of Czechoslovakia; this issue had, however, been reserved for settlement between the Czechs and the Poles.

b) Dr. Beneš agreed with Molotov that Polish-Czechoslovak Confederation would be dependent upon the Poles agreeing to satisfy Soviet demands generally, and their territorial demands in particular. Dr. Beneš has therefore, in effect, supported Soviet claims against those of his own partner, Poland.[1]

---

1. Bogomolov put similar arguments to Ripka in late July in favour of the abandonment of plans for a Polish-Czechoslovak Confederation. He stated that he 'could quite understand the reason for a close understanding between Czechoslovakia and Poland, before the German attack on Russia', but that this was now quite unnecessary (F.O. 371. C7636/151/12). On 12 September, Beneš informed Bogomolov that the Czechs were not prepared to push for a Polish-Czechoslovak confederation, 'in the face of direct Soviet opposition' (F.O. 371. C9156/151/12). The British too were increasingly aware that, as Strang minuted on 22 October 1942, the Polish-Czechoslovak confederation could make no progress 'in the present state of Polish-Russian and Polish-Czechoslovak relations' (F.O. 371. C10670/151/12).

No. 40

The Ambassador in the Soviet Union (Admiral Standley) to Cordell Hull: Telegram

KUIBYSHEV, 10 October 1942
F.R.U.S. 1942, III, pp. 194–5

The Polish Minister Counselor[1] has informed the Embassy that he had a cordial interview with Molotov on September 30 during which the latter stated that the existing misunderstandings in Soviet-Polish relations were working to the disinterest of both parties and should be reexamined with a view to clearing them up.[2] The Minister is of the opinion that the recent

---

1. Henryk Sokolnicki.
2. The Soviet Government had in July closed the local offices of Embassy delegates in a number of towns. These had been established to deal with the welfare of Polish deportees in the Soviet Union. Subsequently a large number of these delegates had been arrested on charges of espionage. This had occasioned much correspondence between the Polish Embassy and the Soviet authorities. See D.O.P.S.R.I, Nos. 249, 250, 251, 252, 254, 255, 256, 257, 258, 263, 265, 266, 267, 269, 272, 274.

American and British representations on behalf of the Poles have had a salutary effect and that at least a temporary improvement in Soviet-Polish relations could be expected. He added that a certain improvement had already been noticed explaining that no Polish relief representatives had been arrested for some time and that the Polish Embassy had recently received a note from the Foreign Office couched in favourable terms in which the Soviet Government offered to place more additional quarters at the disposal of Polish children in the Soviet Union and suggested that conversations be initiated with respect to evacuation questions. He stated that there had been no change, however, in the Soviet attitude toward Polish Jews in the Soviet Union.

No. 41

Anthony Eden to Philip Nichols: Letter (Extracts)
LONDON, 2 November 1942
F.O. 371. C10614/151/12

3. . . . The Czech Government [said Beneš] had been placed in a very difficult position *vis-á-vis* both the Poles and the Russians. The Poles tended to regard him, the President, as nothing but the lackey of the Russians, while the Russians regarded him as the friend and intimate of the Poles. He was tired of being kicked by both sides and felt strongly that he did not deserve such treatment. His policy was a clear one: he believed in a Confederation between the Poles and the Czechs supported by the Russians and by ourselves; only thus could we ensure the failure of a future German *Drang nach Osten*. His difficulty had been (as you yourself have reported more than once) that the Russians would not declare themselves particularly in regard to the Polish-Czechoslovak Confederation. But he had had within the last few days a conversation with M. Bogomolov, which had been useful.

4. In this conversation M. Bogomolov had made three points. Firstly, he had said that his Government desired direct, close and friendly relations with the Czechoslovak Government. Secondly, that as regards Polish-Czech relations, which meant the Confederation, his Government were "observing and examining the situation". Thirdly, that they welcomed friendly relations and collaboration between the Poles and the Czechs. This, said Dr. Beneš, was a distinct advance on anything the Russians, and particularly M. Bogomolov, had said hitherto.

5. I took the opportunity of assuring Dr. Beneš that we for our part were strongly in favour of a Polish-Czechoslovak Confederation. I asked him whether he thought that a meeting between his Government, the Poles, the Russians and ourselves would serve any useful purpose. I gathered from his reply that he thought that such a meeting would need to be very carefully prepared beforehand, but that meanwhile he was considering whether a very simple treaty of alliance and friendship between the Czechoslovak Government

and the Polish Government, blessed by both His Majesty's Government and the Soviet Government, might not be appropriate and timely.[1] Such a treaty, to be of value, would, of course, have to cover the peace years as well as the war. I said that this was a very interesting idea of which we should be glad to hear further; meanwhile we would ourselves study it.

1. In a letter to Jan Masaryk on 19 November, Eden stressed that the proposed treaty should not be regarded as a substitute for a Polish-Czechoslovak confederation (F.O. 371. C10614/151/12). Beneš suggested the treaty to Raczyński on 23 November, but also raised his terms, arguing that before it could be signed two questions would have to be dealt with, 'Russia' and 'Teschen' (F.O. 371. C12165/151/12). This made further progress towards a confederation impossible, and Beneš' new line of policy was therefore strongly criticized by the Foreign Office (F.O. 371. C12165/151/12).

No. 42

Minute by G. D. Allen, Central Department (Extracts)
LONDON, 20 January 1943
F.O. 371. C923/258/55

During his visit to Washington[1] General Sikorski gave Lord Halifax what purported to be an account of his conversation with President Roosevelt in which they had dwelt on the necessity of settling Polish-Soviet relations.[2] Among other things General Sikorski said that the President had told him that in his opinion Stalin would be satisfied with the following conditions: Petsamo to be a Russian port, a neutral area to be created in Karelia, Soviet Russia to incorporate Estonia and Latvia but not Lithuania, Bessarabia but not Bukovina. No details were given of the actual Polish eastern frontier, but the towns of Vilna and Lwów were to be Polish. General Sikorski said that on such lines he was prepared to do a deal with Stalin at any time. He also said that the President had spoken in favour of giving East Prussia and Danzig to the Poles.

We had no grounds for supposing that the Soviet government would be ready to give up Lithuania, Bukovina, Vilna and Lwów, and asked Lord Halifax if he could find out what the President had in fact said. Lord Halifax subsequently saw Mr. Sumner Welles, who told him that the account given by General Sikorski of his conversation with the President was completely incorrect. General Sikorski had in fact done all the talking and it was he who had expressed the hope or the view that Stalin would be satisfied with the conditions set out above. The President had made very little comment on these observations except to say that he thought the Danzig Corridor had provde a very bad arrangement and that we should all have to consider the future position of East Prussia. In response to a lead from Lord Halifax, Mr. Welles stated that there would be no

1. In late December 1942.
2. See Halifax's telegram to Eden of 5 December 1942 (F.O. 371. C12148/19/55).

question of the United States Government undertaking any territorial commitments about the eastern or the western boundaries of Poland. . .[3]

3. In a memorandum of 9 December, Ray Atherton, Acting Chief of the Division of European Affairs in the State Department, had argued, while still defending the policy that the U.S. should not negotiate on European frontiers 'at this stage of the war', that no attempt should be made to re-establish the 1921 frontier of Poland in the east. He stated that the Curzon Line had been 'suggested in accordance with ethnic considerations', but that the problem of Vilna and the Baltic States was of a different type and should be left for subsequent consideration (F.R.U.S. 1942, III, pp. 201–7).

No. 43

The People's Commissariat for Foreign Affairs to the Polish Embassy: Note
KUIBYSHEV, 16 January 1943
D.O.P.S.R.I, No. 285

The People's Commissariat for Foreign Affairs has the honour to inform the Embassy of the Polish Republic of the following:

In connection with the exchange of Notes in the years 1941–1942 between the People's Commissariat for Foreign Affairs and the Embassy, concerning the citizenship of persons who previously lived in the Western districts of the Ukrainian and White Ruthenian Soviet Socialist Republics, the People's Commissariat for Foreign Affairs informed the Embassy on December 1, 1941,[1] that all inhabitants of the above-mentioned districts who found themselves on the territories of these districts at the time of their entry into Union of Soviet Socialist Republics (November 1–2, 1939), had acquired Soviet citizenship in accordance with the Decree of the Supreme Council of the USSR dated November 29, 1939, and the Citizenship of the USSR Act of August 19, 1938.

In its Note of December 1, 1941, the People's Commissariat for Foreign Affairs informed the Embassy that the Soviet Government were prepared, by way of exception, to regard as Polish citizens persons of Polish origin living in the territories of the above-mentioned districts on November 1–2, 1939. The People's Commissariat for Foreign Affairs is bound to state thate despite the good will of the Soviet Government thus manifested, the Polish Government had adopted a negative attitude to the above statement of the Soviet Government and has refused to take the appropriate steps, putting forward demands contrary to the sovereign rights of the Soviet Union in respect to these territories.

In connection with the above, the People's Commissariat for Foreign Affairs, on instructions from the Soviet Government, gives notice that the statement included in the Note of December 1, 1941, regarding the readiness to treat some categories of persons of Polish origin on an exceptional basis must be considered as without validity and that the question of the possible non-applicationsto such persons of the laws governing citizenship of the Union of Soviet Socialist Republics has ceased to exist.[1]

1. On 26 January, Raczyński addressed a note to Bogomolov, Ambassador to the
Polish Government protesting that the Soviet note was incompatible with the spirit of
the Polish-Soviet Agreement (D.O.P.S.R.I, No. 286). On 2 February, he pressed Eden
to react to the Soviet note, since otherwise he felt it would be followed by further
unilateral decisions at the expense of the Poles (F.O. 371. C1279/258/55). A similar
plea was made in a letter by Sikorski to Churchill on 9 February (D.O.P.S.R.I, No. 289).

Bogomolov replied to Raczyński on 17 February, reaffirming the Soviet position
(D.O.P.S.R.I, No. 290) which provoked the Polish Government to issue a statement on
25 February, in which it repudiated 'most definitely the malicious propaganda which
accuses Poland of indirect or direct inimical tendencies towards Soviet Russia. It is
absolutely absurd to suspect Poland of intentions to base the eastern boundaries of the
Polish Republic on the Dnieper and the Black Sea, or to impute to Poland any
tendencies to move her frontier farther to the East.

'The Polish Government, representing Poland, took up the fight imposed on her,
have, from the moment of the conclusion of the Polish-Soviet Treaty of July 30, 1941,
maintained the unchangeable attitude that so far as the question of frontiers between
Poland and the Soviet Union is concerned, the *status quo* previous to September 1,
1939, is in force, and they consider the undermining of this attitude, which is in
conformity with the Atlantic Charter, as detrimental to the unity of the Allied
nations' (D.O.P.S.R.I, No. 294).

No. 44

Anthony Eden to Sir Cecil Dormer: Dispatch (Extracts)
LONDON, 22 January 1943
F.O. 371. C910/258/55

. . . 5. General Sikorski then handed me the annexed memorandum,[1] which
sets out the view of the Polish Government as regards the Polish-Soviet
frontier. I told him that, while I entirely agreed with the first paragraph of
the memorandum, this paper seemed to represent a more rigid attitude on
the part of the Polish Government than that which had been developed to
me in confidence by General Sikorski in the past. If I had understood him
rightly, his view had been that he would not discuss frontiers with the
Russians now, but that, provided Poland could secure East Prussia and
possibly an adjustment in Silesia, she would not exclude the possibility of
adjustments in favour of the Soviet Union in the East.[2] Now, however, her
programme appeared to be the maintenance of the frontier laid down in the
Treaty of Riga and the acquisition of East Prussia as well. There therefore
appeared to have been a hardening on both sides, and it seemed to me that
the more the Russians suspected that the Poles were trying to secure support
from Great Britain and the United States for their eastern frontier, and to
mobilise the smaller Allies against Russia, the more rigid would the Soviet
attitude become.

6. General Sikorski said that he was convinced that the Soviet
Government were moved by imperialistic aims. The Comintern had of late
had a new lease of life and was now being used in support of Soviet imperialism.
The reason why the Soviet Government wanted the Molotov-Ribbentrop
line was in order to have access to Central Europe. . .

7. General Sikorski said that, in this situation, he was wondering whether he ought not to make another journey to Moscow in order to negotiate a treaty of friendship with M. Stalin. If, however, he did so, the question of the Polish-Russian frontier would necessarily be discussed, and if he undertook this journey he would wish to do so with the assurance that both the British and United States Governments would support him in his claims as regards Poland's eastern frontier.

8. I told him that nothing that I had heard from Washington gave me any reason to belive that the United States Government would be willing to commit itself to support any particular frontier, and I gave him no encouragement to think that His Majesty's Government could do so either. . .

1. Not printed.
2. On 1 December 1942, the Polish Government had submitted to the British a memorandum on their territorial demands in the West in which they had claimed East Prussia, Danzig and Opole Silesia. In addition the memorandum had stated that 'Poland's line of national security in relation to Germany is that of the Oder. This line may be compared with that of the Rhine as a line of national security for Belgium and France' (F.O. 371. C12169/464/55).

No. 45

The British Ambassador to the Soviet Union, Sir Archibald Clark-Kerr to Anthony Eden: Telegram
KUIBYSHEV, 3 March 1943
F.O. 371. C2463/258/55

I am relieved to hear from Polish Embassy that Stalin was already aware of the terms if the Polish declaration published in London on February 25th when he saw the Polish Ambassador on February 26th.[1] He mentioned it to M. de Romer (who had not seen it) and said something to the effect that Polish Government had now had their say about frontiers, that Soviet Government would reply in a public statement and that then the two would

1. For the declaration see above, No. 43, note 1. During this conversation, Stalin made a number of fairly conciliatory remarks on the citizenship question. At the same time, however, he unsuccessfully pressed Romer to start negotiations on the problem of the Polish Eastern frontier. (D.O.P.S.R.I, No. 295).
    In spite of this seeming improvement in the atmosphere, the statement issued by *Tass* on 1 March took an extremely hard line claiming that the 'declaration of the Polish Government in London [of 25 February] bears witness to the fact that the Polish Government refuses to recognize the historic rights of the Ukrainian and Byelorussian peoples to be united within national states' (D.O.P.S.R.I, No. 296). This provoked another Polish statement on 5 March claimed that until the outbreak of the war, the Soviet Union had never called into question the Riga frontier (D.O.P.S.R.I, No. 297). When Romer met Molotov on 9 March, he was again pressed to initiate discussions on the frontier. He refused, pleading he had no instructions (F.O. 371, C2836/258/55). This is not mentioned in the Polish version of these conversations, although this does make clear Romer's refusal to discuss the border (D.O.P.S.R.I, No. 299). Another indication of the increased Soviet pressure on the Poles was the publication on 8 March of the first issue of *Wolna Polska* (Free Poland), organ of the communist-dominated Union of Polish Patriots in the U.S.S.R.

be quiet.

Some elements in the Polish Embassy have the impression that Stalin is anxious to discuss the question of the frontier without delay and are urging their Ambassador to do so. They have begged me to use my influence in this sense with the Ambassador. But I do not propose to do so. I should however be glad to have some guidance from you as to the general views of HMG on this subject.[2]

2. The Foreign Office cabled back that the frontier question should be settled directly between the Polish and Soviet governments and that the present time was not suitable for such negotiations (F.O. 371. C2836/258/55).

No. 46

Anthony Eden to Sir A. Clark-Kerr: Telegram (Extracts)
LONDON, 10 March 1943
F.O. 371. N1605/499/38

. . . 4. As regards Poland, the attitude of the Soviet Government [said M. Maisky] had not changed. They were prepared that Poland should have East Prussia, they wished to see her strong and homogeneous, and did not wish to see foreign minorities included in Poland. As far as the eastern frontier of Poland was concerned, something in the nature of the Curzon Line would be agreeable to the Russians. There would have to be minor adjustments, no doubt, but broadly speaking this line was acceptable. Western Ukraine and White Russia would have to be included as autonomous republics in the Soviet Union. If the future Polish Government were democratic and prepared to be friendly, then relations between the two countries should certainly be good. If, however, the Government was of the same character as that which had existed in Poland before the war, and if there was the same outlook as that shown by a number of Polish *émigrés* now in this country (M. Maisky specificially excepted General Sikorski and Count Raczynski from his strictures), then there would still be an independent Poland but the relations with Russia would be bad.

. . . 6. We then had some discussion about Poland's eastern frontier and about Russia's requirements in respect of bases in Roumania and Finland. I said that, while I was grateful to the Ambassador for telling me thus frankly his view, he must not take my silence on any one point that he had mentioned as acquiescence, nor could I undertake to be a protagonist for the Russian point of view on these issues in the United States. The Ambassador fully understood this, but said that he thought I would find it useful to know what he believed to be in the mind of his Government before I went to the United States, for I might thus be able to correct any wrong impressions the United States Government might have in this respect.

7. We then spoke of the future of federation in Europe. The Ambassador

said his Government was not enthusiastic. There was too much of an in-
clination to regard federation as a panacea.[1] . .

8. I asked what was now the Soviet Government's attitude towards
Polish-Czech federation. The Ambassador said the difficulty for his Government was that they did not yet know "what Poland is going to be". If the
country were going to be friendly, then there was something to be said for
such federation, but not otherwise. In essentials the Ambassador thought
that his Government had come to the conclusion that out of this war there
should be a *bloc* of the United Nations. That *bloc* should be led by ourselves
and the Soviet Union, and in it there might be a number of groupings of
economic units, but not, he thought, political units. All the nations in
Europe should not have an equal voice in whatever was the post-war
organisation of Europe. Albania, for instance, could not have the same vote
as Britain.

I am, &c.
ANTHONY EDEN.

1. The State Department view on federations had been set out in a memorandum by
Ray Atherton, Acting-Chief of the Division of European Affairs, on 9 December. He
argued that to be successful, any federation should not have anti-Soviet aims, should
make provision for the adherence of non-member states (such as Hungary, Bulgaria
and Rumania) and should take regard of economic factors (F.R.U.S. 1942, III, p. 206).

No. 47

Anthony Eden to Winston Churchill: Telegram
16 March 1943
F.O. 371. N1748/499/38

. . . 2. We discussed in some detail Russian demands as given to me by
Maisky.[1] The President, somewhat to my surprise, did not seem to find any
great difficulty in the Polish question. He thought that if Poland had East
Prussia and perhaps some concessions in Silesia, she would gain rather than
lose by agreeing to the Curzon line. In any event we, the United States, and
Russia should decide at the appropriate time what was a just and reasonable
solution, and if we were agreed, Poland would have to accept. Though he
mentioned that he liked Sikorski, he clearly did not think the Poles had
played their cards wisely. The big question was whether it was possible to
work with Russia now and after the war. Bullitt had expressed the view to
him that Russia wished to see all States in Europe Communistic and to over-
run the Continent herself. What did I think? I said I thought it impossible
to give a definite view. One could only proceed in foreign policy on the
basis of certain assumptions. Even if Bullitt's fears were to prove correct, we
should make the position no worse by trying to work with Russia and by
assuming that Stalin meant what he said in the treaty which he had signed

1. See above, No. 46.

with us. The President agreed; nor did he take exception to the Russian
claim to the Baltic States. I think that his view of this is that if Russia takes
these States nobody is going to be able to turn her out, though he did
mention that he hoped that some arrangements for a plebiscite, a method
of resolving difficulties to which he seems over-optimistically attached,
would be possible. The President suggested it might be desirable if at some
stage we, Russia, and the United States were to try to come to an agreement
about Poland. The President added that he did not feel any difficulty now in
agreeing to Russian demands about Finland.

No. 48

Sir Alexander Cadogan to the Prime Minister: Minute
LONDON, 31 March 1943
F.O. 371. C3386/258/55

As you know, Polish-Soviet relations have become very strained in recent
weeks. The trouble began in January, when the Russians insisted upon
regarding as Soviet citizens not only White Russians and Ukrainians, but also
racial Poles from the Polish Eastern provinces. This affected large numbers
of Poles exiled in the Soviet Union, many of whom are relatives of the Polish
Forces in this country and in the Middle East. Polish relief activities in Russia
have since been seriously curtailed and there is evidence that some Poles
have been recruited into the Soviet Forces and others illtreated to compel
them to accept Soviet citizenship.

On February 26th the Polish Ambassador had a promising interview with
Stalin, but the situation has since further deteriorated, possibly because of
Soviet irritation at various public statements issued by the Poles concerning
Polish-Soviet frontier questions. The Russians were also annoyed by General
Sikorski's visit to the U.S.A. last December to obtain American support for
the Poles.[1] On their side the Poles have been irritated by the recent "Times"
articles on the future role of Russia, as you will remember from your
correspondence with General Sikorski.[2]

With this background I submit a record of a talk I had with the Polish
Ambassador on March 27th[3] when he pleaded for our intervention at Moscow
to break the present deadlock. This is so serious that the head of the Polish
Ministry for Foreign Affairs has warned H.M. Ambassador that the Polish
Government might be compelled to break off relations with the Soviet
Government.[4] We are of course discouraging them from any rash action of
this kind.

The indications are that the Russians are trying to force the Poles to
agree to accept the Curzon Line frontier under the threat of working against
General Sikorski's Government and of making the position of the Poles in
Russia impossible. General Sikorski cannot accept such a frontier settlement
now and neither we nor the United States Government could advise him to

do so. The Russian attitude is, therefore, playing into the hands of German propaganda by stirring up disunity among the United Nations, and by encouraging anti-Soviet feelings in the U.S.A. and among the smaller European nations. It is also undermining the morale of the Polish Fighting Forces here and in the Middle East, which is a matter of very direct interest to us.

I therefore submit that we should intervene at Moscow, despite our general preference for leaving the Poles and the Russians to deal with such questions themselves. It would be useless to put forward the Polish Ambassador's suggestion for an international relief organisation in Russia, although it might be possible to suggest removing certain categories of Poles from Russia if the numbers are not very large — we are looking into this in greater detail. Our intervention should, I think, be based mainly upon the higher interests of the United Nations, coupled with our own special interest in the morale of the Polish Fighting Forces. We should seek American support for such intervention.

H.M. Ambassador at Moscow has advised that our intervention should be at a high level. If you agree that we should intervene, you might either (a) send a personal message to Premier Stalin, who has sometimes shown himself better disposed towards the Poles than some of his advisers, or (b) send for M. Maisky and speak to him firmly. On the whole I should recommend (b), since it would be difficult to deal with so complicated a matter within the compass of a message.

You might take the line with M. Maisky that, despite all past difficulties, Polish-Soviet relations had seemed to be reasonably satisfactory until the end of last year. You could not understand how or why all the present troubles had arisen but the general result was obviously only to help our common enemy. We were naturally interested in the matter in view of the part we had played in helping to bring about the Polish-Soviet Treaty of 1941 and of our responsibility for the morale of Polish troops serving with us. Could not the Russians therefore restore the situation as it existed at the end of last year? If M. Maisky complained of Polish provocation you could then say that you understood he had himself spoken highly of General Sikorski and Count Raczyński to the Secretary of State, and that you assumed that he had explained to his Government their difficulties in controlling public statements in this country, where there was liberty of the press, and his opposition. Surely the Soviet Government did not wish to undermine General Sikorski's position.

I realise that this is not an ideal moment for such action, in view of our recent message to Stalin about convoys. But, if we do nothing, the crisis may grow worse and General Sikorski will want to know where he stands before he pays his first visit to his troops in the Middle East about the middle of next month. If you approve either of the above suggestions, it would be well to ask the President to make a similar communication either at Moscow or to M. Litvinov.

1. This view was shared by Admiral Standley, U.S. Ambassador to the U.S.S.R., who cabled the State Department on 9 March that '. . . From various sources here I am informed that it is precisely because of the fact that Sikorski took his problem to Washington before discussing them with Stalin that Soviet-Polish relations have deteriorated to their present stage' (S.D. 760 C61/1007). Already on 22 January, Eden had counselled Sikorski to give Bogomolov a full account of what had passed during his talks in Washington (F.O. 371. C910/258/55).
2. *The Times* had published on 10 March an article by E. H. Carr which had claimed that the only power which could check Germany's eastward expansion was the Soviet Union.
3. Not printed. On this occasion Raczyński had asked the British to request the Soviets to allow Polish children to be evacuated and to permit a Polish relief organization to function (F.O. 371. C3386/258/55). On 1 April, he informed Cadogan that the entire Polish welfare organization had been taken over by the Soviet Government (F.O. 371. C3741/258/55). On 9 April, Raczyński appealed to Eden to intercede with the Soviets to allow some 50,000 Polish citizens to leave the Soviet Union and to permit an international organization to look after the remaining 200,000 who had been in receipt of relief from Polish agencies (F.O. 371. C4020/258/55).

4. Sikorski in a letter to Roosevelt on 16 March had stated that 'we are prepared to do all in our power to prevent the breaking off of Poland's relations with Soviet Russia if only we are met with good will and some response on the other side' (F.R.U.S. 1943, III, p. 349).

No. 49

Minutes on a Memorandum by Sir Orme Sargent, Deputy Under Secretary of State for Foreign Affairs (Extracts)[1]
LONDON, 15–26 April 1943
F.O. 371. C4133/258/55

Cadogan, 15/4:

. . . I had had a similar idea myself, but the difficulty is that, although President Roosevelt has, it is true, expressed himself as indicated here, I should suggest that he could only go as far as this as part of a general settlement. If

1. The memorandum (dated 15 April 1943) quoted Roosevelt's statement to Eden that if the Poles were compensated in the West they would 'gain rather than lose by agreeing to the Curzon Line.' Roosevelt had further proposed joint intervention by the U.K., U.S.A. and Soviet Union to compel the Poles to accept a just and reasonable solution. (See above No. 47). Sargent felt that the Russo-Polish conflict had now become so acute that a direct British approach to the Soviets in collaboration with the United States was necessary to settle the question of the Russo-Polish conflict. 'It is quite evident,' he wrote, 'that the Polish-Soviet frontier question cannot be settled by direct negotiation between the Soviet Government and the present exiled Polish Government. But even the exiled Government might acquiesce – even though under protest – in the imposition by the three powers of a comprehensive settlement, provided that it stated not only what Poland was to give up in the way of territory, but also what she would gain in compensation, and provided that the Poles were not required to sign the document embodying the agreement.' He thus suggested a comprehensive settlement of the Soviet Western border, in terms of which the Curzon Line, with the extension which would leave Lwów in Poland, would be the Russo-Polish frontier and the Soviet Union would also receive Bessarabia, Northern Bukovina, the Baltic States and its 1940 frontier with Finland.

we pick out these particular statements of his and propose to hold him to them for the early settlement of a European difficulty, I should think he would back out. And he might even resent such an approach. . .

Cadogan, 20/4:

. . . My own view is as stated in my minute above, i.e. that we shall *not* get Soviet-Polish agreement during the war save by a settlement of this frontier problem, and it *might* be a good thing to get from the Russians an admission that they would be satisfied with something, still a long way from their grasp, before they are actually overrunning that region, and perhaps more besides. But I don't think we could get the President to face it.

On the whole I don't think there would be much harm — if you think it worthwhile — in putting it to the President on these lines:—

'We have asked you [or you have agreed] to intervene between Poles and Russians in the immediate crisis. Even if this is surmounted, we believe difficulties will recur until this Russian frontier question is settled. To tackle it now would be against our rule of leaving such questions till the general settlement, and raises (and would focus attention on) all sorts of awkward questions. What do you think about it?'

Eden, 26/4:

I am glad that Sir. O. Sargent has written this paper. I fear that the arguments against the course he proposes are too strong, but, in so complex a business as Polish-Russian relations it is wise to examine even out 'taboos' from time to time.

I shall be glad to discuss this paper. . .

CHAPTER THREE

FROM APRIL 1943 TO THE TEHERAN CONFERENCE (DECEMBER 1943)

No. 50

Statement by the Polish Government
LONDON, 17 April 1943
D.O.P.S.R.I, No. 308

No Pole can help but be deeply shocked by the news, now given the widest publicity by the Germans, of the discovery of the bodies of the Polish officers missing in the USSR in a common grave near Smolensk, and of the mass execution of which they were victims.[1]

The Polish Government has instructed their representative in Switzerland to request the International Red Cross in Geneva to send a delegation to investigate the true state of affairs on the spot. It is to be desired that the findings of this protective institution, which is to be entrusted with the task of clarifying the matter and of establishing responsibility, should be issued without delay.

At the same time, however, the Polish Government, on behalf of the Polish nation, denies to the Germans any right to base on a crime they ascribe to others, arguments in their own defence. The profoundly hypocritical indignation of German propaganda will not succeed in concealing from the world the many cruel and reiterated crimes still being perpetrated against the Polish people.

The Polish Government recalls such facts as the removal of Polish officers from prisoner-of-war camps in the Reich and the subsequent shooting of them for political offences alleged to have been committed before the war, mass arrests of reserve officers subsequently deported to concentration camps, to die a slow death, – from Cracow and the neighbouring district alone 6,000 were deported in June, 1942; the compulsory enlistment in the German army of Polish prisoners of war from territories illegally incorporated in the Reich; the forcible conscription of about 200,000 Poles from the same territories, and the execution of the families of those who managed to escape; the massacre of one-and-a-half-million people by executions or in concentration

1. The Germans had made the announcement of the discovery of the mass grave on 13 April (D.O.P.S.R.I, No. 305). On 15 April, the Soviet Information Bureau issued a communiqué claiming that 'the German Fascist reports on the subject leave no doubt as to the tragic fate of the former Polish prisoners of war, who in 1941 were engaged in construction work in areas west of Smolensk and who . . . fell into the hands of the German-Fascist hangmen in the summer of 1941. . .' (D.O.P.S.R.I, No. 306).

camps; the recent imprisonment of 80,000 people of military age, officers and men, and their torture and murder in the camps of Maydanck and Tremblinka.

It is not to enable the Germans to make impudent claims and pose as the defenders of Christianity and European civilization, that Poland is making immense sacrifices, fighting and enduring suffering. The blood of Polish soldiers and Polish citizens, wherever it is shed, cries for atonement before the conscience of the free peoples of the world. The Polish Government condemn all the crimes committed against Polish citizens and refuse the right to make political capital of such sacrifices, to all who are themselves guilty of such crimes.[2]

2. This statement was much more restrained than that issued by General Kukiel, the Polish Minister of National Defence on 16 April. This, with considerable circumstantial evidence, implied that the Soviets were responsible for the Katyn murders (D.O.P.S.R.I, No. 307).

No. 51

Joseph Stalin to Winston Churchill: Letter
MOSCOW, 21 April 1943
Stalin Correspondence, I, No. 150

The behaviour of the Polish Government towards the U.S.S.R. of late is, in the view of the Soviet Government, completely abnormal and contrary to all the rules and standards governing relations between two allied states.

The anti-Soviet slander campaign launched by the German fascists in connection with the Polish officers whom they themselves murdered in the Smolensk area, in German-occupied territory, was immediately seized upon by the Sikorski Goverment and is being fanned in every way by the Polish official press. Far from countering the infamous fascist slander against the U.S.S.R., th Sikorski Government has not found it necessary even to address questions to the Soviet Government or to request information on the matter.[1]

The Hitler authorities, having perpetrated a monstrous crime against the Polish officers, are now staging a farcical investigation, using for the purpose certain pro-fascist Polish elements picked by themselves in occupied Poland, where everything is under Hitler's heel and where no honest Pole can open his mouth.

Both the Sikorski and Hitler Governments have enlisted for the "investigation" the aid of the International Red Cross, which, under a terror regimé of gallows and wholesale extermination of the civil population, is forced to take part in the investigation farce directed by Hitler. It is obvious that this "investigation", which, moreover, is being carried out behind the Soviet Government's back, cannot enjoy the confidence of anyone with a

1. On April 20, Raczynski had asked Bogomolov for information about the missing Polish prisoners, who numbered about 15,000, including 8,700 officers (D.O.P.S.R.I, No. 309).

semblance of honesty.

The fact that the anti-Soviet campaign has been started simultaneously in the German and Polish press and follows identical lines is indubitable evidence of contact and collusion between Hitler – the Allies' enemy – and the Sikorski Government in this hostile campaign.

At a time when the peoples of the Soviet Union are shedding their blood in a grim struggle against Hitler Germany and bending their energies to defeat the common foe of the freedom-loving democratic countries, the Sikorski Government is striking a treacherous blow at the Soviet Union to help Hitler tyranny.

These circumstances compel the Soviet Government to consider that the present Polish Government, having descended to collusion with the Hitler Government, has, in practice, severed its relations of alliance with the U.S.S.R. and adopted a hostile attitude to the Soviet Union.

For these reasons the Soviet Government has decided to interrupt relations with that Government.

I think it necessary to inform you of the foregoing, and I trust that the British Government will appreciate the motives that necessitated this forced step on the part of the Soviet Government.[2]

2. An almost identical letter was sent to Roosevelt (Stalin Correspondence, II, No. 89).

No. 52

Winston Churchill to Joseph Stalin: Letter
25 April 1943
Stalin Correspondence, I, No. 153

Mr. Eden saw General Sikorski yesterday evening.[1] Sikorski stated that so far from synchronising his appeal to the Red Cross with that of the Germans his Government took the initiative without knowing what line the Germans would take. In fact the Germans acted after hearing the Polish broadcast announcement. Sikorski also told Mr. Eden that his Government had simultaneously approached Monsieur Bogomolov on the subject. Sikorski emphasised that previously he had several times raised this question of the missing officers with the Soviet Government and once with you personally. On his instructions the Polish Minister of Information in his broadcasts has reacted strongly against the German propaganda and this has brought an angry German reply. As a result of Mr. Eden's strong representations Sikorski has undertaken not to press the request for the Red Cross investigation and will so inform the Red Cross authorities in Berne.[2] He will also

1. Churchill had written to Stalin on 24 April, stating that the British would oppose a Red Cross investigation and that Eden would inform Sikorski of this. He also stated that he had prepared a telegram to Stalin asking him to allow more Poles to go to Iran, but was deferring sending it (Stalin Correspondence, I, No. 151).
2. On 30 April, the Polish Government stated that it regarded its appeal to the Red Cross 'as having lapsed' (D.O.P.S.R.I, No. 321).

restrain the Polish press from polemics. In this connection I am examining the possibility of silencing those Polish newspapers in this country which attacked the Soviet Government and at the same time attacked Sikorski for trying to work with the Soviet Government.

In view of Sikorski's undertaking I would now urge you to abandon the idea of any interruption of relations.

I have reflected further on this matter and I am more than ever convinced that it can only assist our enemies, if there is a break between the Soviet and Polish Governments. German propaganda has produced this story precisely in order to make a rift in the ranks of the United Nations and to lend some semblance of reality to its new attempts to persuade the world that the interests of Europe and the smaller nations are being defended by Germany against the great extra-European Powers, namely the Union of Soviet Socialist Republics, the United States and the British Empire.

I know General Sikorski well and I am convinced that no contacts or under standing could exist between him or his Government and our common enemy, against whom he has led the Poles in bitter and uncompromising resistance. His appeal to the International Red Cross was clearly a mistake though I am convinced that it was not made in collusion with the Germans.

Now that we have, I hope, cleared up the issue raised in your telegram to me, I want to revert to the proposals contained in my draft telegram to which I referred in my message of April 24th. I shall therefore shortly be sending you this earlier message in its original form. If we two were able to arrange to link the matter of getting these Poles out of the Soviet Union it would be easier for Sikorski to withdraw entirely from the position he has been forced by his public opinion to adopt. I hope that you will help me to achieve this.

No. 53

Commissar Molotov to Tadeusz Romer, Polish Ambassador in the Soviet Union: Note
MOSCOW, 25 April 1943
Dokumentyi Materiały, No. 243

On behalf of the Government of the Union of Soviet Socialist Republics, I have the honour to notify the Polish Government of the following:

The Soviet Government consider the recent behaviour of the Polish Government with regard to the USSR as entirely abnormal, and violating all regulations and standards of relations between two Allied States. The slandero campaign hostile to the Soviet Union launched by the German Fascists in connection with the murder of the Polish officers, which they themselves committed in the Smoleńsk area on territory occupied by German troops, was at once taken up by the Polish Government and is being fanned in every way by the Polish official press.

Far from offering a rebuff to the vile Fascist slander of the USSR, the

Polish Government did not even find it necessary to address to the Soviet Government any enquiry or request for an explanation on this subject.

Having committed a monstrous crime against the Polish officers, the Hitlerite authorities are now staging a farcical investigation, and for this they have made use of certain Polish pro-Fascist elements whom they themselves selected in occupied Poland where everything is under Hitler's heel, and where no honest Pole can openly have his say.

For the 'investigation', both the Polish Government and the Hitlerite Government invited the International Red Cross, which is compelled, in conditions of a terroristic régime, with its gallows and mass extermination of the peaceful population, to take part in this investigation farce staged by Hitler. Clearly such an 'investigation', conducted behind the back of the Soviet Government, cannot evoke the confidence of people possessing any degree of honesty.

The fact that the hostile campaign against the Soviet Union commenced simultaneously in the German and Polish press, and was conducted along the same lines, leaves no doubt as to the existence of contact and accord in carrying out this hostile campaign between the enemy of the Allies – Hitler – and the Polish Government.

While the peoples of the Soviet Union bleeding profusely in a hard struggle against Hitlerite Germany, are straining every effort for the defeat of the common enemy of the Russian and Polish peoples, and of all freedom-loving democratic countries, the Polish Government, to please Hitler's tyranny, has dealt a treacherous blow to the Soviet Union.

The Soviet Government is aware that this hostile campaign against the Soviet Union is being undertaken by the Polish Government in order to exert pressure upon the Soviet Government by making use of the slanderous Hitlerite fake for the purpose of wresting from it territorial concessions at the expense of the interests of the Soviet Ukraine, Soviet Byelorussia and Soviet Lithuania.

All these circumstances compel the Soviet Government to recognize that the present Government of Poland, having slid on the path of accord with Hitler's Government, has actually discontinued allied relations with the USSR, and has adopted a hostile attitude towards the Soviet Union.

On the strength of the above, the Soviet Government has decided to sever[1] relations with the Polish Government.[2]

. The Soviet note used the word 'IIpepBatb', which could mean either 'break' or 'interrupt'. Sikorski told Biddle, the American Ambassador to the Polish Government on 7 April that the Soviet use of the word 'suspend' was believed by Romer to indicate that the door was still 'open for discussion' (F.R.U.S. 1943, III, pp. 397–8). On 28 April, however, foreign correspondents were permitted to use the phrase 'break' of relations instead of the previously obligatory 'suspension' (F.R.U.S. 1943, III, p. 401).
. On 28 April, the Polish Government replied to Molotov's note, affirming the terri- torial integrity of the Polish Republic, but denying any claim on Soviet territory. D.O.P.S.R.I, No. 318). In conversation with Eden on 29 April, Maisky objected to this emphasis on 'the frontiers of 1939' (F.O. 371. C4778/258/55).

No. 54

Joseph Stalin to Winston Churchill: Letter (Extract)
4 May 1943
Stalin Correspondence, I, No. 156

In sending my message of April 21 on interrupting relations with the Polish Government, I was guided by the fact that the notorious anti-Soviet press campaign, launched by the Poles as early as April 15 and aggravated first by the statement of the Polish Ministry of National Defence and later by the Poli Government's declaration of April 17, had not encountered any opposition in London; moreover, the Soviet Government had not been forewarned of the anit-Soviet campaign prepared by the Poles, although it is hard to imagine that the British Government was not informed of the contemplated campaign I think that from the point of view of the spirit of our treaty it would have been only natural to dissuade one ally from striking a blow at another, particularly in the blow directly helped the common enemy. That, at any rate, is how I see the duty of an ally. Nevertheless, I thought it necessary to inform you of the Soviet Government's view of Polish-Soviet relations. Since the Pole continued their anti-Soviet smear campaign without any opposition in Londo the patience of the Soviet Government could not have been expected to be infinite.

You tell me that you will enforce proper discipline in the Polish press. I thank you for that, but I doubt if it will be as easy as all that to impose discipline on the present Polish Government, its following of pro-Hitler boosters and its fanatical press. Although you informed me that the Polish Government wanted to work loyally with the Soviet Government, I question its ability to keep its word. The Polish Government is surrounded by such a vast pro-Hitler following, and Sikorski is so helpless and browbeaten that ther is no certainty at all of his being able to remain loyal in relations with the Soviet Union even granting that he wants to be loyal.

As to the rumours, circulated by the Hitlerites, that a new Polish Government is being formed in the U.S.S.R., there is hardly any need to deny this fabrication. Our Ambassador has already told you so.[1] This does not rule out Great Britain, and the U.S.S.R. and the U.S.A. taking measures to improve the composition of the present Polish Government in terms of consolidating the Allied united front against Hitler. The sooner this is done, the better.

1. Churchill had expressed fears to this effect in his letter to Stalin of 30 April. (Stalin Correspondence I, No. 154). Eden had also expressed similar fears to the War Cabinet on 27 April (W.M. (43) 59). Maisky told Churchill on 30 April that the Soviet Government had no intention of setting up an alternative Polish Government in Moscow He added that he could say with equal assurance that they would not renew relations with the present Polish Government. In reply to a question, he admitted that his Government did not wish to displace General Sikorski or Count Raczyński, but he said a 'reconstruction would be necessary' (F.O. 371. C5136/258/55). The Soviets objected particularly to General Kukiel, the Minister of War because of his communique, Stanislaw Kot, Minister of Information and Marian Seyda, Minister of Justice.

on his return from the U.S.A. Mr. Eden told Maisky that President
osevelt's adherents in the U.S.A. thought that the present Polish Government
d no prospects for the future and doubted whether it had any chance of
urning to Poland and assuming power, although they would like to retain
orski. I think the Americans are not so very far from the truth as regards
prospects of the present Polish Government.

As regards the Polish citizens in the U.S.S.R., whose number is not great,
d the families of the Polish soldiers evacuated to Iran, the Soviet Govern-
nt has never raised any obstacles to their departure from the U.S.S.R. . .

. 55

Archibald Clark-Kerr to Anthony Eden: Telegram
SCOW, 8 May 1943
. 371. C5189/258/55

Stalin received me last night.

2. I began by saying that His Majesty's Government were unhappy about
course events had taken. At this word he jibbed a little, asking why. I then
ke of the disturbance of Allied unity and of the unwisdom of driving
orski out of office. He said that he and his Government had been brooding
r Sikorski whom you and the Prime Minister considered to be "un-
eachable". He did not know, but he was ready to take your word for that.
ertheless, he felt strongly that Sikorski was politically weak and that he
wed himself to be swept along by pro-Hitler people about him, whom he
not the strength to resist. That spoilt the Soviet Government's relations
h him.

. He then asked why I had not been shown his last message to the Prime
ister and he sent Molotov to get it. It was translated for me. I then
rted to the unfortunate effects of the interruption of relations and said
we were most anxious to see them restored, and I asked how he thought
this could best be done. He replied at once "by reconstruction of the
sh Government" and went on to say that it needed "solider" men. Its
ent members did not want to live in peace with this country. They had
ed to the Soviet Government all the old hatred that they had felt for the
ist Government. They did not understand the changes that had taken
e. They persisted in trying to play one ally off against the other, coming to-day to us and the Americans about the Russians, and to-morrow
e Russians about us. They thought that this was clever, but in fact
d had given them no brains' . Nevertheless there were plenty of cpable
s and he felt sure that if the Prime Minister were to make a search, he
ld be able to find some suitable men to replace the 'abnormal' people
surrounded Sikorski. Meanwhile he was not impatient, for he was not
tly concerned about the interruption of relations.

. I then turned to the question of Poles in the U.S.S.R. and he reminded me that, in his message to the Prime Minister, he had said that no obstacles would be put in the way of their leaving this country.[1] But he understood that some of the soldiers' families did not want to go. He seemed reluctant to discuss this question any further.

5. He made no reference to frontiers.

1. See above No. 54.

No. 56

Anthony Eden to Sir Archibald Clark-Kerr: Telegram
LONDON, 11 May 1943
F.O. 371. C5295/258/55

THE Soviet Ambassador called this afternoon to offer the warm congratulations of his Government on the North African victories.

2. We then discussed Russian-Polish relations on the Ambassador's initiative. He asked me what progress was being made in our work with the Poles. I said that General Sikorski and Count Raczyński had declared themselves in complete agreement as to the need for the control of the Polish press, and even offered one of their staff to help in the censorship.[1] The next matter with which we wished to make progress was the evacuation of a number of Poles from the Soviet Union. The Ambassador indicated that M. Stalin had already given a favourable reply on this subject. I replied that I was asking you to take up the matter in detail. The Ambassador then asked if there was any information as to the reconstruction of the Polish Government. I replied that this was a matter of very considerable delicacy.[2] No Goverment could be expected to reconstruct itself under foreign pressure. The Ambassador did not dissent from this, but launched out into an account of his Government's general views towards Poland. He maintained that the Soviet Government wished to see a Polish Government of liberal and democratic tendencies. They did not wish to see a Communist Government, nor one animated by hostility towards Russia. Admittedly, the Poles and Russians could not be friends at once. There was too much past history, but they should be able to

1. On 7 May, Eden had met Sikorski and Raczyński and agreement had been reached on tighter control of the Polish press (F.O. 371. C5186/258/55).
2. Later on 7 May, Eden had broached with Sikorski the question of a reconstruction of the Polish Goverment. Sikorski had agreed to consider setting up a smaller 'War-Council' within his Cabinet (F.O. 371. C5139/258/55). However, Vyshinsky's uncompromising statement to the press on Soviet Polish relations on 7 May (D.O.P.S.R.II, No. 7) led Sikorski to write to Eden that 'This unprovoked attack confirms me in my decision not to move one inch from my position, and, therefore, with regret it does not seem possible to me to follow your last suggestion' [concerning the reconstruction of the Polish Government] (F.O. 371. C5179/258/55). On the same day Eden told the Cabinet that 'He thought it would be very difficult for General Sikorski to reconstitute his Government, in view of the attitude taken by the Soviet Government. He was, therefore, increasingly disturbed about the position' (W.M. (43) 66).

get on reasonably well with each other. If after the war the Polish Government was one of extreme Right tendencies this would be impossible and relations with Poland would be bad; even so, Russia would leave Poland alone, but it was much to be desired that Poland, under a more democratic régime, should be Russia's friend as well as neighbour. What I had told him about the press would help, because it was not only about the Polish Government that his Government was anxious but also about the Polish army, where the Polish press had considerable influence and where anti-Soviet tendencies were strong. I said that the difficulty of any reconstruction was to find men who would strengthen the Government in their persons and whose policy was in accord with General Sikorski's own, *i.e.*, to work with the Soviet Union. The only Polish political figures of importance who were outside the present Government were all more anti-Soviet than those who were in it. M. Maisky did not contest this, though he indicated vaguely that there must be some good men who could be found. He mentioned no name.

3. I then said that it had been General Sikorski's intention, before recent events had come about, to pay a visit to his troops in the Middle East. I was inclined to think, subject to the Prime Minister's approval, that this plan should be proceeded with. I had no doubt that General Sikorski's influence in the Middle East would be helpful. In the meanwhile, this question of the reconstruction of the Polish Government could be quietly considered, and it might be that a little later on some steps could be taken by the Polish Government on their own account which would enable diplomatic relations to be restored. I thought it unwise to attempt to secure a rapid solution of this question. M. Maisky did not demur either to the project of the visit or to my comments on the need for time. He argued, however, that, if only the Poles had behaved throughout as the Czechs had done, matters need never have come to the present pass. He wished that there had been a Polish military force fighting on the Soviet front. The fact that the Czechs were doing so had created a very good effect.

4. The conversation was friendly throughout and M. Maisky seemed more ready to adopt an understanding tone towards Polish problems than at our last meeting.

No. 57

Winston Churchill to Joseph Stalin: Letter (extracts)
LONDON, 12 May 1943
Stalin Correspondence, I, No. 159

I am much obliged to you for your message about the Polish affair.

The Poles did not tell us what they were going to do and so we could not warn them against the peril of the course which they proposed to take.

The Polish press will be disciplined in future and all other foreign language publications.

I agree that the Polish Government is susceptible of improvement, though there would be a great difficulty in finding better substitutes. I think like you that Sikorski and some others should in any event be retained. If Sikorski were to reconstruct his Government under foreign pressure he would probably be repudiated and thrown out and we should not get anyone so good in his place. Therefore he probably cannot make changes at once, but I will take every opportunity to urge him to this direction as soon as may be. I will discuss this with President Roosevelt.

I note from your intimation that it is not the policy of the Soviet Government to put obstacles in the way of the exit of Polish subjects in the Union of Soviet Socialist Republics or families of Polish soldiers, and will communicate with you further on this subject through the Ambassador. . .

No. 58

Sir Archibald Clark-Kerr to Anthony Eden: Telegram
MOSCOW, 19 May 1943
F.O. 371. C5652/258/55

I had it out with M. Molotov last night.

2. With regard to the new Polish Legion[1] he made a distinction between nationality and citizenship but said that recruits would largely be drawn from people formerly living in the Western Ukraine and Western White Russia who, though Polish by nationality, were in fact Soviet citizens. In this he saw nothing incongruous.

3. In reply to my question whether the Union of Polish Patriots approximated in any way to Czechoslovak or French National Committees, he gave me a most categorical 'no', insisting that there was no similarity of any kind. I then asked whether it was to be regarded as a competent united Polish authority in Moscow. To this his 'no' was just as emphatic and, when I pressed him for more elucidation, he said that the activities of the Union would be purely a matter of internal policy and in no sense connected with Soviet foreign policy.[2]

4. About the dividing line between the Union's activities and those of office in charge of Polish interests, he claimed that there was no room for misunderstanding or conflict. The line was sharply drawn. The definition of Soviet citizens was known to us. It embraced all those domiciled in the Western Ukraine and Western White Russia. The question of Polish citizenship was a different one. It was true that no common ground has been reached with the Polish Government on this issue, but the Soviet Government

1. On 8 May, *Wolna Polska* had issued a communique announcing that the Soviet Government had agreed to the request of the Union of Polish Patriots to form a Polish Division the Soviet Union (*Wolna Polska*, 8 May 1943). The Polish Government had protested against this in a note to the Foreign Office and the State Department on 13 May (D.O.P.S.R.II, N
2. Similar assurances were given by Maisky to Eden on 18 May (F.O. 371. C5624/258/5

dheres to its standpoint, which was to the effect that Polish nationals vacuated from Western Poland to the Western Ukraine and Western White Russia remained Polish irrespective of their extraction. The people he referred o were mostly refuges from German occupied Poland at the time there were ome border line cases which were susceptible of discussion.

5. He went on to say that it had been foreseen that there might be some misgivings about the Union and the formation of Polish Legion, therefore it ad been in order to forestall and dispel these misgivings that the Soviet Government had caused the facts to be made public. They had wanted every-hing to be open and above-board.

6. Throughout it was clear he was anxious that all our doubts should be et at rest.

No. 59

Anthony Eden to Philip Nichols: Dispatch (Extracts)
LONDON, 16 June 1943
F.O. 371. N3835/3835/38

PRESIDENT BENEŠ, on his return from the United States, asked me to uncheon to-day and gave me an account in some detail of his experiences. . .

6. Returning again to his general Russian policy, Dr. Beneš told me that he Americans had expressed agreement with and approval of his intentions, nd Mr. Roosevelt, oon his side, had asked him whether he would, during his isit to Moscow, do his best to assist United States policy. In particular the .merican President had asked him to help on two points. The first, xplained Dr. Beneš, who asked that I should treat these matters as highly onfidential, concerned the Baltic States. Here Mr. Roosevelt was in general ady to accept the Russian standpoint, but the matter must be arranged in a anner which would give the least offence to American public opinion. Vould Dr. Beneš see what he could do to obtain this? Secondly, the President elieved that the Curzon Line represented an equitable solution of the Polish-ussian frontier problem, but he wondered whether it would be possible to btain from the Russians any concessions which would render this line more alatable to the Poles. Dr. Beneš had said that he was ready to undertake ese two tasks. . .

No. 60

Sumner Welles to Anthony Biddle: Letter (Extracts)
WASHINGTON, 16 June 1943
F.R.U.S. 1943, III, p. 431

. We have of course followed closly the Soviet-Polish controversy and have ome to the conclusion that any restoration of relations must be of such a aracter as to provide an elimination of as many as possible of the factors which were responsible for the present breach. We are quite firm, however, in our determination not to be a party to any discussions of future frontiers at the present stage of the war.

We have received the same impression as yourself that the immediate desire of the Soviet Government is to bring about a change in the composition of the Polish Government-in-exile. While some changes might prove advantageous after the restoration of relations, on the basis indicated above, we do not feel that it would be proper for us to bring pressure on Sikorski to change the composition of the Polish Government in order to satisfy the Soviet Government.[1] In our opinion it would be unfortunate for a precedent to be established under which the government of one United Nation could successfully force changes in the composition of another government of the United Nations.

We are endeavouring to work out with the British some form of joint approach which will offer the best possibility of an equitable solution of the Polish-Soviet dispute and you will be informed when we have arrived at some common ground with them.

1. In a letter to Welles on 2 June, 1943 (F.R.U.S. 1943, III, pp. 424–6) Biddle argued that the resumption of relations between the Poles and the Soviets depended on the satisfaction of three Soviet preconditions:–
   1) changes in the composition of the Polish Government;
   2) censorship of anti-Soviet articles in the Polish press;
   3) 'tranquilization of the anti-Soviet attitude of the Polish forces, both here and in the Middle East.'
Earlier on 2 May, Biddle had claimed that the Soviets had prepared their case against the Poles at the time of the dispatch of their note of 16 January and had used the Polish appeal to the Red Cross as a useful pretext to break off relations. Soviet asperations went beyond the Polish Soviet frontier to 'other Russian post-war "security-frontier" asperations in the "middle zone" ' (F.R.U.S. 1943, III, pp. 404–5).

No. 61

Minutes by William Strang, Sir Orme Sargent, Sir Alexander Cadogan and Anthony Eden on Memorandum by G. M. Wilson of the Central Department on Russia's Western Frontier[1]
LONDON, 29 June – 11 July 1943
F.O. 371. N4905/4069/38

If we have made up our minds as to the future frontiers of Poland, I do no see why we should not, informally and without commitment, intimate to the

1. In this memorandum, submitted on 22 June, Wilson argued, much on the lines of Strang's memorandum of 15 April 1943 (See above, No. 49 notes) that an improvement of Polish-Soviet relations could only be lasting if an agreement on the Polish Eastern frontier were reached. Similar views had been expressed by Clark-Kerr in a telegram to Eden on 25 April 1943 (F.O. 371. C4464/258/55). Eden had replied that 'Sikorski is the best Polish leader we or the Russians can hope to work with and it would be foolish to precipitate his fall on an issue which is not yet a practical one since the Soviet armies are still far from the former Polish frontier' (F.O. 371. C4806/258/55).

Soviet Government what our views are.

I assume that we should think it reasonable that the Poles should receive

(1) East Prussia

(2) an adjustment in their favour in Upper Silesia, including the whole industrial basin;

and that they should be content with

(3) the Curzon Line, with possible adjustment of it in their favour including the city of Lwów.[2]

What we might say to the Russian would be that, while we still maintain our non-recognition of the territorial changes effected in Poland since August 1939 (as stated to the Poles at the time of the conclusion of the Polish-Soviet Treaty of July 1941), we think that the Poles would be wise to accept a settlement on the above lines when the time comes.

It would be better if this statement were made to the Russians as part of a general conversation about the post-war settlement than as an isolated statement.

We must be careful not to make any agreement, written or unwritten, with the Russians on the point of view of our undertaking to the Poles not to conclude any agreement affecting or compromising the territorial status of the Polish Republic.'[3]

We should also take a suitable opportunity to inform the Polish Government that our views about the post-war territorial settlement are as stated above; we might, when doing so, add that we understand that President Roosevelt shares these views.[4] (We have already told the Soviet and Czechoslovak Governments of the President's views, and there is therefore a good deal to be said for telling the Poles also.)

I think that this is as far as we ought to go at the present stage. I should not be in favour of trying to persuade the Poles to reach a frontier settlement with the Russians here and now.

> W. Strang
> 29th June, 1943

I naturally agree with Mr. Strang as his proposal is in conformity with that which I put up in paragraph 18 of my memorandum of April 15th. . .

. On 25 July Wilson prepared a paper suggesting two possible lines of approach which the British could pursue to secure Lwów for the Poles (F.O. 371. N4447/499/38). He argued that a British assertion of the Polish claim would be unlikely to produce the desired results. Rather he favoured a statement to the Russians that the British were prepared to endorse their 'claim to the 1941 frontier (roughly)' while expressing the hope that in the interests of Polish-Soviet relations, Lwów would be left to the Poles. Harrison, however, argued that '. . . I cannot see that we can usefully consider at the moment what our final attitude on the subject of Lwów will be at the peace settlement.'

In Eden's letter to Sikorski on 21 April 1942. See above No. 36, note 1. Eden minuted 'When *did* we say this?'

Eden minuted, 'We could hardly do this without American permission.'

But I think I ought to put in a word of warning to the effect that it may be very difficult to discuss Polish frontier questions with Russia without being required to commit ourselves simultaneously with regard to the Baltic States, Finland and Roumania.[5]

On one point. I do not think it would be enough, as Mr. Strang suggests, merely to say that we understand that President Roosevelt shares our views. I am sure that in a matter of this importance we and the Americans ought to act jointly.

Since this question was previously discussed on my memorandum of last April further reasons for grasping this particular nettle have cropped up. For instance, (1) it looks as though the President intends to employ Dr. Beneš to discuss the subject with Stalin.[6] In any case it is more than probable that Dr. Beneš has made up his mind to discuss it, if not as the President's mouth-piece then on his own responsibility during his Moscow visit. (2) As the war moves towards the Balkans and our planning for a Balkan campaign takes more definite form, it becomes more and more clear that we shall have to reach some understanding with the Soviet Government for co-operating in the re-establishment of order in Central Europe if and when there is an Axis collapse. . . It will, however, be very difficult to make any progress with the Soviet Government on this very delicate matter unless we are prepared at the same time to discuss the Soviet Union's own frontiers with Central Europe and the Balkans. (3) Recent correspondence with Stalin has shown how important it is that we should establish some working arrangement for periodic three-party discussions to include ourselves, the Americans and the Russians. It is to be hoped that it will be possible to make an arrangement but, if the ensuing discussions are to make any progress or inspire any confidence in Stalin's mind, we shall have to be ready to discuss the questions which the Russians wish to discuss, however embarrassing it may be to ourselves to do so. Among these the question of the Soviet Union's western frontiers will certainly bulk large.

O. G. Sargent,
5th July, 1943

I am still disposed to agree that this question is at the root of all the trouble. But nearly all the difficulties in the way of attempting to settle it now still exist.

The final stage would in any case have to be agreement between ourselves and the Americans. In connection with Dr. Beneš' forthcoming visit to Moscow we have already made an approach to the U.S. Government, which might lead to a thorough and frank discussion of the question with them. (We must await the reply to that).

5. Eden minuted, 'I agree.'
6. See above, No. 59.

Gen. Sikorski's remark has added another complication: we do not know what sort of a Polish Government they will have nor how M. Stalin will regard them.

A. C. [Cadogan]
5th July, 1943

I think that I should be disposed to go at least as far as Mr. Strang suggests. All this has to be further examined in the light of a possible visit to Moscow by me a little later. We might have a discussion after this visit.

A. E. [Eden]
11th July, 1943

No. 62

The Ambassador to the U.K., John Winant to Cordell Hull: Telegram
LONDON, 20 July 1943
F.R.U.S. 1943, III, pp. 447–9

After sending you my 4526, July 10,[1] I asked Mr. Eden if at a later date he could give me a more detailed and considered judgment on the new Polish Government. I have just received the following letter from him which I think you will find of particular interest as representing the British Government's view:

'When you came to see me on the 14th of July I promised to let you have a short statement about the Polish political situation. As you will have gathered, the formation of the new Polish Government which was announced in the press on the 15th of July was not achieved without considerable difficulties. These difficulties arose chiefly out of the question of the constitutional relationship between the President, the Commander-in-Chief and the Prime Minister and were connected with the problem of the interpretation to be placed upon those articles of the Polish Constitution of 1935 which dealt with that relationship. The 1935 Constitution, which was adopted at the end of the Pilsudski era, placed far-reaching powers in the hands of the President of the Republic. The Polish Democratic and Left Wing parties have never willingly accepted this aspect of the Constitution and when the Polish Government was first reconstituted in France at the end of 1939 an understanding was reached that the President would not exercise his full prerogatives during the period of emigration.

Under the Constitution, the President of the Republic is empowered in time of war to nominate his own successor. President Raczkiewicz had himself been so nominated by his predecessor, President Mościcki, and he in his turn

1. In this Winant stated, 'Today Mr. Eden told me in his opinion the reorganization of the Polish Government was reasonably good. . . ' (F.R.U.S. 1943, III, p. 447).

had nominated as his eventual successor General Sosnkowski. The President also enjoys under the Constitution the power to appoint and dismiss the Commander-in-Chief of the Polish Armed Forces. It was in the exercise of this power that President Raczkiewicz decided shortly after General Sikorski's death to nominate General Sosnkowski to succeed him in his capacity as Commander-in-Chief. In taking this decision he was primarily influenced by the need of stabilizing opinion in the Polish Armed Forces both here and in the Middle East, whose discipline and loyalty he felt might be seriously affected if there were a long delay.

This decision was not pleasing to the Left Wing parties and in particular to M. Mikolajczyk himself who, as Deputy Prime Minister under General Sikorski became Acting Prime Minister on the latter's death. He felt that adequate arrangements should be made to ensure that the Commander-in-Chief did not occupy too commanding a position which he might welcome. In addition to commanding the Polish Armed Forces he also directed the underground military movement in Poland. He would have preferred that an [*no?*] appointment be made to the post of Commander-in-Chief or that at least, if one were made, the man chosen should be someone less influential than General Sosnkowski.[2] M. Mikołajczyk was undoubtedly influenced by the wish to ensure that his party and those of like mind should retain their influence in Poland itself against the day of the Polish Government's return to their country.

These considerations led M. Mikołajczyk to inform the President that he was unable to accept office as Prime Minister and form a government unless means could be found of limiting the authority of the Commander-in-Chief.[3] After protracted discussions, it appears that satisfactory arrangements to this end have been made and M. Mikołajczyk has succeeded in forming an all party Government of National Union in which representatives of his own Party (the Peasant Party) and the Socialist Party, predominate. This Government seems to us as satisfactory as can be hoped for. Its democratic character, and the fact that M. Mikołajczyk has pledged it to continue General Sikorski's policy, suggest that it should not be unduly provocative of Soviet-Russian susceptibilities.[4] It should also be in a position to command the loyalty both of the Polish Armed Forces abroad and of the vast majority of Poles in Poland itself and to ensure the maintenance of the resistance movement inside the country. From the military point of view, the choice of General Sosnkowski also appears to have a good deal to commend it. He is the senior general in the Polish Army, whose loyalty he is believed to command. It is true that he was an ardent follower of Pilsudski, and that he opposed General Sikorski's action in signing the treaty with Soviet Russia in July 1941. However, if, as appears to be the case, adequate measures have been taken to ensure that he is subordinated to the Government as a whole, this aspect should assume less importance.'

2. Mikołajczyk would have preferred General Kopański, or failing him, General Anders,

who had commanded the Polish forces in Russia.

3. Mikołajczyk had laid down four conditions:−

    1. The Commander-in-Chief should be subject to the directions of the Government and not responsible only to the President.

    2. The Commander-in-Chief should not have a right to the succession to the Presidency.

    3. He wanted an assurance that he would in no circumstances be dismissed by the President.

    4. All control of Polish secret organizations should be brought under the control of the Government, ending the situation whereby some control lay with the Commander-in-Chief (W.M. 97 (43)).

4. In a minute for the Prime Minister on 7 July, Eden accepted the Polish argument that 'there is no reason to believe that he [Sosnkowski] would be more unacceptable to Russia than Anders. . . If the Russians want to make trouble for the Polish Government they will do so whoever is appointed Commander-in-Chief' (F.O. 371. P.M. 43/207). This was in spite of the fact that, as G. W. Harrison of the Central Department reported on 8 July, Bogomolov, when asked by Biddle for his views on Sosnkowski, had replied that ' . . . there should be no Commander-in-Chief at all since under the Polish Constitution the Commander-in-Chief could at any moment walk into the Cabinet and take over dictatorial power' (F.O. 371. C7960/259/55).

No. 63

Documents handed to Stalin by Sir Archibald Clark-Kerr and Admiral Standley[1] (Extracts)
MOSCOW, 11 August 1943

1. Statement by Sir Clark-Kerr − S.D. 760c. 61/2097

As the Soviet Government are aware, His Majesty's Government are greatly concerned to promote and to maintain solidarity between the United Nations and have recently been considering whether they could make any constructive proposals regarding the improvement of Soviet-Polish relations and the removal of possible causes of friction between the two Governments. This seems to them to be all the more important on account of the unhappy death of General Sikorski. His Majesty's Government have been imposing, and will continue to impose, upon the foreign newspapers published in the United Kingdom a control which will have, they hope, the effect of putting an end to discussion in the press of controversial issues affecting inter-allied relations.

It will be remembered that in his message of the 6th May to Mr. Churchill,

1. Considerable delay had occurred in making this joint approach to the Soviets because of the difficulty of harmonzing the British and American positions. For the formulation of American policy on this question, see the telegrams from Hull to Standley of 12 June, 29 June and 10 July (F.R.U.S. 1943, III, pp. 428−31, 434−7, 440−3). For Standley's unavailing attempts to modify State Department policy, see his telegrams of 18 June and 5 July (F.R.U.S. 1943, III, pp. 432−4, 437−9). The marked disinclination of the U.S. Government to enter into discussion about post-war frontiers emerges clearly in Hull's telegrams. For the development of the British position, see the following telegrams:− Clark-Kerr to Eden, 17 June 1943 (F.O. 371. C7000/258/55), Eden to Clark-Kerr, 23 June (F.O. 371. C7000/258/55), Eden to Halifax, 24 June (F.O. 371. C7491/258/55), Halifax to Eden, 30 June (F.O. 371. C7491/258/55), Eden to Halifax, 4 July (F.O. 371. C7491/258/55), Eden to Clark-Kerr, 11 July (F.O. 371. C7933/258/55).

Marshal Stalin said that the Soviet Government had never put obstacles in the way of the departure from the U.S.S.R. of Polish subjects and the families of Polish troops evacuated to Iran. In the light of this assurance, His Majesty's Government have been in consultation with the United States Government about the possibilities and advantages of such an evacuation. The two Governments have been considering whether, by the evacuation of certain categories of Poles, it would not be possible to lighten the burden of the Soviet Government in feeding and maintaining on its territory a considerable foreign population, and, at the same time, to mitigate the hardship of separation for a large number of Polish families. Such a result could, in the opinion of both the British and the United States Governments, serve only to strengthen and improve relations between the peoples of Poland and the Soviet Union.

With this end in view, His Majesty's Government wish to bring to the attention of the Soviet Government proposals for the evacuation of certain categories of Poles to the Middle East whence they would subsequently be dispersed to those destinations where they could be most suitably accommodated or employed in the interests of the common war effort. The categories in question are as follows:

1) The families of all Polish troops who were not evacuated with their men folk in 1942, and also the families of those Polish troops who, although they have never been in this country, are at present serving in the Polish forces in other parts of the world. It is believed that this category would not be likely to exceed 30,000 people;

2) Polish orphans, whose numbers are uncertain;

3) The families of Polish civilians at present outside the U.S.S.R.;

4) Certain Polish technicians and the personnel of the former Polish welfare organizations, who would together amount to something over 5,000.

The evacuation would be spread over such a period as might prove to be appropriate and necessary. . .

Finally, it is suggested that the Soviet Government would be well advised to consider the evacuation of Polish nationals from Western Poland, whose nationality is not in dispute.

His Majesty's Government are of the opinion that the foregoing proposals would, by reducing the number of Polish refugees in this country, go a long way towards putting an end to the present abnormal conditions which, in their view, can only serve to aggravate relations between two of the United Nations. The disappearance of these abnormal conditions would, it is felt, help to restore mutual confidence and render more easy an eventual resumption of friendly relations between the two Governments. Such a solution by putting an end to inter-allied differences, would at once deprive the Axis propaganda machine of a fruitful field of exploitation and would assist in re-establishing that harmony between the United Nations which is so necessary for the solution of common problems both during the war and fter it.

2. Aide-Memoire of the United States Government — S.D. 760c. 61/2091

The Government of the United States regret that the Soviet and Polish Governments have been unable thus far to resolve their problems under dispute and to resume diplomatic relations. It has not heretofore approached the Soviet Government in regard to the question since it hoped that the unfortunate breach might be healed by the two Governments. In view of the continued suspension in relations and of the extreme importance placed on the question of the necessity for unity among all the United Nations, the American Government, in an endeavor more firmly to close the ranks of the United Nations in order that they may even more resolutely bring their full and combined weight to bear in the prosecution of the war, desires to offer its assistance in bringing about a resumption of relations between the Soviet and Polish Governments.

The American Government believes that the principal objective of the solution of the question at issue is the formal resumption of diplomatic relations on a sound basis under which the grievances of the past should not be permitted to plague the future. From a study of the practical problems involved in recent Soviet-Polish relations it feels that an attempt should be made to eliminate the principal defects of the Soviet-Polish Agreement of July 1941, as supplemented by subsequent informal agreements. With this in mind, it desires to offer the following proposals for settling the dispute on a basis as just and permanent as the difficult situation permits:

1. Polish Relief and Welfare Work in the Soviet Union.

The establishment of what amounted to an extra-territorial apparatus of a foreign government functioning in the Soviet Union would appear to have given rise to misunderstandings between the two governments. The American Government is inclined to the belief therefore that a more workable solution could be reached if the Poles would agree to permit relief and welfare work to be carried on by Soviet organizations, with, of course, the understanding that Polish citizens would receive treatment no less favorable than that granted to Soviet citizens in similar circumstances. If this proposal is acceptable to the Polish Government, the Soviet Government on its part might be prepared to permit Polish citizens in the Soviet Union to have contact with appropriate Polish consular officers when diplomatic relations are resumed.

2. Citizenship.

The American Government feels that the question of citizenship must be resolved before any just or lasting resumption of relations can be brought about. It also feels that the unfortunate persons resident in Polish territory in the fall of 1939 who were uprooted from their homes as a result of the war and who now find themselves in the Soviet Union should at least be given the opportunity of deciding for themselves the country of which they desire to be citizens. . .

In view of the complexities of the question of citizenship it is felt that an approach on the following broad lines would be practicable:

    a. Non-racial Poles in the Soviet Union shall be permitted by the Soviet and Polish Governments to opt for Soviet or Polish citizenship.

    b. All racial Poles in the Soviet Union who were domiciled in Poland on September 1, 1939, shall be recognized by the Soviet Government as Polish citizens and shall therefore not be called upon to opt.

3. The Evacuation of Polish Citizens from the Soviet Union.

The American Government feels that the discussions in respect to relief and citizenship should not interfere with any plans already under consideration for the evacuation of special categories of Polish citizens from the Soviet Union. It therefore desires it to be made clear that in its opinion the evacuation of certain groups of Polish citizens should not await a more basic settlement of the Soviet-Polish disagreement. In the opinion of the American Government a generous attitude on the part of the Soviet Government reflected in the immediate evacuation of certain groups of Polish citizens will not only represent a concrete contribution to the united war effort but will also assist in the creation of a more favorable atmosphere for the reestablishment of diplomatic relations between the Soviet Union and Poland on a basis which will make possible an era of real friendship between the two countries.

The American Government places particular importance upon the problem of evacuating from the Soviet Union Polish citizens who have close relations abroad, especially those who are members of the immediate families of men in the Polish armed forces. At the same time it believes that every effort should be made for the evacuation of Polish orphans and other Polish children who cannot be properly cared for in the Soviet Union as soon as suitable arrangements can be made for their care elsewhere.

The American Government feels that the Soviet Polish dispute is so important in connection with bringing the full weight of all the United Nations to bear on the prosecution of the war against the common enemies that every effort should be made at this time to try to resolve the aforementioned fundamental questions at issue.

3. Statement by the United States Ambassador – F.O. 371. C10042/258/55

The Government of the United States does not feel that at this time, when the energies of the United Nations should be concentrated on the winning of the war controversies with respect to future boundaries should be permitted to develop. It is convinced that the liquidation of difficulties with respect to boundaries, unless such difficulties may be settled amicably without friction between the Governments concerned, should await the termination of the war and be included in the general post-war settlement.[2]

2. When these documents were presented by Standley and Clark-Kerr, Molotov and Stalin listened 'in complete silence' and refused to

No. 64

Anthony Eden to Sir Alexander Cadogan: Telegram (Extracts)
QUEBEC, 19 August 1943
F.O. 371. N5066/499/38

I had a talk with Harry Hopkins this morning... We then spoke of Russia. I said that I was much troubled at the prospect of this proposed meeting of Foreign Secretaries. Two subjects in the main interested Joe, (1) the Second Front, and (2) his Western frontiers. H.H. agreed and added a third condition, the treatment of Germany after the war. I said that I thought two and three related. If I were to go to meet Molotov or Stalin accompanied by some American opposite number, and made plain that we had not advanced at all in our consideration of Russian frontier claims, then I thought the meeting would almost certain do more harm than good. H.H. agreed and said it was just because of this that the President had originally wished to meet Stalin himself. He could say things to Stalin which he felt sure the President would not allow anyone else to say for him. In fact, H.H. knew that the President's mind about Russia's frontiers was almost exactly the same as my own. He had said as much to Molotov and Litvinov also. He could not therefore go back on this, but H.H. felt quite sure that he would not authorise Welles to speak in this way. Moreover, if Welles went Hull would certainly do his best to torpedo the meeting. I said that this sounded altogether a very agreeable enterprise for me to set out upon. Why could not H.H. go with me instead? H.H. said that he thought Hull would certainly prefer this, but the President might be reluctant. He himself would be prepared to go if he could be given sufficient latitude...

No. 65

Conversation between President Benes and a senior Polish Official[1] (Extracts)
LONDON, 19 August 1943
F.O. 371. C10484/525/12

... President Benes turned to political problems. 'Czechoslovakia', said Dr. Benes, 'is faced by three alternative solutions in so far as the post-war settlement is concerned: 1) a federation with Poland and other states of Central Europe, 2) a Danubian federation in a different set of states, and finally 3) a close understanding and Alliance with Russia. Czechoslovakia has chosen the third solution and no power on earth will be able to detach Czechoslovakia from this collaboration with Russia. We have lost confidence in the Western countries after what happened in Munich. The Czechoslovak people have no confidence in France, Britain or America. We do not want to be regarded as a Western European nation, we are more closely bound up with the East. Only Russia was ready to help us in our misfortune in 1938 after we had been

1. The official was probably Mgr. Edmund Kaczynski, Polish Minister of Education.

betrayed by the Western states. But she was not allowed to do so.' ...

No. 66

Conversation between Anthony Eden and Cordell Hull (Extracts)
QUEBEC, 19 August 1943
F.O. 371. C10847/231/55

... I read to Mr. Hull the minute which I submitted to the Prime Minister. . .[1]
on this subject, together with parts of the draft telegram to Washington.[2]

Mr. Hull said this raised difficult questions and he emphasized that if we
were to make considerable concessions to the Soviet Government we must ask
something from them in return. We agreed that the matter ought certainly to
be considered, as in any negotiations which we might hold with the Soviet
Government about post-war matters the latter would be certain to raise this
frontier question. We might be able to make any concessions on this question
dependent upon the Soviet Government's falling in with our ideas on the
general post-war plan. I promised to give Mr. Hull a note on the subject which
would follow the line of the draft telegram to Washington which I submitted
to the Prime Minister.[3]

1. In this minute, Eden had argued that cooperation with Russia was becoming
increasingly vital and that it would greatly improve if the British made clear their
position on the western frontier of the Soviet Union (F.O. 371. N5060/422/38).
2. The essence of this is contained in the Memorandum Eden submitted to Hull on 23
August. See below, No. 67.
3. Ibid.

No. 67

Memorandum communicated to Cordell Hull by Anthony Eden
QUEBEC, 23 August 1943
F.O. 371. N5060/499/38

In December 1941 Stalin informed the Foreign Secretary that he regarded
the question of U.S.S.R.'s western frontiers as 'the main question for us in the
war'.

Stalin during the Foreign Secretary's visit to Moscow in 1941, Molotov in
London in 1942, and Maisky speaking to the Foreign Secretary in March 1943
have all said that Curzon Line with minor modifications would be satisfactory
basis for frontier settlement.

Neither H.M.G. nor, so far as we are aware, U.S. Government, have indicated
to Soviet Government what their views on this question are. We have little
doubt, however, that the Soviet Government would be much easier to deal with
on Polish and other matters if H.M.G. and U.S. Government could let them
know that we are prepared in practice to contemplate a substantial measure
of satisfaction on what we understand Soviet territorial claims to be, while

not abandoning our principle of not recognising during the war any territorial changes.

H.M.G. consider that an equitable solution of Russian claims would be something on the following lines: (a) *Poland* to receive in the west Danzig, East Prussia and Upper Silesia, and to be content in the east with the Curzon Line adjusted to include city of Lwów in Poland. (b) *Other frontiers.* Eventual recognition of Russia's 1941 frontiers with Finland and Roumania, and of Soviet sovereignty over the Baltic States.

If the views of the U.S. Government do not differ radically from the above, there might be a basis for a joint intimation of our views to Soviet Government, in the course of any discussion with them of the general post-war settlement. H.M. Government wish to consider advisability of such action *now* because:

(a) Recent exchanges of personal telegrams between the Prime Minister and Stalin show that the latter desires closer consultation on future operations. This is natural now that we are embarked on operations in Europe which are likely soon to affect south-eastern Europe more or less directly. The views of Soviet Government will have to be taken into consideration and their attitude is likely to be suspicious and unco-operative unless they get some reassurances upon this 'main question' of frontiers.

(b) When some time ago His Majesty's Ambassador in Moscow broached with M. Molotov the question of the Soviet attitude to post-war questions in Germany, he received a definite indication that the Soviet Government wished to discuss such matters with H.M.Government and U.S. Government, with a view to reaching firm agreement. The matter has not been pursued pending discussion with U.S. Government, but if we want to break down Soviet suspicions and get into real contact with them on major matters we think it unwise to leave discussions further in suspense. The Organisation of a Free German Movement is an added reason for resuming discussions.

There could, of course, be no question at this stage of any agreement written or unwritten with the Soviet Government on frontier question. This would be contrary to the assurances we gave Poland in 1941 when the Soviet Polish Treaty was signed and again in 1942 at time of the negotiations for an Anglo-Soveit treaty. We should therefore propose to inform the Polish Government that in our view no final settlement of Polish-Soviet difficulties can be found so long as there is no agreement on the frontier question. This question will have to be solved sooner or later. It could be left until the Soviet armies re-enter Polish territory, but it is our belief that a satisfactory solution would then be all the harder to obtain. We and the U.S. Government would propose therefore to approach the Soviet Government in the matter and discuss it with them.

It is probable that the Soviet Government would agree to something on the lines of para. 3(a) above. We know that it is difficult, maybe impossible, for this or any Polish Government, during the course of the war, to accept any surrender of former Polish territory. But it might perhaps help them if the U.S. and U.K. Governments were to recommend to them such a solution, conditional on Poland receiving the compensation indicated.

We for our part would not wish to announce formally any understanding that might be reached with the Soviet on these lines, and we should also ask them to keep it to themselves until such time as it could be presented as part of a general territorial settlement.

We must face the fact that, if we do proceed thus, we cannot be certain that publicity will not be given to the facts either from the Soviet or the Polish side.

There could of course be no intention of giving the Soviet Government satisfaction on the point of frontiers unless they, on their side, are willing to play a useful part in post-war organisation as we conceive it. But it is so certain that the Russians will raise this point if we get into discussion that it seems essential that we should know how we propose to deal with it.

No. 68

Anthony Eden to Sir Archibald Clark-Kerr: Telegram (Extracts)
LONDON, 31 August 1943
F.O. 371. N4577/66/38

9. M. Maisky then spoke of incidents which he maintained had caused considerable friction in Moscow. . .

. . . M. Maisky continued that there were two possible ways of trying to organise Europe after the war. Either we could agree each to have a sphere of interest, the Russians in the East and ourselves and the Americans in the West. He did not himself think this was a good plan, but if it were adopted we should be at liberty to exclude the Russians from French Affairs, the Mediterranean and so forth, and the Russians would claim similar freedom in the East. If, on the other hand, we would both, and the United States also, agree that all Europe was one, as his Government would greatly prefer, then we must each admit the right of the other to an interest in all parts of Europe. If we were concerned with Czechoslovakia and Poland, and the United States with the Baltic States, then we must understand Russian concern in respect of France and the Mediterranean. I said that all this was admitted. There was no dispute about it and it might even be found possible to find a form of words at our meeting of Foreign Secretaries and to give expression to it if the Russians so desired. . .

No. 69

Minute by Sir William Strang
LONDON, 9 September 1943
F.O. 371. C10409/231/55

At luncheon with the Polish Prime Minister today, the Secretary of State said he would like to ask an indiscreet question. Supposing it were proposed that Poland should receive East Prussia and a substantial accession of territory in Silesia, together with a frontier in the east approximately to the Curzon Line but including Lwów, would this be a very shocking proposal in Polish eyes?[1]

M. Mikołajczyk said that in the first place, he noticed there was no reference to Vilna. Vilna, like Lwów, was a indispensable bastion of the Polish eastern frontier.

Apart from this, M. Mikołajczyk said he had two observations to make. The first was that no Polish Government in exile could possibly make itself responsible for any territorial concession. The second was that what was at stake between Poland and Russia was not merely a question of frontiers but a question of general relations and indeed the question of the survival of Poland as an independent state. The Ribbentrop-Molotov Line was still a live issue and not a dead letter and would have a bearing not only upon the future organization of Poland but upon Soviet-German relations.

The Polish Ambassador, who was present, intervened to say that the Curzon Line had serious dangers for Poland from a strategical point of view. The frontier drawn at Riga was a good natural frontier from the political, economic and geological point of view, since it was firmly based upon the Pripet marshes and gave Poland reasonable military security in the east.

1. Already on 26 July, Churchill had told the Polish President that while he was determined to secure a strong and 'completely independent Poland' at the end of the war, he was not ready to give any kind of assurance as to exactly where the frontiers of Poland would lie' (F.O. 371. C9006/258/55).

No. 70

The People's Commissariat of the Soviet Union to the American Embassy in the Soviet Union (Extracts)[1]
MOSCOW, 27 September 1943
F.R.U.S. 1943, III, pp. 161–7

On August 11, 1943, the American Ambassador, Mr. Standley, and the British Ambassador, Mr. Kerr, made to the President of the Council of People's Commissars of the USSR, J. V. Stalin, a joint statement concerning Soviet-Polish relations,[2] submitting at the same time in the name of their Governments *aide-mémoires* on this subject. . .

The Soviet Government duly appreciates the motives guiding the Governments of the United States of America and Great Britain in the matter of regularizing Soviet-Polish relations. The Soviet Government, however, cannot fail to express its regret that at the same time they did not make use of their

1. An identical *Aide Memoire* was communicated to the British Embassy (F.O. 371. C13460/258/55).
2. See above, No. 63.

influence in order to prevent acts of the Polish Government hostile to the Soviet Union and injurious to the cause of unity among the United Nations which obliged the Soviet Government to take the decision to interrupt diplomatic relations with the Polish Government. . .

The Soviet Government . . . considers it necessary to draw the attention of the Government of the United States of America to the fact that the disruption of normal diplomatic relations between the USSR and Poland was directly connected not with these questions but with the generally hostile direction of the policies of the Polish Government in relation to the USSR, which found its specific expression in the attempt of the Polish Government to use the German fascist provocation concerning the Polish officers killed by the Hitlerites in the Smolensk District for the purpose of wringing from the Soviet Union territorial concessions at the expense of the interests of the Soviet Ukraine, Soviet Belorussia, and Soviet Lithuania.

It is impossible not to draw attention to the fact that the British and American proposals almost coincide with the pretensions of the Polish Government formulated by General Sikorski, notably in his speech of May 4, 1943, and at present supported by the Polish Premier, Mikolajczyk, which refer in demagogic fashion to the necessity for 'liberating' and evacuating from the Soviet Union 'unfortunate' Polish citizens. This type of statement is lacking in any foundation whatsoever and cannot be considered other than as an insulting attack against the Soviet Union to which the Soviet Government does not consider it necessary to react.

Referring to the questions raised in the above-mentioned *aide-mémoires,* the Soviet Government considers it necessary to communicate the following:

1. *Concerning Polish relief and welfare work in the Soviet Union.*

In the first place it is necessary to note that the establishment in the Soviet Union of agencies of the Polish Embassy to extend assistance to Polish citizens was not at all the cause for misunderstandings between the Soviet and Polish Governments, as is stated in the proposal in the note of the American Government. If one is to speak of such misunderstandings, the reason for them was not the establishment of such organizations, but the fact that the Polish agencies and a number of their personnel and trusted representatives, instead of honestly doing their duty and fulfilling their obligations for cooperation with the Soviet authorities, embarked on espionage activities which were inimical to the Soviet Union. . .

These are the real and not the imaginary grounds for those 'misunderstandings' which are mentioned in the *aide-memoire* of the Government of the United States of America dated 11 August, 1943.

It is therefore entirely understandable that it is impossible to link the question of these 'misunderstandings' to the question of the organization of relief for Polish nationals and to the question of the forms and methods of extending such relief. It is apparent that the causes of these misunderstanding do not lie in this plane at all. They lie in the fundamentally hostile policy of the Polish Government toward the USSR.

With reference to the proposal of the Government of the United States of America for the concentration of all matters pertaining to the relief of Polish citizens in the hands of Soviet organizations, that is exactly the manner in which relief for Polish citizens is organized in the USSR at the present time. To the foregoing it is necessary to add that Poles who were evacuated to regions in the rear of the USSR, in addition to the relief extended to them on an equal basis with all Soviet citizens, receive additional relief through a specially created system of Soviet institutions which look after Poles evacuated to regions in the Soviet rear. The submission of this proposal by the American Government is evidently explained by the insufficient information thus far at its disposal.

2. *Citizenship*

All former Polish citizens who resided in the western regions of the Ukrainian and Belorussian Soviet Republics at the time of the admission of these regions into the Union of Soviet Socialist Republics (November 1–2, 1939) acquired Soviet nationality by virtue of the freely expressed will of the population of these regions and on the basis of the laws for the incorporation of the Western Ukraine and Western Belorussia in the Union of Soviet Socialist Republics through their reunion with the Ukrainian and Belorussian Soviet Socialist Republics, adopted by the Supreme Council of the USSR on November 1–2, 1939, and also on the basis of the decree of the Presidium of the Supreme Council of the USSR of November 29, 1939, and in accordance with the 'Law Concerning Soviet Citizenship' of August 19, 1938. . .

In the same way the question of the territorial status of the Western Ukraine and of Western Belorussia and the citizenship of persons who were residents of these territories was fully decided at that time. The Soviet Government cannot agree with the considerations set forth in the *aide-memoire* of the Government of the United States in favor of some other decision of this question with relation to separate categories of Polish citizens, in as much as such a decision would be a violation of the laws of the USSR. It is impossible, of course, to agree with arguments such as these advanced to the effect that all persons of Polish nationality who were formerly Polish citizens and are now in the Soviet Union should be recognized as Polish citizens because they formerly were domiciled in Poland. Does the Government of the United States of America consider as Polish citizens Poles who formerly were domiciled in Poland, but who at the present time are domiciled in the United States of America, any more than the British Government recognizes as French citizens Frenchmen who are domiciled, for instance, in Canada? It is clear that the question of citizenship cannot be decided from the point of view of the former citizenship or place of residence of these or other persons but must be decided on the basis of the laws in effect in the given country.

With reference to persons who were not residents of the Western Ukraine or of Western Belorussia who found themselves on Soviet territory because of war conditions, the Soviet Government has never raised and does not raise the question of their recognition as Soviet citizens against their will. These persons have always been allowed and are being allowed the full possibility of deciding for themselves the country of which they wish to be citizens.

In view of the foregoing the proposals of the American Government set forth in paragraphs (a) and (b) of section 2 of the *aide-mémoire* of August 11 are inadmissible for the Soviet Government.

3. *The evacuation of Polish citizens from the Soviet Union.*

As the Governments of Great Britain and the United States know, the Soviet Government, guided by its good will, in due course met the wishes of the Polish Government and permitted the evacuation from the Soviet Union, apart from 75,491 Polish troops, of 37,756 members of their families, among whom were also a considerable number of Soviet citizens. The Soviet Government on several occasions has stated and states again that from the side of the Soviet Government no obstacles were placed in the way of the departure from the Soviet Union of Polish citizens in the USSR, the number of which was not large, or of the families of Polish soldiers who have been evacuated to Iran. There are, furthermore, no obstacles with regard to this category of persons at the present time. . .

In its *aide-mémoire* the British Government, in considering the question of steps for the improvement of Soviet-Polish relations and the removal of possible causes of friction in these relations, declares that it has been imposing and will continue to impose upon the foreign newspapers published in the United Kingdom a control which, it hopes, will have the effect of putting an end to discussion in the press of controversial issues affecting inter-Allied relations. The Soviet Government cannot fail to express serious doubt concerning the effectiveness of measures of this kind on the part of the British Government, since the measures taken thus far, judging by the unceasing hostile campaign against the Soviet Union in certain parts of the Polish press, have led to no positive results whatsoever.

The Soviet Government shares the opinion of the Governments of Great Britian and the United States of America concerning the great importance of the resumption of friendly relations between the Soviet Government and the Polish Government. The Soviet Government, however, for the reasons set forth above, cannot agree that the task of reestablishing Soviet-Polish relations can be resolved on the basis of the proposals presented to the Soviet Government by the Governments of the United States of America and Great Britain in their *aide-mémoires* of August 11, 1943.

No. 71

Memorandum by the Secretary of State for Foreign Affairs: The Western
Frontiers of the U.S.S.R. (Extracts)
LONDON, 5 October 1943
W.P. (43) 438

IN December 1941, Stalin informed me that he regarded the question of
the U.S.S.R.'s western frontiers 'as the main question for us in the war'. We
believe that this is still the Soviet view, although the question has not been
raised from the Soviet side in recent months.

2. The Soviet attitude in our forthcoming discussions on the future settlement of Europe will therefore presumably be very much influenced by our
views about their western frontiers.

3. The question has in any case become one of imminent practical importance with the approach of the Soviet armies to the former Polish frontier. The
resulting problems will be very difficult to handle unless we and the other
Governments concerned know where each stands in the matter.

4. Soviet territorial claims can be divided into those affecting (a) Poland
and (b) other countries. viz: (1) the Baltic States, (2) Finland and (3)
Roumania.

(a) *Poland.*

5. On various occasions MM. Stalin, Molotov and Maisky have indicated
that they would regard the Curzon Line with minor modifications as a
satisfactory basis for a frontier settlement with Poland. We have hitherto
maintained that we recognise no territorial changes which have been effected
in Poland since August 1939, but have given the Russians no more precise
indication of our views.

6. The Soviet-Polish frontier is the core of the problem. The Polish
Government's attitude is that they cannot accept during the course of the
war any surrender of former Polish territory, without forfeiting the confidence
of the Polish people at home or the loyalty of the Polish armed forces abroad
(a matter of direct interest to us). We ourselves cannot enter into any agreement, written or unwritten, with the Soviet Government involving the
surrender of Polish territory, since we are bound by the assurances which we
gave to Poland in July 1941, when the Soviet Polish Treaty was signed, and
again in 1942, at the time of the negotiations for an Anglo-Soviet Treaty.[1]

7. There are, however, signs that even the Polish Government do not wish
to postpone consideration of this problem until the Soviet armies cross the
August 1939 Polish frontier. Decisions must be taken soon regarding the
attitude of the well-organized Polish underground forces to the Russians
and *vice-versa*. I am circulating a separate paper to my colleagues on this

1, See above Nos. 18, 36.

question.[2] The problem of resuming Polish-Soviet diplomatic relations will then become acute. We shall be faced with a deadlock on all such issues unless, without abandoning our principle of not recognising during the war any territorial changes, we can show the Soviet Government that we do not intend to oppose their essential territorial aims in the west.

8. I suggest that our policy should be not to oppose the Soviet claim that the Curzon Line should form the basis of the new Soviet-Polish frontier, but to make every effort to secure a modification whereby the City of Lwów would be included in Poland. The further Polish claim to Vilna, to which they also attach the greatest importance, would be unrealisable, if only for geographical reasons. We might, however, emphasise to the Soviet Government the importance attached to Vilna by the Poles and use it as a bargaining counter to secure at least Lwów for them. Poland should receive as compensation in the west, Danzig, East Prussia and Upper Silesia. The Soviet Government have consistently favoured these arrangements at the expense of Germany. These territorial changes might involve substantial transfers of population.

9. At Quebec I discussed the above proposal with Mr. Hull.[3] He said that it raised difficult issues but that the matter would have to be considered as the Soviet Government would be sure to raise it at any discussion of post-war matters. Mr. Hopkins told me that he knew President Roosevelt's mind about Russia's frontiers was almost exactly the same as mine and that the President had already said as much to M. Molotov and M. Litvinov.[4]

10. I am, however, by no means confident that the United States Government would formally endorse the views which the President has apparently expressed . Mr. Cordell Hull, who will be my opposite number at the Moscow talks, is particularly likely to hold back on this issue. The United States Government have always taken a very firm line against the recognition of any

2. W.P.(43)439. This argued that given Soviet hostility to the London-controlled underground, the question of arming this underground should be discussed at the coming Foreign Ministers' conference in Moscow. See below No. 74. The Poles saw their powerful underground as a valuable weapon in inducing the Soviets to cooperate with them. On 27 October 1943 a new Instruction had been sent to the underground by the Polish cabinet and commander-in-chief. This laid down that the government might in the future order the underground to 'intensify the armed operations against the Germans, either in the form of a general uprising or of intensified sabotage. If possible this action would be coordinated with the western allies and would aim at liberating as much of Polish territory as possible from the Germans.' It also laid down that if Soviet-Polish relations had not been re-established when Soviet troops entered Poland, this entry should be preceded by 'armed action against the Germans . . . The Polish Government makes a formal protest to the United Nations, informing them at the same time that Poland will not collaborate with the U.S.S.R. The Polish Government also issues a warning that in the case of imprisonment of the representatives of the Polish underground organization and of any reprisals directed against Polish citizens, the Polish underground organization will act in self-defence. The authorities and the Secret Army in Poland remain clandestine awaiting further instructions from the Polish Government.' (D.O.P.S.R. II, No. 44).
3. See above, No. 66.
4. See above, No. 64.

territorial changes effected by force and in an election year they will pay great attention to the well-organised Polish vote of approximately three millions. On an issue of this kind I consider it important that we should only act together with the United States Government, more particularly as we, unlike the United States Government, have treaty and other commitments to Poland. Otherwise the Poles will be unable to resist the temptation to stir up opposition in the United States.

11. The forthcoming 'Foreign Secretaries' meeting' is, however a preliminary meeting to explore the ground and prepare the way for the forthcoming meeting between the Prime Minister, Premier Stalin and President Roosevelt. I suggest, therefore, for the approval of my colleagues, that without committing His Majesty's Government, I should use the opportunity afforded by the Moscow talks to explore the position with a view to subsequent discussion at the meeting between the President and the two Prime Ministers. This course will have the advantages (1) that the President is likely to be more forthcoming than Mr. Hull; and (2) it will give us time to see whether the Soviet advance is likely to take them as far as Poland this year.

12. In exploring this question, which is in any case bound to come up at the meeting, I should take the line with the Soviet Government that I should like to know what they would do on their side if the Polish Government were prepared to accept a frontier settlement on the lines of paragraph 8 above. I should indicate that if we decided not to oppose at the final settlement an arrangement as regards Poland on the lines set out in paragraph 8 above and if the Poles were prepared to accept this, we should expect the Soviet Government to show a real willingness to co-operate in post-war matters in Europe and to demonstrate their good will by (1) resuming relations with the Polish Government; (2) co-operating with us and the Polish Government in finding a satisfactory solution to problems concerning (a) Polish underground resistance (see paragraph 7 above); (b) the position of Poles in the U.S.S.R.; (c) their support of the Union of Polish Patriots and of the rival Polish army in the U.S.S.R. Soviet action on the above lines would go far to remove the anxieties now being felt in Polish circles that the U.S.S.R. is not so much interested in frontier questions as in turning Poland into a puppet-State.

13. I should feel bound, in view of our treaty and other commitments, to inform the Polish Government, before the Conference opens, that we intend to explore with the Soviet Government the question of Polish-Soviet relations, not excluding the frontiers.

(b) *Other frontiers.*

(1) *Baltic States.*

14. The Russians contend that the Baltic States voted themselves into the Soviet Union in the summer of 1940, and thus formed an integral part of the U.S.S.R. at the date of the German attack. There is not the smallest chance of

the Russians abandoning any part of this claim...

(2) *Finland.*

In December 1941, Stalin told me that he would like to see the frontier in Finland restored to its position in 1941 immediately before the outbreak of war...

(3) *Roumania.*

In December 1941, Stalin said that the Roumanian frontier should be so formed as to include Bessarabia and North Bukovina in the Soviet Union...

15. There can be no question of entering into any written agreement with the Russians as regards any of these frontier claims. But I would ask my colleagues to authorise me to conduct explanatory conversations with the Soviet and United States representatives in the same spirit as I have already proposed in paragraphs 11 and 12 in connexion with the Polish-Soviet frontier on the assumption that, while we do not propose to reverse our decision not to recognise any territorial changes made during the war. His Majesty's Government would, when the appropriate moment came, raise no objection to the Soviet claim to have the 1941 position restored as regards their territorial claims in respect of Finland, the Baltic States and Roumania.

(c) *Other Points.*

16. I further ask my colleagues to agree that I should take the following line with regard to other points that may arise:—
(a) Provision should be made at the final settlement for inhabitants of any territories transferred thereunder to depart elsewhere with their movable property. This would help the Baltic settlement and also that of the Polish eastern frontiers, but would be of general application and thus perhaps easier for the Russians to accept.
(b) As regards probable Soviet proposals for alliances or mutual assistance pacts with Finland and Roumania, His Majesty's Government would be prepared to consider these at the peace settlement.
(c) The claim to Petsamo falls into a different category from other Soviet frontier demands inasmuch as it was not included in the frontiers of the Union of Soviet Socialist Republics on the 22nd June, 1941, but His Majesty's Government would be prepared to consider this claim too if it is put forward at the peace settlement.[5]

5. During the debate in the War Cabinet on 8 October, the Prime Minister stated that while 'the cardinal point in this matter must be that we should welcome an agreement between the Russians and the Poles; and that while we could not force the Poles to come to an agreement which would mean ceding to Russia territory in the Eastern part of their country we would urge them to come to a settlement on the grounds that this was in their own best interests.' Eden stated that the Poles had definitely asked him not to rasie frontier questions at the Moscow conference (W.M.(43)137).

No. 72

Conversation between President Roosevelt, Cordell Hull and Sumner Welles (Extract)[1]
WASHINGTON, 5 October 1943
F.R.U.S. 1943, I, p. 542.

. . . IV. *Baltic States and Poland.*

When he meets with Stalin, the President intends to appeal to him on grounds of high morality. He would say to him that neither Britain nor we would fight Russia over the Baltic States, but that in Russia's own interest, from the viewpoint of her position in the world, it would be a good thing to say that she would be willing, in two years or so after the war, to have a second plebiscite, since, while she is satisfied that the earlier plebiscite was conclusive, the rest of the world does not seem to think so. The same idea might be applied to Eastern Poland. The President thinks that the new boundary should, in any event, be somewhat east of the Curzon Line, with Lemberg going to Poland, and that a plebiscite should take place after the shell-shock of war had subsided.

1. Also present were Admiral Leahy, Chief of Staff to the Commander-in-Chief of the Army and Navy and H. Freeman Matthews, Chief, Division of European Affairs, State Department.

No. 73

Anthony Eden to Sir Owen O'Malley: Dispatch (Extracts)
LONDON, 6 October 1943
F.O. 371. C11782/258/55

I LUNCHED with the Polish Prime Minister on the 6th October. The Polish Minister for Foreign Affairs, the Polish Ambassador, Sir. A. Cadogan and your Excellency were also present. . .

3. I said that I entirely agreed with the desirability of a resumption of friendly relations between Poland and Russia before the Russian armies reached the Riga frontier, but asked whether I had rightly understood M. Mikołajczyk to have said earlier in the conversation that no discussion of the Polish-Russian frontier would be permissible at the present date. If this were indeed the Polish Government's view it seemed most unlikely that any agreement between Poland and Russia would be reached. The probability was that the Russian armies would reach the Riga frontier in the spring. When they did so, and if no previous agreement had been reached, Poland would be in a very dangerous situation. Stalin was, in my belief, ready to discuss the Russo-Polish frontier and firmly determined not to make friends with Poland till the future frontier had been settled. It seemed to me hopeless to expect any *détente* if the Polish attitude was completely negative.

4. M. Mikołajczyk said that the Russo-Polish question was not really a

question of frontiers at all. Stalin's ambitions were world-wide. They certainly did not stop at the Curzon Line.

5. I said that the last time I had discussed the matter with Stalin, the latter had indicated pretty clearly that this line would satisfy him and that this line he was determined to have. In my personal view, a Poland plus East Prussia, Silesia and Lwów, but minus certain eastern provinces, would be stronger than the Poland of 1939. If the Polish Government would be ready to agree that Poland should be reconstituted on these lines after the war, it might be possible to get Russia to accept such a settlement as final and satisfactory. If the Polish Government maintained their negative attitude I would not see how any progress towards a better relationship between Poland and Russia could be hoped for.

6. Count Raczyński said that a resumption of diplomatic relations between Poland and Russia should anyhow precede a general settlement between the two countries. Russian readiness or unreadiness to resume relations would be a test of the genuineness or otherwise of Russian intentions.

7. Sir A. Cadogan said that the advance of the Russian armies would confront Poland with a problem of the greatest gravity; and, that in his view, no solution could be found without a discussion of frontiers.

8. M. Mikołajczyk said that it was out of the question for an emigrant Government to surrender national territory to a foreign Power.

9. I said that the question of frontiers would certainly be raised at the forthcoming meeting between myself and Mr. Hull and M. Molotov. I must put on the Polish Government the responsibility for deciding what answer I should give if the Russians made frontier concessions a condition for friendly relations with the Poles. I had no right to dictate this answer to the Polish Government, but I had small hopes of a happy issue unless the Poles gave me something to bargain with.

10. M. Mikołajczyk said that even if he and his Government were actually in Poland now he would not discuss the frontier question simply because he did not believe it was fundamental. The general attitude of Stalin towards Poland, towards Germany and the Free German movement and towards questions touching other occupied countries, as well as his record and his whole mentality implied more extensive ambitions than ambitions only in the eastern provinces of Poland which were strategically important to Poland but in no sense vital to Russia. Stalin would not have behaved as he had if the frontier was a crucial problem. If it was not the crucial problem, frontier concessions would leave Poland the poorer with no final solution in sight, and would have whetted Stalin's appetite for the fruits of intimidation.

11. I said that British experience suggested that Stalin was much less intransigent than M. Mikołajczyk thought. . .

16. Count Raczyński said that if Great Britain and the United States put their full weight behind a recommendation for a resumption of relations Russia would agree to this. Failing such agreement so arrived at there would

certainly be no agreement on other questions.

17. I summed up by saying that I had at any rate got a clear answer to my question. The Poles were not ready to discuss the frontier line and I would accordingly have to go as a mediator with a very weak hand to the three-Power meeting. I was not unmindful of British obligations to Poland and would do my best; but while not contesting the right of Poland to give this answer I thought it unwise in Poland's own interest.[1]

1. On 7 October, when communicating a memorandum to the Foreign Office, Raczyński was rather less intransigent. On this occasion, he told Eden that 'speaking entirely personally he thought that an element of what he might call violence might be necessary in reaching a territorial settlement between Poland and Russia by the action of the Great Powers. But such violence ought to be open and above board and accompanied by firm international guarantees for the protection of Poland against a repetition of the post-Munich procedure. He emphasized that the territories in the east of Poland were of great economic importance and unless the concessions required of Poland were of a moderate character the Great Powers would be imposing too heavy a sacrifice on Poland' (F.O. 371. C11657/258/55).

Of the memorandum itself (D.O.P.S.R.II, No. 42), Eden minuted 'This paper seems to me to have been written in a Polish cloud cuckoo land. If Poles persist in this utter lack of realism, there will be no Poland after the war and we will be powerless to prevent this misfortune' (F.O. 371. C11657/258/55).

No. 74

Anthony Eden to Foreign Office: Telegram (Extract)
6 November 1943
F.O. 371. C13111/258/55

Polish Affairs were discussed at restricted meeting of Conference on October 29.[1] Both Mr. Hull and I showed our anxiety to see normal relations between Soviet Russia and Poland restored at the earliest moment possible. Mr. Molotov was non-commital. He would only say that the Soviet Government stood for an independent Poland and was ready to help her; but that Poland must have a Government with friendly relations towards Soviet Russia and this was lacking. Mr. Molotov showed marked suspicion of General Sosnkowski. He praised the Polish division fighting on the Eastern front and was considerably interested when I said I hoped Polish troops would shortly be fighting in Italy. I have no doubt that if in fact these Polish troops fight the Germans anywhere, this would be the best contribution now in the power of the Polish Government.

2. When I asked what the Russian view would be of our arming the Polish Secret Army, he said that the arms should only be given into safe hands. 'Were there any safe hands in Poland?' The question of arms depended on the

1. For more detailed accounts of the discussions at Moscow, see F.R.U.S. 1943, I, pp. 667–8 and F.O. 371. C13335/258/55. It should also be noted that during the conference, Molotov, who read a prepared statement on the subject, again made clear that the Soviet government considered 'the active consideration or encouragement' of schemes for federation as 'premature and even harmful' (For the Soviet statement, F.R.U.S. I, p. 762–3, for the discussion, ibid., p. 639).

reliability of the people to whom you gave them.

3. I shall no doubt have to see the Poles when I get back to London. Meanwhile I think it would be best if you simply informed them that both Mr. Hull and I impressed on Molotov our anxiety to see Soviet-Polish relations restored, that Molotov said that this was his wish also, but remained non-committal as to when and how. Frontier questions were not discussed. This was, of course, in accordance with the declared view of the United States Government and with the request of the Polish Government. . .

No. 75

War Cabinet Conclusions (Extract)
LONDON, 17 November 1943
W.M.(43)156

2. THE SECRETARY OF STATE FOR FOREIGN AFFAIRS said that from an interview which he had had with the Polish Ambassador that morning, it seemed that the Polish Government at last recognised that it was in their interests that a settlement should be reached on the questions in dispute between Russia and Poland; but that the Polish Government might, in all the circumstances welcome the imposition of a settlement by the British and United States Governments.[1]

The War Cabinet took note of this statement.

1. When presenting a Polish memorandum (D.O.P.S.R.II, No. 15) to the Foreign Office, Raczyński had told Eden that 'it was impossible for the Polish Government to propose concessions which would affect the future of the Polish state at a time when the Government were in exile and without the support of the Polish Parliament. If, however, Poland's friends were to tell the Government that they must accept such and such a settlement in order to safeguard the future of Poland, this would create a new situation. But even so, Count Raczyński added that he hoped that M. Mikołajczyk would be given an opportunity of expressing his views and discussing any schemes which might be worked out. Above all, it would be essential in Count Raczyński's view that any settlement should include provisions for the future security of Poland. In this connexion he called attention to point (3) on page 2 of M. Mikołajczyk's memorandum. Evidently by this he meant that any settlement between Poland and the Soviet Union should be underwritten by Great Britain and the United States' (F.O. 371. C13615/231/55). This was not the only statement of this type made at this time. On 12 November Raczyński in reply to Sir Orme Sargent's reproaches that the Poles had prevented the Moscow conference from dealing with the Polish question had stated that 'we could not expect an exiled Government like the Polish to take the initiative of proposing a surgical operation on the body of their country. This was his own expression. But he went on to imply, if I understood him aright, that if H.M. Government considered that such an operation was unnecessary the Polish Government would bow to the inevitable' (F.O. 371. C13642/258/55). Eden minuted, 'I have long been considering whether the Poles are awaiting for this.' On 17 November, Romer told Richard Law, The Minister of State at the Foreign Office, that 'it was impossible for the Poles to meet the Russian point of view on further questions until they knew how they stood with regard to East Prussia, Silesia, etc. I asked M. Romer whether that meant they would, at an appropriate moment, consider some arrangement with the Russians on their eastern frontier. He replied yes, when they knew more about how they stood within the general picture' (F.O. 371. C13861/258/55).

No. 76

Anthony Eden to Sir Owen O'Malley: Dispatch (Extracts)
LONDON, 22 November 1943
F.O. 371. C13865/258/55

I RECEIVED on the 22nd November, at his request, the Polish Prime Minister, who was accompanied by the Polish Ambassador and the Minister for Foreign Affairs.

3. ... In reply to a question from M. Mikołajczyk I told him that the European Advisory Commission was not intended to deal with the Polish frontier question, which would have to be dealt with on a higher level. I went on to say that I had hitherto been unable to raise the Polish frontier question at all because the Polish Government did not wish this. I might have done so during the Mosocw talks and I wished to be able to raise the matter on my onw and not on the Polish responsibility if the atmosphere were propitious.

4. M. Mikołajczyk said he understood the position and the Polish Government certainly did not wish to dissuade me from such discussions which would, they understood, cover the whole range of Polish-Soviet problems, and would be especially designed to lead ultimately to a renewal of relations and a settlement of the frontier question. He wished, however, to be assured that any discussions about frontiers would also cover Polish claims in the west and that no definite and binding decisions would be reached by His Majesty's Government without the Polish Government being given an opportunity of expressing their views on the results of my exploratory talks. M. Mikołajczyk then explained that his idea would be to give me the Polish Government's views after consulting the underground movement at home, which could be done at short notice.[1]

5. I reminded M. Mikołajczyk that we were still far from that stage. The furthest we could hope to go in the near future was, for example, for the Soviet Government to inform us that they favoured a frontier on the basis of the Curzon Line with compensation for Poland in the west. All I could then do would be to take note of this and consult the Polish Government. I should not, however, commit either His Majesty's Government or the Polish Government. M. Mikołajczyk commented that even the Curzon Line was very different from the Ribbentrop-Molotov Line of 1939...

14. In conclusion, I told M. Mikołajczyk that I would discuss the whole matter with the Prime Minister. I assured him that I had no intention of disinteresting myself in the Polish case or of forgetting her role. No one would have welcomed it more than I if the Poles and the Russians had been able to settle their difficulties together, and I had therefore done my best to promote

---

1. According to Beneš, Mikołajczyk went even further in conversation with him on 23 November. On this occasion the Polish Premier stated that he realized that his government would have to make great concessions to the Soviet Union 'in the matter of frontiers. His concern was thus to keep Lwow and a part of East Galicia and to prevent Soviet intervention in Polish internal affairs' (Beneš, *Memoirs,* p. 264).

a rapprochement in 1941. I would continue to do my best, although the Polish Government should not expect too much from the forthcoming meeting. I might have some difficulty over the American attitude, which seemed disposed to leave this and other similar territorial questions until the end of the war. I myself thought this unwise. I must, therefore, have some latitude in which to take the matter up, if I could, but I would not commit the Polish Government to any particular solution. . .[2]

2. Eden has spoken in a similar vein to Raczyński on 19 November (F.O. 371. C13768/258/55).

No. 77

Memorandum submitted to the War Cabinet by the Secretary of State:
Possible Lines of a Polish-Soviet Settlement (Extracts)
LONDON, 22 November 1943
W.P.(43)528

MY colleagues may be interested to see the annexed memorandum on the possible lines of a Polish-Soviet settlement, by which I would propose to be guided should it prove practicable to take this question up in the near future.[1]

A.E.

ANNEX.

OUR view has been that the main difficulty is the question of frontiers. We consider that the only possible solution, which would in fact be in Poland's own interest, is for the future frontier to be based on the Curzon Line. This is more favourable to the Poles than the Ribbentrop-Molotov Line, for which the Soviet Government will no doubt press, in that it includes in Poland the Bialystok area in the north, whose inhabitants are mainly racial Poles. We should try as part of a comprehensive settlement to persuade the Russian to be generous and allow the Poles to keep Lwów. It would, I think, be out of the question to press for Vilna for the Poles, except possibly as an opening bargaining gambit. We should, I think, suggest that such a settlement should be accompanied by transfers of populations, more particularly in Eastern Galicia, to remove, so far as possible, racial minorities from each side of the frontier.

In return, the Poles should receive a definite assurance from the Soviet Government and His Majesty's Government, and, if possible, the United States Government, that they will receive in compensation East Prussia, Danzig, and the Oppeln district of Upper Silesia. This arrangement would also be accom-

1. This paper had been written by Sir Orme Sargent and submitted to Eden on 19 November. Eden accepted the paper except for a section advocating British participation in the Soviet-Czech-Polish treaty. (See the memorandum, p. 162). He commented, 'I am reluctant to do this. It is an engagement in an area where our influence cannot be great and where militarily we should be ineffective' (F.O. 371. C14592/258/55).

panied by transfers of population if this were considered desirable.

The Poles, however, fear that what is at stake is not so much the frontiers as the future existence of Poland. Their anxieties are (1) that Russia's long-term aim is to set up a puppet Government in Warsaw and turn Poland into a Soviet republic, (2) that disorders would be provoked on the entry of Soviet forces, (3) that it will then be impossible to maintain the present instructions of the Polish Government restraining the Polish population from taking action against the Russians, and (4) that all the leading resistance elements in Poland will be disposed of by the Soviet forces of occupation.

It is therefore necessary to secure from the Russians, in return for our undertaking to impose on the Poles a frontier settlement on the above lines, assurances to the following effect:—

(1) Diplomatic relations should be restored at once between the Soviet and Polish Governments;

(2) Arrangements should be made on similar lines to those contemplated for our other European Allies for the Polish Government to return to Poland and be associated with the Administration of the country as soon as military necessities permit;

(3) The Polish Government should submit themselves to the approval of the Polish people as soon as possible and the latter should be free to choose their own Government without any outside pressure;

(4) The Polish Government should at once be encouraged to accede to the Soviet-Czechoslovak Treaty, as provided for under the Protocol attached to the treaty, thus instituting a tripartite system of security in Eastern Europe, for which Poland will be one of the main beneficiaries;

(5) These arrangements should be formally approved by His Majesty's Government and if possible the United States Government. They might be associated with them in whatever way is considered most appropriate, *e.g.*, either through some public declaration, participation in the Tripartite Treaty (see under (C) below), or through arrangements to be worked out in the London Commission.

The following are among the major difficulties which may arise in the above programme:—

(A) The Soviet Government may insist upon some changes in the Polish governmental machine. So far as the Government itself is concerned, there is no adequate reason for any such changes. The Polish Government is composed of all parties from the Centre to the Left and contains no members to whom the Soviet Government could legitimately object. There is certainly no way in which it could be reconstituted to make it more acceptable to the Russians, since the only important people outside the Government are Soviet "bogies", such as Messrs. Bielecki[2] and Zaleski.[3] The Soviet Government really object

. Leader of the right-wing National Democrats.
. Former Foreign Minister, now in the President's Chancellery.

to the President and to General Sosnkowski as Commander-in-Chief of the Polish forces. Clearly the President cannot be removed at the behest of a foreign Government. Moreover, both he and General Sosnkowski have been much more "reasonable" in recent months, and all our evidence suggests that the divergences which once existed between them and M. Mikołajczyk have been removed, and that General Sosnkowski has refrained from intervening in political matters. . .

(B) The Soviet Government may press for the association of the Union of Polish Patriots in some way with the Polish Government. I do not think we could or should persuade the Poles to accept, say, Wanda Wasilewska or General Berling in their Government. There may possibly be other Poles in Russia who could be brought in in some way, but I doubt whether this is a really important point on which the Soviet Government would insist. . .

(C) The Polish Government on their side wish to be assured that we shall not simply throw them into the arms of the Russians and then abandon them.

They have the Munich precedent very much in mind. It is, I submit, essential for our own good name, as well as to satisfy the Poles that we should make it crystal clear that this settlement differs from Munich in that (I) the Poles receive adequate compensation in the West for their losses in the East; and (II) that they receive an effective instead of an ineffective guarantee of their future security from the Western Powers as well as from Russia. General declarations of approval will not, I submit, suffice. It will, I think, be necessary to contemplate the arrangement already suggested in the War Cabinet Paper W.P.(43)423 of the 28th September, paragraph 8 of which reads as follows:—

There remains the question of our own participation [i.e. in the proposed Soviet-Czech-Polish treaty]. Unless we participate in some way, there is little change of reaching a stable and satisfactory solution of this European question. We are still bound by our alliance with Poland, and although we refused a request from the Polish Government in 1942 to negotiate a new Anglo-Polish treaty to replace that of August 1939, we then informed the Polish Government that 'we should of course enter into consultation with them in good time before August 1944' (when the 1939 treaty can be terminated by either party) 'so that the two Governments might consider how best to maintain and prolong its effects. . .'

I submit that our approach to the Russians should be based upon the consideration that Anglo-Soviet relations having now been placed upon a footing of mutual confidence by the Anglo-Soviet Treaty and the Moscow Conference, we are most anxious to remove any possible sources of friction. Having regard to our treaty and other obligations to Poland and to the outstanding part played by Poles at home and abroad in resistance to Germany since 1939, His Majesty's Government and British public opinion are bound to do all in their power to ensure that a strong and independent Poland emerges from the war. This they also feel to be in the general European interests, as well as in the interest of good Anglo-Polish and Anglo-Soviet relations. Any failure to achieve a reasonable settlement would inevitably become a running sore in Anglo-Soviet relations and this His Majesty's Government are determined to make every effort to avoid.

No. 78

The Polish Question at the Teheran Conference

1. Conversation between Churchill and Stalin (Extracts)[1]
TEHERAN, 28 November 1943
W.P.(44)8

. . THE PRIME MINISTER suggested that they should discuss the Polish question.

MARSHAL STALIN agreed and invited the Prime Minister to begin.

THE PRIME MINISTER said we had declared war on account of Poland. Poland was therefore important to us. Nothing was more important than the security of the Russian western frontier. But he had given no pledges about frontiers. He wanted heart-to-heart talks with the Russians about this. When the Marshal felt like telling us what he thought about it, the matter could be discussed and they could reach some agreement, and the Marshal should tell him what was necessary for the defence of the western frontiers of Russia.

MARSHAL STALIN said he did not feel the need to ask himself how to act. So far his heart did not feel stimulated.

[He meant that the Prime Minister should become more precise.]

THE PRIME MINISTER said that after this war in Europe, which might end in 1944, the Soviet Union would be overwhelmingly strong and Russia would have a great responsibility for hundreds of years in any decision she took with regard to Poland. Personally, he thought Poland might move westwards like soldiers taking two steps left close. If Poland trod on some German toes, that could not be helped, but there must be a strong Poland. This instrument was needed in the orchestra of Europe.

MARSHAL STALIN said the Polish people had their culture and their language, which must exist. They could not be extirpated.

THE PRIME MINISTER agreed and asked if we were to draw frontier lines.

MARSHAL STALIN said Yes.

THE PRIME MINISTER said he had no power from Parliament, nor he believed had the President, to define any frontier lines. He suggested that they might now, in Tehran, see if the three Heads of Government, working in agreement, could form some sort of policy which might be pressed upon the Poles and which we could recommend to the Poles, and advise them to accept.

MARSHAL STALIN said we could have a look.

THE PRIME MINISTER said we should be lucky if we could.

. The conversation took place at a dinner after Roosevelt had gone to bed. For the American minutes, see F.R.U.S. Teheran, p. 512. There are no published Soviet minutes.

MARSHAL STALIN asked whether it would be without Polish participation

THE PRIME MINISTER replied in the affirmative and said that this was all informally between themselves, and they could go to the Poles later.

MARSHAL STALIN agreed.

MR. EDEN said he had been much struck by what the Marshal had said that afternoon to the effect that the Poles could go as far west as the Oder. He saw hope in that and was much encouraged.

MARSHAL STALIN asked whether we thought he was going to swallow Poland up.

MR. EDEN said he did not know how much the Russians were going to eat. How much would they leave undigested?

MARSHAL STALIN said the Russians did not want anything belonging to other people, although they might have a bite at Germany.

MR. EDEN said what Poland lost in the east she might gain in the west.

MARSHAL STALIN said possibly they might, but he did not know.

THE PRIME MINISTER demonstrated with the help of three matches his idea of Poland moving westwards, which pleased Marshal Stalin.

2. Conversation between Roosevelt and Stalin (Extracts)
TEHERAN, 1 December 1943, 3.20 p.m.
F.R.U.S. Teheran, p. 594

THE PRESIDENT said he had asked Marshal Stalin to come to see him as he wished to discuss a matter briefly and frankly. He said it referred to internal American politics.

He said that we had an election in 1944 and that while personally he did not wish to run again, if the war was still in progress, he might have to.

He added that there were in the United States from six to seven million Americans of Polish extraction, and as a practical man, he did not wish to lose their vote. He said personally he agreed with the views of Marshal Stalin as to the necessity of the restoration of a Polish state but would like to see the Eastern border moved further to the west and the Western border moved even to the River Oder.[1] He hoped, however, that the Marshal would understand that for political reasons outlined above, he could not participate in any

1. The exact meaning of this statement was to occasion much later difficulty, particular at the talks between Stalin, Churchill and Mikolajczyk in October 1944. On 18 October 1944, Churchill telegraphed to Roosevelt,
   'I shall mention though no doubt Averell [Harriman] will have reported (see F.R.U.S Yalta, pp. 202–5) that Molotov stated at our opening meeting with the London Poles tha you had expressed agreement with the Curzon Line at Teheran. I informed Stalin afterwa that neither Eden nor I could confirm this statement. Stalin thereupon stated that he had had a private conversation with you, not at the table, when you had concurred in the policy of the Curzon Line, though you had expressed a hope about Lwow being retained by the Poles. I could not, of course, deal with this assertion' (F.R.U.S. Teheran, p. 885). Eden commented later, Roosevelt's remarks were 'hardly calculated to restrain the Russians. . .' (Eden, *The Reckoning*, p. 428).

decision here in Tehran or even next winter on this subject and that he could not publicly take part in any such arrangement at the present time.

MARSHAL STALIN replied that now the President explained, he had understood. . .[2]

2. Roosevelt also told Stalin that he was prepared to see the Baltic States incorporated into the Soviet Union, but he would like to see this done with some measure of approval by the inhabitants of these areas.

3. Conversation at the Soviet Embassy[1] (Extracts)
TEHERAN, 1 December 1943, 6 p.m.
W.P.44(8)

Present: Prime Minister Churchill
              President Roosevelt
              Marshal Stalin
              Anthony Eden
              Vyacheslav Molotov
              Harry Hopkins
              Sir Archibald Clark-Kerr
              Averell Harriman

. . . PRESIDENT ROOSEVELT began by saying that it was his hope that there could be a resumption of relations between the Polish and Soviet Governments, so that any decision taken could be accepted by the Polish Government. Thus it would be much easier. But he had to recognise that there were difficulties.

MARSHAL STALIN asked with what Government he would have to negotiate. The Polish Government and their friends in Poland were in contact with the Germans. They killed the partisans. Neither the President nor the Prime Minister could have any idea of what was now going on in Poland.

PRESIDENT ROOSEVELT remarked that he had recognised that there were difficulties.

THE PRIME MINISTER said that the Polish matter was an important one for us in the United Kingdom, because we had declared war on Germany on account of her invasion of Poland. . .

THE PRIME MINISTER went on to say that he had in mind the picture of the three matches — Germany, Poland and the Soviet Union. One of the main objects of the Allies was to achieve the security of the Soviet western frontier and so to prevent an attack by Germany in the future. Here he reminded Marshal Stalin that mention had been made by the Marshal of the line of the Oder in the west.

MARSHAL STALIN (interrupting) said that the day before yesterday there had been no mention of re-establishing relations with the Polish Government.

. . For the American minutes of this conversation, see F.R.U.S. Teheran, pp. 596–604, or the Soviet minutes, Soviet Protocols, pp. 38–44.

It had been a question of prescribing something to the Poles. To-day the matter had been put quite differently. Russia, even more than other States, was interested in good relations with Poland because for her it was a question the security of her frontiers. Russia was in favour of the reconstruction, development and expansion of Poland mainly at the expense of Germany. But he separated Poland from the Polish Government in exile. He had broken off relations with the Polish Government in exile not on account of caprice, but because the Polish Government in exile had joined with Hitler in slanderous propaganda against Russia. It had all been in the press. What was there to guarantee that it would not happen again? He would like to have a guarantee that the Polish Government in exile would not kill partisans, but on the contrary would urge the Poles to fight the Germans and not concern themselves with any machinations. He would welcome any government which would take active measures and he would be glad to renew relations with them. But he was by no means sure that the Polish Government in exile was ever likely to become the kind of government it ought to be. If the Polish Government were to go hand in hand with the partisans and have no relations with the Germans in Poland, he would be glad enough to see the question settled. Here he reverted to the matter of the three matches.

THE PRIME MINISTER said that it would be a great help if round that very table we could learn what were the Russian ideas about the frontiers. He would then be glad to put the matter before the Poles and to say frankly if he thought the conditions fair. His Majesty's Government (he was only speaking for His Majesty's Government) would like to be able to tell the Poles that the plan was a good one and the best that they were likely to get, and that His Majesty's Government would not argue against the Soviet Government at the peace table. Then we could get on with the President's idea of resuming relation What we wanted was a strong and independent Poland, friendly to Russia.

MARSHAL STALIN said that that was true, but that the Poles could not be allowed to seize the Ukraine and White Russian territory. That was not fair According to the 1939 frontier the soil of the Ukraine and White Russia was returned to the Ukraine and to White Russia. Soviet Russia adhered to the frontiers of 1939, for they appeared to be ethnologically the right ones.

MR. EDEN asked if this meant the Ribbentrop Molotov line.

MARSHAL STALIN said: 'Call it whatever you like.'

M. MOLOTOV remarked that it was generally called the Curzon Line.

MR. EDEN said no, there were differences which were important.

M. MOLOTOV said there were no essential differences.

THE PRIME MINISTER then produced a map and showed the Curzon Line and the 1939 line and indicated also the line of the Oder.

MR. EDEN suggested that the south end of the Curzon Line had never been defined in terms.

At this point the meeting broke up into groups. There was a general gathering round the Prime Minister's map and round a map which was produce by the Americans, and it was difficult to take notes of the conversation.

MR. EDEN suggested that the Curzon Line was intended to pass to the east of Lvov.

MARSHAL STALIN replied that the line on the Prime Minister's map had not been drawn right. Lvov should be left on the Russian side and the line should go westwards towards Przemysl, adding that M. Molotov would get a map of the Curzon Line and a description of it.

THE PRIME MINISTER said he would be grateful.

MARSHAL STALIN here remarked that he did not want any Polish population, and that if he found any district inhabited by Poles he would gladly give it up.

PRESIDENT ROOSEVELT asked if he might put a question. Did the frontier of East Prussia and the territory east of the Oder approximate to the size of the eastern provinces of Poland itself.

MARSHAL STALIN said that he did not know and that it had not been measured.

THE PRIME MINISTER suggested that the value of this land was much greater than the Pripet Marshes. It was industrial and it would make a much better Poland. We should like to be able to say to the Poles that the Russians were right, and to tell the Poles that they must agree that they had had a fair deal. If the Poles did not accept, we could not help it. And here he made it clear that he was speaking for the British alone, adding that the President had many Poles in the United States who were his fellow-citizens.

MARSHAL STALIN said again that if it were proved to him that any district were Polish, he would not claim it, and here he made some shadowing on the map west[2] of the Curzon Line and south of Vilna, which he admitted to be mainly Polish.

At this point the meeting again broke up, and there was a prolonged study of the Oder Line on a map. When this came to an end—

THE PRIME MINISTER said that he liked the picture, and that he would say to the Poles that if they did not accept it they would be fools, and he would remind them that but for the Red Army they would have been utterly destroyed. He would point out to them that they had been given a fine place to live in, more than 300 miles each way.

MARSHAL STALIN said that it would indeed be a large, industrial State.

THE PRIME MINISTER said that it would be a State friendly to Russia.

MARSHAL STALIN replied that Russia wanted a friendly Poland.

THE PRIME MINISTER said to Mr. Eden, with some emphasis, that he was not going to break his heart about this cession of parts of Germany to Poland or about Lvov.

MR. EDEN said that if Marshal Stalin would take the Curzon and Oder Lines as a basis on which to argue that might provide a basis.

At this point M. MOLOTOV produced the Russian version of the Curzon

2. This should read 'east'.

Line, and a text of a wireless telegram from Lord Curzon giving all the place names.

THE PRIME MINISTER asked whether M. Molotov would object to the Poles getting the Oppeln district.

M. MOLOTOV replied that he did not foresee any objection.

THE PRIME MINISTER said that the Poles would be wise to take our advice. They were getting a country 300 miles square, and that he was not prepared to make a great squawk about Lvov, and (turning to Marshal Stalin) he added that he did not think that we were very far off in principle.

PRESIDENT ROOSEVELT asked Marshal Stalin whether he thought a transfer of population on a voluntary basis would be possible.

MARSHAL STALIN said that probably it would be. . .

. . . At this point the PRIME MINISTER brought the discussion back to Poland. He said that he was not asking for any agreement, nor was he convinced on the matter himself, but he would rather like to get down something like what he had just put on paper, and he produced the following formula: 'It was thought in principle that the home of the Polish State and the nation should be between the so-called Curzon Line and the line of the Oder, including for Poland East Prussia (as defined) and Oppeln: but the actual tracing of the frontier line required careful study and possibly disentanglement of population at some points.' . . .

The Poles would make a clatter. Why not a formula on which he could say something like this to them: 'I do not know if the Russians would approve, but I think that I might get it for you. You see you are being well looked after.' He added that we would never get the Poles to say that they were satisfied. Nothing would satisfy the Poles.

MARSHAL STALIN (with a grin) 'The Poles in London seem to be most reasonable people.' The Marshal then said that the Russians would like to have the warm water port of Königsberg and he sketched a possible line on the map. This would put Russia on the neck of Germany. If he got this he would be ready enough to agree to the Prime Minister's formula.

THE PRIME MINISTER asked what about Lvov.

MARSHAL STALIN said he would accept the Curzon Line.

CHAPTER FOUR

FROM THE TEHERAN CONFERENCE TO THE FALL OF MIKOŁAJCZYK
(DECEMBER 1943 – NOVEMBER 1944)

No. 79

Protocol to the Soviet-Czechoslovak Treaty[1]
MOSCOW, 12 December 1943
F.O. 371. C14740/525/12

In concluding the Treaty of Friendship, Mutual Assistance and Post-war
Collaboration between the U.S.S.R. and the Czechoslovak Republic, the
Contracting Parties have agreed that in the event of some third country which
borders on the U.S.S.R. or on the Czechoslovak Republic and which forms the
object of German aggression in the present war, desiring to join in this Treaty,
she will be accorded the opportunity, on the mutual consent of the Government of the U.S.S.R. and of the Czechoslovak Republic, of signing this Treaty
which will thus acquire the character of a Tripartite Treaty.[2]

1. Beneš had just informed Eden of his intention to conclude a treaty with the U.S.S.R.
'analagous to the Anglo-Soviet treaty' on 16 June 1943 (F.O. 371. N3835/3835/38). Eden
objected on the grounds that such a treaty would constitute a breach of the 'self-denying
ordenance' agreed on between him and Molotov in 1942 against concluding agreements
with the smaller allied powers. He was also concerned at the effect the treaty would have
on the Poles. The Soviets subsequently denied the existence of this 'self-denying
ordinance', and on 31 August Maisky told Eden of Soviet intention at British objections
by the proposed treaty (F.O. 371. N4977/66/55).
2. While in Moscow, for the signing of the Treaty, Beneš stated; 'This treaty is of special
importance for the three Slav peoples – Poles, Czechoslovaks and Ukrainians – who have
for centuries been endangered by German imperialism' (*Soviet War News,* 24 December
1943). Ripka, for his part, informed the Czechoslovak State Council on 15 December
that the treaty would enable 'other nations of Central Europe, and in particular the Polish
nation, to achieve the same degree of co-operation with the neighbouring power, as
distinguishes the Soviet-Czechoslovak relationship. . .' (*Czechoslovak News Letter,* 17
December 1943).

No. 80

Winston Churchill to Anthony Eden: Telegram (Extracts)
MARRAKESH, 20 December 1943
F.O. 371. C15015/285/55

2. . . . I think you should now open the Polish frontiers question with the
Poles, stating it is at my personal wish and that I would have done it myself
but for my temporary incapacitation. You should show them the formula
and the rough line on the map on the eastern side, and the line of the Oder

including the Oppeln district on the west.[1] This gives them a magnificent piece of country three or four hundred miles across each way and with over 150 miles of seaboard, even on the basis that they do not begin till west of Konigsberg. The Poles should understand of course that these are only very broad, tentative suggestions, but that they would be most unwise to let them fall to the ground. Even if they do not get Lemberg I should still advise their acceptance and that they put themselves in the hands of their British and American friends to try to turn this plan into reality. You should put it to them that by taking over and holding firmly the present German territories up to the Oder they will be rendering a service to Europe as a whole as well as making for themselves a secure, solid and integral homeland which, on the basis of a friendly policy towards Russia and close association with Czecho-Slovakia, would give a chance for the rebirth of the Polish nation brighter than any yet seen.

3. Once we know that they will accept and endorse these proposals we will address ourselves to the Russians and endeavour to make matters firm and precise. On the other hand if they cast it all aside I do not see how His Majesty's Government can press for anything more for them. The Russian armies may in a few months be crossing the frontiers of pre-war Poland, and it seems of the utmost consequence to have friendly recognition by Russia of the Polish Government and a broad understanding of the post war frontiers settlement agreed before then. I shall be most interested to hear what their reaction is.[2]

1. The Russian claims were outlined to Churchill by Beneš on 4 January (F.O. 371. C253/8/55). On this occasion, Beneš argued that the Russians were willing to cede Łomza and Białystok to the east of the Curzon Line, but would not give way on Lwów. On 20 December, he had expressed similar views to Harriman (F.R.U.S. 1943, III, pp. 731−3).
2. At this time, Churchill was, in general, more sympathetic to the Soviet position and more prepared to put strong pressure on the Poles. On 7 January, for instance, he cabled Eden from Marrakesh stressing the need for the Poles to make concessions and asserting, 'they must be very silly if they imagine war with Russia for the sake of the Polish Eastern frontier' (F.O. 371. C953/8/55). He even sent to the Foreign Office a draft message for Stalin which asserted that he would do his best 'to bring the Poles to reason' (Prem. 111/355). Foreign Office pressure secured the modification of this sentence, but in the event the letter was not sent.

No. 81

Anthony Eden to Winston Churchill: Telegram
LONDON, 24 December 1943
F.O. 371. C15353/258/55

1. I had the Polish Prime Minister, Foreign Secretary and Ambassador to dinner last night and we went over the whole ground of Polish-Soviet relations once again at length. There were no new developments of importance.[1]
2. I pressed the Poles strongly to produce a statement of their plans for anti-

German operations in Poland and an indication on their part of willingness
to co-operate with the Russians inside their territory.

You will remember that Stalin complained of the Polish attitude towards
his partisans and if we can clear away these suspicions, as we should be able to
do, this should help us in bringing about resumption of relations and eventually
an agreement as to the attitude of both countries when Russian troops cross
the Polish border. But we have many difficulties yet to surmount and Poles are
uncertain folk.[2]

3. We also discussed frontier problem. Poles are clearly still very unhappy
about this and it is difficult to make them understand the realities of the
situation. Mikołaczyk explained that all his communications from inside Poland
showed how his people were expecting Poland as a reward for Polish suffering
and fighting to emerge from this war with victors, her eastern provinces intact
and her western provinces increased. The poor man clearly does not relish
the task of educating his people and is not comforted by the offer of large
areas of German territory which he fears a weakened Poland would have
difficulty in digesting. But none the less we are pegging away and I do not
despair.

4. The only Soviet demand which I did not mention to the Poles was
Konigsberg. I am sure that if I had done so their suspicions of Russian plans
for their encirclement would have been confirmed and this would have closed
their minds to all reason. O'Malley also shares this view strongly. The more I
think over Stalin's Konigsberg demand the more I think that if the Poles are
willing to talk on the basis of the Curzon Line we should press him very
strongly to drop it. From our investigations here I do not believe there is
anything in the warm water port pretext. You will remember that he added
this demand at the end of the conversation and it may have been an after-
thought. At any rate when the time comes I think we should try hard to
save Konigsberg for the Poles, but this is all in the future.[3]

1. Eden had seen Raczyński on 17 December (F.O. 371. C1495/258/55) and Mikołajczyk
on 20 December (F.O. 371. C14281/258/55; D.O.P.S.R.II, No. 66). On both occasions he
had stressed the importance of the Poles making concessions on their eastern frontier and
has also pressed the Poles to provide information which would enable him to show that
the London-controlled underground was not anti-Soviet.
2. On 30 December, the Poles responded to these suggestions by presenting an *Aide-
Mémoire* to the Foreign Office (D.O.P.S.R.II, No. 68). This denied that members of the
Polish underground had ever been ordered to kill Soviet partisans and stressed the Polish
desire for cooperation between the two underground movements and between the Polish
Home Army and the Soviet command.
3. The Foreign Office had been extremely taken aback by Stalin's claim at Teheran for
Königsberg, the more so since a Research Department paper showed that the claims that
he needed it because he required an ice-free port was largely spurious (The paper argued
that other Baltic ports such as Memel, Libau and Windau were also ice-free). O'Malley felt
that the cession of Königsberg to the Soviets would take 'most of the gilt off the East
Prussian gingerbread for Poland' (14 December, F.O. 371. C14985/258/55). Sir Orme
Sargent wrote 'As regards Stalin's claim to Konigsberg, this looks like a piece of bluff
which I trust we shall call' (Ibid). This provoked Eden to write, 'I should like to see
Sir O. Sargent do it.'

No. 82

Statement by the Polish Government
LONDON, 5 January 1944
D.O.P.S.R. II, No. 70

IN their victorious struggle against the German invader, the Soviet forces are reported to have crossed the frontier of Poland.

This fact is another proof of the breaking down of the German resistance and it foreshadows the inevitable military defeat of Germany. It fills the Polish nation with the hope that the hour of liberation is drawing near.

Poland was the first nation to take up the German challenge, and it has been fighting against the invaders for over four years at the cost of tremendous sacrifices and sufferings without producing a single quisling, and rejecting any form of compromise or collaboration with the aggressor.

The underground movement, among its many activities, concentrated upon attacking the Germans in their most sensitive spots, upon sabotage in every possible form, and in the carrying out of many death sentences on German officials whose conduct had been particularly outrageous.

The Polish forces, twice reorganised outside their country, have been fighting ceaselessly in the air, at sea and on land, side by side with our Allies. There is no front on which Polish blood has not been mingled with the blood of other defenders of freedom; there is no country in the world where Poles did not contribute to furthering the common cause.

The Polish nation, therefore,·is entitled to expect full justice and redress as soon as it will be set free of enemy occupation. The first condition of such justice is the earliest re-establishment of Polish sovereign administration in the liberated territories[1] of the Republic of Poland and the protection of life and property of Polish citizens.

The Polish Government, as the only and legal steward and spokesman of the Polish nation, recognised by Poles at home and abroad as well as by Allied and free Governments, is conscious of the contribution of Poland to the war and is responsible for the fate of the nation. It affirms its indestructible right to independence confirmed by the principles of the Atlantic Charter, common to all the United Nations, and by binding international treaties. The provisions of those treaties, based on the free agreement of the parties, not on the enforcement of the will of one side to the detriment of the other, cannot be revised by accomplished facts. The conduct of the Polish nation in the course of the present war has proved that it has never recognised, and will not recognise, solutions imposed by force.

The Polish Government expects that the Soviet Union, sharing its view as to the importance of future friendly relations between the two countries, in the interest of peace and with the view to preventing a German revenge, will

1. The phrase originally read 'in all the liberated territories', but was modified as a result of British pressure.

not fail to respect the rights and interests of the Polish Republic and of its citizens.

Acting in that belief, the Polish Government instructed the underground authorities in Poland, on the 27th October, 1943,[2] to continue and intensify the resistance against the German invaders, to avoid all conflicts with the Soviet armies entering Poland in their battle against the Germans, and to enter into co-operation with the Soviet commanders in the event of the resumption of Polish-Soviet relations.

If a Polish-Soviet agreement such as the Polish Government had declared itself willing to conclude had preceded the crossing of the frontier of Poland by the Soviet forces, such an agreement would have enabled the underground Polish army to co-ordinate its action against the Germans with the Soviet military authorities. The Polish Government still considers such an arrangement highly desirable.

At this crucial moment, the importance of which for the course of the war and for its outcome in Europe is evident to everyone, the Polish Government issues the above declaration, confident in a final victory and in the triumph of the just principles for which the United Nations stand.[3]

2. See above No. 71, note 2.
3. This statement provoked Stalin to write to Churchill on 5 January '. . . if we are to judge by the latest declaration of the Polish émigré Government and other statements by Polish leaders, we will see that there are no grounds for thinking that these circles can be made to see reason. They are incorrigible' (Stalin Correspondence, I, No. 222). The Soviet government replied in a statement on 11 January, asserting that 'western Ukraine' and 'western Byelorussia' had entered the Soviet Union in 1939 as a result of the expression of the popular will. It expressed its willingness to accept the Curzon Line as the eastern frontier of Poland and proposed the expansion of Poland westwards. It concluded that 'the interests of Poland and the Soviet Union lie in the establishment of solid friendly relations between our countries, and that the people of Poland and the Soviet Union should unite in the struggle against the common external enemy as is demanded by the cause of all the Allies' (D.O.P.S.R. II, No. 74).

The Foreign Office felt that this statement, and, in particular, its last sentence should be construed as evidence of a Soviet desire for a negotiated solution of the Polish question. Accordingly, strong pressure was exercized on the Polish Government to make a conciliatory reply. The first Polish draft was rejected and two passages from the second draft were rewritten. Of these, the more controversial originally read, 'They [the Polish Government] cannot however recognize unilateral actions or *faits accomplis*, nor the strength of arguments designed to justify the loss by Poland of about half her territory and of more than 11 millions of her population.' In the final draft this last clause was dropped and the statement, issued on 14 January was thus given a generally conciliatory character (For the discussion on the Polish draft, see D.O.P.S.R.II, No. 75; F.O. 371. C995/8/55; W.M.(44)6.1.CA; F.R.U.S. 1944, III, p. 1224. For the statement, see D.O.P.S.R.II, No. 77).

This did not prevent the Soviets on 17 January issuing a harsh rejoinder (D.O.P.S.R.II, No. 80) attacking the Polish Government for failing to take the Curzon Line as the basis for discussion of the Polish eastern frontier. This uncompromising stand was resented by the British and Eden made this known to the Soviet Ambassador Gusev on 17 January (F.O. 371. C736/8/55). Gusev had replied that the Soviet government felt that they 'had offered Curzon Line and the Poles had not accepted.' 'Further progress' was, however, not to be ruled out.

No. 83

Cordell Hull to Averell Harriman: Telegram
WASHINGTON, 15 January 1944
F.R.U.S. 1944, III, pp. 1228–9

I have talked over with the President the request of the Polish Government for this Government to act with the British Government 'with a view to securing through their intermediary the discussion by Polish and Soviet Governments with the participation of British and American Governments of all outstanding questions,'[1] and we desire that you take up the matter with the Soviet Government along the following lines:

As the Soviet Government well knows, we are committed to the principle of the settlement of disputes by peaceful accord, and the most important recent official declarations on the part of the leading peace-loving nations of the world have been along these lines.

Without regard to the merits of the case, it is the hope of this Government that the Soviet Government will give the most favorable consideration to the Polish offer to discuss outstanding questions, presumably on the basis of a renewal of official relations between the two Governments. The effect of any hesitancy or refusal by the Soviet Government at this time would adversely affect the cause of general international cooperation. Conversely, an amicable solution of the Polish-Soviet differences, in conformity with the principles of international cooperation, would have far-reaching effects on world opinion.

We must not overlook the very considerable advantages to our common war effort of the restoration of unity in the ranks of the United Nations. Our interest in the resumption of relations between the Polish and Soviet Governmens and the amicable settlement by mutual agreement between them of outstanding questions is directly related to the furtherance and the acceptance by all peace-loving peoples of the reality of the basis for international cooperation established at Moscow and Tehran.

If the Soviet Government finds it agreeable and desirable, this Government would be glad to extend its good offices in the matter of arranging for the initiation of discussions between the two Governments with a view to resumption of official relations between them.

For your own individual information, this is intended primarily as an earnest, friendly effort to be of aid to Russia in reaching a settlement of this difficult problem. The effect on opinion in this country of the *Pravda* reply to Mr. Willkie's article[2] and the interpretation by the public and press here of this reply as an indication that the Soviet Government proposed to follow a course of unilateral action, has been far-reaching. Very considerable and important elements in this country are viewing the attitude and actions of

1. The last sentence of the Polish statement of 14 January. See above No. 82, note 3.
2. Wendell Willkie, Roosevelt's personal representative had visited the U.S.S.R. in September 1942 and described his conversations with Stalin in *Life* of 5 October 1942.

the Soviet Government with regard to the Polish boundary question as a test of the reality of international cooperation in its broad future aspects on a basis of friendly accord and respect for the rights of nations. We have had encouraging results in this country from the declaration of Moscow and the meeting of Tehran but we would not be frank if we did not point out the danger to the cause of cooperation in an international security system which would result from an arbitrary dealing with the Polish-Soviet differences.

These observations are not intended to reflect or deal with the merits of the case in question.[3]

3. When Harriman delivered this note on 18 January, Molotov claimed that at Teheran, Stalin had made clear that he could not deal with the existing Polish Governmnet, 'because it contained Fascist elements'. He further claimed that 'the Soviet Government envisioned an entirely new Polish Government including perhaps some of the present members of the London Government, prominent Poles in the United States and Poles now in the Soviet Union.' This seemed to Harriman to go beyond Molotov's statements to him and also to John Balfour, the British Minister on 16 January when he had merely claimed that persons 'hostile to the U.S.S.R.' must be eliminated from the Polish Government (F.R.U.S. 1944, III, pp. 1230–1). Harriman felt nevertheless that the Soviets would still recognize Mikołajczyk's government provided that the most irreconcilably anti-Soviet elements in it were removed. In addition, the Curzon Line would have to be accepted 'as a basis for negotiation of the boundary' (Ibid, pp. 1232–3; S.D.760c 61/2188).

Molotov replied to Hull's offer to mediate on 23 January. He claimed that conditions were 'not yet ripe' for mediation, since the Polish government had refused to accept the Curzon line as a basis for the settlement of the frontier. What was required was 'a radical improvement of the composition of the Polish Government, one that would exclude pro-facist imperialist elements and include democratic elements.' (Stalin Correspondence, II, pp. 291–2). Harriman argued that a reconstruction of the Polish goverment would require 'the strongest pressure' from the British. 'How far we should go I would not feel qualified to say' (S.D. 760c. 61/2188). Hull made his own position clear in a telegram to Harriman on 25 January in which he stated that 'Present Russian insistence on an almost complete reconstitution of the Polish Government-in-exile as an essential prerequisite to any direct discussion of mutual problems is an approach which American public opinion will not understand' (F.R.U.S., 1944, III, pp. 1234–5).

No. 84

War Cabinet Minutes (Extracts)
LONDON, 25 January 1944
W.M.(44)11. I.C.A.

The War Cabinet had before them the note of a conversation between the Prime Minister and the Polish Ministers on the 20th January (W.P.(44)48),[1] about the Polish-Soviet problem, and in particular the Polish-Soviet frontier question.

1. For the record of this conversation see D.O.P.S.R.II, No. 83, F.O.371. C1238/8/55 and F.R.U.S. 1944, III, pp. 1236–7. Mikołajczyk objected to Churchill's advocacy of compensation in the west for territorial losses in the east, arguing that the loss would be out of all proportion to the compensation, which was, in addition, by no means assured. He further claimed that there was no clear evidence that the Soviet Union was prepared to tolerate an independent Poland.

THE PRIME MINISTER referred to the extreme difficulty of the problem which the Cabinet had to consider. As the record of the conversation showed, the Polish Ministers had not been prepared to go very far. We had to face the fact that, once we agreed to Russia having the Baltic States, and to the transfer of other areas of large masses of German population in East Prussia and East of the Oder to make room for dispossessed Poles, we should be challenged on the ground that such action was contrary to the Atlantic Charter. The ideal position would be to postpone any decision about frontiers until after the war, and then to consider all frontier questions together. But we were not free agents in the matter. The Russian armies were advancing into Poland. If no settlement was reached between Russia and Poland, we had to face the fact that when the Russians reached Warsaw they would probably set up a Polish Government, based on a plebisite, having every aspect of democratic and popular foundation, and in full accord with the Russian view. Nor ought we to ignore the fact that only Russian sacrifices and victories held out any prospect of the restoration of a Free Poland. He was certain that it would be in the best interests of Poland to accept the Curzon Line as the basis for the Polish-Soviet frontier.

THE FOREIGN SECRETARY reported that he had now received a further communication from the Polish Government. This was under examination, and sought clarification or guarantees on a number of important and difficult points. . .[2]

The War Cabinet's conclusions were as follows:—

(1)   An immediate approach should be made to Premier Stalin by the Prime Minister, on the following lines.

The Prime Minister would state that, with the Foreign Secretary and with the full authority of the Cabinet, he had discussed the whole position with the Polish Government. The result of these discussions was that the Polish Government had not refused a settlement of the frontier question on the basis of the Curzon Line, subject to certain ethnographical considerations. But, as was natural, the Polish Government required further information on a number of points. If the Russian Government were willing to proceed with negotiations on the same basis as that adopted by

---

2. The essence of these questions was contained in paragraph 4 of Churchill's letter to Stalin of 28 January (See below No. 85). For Raczyński's letter see D.O.P.S.R.II, No. 85 and F.O. 371. C1059/8/55. Eden replied to Raczyński on 1 February that 'The issues raised in your Excellency's letter are in the view of His Majesty's Government closely bound up with the approach now contemplated to the Soviet Government, in which, as you are aware, it is intended to link up in broad and general terms the frontier question with those of assuring the restoration of the legal authorities in liberated territories of maintaining the strength and independence of Poland in the post-war years and of providing adequate guarantees to prevent any recurrence of aggression against Poland. But until His Majesty's Government have elicited the views of the other Governments concerned upon these matters, and, in particular, have more definite information regarding the basis upon which agreement might be reached between the Polish and Soviet Government, they are not in a position to return any final answer to the detailed questions contained in your letter' (F.O. 371. C1059/8/55).

the Prime Minister in his discussions with the Poles, and would afford the clarifications which the Poles desired, H.M.G., for their part, undertook that at the Peace Conference their attitude on the Russian-Polish frontier would be that which the Prime Minister had taken in his conversation with the Polish Government.

The message should continue that it seemed a great pity that Premier Stalin should attack the Polish Government in exile. Clearly, when Poland had been liberated, its government would once more be based on the people of that country. But, at the present time, the established Polish Government were the only persons with whom it was possible to have negotiations on this matter. . .

No. 85

Mr. Churchill to Marshal Stalin: Letter
LONDON, 28 January 1944
Stalin Correspondence, I, No. 235

On Thursday last accompanied by the Foreign Secretary and with the authority of the War Cabinet I saw representatives of the Polish Government in London.[1] I informed them that the security of the Russian frontiers against Germany was a matter of high consequence to His Majesty's Government and that we should certainly support the Soviet Union in all measures we considered necessary to that end. I remarked that Russia had sustained two frightful invasions with immense slaughter and devastation at the hands of Germany, that Poland had had her national independence and existence restored after the First World War, and that it was the policy of the great Allies to restore Poland once again after this war. I said that although we had gone to war for the sake of Poland we had not gone for any particular frontier line but for the existence of a strong, free, independent Poland which Marshal Stalin declared himself as supporting. Moreover although Great Britain would have fought on in any case for years until something happened to Germany, the liberation of Poland from Germany's grip is being achieved mainly by the enormous sacrifices of the Russian armies. Therefore, the Allies had a right to ask that Poland should be guided to a large extent about the frontiers of the territory she would have.

2. I then said that I believed from what had passed at Tehran that the Soviet Government would be willing to agree to the easterly frontiers of Poland conforming to the Curzon Line subject to the discussion of ethnographical considerations, and I advised them to accept the Curzon Line as a basis for discussion. I spoke of the compensations which Poland would receive in the North and in the West. In the North there would be East Prussia; but here I did not mention the point about Königsberg. In the West they would be secure and aided to occupy Germany up to the line of the

1. This is the meeting on 20 January. See above, No. 84, note 1.

Oder. I told them it was their duty to accept this task and guard their frontiers against German aggression towards the East in consequence of their liberation by the Allied forces. I said in this task they would need a friendly Russia behind them and would, I presume, be sustained by the guarantee of the three Great Powers against further German attack. Great Britain would be willing to give such a guarantee if it were in harmony with her ally, Soviet Russia. I could not forecast the action of the United States but it seemed that the three Great Powers would stand together against all disturbers of the peace, at any rate until a long time after the war was ended. I made it clear that the Polish Government would not be committed to agree to the Curzon Line as a basis of examination except as part of the arrangement which gave them the fine compensations to the North and to the West which I had mentioned.

3. Finally, I said that if the Russians' policy was unfolded in the sense I had described, I would urge the Polish Government to settle on that basis and His Majesty's Government would advocate the confirmation of such a settlement by the Peace Conference or by the conferences for the settlement of Europe following the destruction of Hitlerism, and would support no territorial claims from Poland which went beyond it. If the Polish Ministers were satisfied that agreement could be reached upon these lines, it would be their duty at the proper time not merely to acquiesce in it but to commend it to their people with courage, even though they ran the risk of being repudiated by extremists.

4. The Polish Ministers were very far from rejecting the prospects thus unfolded but they asked for time to consider the matter with the rest of their colleagues, and as a result of this they have asked a number of questions none of which seem to be in conflict with the general outline of my suggestions to them. In particular they wish to be assured that Poland would be free and independent in the new home assigned to her; that she would receive the guarantee of the Great Powers against German revenge effectively; that these Great Powers would also assist in expelling the Germans from the new territories to be assigned to Poland; and that in the regions to be incorporated in Soviet Russia such Poles as wished would be assisted to depart for their new abodes. They also inquired about what their position will be if a large part of Poland west of the Curzon Line is to be occupied by the advancing Soviet armies. Will they be allowed to go back and form a more broad-based government in accordance with the popular wish and allowed to function administratively in the liberated areas in the same way as other goverments who have been overrun? In particular they are deeply concerned about the relations between the Polish underground movement and the advancing Soviet forces, it being understood that their prime desire was to assist in driving out the Germans. This underground movement raises matters important to our common war effort.[2]

5. We also attach great importance to assimilating our action in the different regions which we hope to liberate. You know the policy we are

following in Italy. There we have taken you fully into our councils, and we want to do the same in regard to France and the other countries to whose liberation we look forward. We believe such uniformity of action is of great importance now and in the future to the cause of the United Nations.

6. The earliest possible agreement in principle on the frontiers of the new Polish State is highly desirable to allow of a satisfactory arrangement regarding these two very important points.

7. While, however, everyone will agree that Soviet Russia has the right to recognise or refuse recognition to any foreign government, do you not agree that to advocate changes within a foreign government comes near to that interference in internal sovereignty to which you and I have expressed ourselves opposed? I may mention that this view is strongly held by His Majesty's Government.

8. I now report this conversation, which expresses the policy of His Majesty's Government at the present time upon this difficult question, to my friend and comrade Marshal Stalin. I earnestly hope these plans may be helpful. I had always hoped to postpone discussions of frontier questions until the end of the war when the victors would be round the table together. The dangers which have forced His Majesty's Government to depart from this principle are formidable and imminent. If, as we may justly hope, the successful advance of the Soviet armies continues and a large part of Poland is cleared of German oppressors, a good relationship will be absolutely necessary between whatever forces can speak for Poland and the Soviet Union. The creation in Warsaw of another Polish Government different from the one we have recognised up to the present, together with disturbances in Poland, would raise an issue in Great Britain and the United States detrimental to that close accord between the three Great Powers upon which the future of the world depends.[3]

9. I wish to make it clear that this message is not intended to be any intervention or interference between the Governments of the Soviet Union and Poland. It is a statement in broad outline of the position of His Majesty's Government in Great Britain in regard to a matter in which they feel themselves deeply concerned.

10. I should like myself to know from you what steps you would be prepared to take to help us all to resolve this serious problem. You could certainly count on our good offices for what they would be worth.

11. I am sending a copy of this message to the President of the United States with a request for complete secrecy.

2 . On 26 January the Polish Government had also asked the Americans if they believed that the time was ripe for the final settlement of European territorial problems, if the United States would guarantee such a settlement and if the United States supported Churchill's initiative on the Polish question (F.R.U.S. 1944, III, pp. 1236–7). The State Department replied on 1 February that although the U.S. in principle thought territorial questions 'should be postponed for settlement at the peace conference, some questions could be directly settled by mutual accord.' While the U.S. Government could not guarantee a Polish-Soviet agreement it would welcome such an accord and supported the

British initiative, (D.O.P.S.R.II, No. 92; F.R.U.S. 1944, III, pp. 1248–9).

3.   Roosevelt objected to the wording of these two paragraphs. He wrote to Churchill on 8 February.

'Isn't there a possibility that the wording of paragraph 7 and 8 will give him the impression that you are wedded to the present personalities of the Polish Government-in-Exile and are determined to see them reinstated as the future government or Poland? He may interpret this as evidence of a design on your part to see established along the borders of the Soviet Union a government which rightly or wrongly they regard as containing elements irrevocably hostile to the Soviet Union' (F.R.U.S. 1944, III, pp. 1245–6).

He also wrote to Stalin on 7 February associating himself with Churchill's initiative. He added –

'I have given careful consideration to the views of your Government as outlined by Mr. Molotov to Mr. Harriman on January 18 (See above No. 82, note 3) regarding the impossibility from the Soviet point of view of having any dealings with the Polish Government-in-Exile in its present form and Mr. Molotov's suggestion that the Polish Government should be reconstituted by the inclusion of Polish elements at present in the United States, Great Britain, and the Soviet Union. I fully appreciate your desire to deal only with a Polish Government in which you can repose confidence and which can be counted upon to establish permanent friendly relations with the Soviet Union, but it is my earnest hope that while this problem remains unsolved nothing should be done to transform this special question into one adversely affecting the larger issues of future international collaboration. . . . I am told by Prime Minister Churchill that he is endeavouring to persuade the Polish Prime Minister to make a clean-cut acceptance as a basis for negotiation of the territorial changes which have been proposed by your Government. Is it not possible on that basis to arrive at some answer to the question of the composition of the Polish Government which would leave it to the Polish Prime Minister himself to make such changes in his government as may be necessary without any evidence of pressure or dictation from a foreign country?

It seems to me, as a matter of timing, that the first consideration at this time should be that Polish guerrillas should work with and not against your advancing troops. That is of current importance and as a first step some assurance on the part of all Poles would be of great advantage' (Stalin Correspondence, II, No. 159).

Stalin replied on 16 February stressing again that the Polish government should be remodelled and should accept the Curzon Line as the basis of its eastern frontier (Stalin Correspondence, II, No. 160).

No. 86

Marshal Stalin to Mr. Churchill: Letter
MOSCOW, 4 February 1944
Stalin Correspondence, I, No. 236

Your message on the Polish question has reached me through Mr. Kerr who arrived in Moscow a few days ago and with whom I had a useful talk.[1]

I see you are giving a good deal of attention to the problem of Soviet-Polish relations. All of us greatly appreciate your efforts.

I have the feeling that the very first question which must be completely cleared up even now is that of the Soviet-Polish frontier. You are right, of course, in noting that on this point Poland should be guided by the Allies. As for the Soviet Government, it has already stated, openly and clearly, its views on the frontier question. We have stated that we do not consider the 1939 boundary final, and have agreed to the Curzon Line, thereby making very important concessions to the Poles. Yet the Polish Government has evaded our proposal for the Curzon Line and in its official statements continues to maintain that the frontier imposed upon us under the Riga Treaty is final. I infer from your letter that the Polish Government is prepared to recognise the Curzon Line, but, as is known, the Poles have not made such a statement anywhere.

I think the Polish Government should officially state in a declaration that the boundary line established by the Riga Treaty shall be revised and that the Curzon Line is the new boundary line between the U.S.S.R. and Poland. It should state that as officially as the Soviet Government has done by declaring that the 1939 boundary line shall be revised and that the Soviet-Polish frontier should follow the Curzon Line.

As regards your statement to the Poles that Poland could considerably extend her frontiers in the West and North, we are in agreement with that with, as you are aware, one amendment. I mentioned the amendment to you and the President in Tehran. We claim the transfer of the north-eastern part of East Prussia, including the port of Königsberg as an ice-free one, to the Soviet Union. It is the only German territory claimed by us. Unless this minimum claim of the Soviet Union is met, the Soviet Union's concession in recognising the Curzon Line becomes entirely pointless, as I told you in Tehran.

Lastly, about the composition of the Polish Government. I think you realise that we cannot re-establish relations with the present Polish Government. Indeed, what would be the use of re-establishing relations with it when we are not at all certain that tomorrow we shall not be compelled to sever those relations again on account of another fascist provocation on its part, such as the 'Katyn affair'? Throughout the recent period the Polish Government, in which the tone is set by Sosnkowski, has not desisted from statements hostile to the Soviet Union. The extremely anti-Soviet statements of the Polish Ambassadors in Mexico and Canada and of Gen. Anders in the Middle East, the hostility displayed towards the Soviet Union by Polish underground publications in German-occupied territory, a hostility which transcends all bounds, the annihilation, on directions from the Polish Government, of Polish guerrillas fighting the Hitler invaders, these and many other pro-fascist actions of the Polish Government are known. That being so, no good can be expected unless the composition of the Polish Government is thoroughly improved. On the other hand, the removal from it of pro-fascist imperialist elements and the inclusion of democratic-minded people would, one is entitled to hope, create the proper conditions for normal Soviet-Polish relations, for solving the problem of the Soviet-Polish frontier and, in general, for the rebirth of Poland as a strong, free and independent state. Those interested in improving the composition of the Polish Government along these lines are primarily the Poles themselves, the broad sections of the Polish people. By the way, last May you wrote to me saying that the composition of the Polish Government could be improved and that you would work towards that end. You did not at that time think that this would be interference in Poland's internal sovereignty.

With reference to the questions posed by the Polish Ministers and mentioned in paragraph 4 of your letter I think there will be no difficulty in reaching agreement on them.[2]

1. For this conversation, see F.O. 371. C1550, 1553/8/55 and Roosevelt papers, President's Secretary's File, Poland; Telegram Churchill-Roosevelt, 5 February 1944. Stalin's tone was friendly but he again stressed that the Polish Government should accept the Curzon line and 'get rid of the intransigeants'. He also gave specific and encouraging answers to the questions raised by Churchill in paragraph 4 of his letter. He repeated his complaint against the Polish underground. Clark-Kerr concluded his telegram to Eden as follows:

'. . . 2. In all the circumstances it now seems to me that we have a fairly clear cut choice to make:

(a) to let things take their course and to face all differences and dangers that this would carry with it; or

(b) to make a supreme effort to bring about a quick settlement by giving Poland such advice as would lead to a reconstruction of their Government.

3. I appreciate that (b) is distasteful to you and the Prime Minister but of the two it seems to me to be the less unhappy. It might be possible to persuade the Polish Prime Minister himself to provoke the resignation of intransigeants by a public acceptance of the Curzon Line.

4. United States Ambassador tells me that he shares my view about (b) and has already expressed it to his Government' (F.O. 371. C1553/8/55).

Churchill cabled back to Clark-Kerr on 5 February, 'Upon receipt of Stalin's reply I will seek Mikołajczyk and try my best to get him to remodel his Government and drop all talk of Riga. If we cannot get the Poles to agree, it may be wise for H.M.G. to reach a definite understanding with Stalin as to the Peace Settlement and then assure him that we will support such a settlement at the peace or armistice conference' (F.O. 371. C1810/8/5

2. See above, No. 85.

No. 87

Mr. Churchill to Marshal Stalin: Letter (Extracts)[1]
LONDON, 21 February 1944
Stalin Correspondence I, No. 243

The Secretary of State for Foreign Affairs and I have had numerous long discussions with the Polish Prime Minister and the Minister for Foreign Affairs. I shall not attempt to repeat all the arguments which were used but only to give what I conceive to be the position of the Polish Government in the upshot.

The Polish Government are ready to declare that the Riga Line no longer corresponds to realities and with our participation to discuss with the Soviet Government, as part of the general settlement, a new frontier between Poland and the Soviet Union together with the future frontiers of Poland in the North and West. Since however the compensations which Poland is to receive in the North and West cannot be stated publicly or precisely at the present time the Polish Government clearly cannot make an immediate public declaration of their willingness to cede territory as indicated above because the publication of such an arrangement would have an entirely one-sided appearance with the consequence that they would immediately be repudiated by a large part of their people abroad and by the underground movement in Poland with which they are in constant contact. It is evident therefore that the Polish-Soviet territorial settlement which must be an integral part of the general territorial settlement of Europe could only formally be agreed and ratified when the victorious Powers are gathered round the table at the time of an armistice or peace.

For the above reasons the Polish Government, until it had returned to Polish territory and been allowed to consult the Polish people, can obviously not formally abdicate its rights in any part of Poland as hitherto constituted, but vigorous prosecution of the war against Germany in collaboration with the Soviet armies would be greatly assisted if the Soviet Government will facilitate the return of the Polish Government to liberated territory at the earliest possible moment; and in consultation with their British and American Allies as the Russian armies advance, arrange from time to time with the Polish Government for the establishment of the civil administration of the Polish Government in given districts. This procedure would be in general accordance with those to be followed in the case of other countries as they are liberated. The Polish Government are naturally very anxious that the districts to be placed under Polish civil administration should include such places as Vilna and Lvov where there are concentrations of Poles and that the territories to the east of the demarcation line should be administered by Soviet military authorities with the assistance of representatives of the United Nations. They point out that thus they would be in the best position to enlist all such able-bodied Poles in the war effort. I have informed them and they clearly under-stand that you will not assent to leaving Vilna and Lvov under Polish ad-ministration. I wish on the other hand to be able to assure them that the area to be placed under Polish civil administration will include at least all Poland west of the Curzon Line.

At the frontier negotiations contemplated in paragraph 2 above the Polish Government, taking into consideration the mixed character of the population of Eastern Poland, would favour a frontier drawn with a view to assuring the highest degree of homogeneity on both sides, while reducing as much as possible the extent and hardship of an exchange of populations. I have no doubt myself, especially in view of the immediate practical arrangements contemplated by the Polish Government set out in paragraph 3 above, that these negotiations will inevitably lead to the conclusion you desire in regard to the future of the Polish-Soviet frontier, but it seems to me unnecessary and undesirable publicly to emphasise this at this stage.

As regards the war with Germany, which they wish to prosecute with the utmost vigour, the Polish Government realise that it is imperative to have a working agreement with the Soviet Government in view of the advance of the liberating armies on to Polish soil, from which these armies are driving the

German invader. They assure me emphatically that they have at no time given instructions to the underground movement to attack "partisans". On the contrary, after consultation with the leaders of their underground movement and with these people they have issued orders for all Poles now in arms or about to revolt against Hitlerite tyranny as follows:

When the Russian army enters any particular district in Poland, the underground movement is to disclose its identity and meet the requirements of the Soviet commanders, even in the absence of a resumption of Polish-Soviet relations. The local Polish military commander, accompanied by the local civilian underground authority, will meet and declare to the commander of incoming Soviet troops that, following the instructions of the Polish Government, to which they remain faithful, they are ready to coordinate their actions with him in the fight against the common foe.

These orders, which are already in operation seem to me, as I am sure they will to you, of the highest significance and importance.[2]

For the first time on February 6th I told the Polish Government that the Soviet Government wished to have the frontier in East Prussia drawn to include, on the Russian side, Königsberg. The information came as a shock to the Polish Government, who see in such a decision substantial reduction in the size and in the economic importance of the German territory to be incorporated in Poland by way of compensation. But I stated that, in the opinion of His Majesty's Government, this was a rightful claim on the part of Russia. . .

As regards the composition of the Polish Government, the Polish Government cannot admit any right of a foreign intervention. They can however assure the Russian Government that by the time they have entered into diplomatic relations with the Soviet Government they will include among themselves none but persons fully determined to cooperate with the Soviet Union. I am of the opinion that it is much better that such changes should come about naturally and as a result of further Polish consideration of their interests as a whole. It might well be in my opinion that the moment for a resumption of these relations in a formal manner would await the reconstitution of a Polish Government at the time of the liberation of Warsaw when it would arise naturally from the circumstances attending that glorious event.[3]

It would be in accordance with the assurances I have received from you that in an agreement covering the points made above the Soviet Government should join with His Majesty's Government in undertaking vis-á-vis each other and Poland, first to recognise and respect the sovereignty, independence and territorial integrity of reconstituted Poland and the right of each to conduct its domestic affairs without interference, and secondly to do their best to secure in due course the incorporation in Poland of the Free City of Danzig, Oppeln, Silesia, East Prussia, west and south of a line running from Königsberg and of as much territory up to the Oder as the Polish Government see fit to accept; thirdly to effect the removal from Poland including the

German territories to be incorporated in Poland of the German population; and fourthly to negotiate the procedure for the exchange of population between Poland and the Soviet Union and for the return to the Mother Country of the nationals of the Powers in question. All the undertakings to each other on the part of Poland, the Soviet Union and the United Kingdom should in my view be drawn up in such a form that they could be embodied in a single instrument or exchange of letters.

I informed the Polish Ministers that should the settlement which has now been outlined in the various telegrams that have passed between us become a fact and be observed in spirit by all the parties to it, His Majesty's Government would support that settlement at the Conference after the defeat of Hitler and also that we would guarantee that settlement in after years to the best of our ability.[4]

1. This message constitued a compromise between the preparedness of the British Government to meet Soviet conditions and the unwillingness and inability of Mikołajczyk to make the concessions the British regarded as necessary. Churchill's first draft, drawn up after a meeting with Mikołajczyk and Romer on 6 February (D.O.P.S.R.II, 96; F.O. 371. C1748/8/55) was criticized by Eden (F.O. 371. C1749/8/55) on the grounds that it was too vague. He argued that it should only be adopted 'once we are quite sure that the Poles will not accept a wider and more clear-cut solution.' The second draft (F.O. 371. C1749/8/55; D.O.P.S.R.II, No. 99) thus stated that the Poles would accept the Curzon Line, subject to minor ethnographical adjustments and would remove Sosnkowski, Kot and Kukiel from the cabinet. A formal Polish recognition of the Curzon Line was not contemplated because of the problems involved in making public the proposed compensation of Poland in the west and north at German expense. But the line of administrative division which was to be laid down would establish the Curzon line as the *de facto* frontier to be ratified at the peace conference. Close collaboration between the London-controlled underground and the Red Army was to be established.

This second draft was submitted to the Poles by O'Malley on 12 February (F.O. 371. C2226/8/55) and rejected by them, primarily because of its explicit recognition of the Curzon line. Mikołajczyk and Romer declared, however, that they were prepared to accept a frontier line drawn somewhere between the Curzon line and the 1921 frontier. Churchill thus reverted to his first draft, and this was shown to the Poles on 16 February after certain minor modifications to make it more acceptable to them (F.O. 371. C2505/8/55; D.O.P.S.R.II, No. 103). After considerable pressure, Mikołajczyk, Romer and Raczyński agreed that the message should be sent. They attached great importance to parallel action by the United States. Accordingly, at the request of Churchill, Roosevelt in a message delivered to Stalin on 28 February stated his support for the British plan (Stalin Correspondence, II, No. 171). Mikołajczyk had been unable to carry his cabinet with him. Indeed on 15 February, the Polish cabinet had expressly declared the Curzon Line to be unacceptable (D.O.P.S.R. II, No. 100; F.R.U.S., 1944, III, pp. 1258–9). In his letter to Stalin of 19 February, Churchill wrote that he thought that the proposals he was sending 'will very likely split the Polish Government' (Stalin Correspondence, I, No. 241). The representative political body of the underground had also declared itself on 15 January against any territorial concessions in the East (D.O.P.S.R. II, No. 78).

2. These orders, which had been communicated to Churchill by Mikołajczyk on 6 February, constituted an abandonment of the line embodied in the order of 27 October 1943 (See above, No. 71, note 3). The initiative for this change had come to a considerable extent from Gen. Bor-Komorowski, Commander of the Home Army, who in a letter to Sosnkowski dated 26 November 1943 and received in London early in January had stated that he was ordering the underground forces to reveal themselves to the Red Army. This policy was approved of by Mikołajczyk, who was able to get it accepted by

his cabinet (See J. Ciechanowski, *The Warsaw Rising*, Cambridge 1974, pp. 164–5; 172).
3. Eden had made the same point in somewhat stronger language to Gusev on 9 February
(F.O. 371. C1868/8/55).
4. Churchill's speech in the House of Commons on 22 February also outlined the
proposals he made in this letter (H. of C. Debates, 397, pp. 697–9).

No. 88

Sir Archibald Clark-Kerr to Anthony Eden: Telegram
MOSCOW, 28 February 1944
F.O. 371. C2793/8/55

I saw Stalin tonight. It was not a pleasant talk. He attempted to dismiss
with a snigger the position of the Polish Government as described in the Prime
Minister's message.

2. He snorted from time to time as I made one by one the points contained
in your telegram No. 457.[1] For instance when I said that the Polish Government had assured us that they would not disavow our action he said: "Is that
serious? How handsome of them!" When I got to point 2 of your paragraph 2
about Curzon line he broke in with "but the Polish Government do not want
to give us Lvov and Vilna.[2] If they did, they should say so." When I explained
that they well understood that they would have to do so, he replied that his
was not clear from the message. Indeed in a recent official statement they had
made it manifest that their view did not tally with the Prime Minister's. I
countered this by drawing on your telegram No. 526, but without much
success.[3]

3. At this stage Molotov confused the issue by evoking the bogey of
Sosnkowski, which haunted us throughout the talk and which I tried in vain to
shoo away. A long wrangle followed during which Stalin said that he had
little hope of settling the matter on basis of the Prime Minister's message. I
said that you and the Prime Minister would be much discouraged by this and
he replied that he must tell the truth. The Polish Government did not want a
settlement. Its purpose was to embroil us with the Soviet Government when I
said that if this were so the Polish Government would fail, he said he feared
that it might succeed. It had indeed made a rift between the Soviet Government and yourself and might do so later with the Prime Minister also. The
Poles always had fresh demands. For instance they had had the effrontery to
suggest something that ignored the sovereignty of the Soviet Government over
territory which belonged to the Soviet Union, when they proposed that
representatives of the United Nations should take a share in the administration
of regions east of the demarcation line.

4. When I scouted all this Stalin said that until the Prime Minister had

1. This had given Clark-Kerr his instructions as to what to say when delivering Churchill's
message to Stalin (F.O. 371. C2461/8/55).
2. See above, No. 87.
3. C2672/8/55.

returned from Africa, Polish affairs had been in your hands. You had offered mediation which he had been obliged to reject. This had been a score for the Poles and you had been displeased. He had been obliged to hurt your feelings. Why? Because of the Poles.

5. I did my best here to explain what was your position in this affair. To this he replied that the Russians and British shed their blood while the Poles sat on your back or hid behind the Prime Minister's.

6. When it became clear that Stalin was determined not to take the Prime Minister's message as the basis of a settlement, I asked him to make some constructive suggestions. He replied that this was simple. He only asked for two things: the Curzon line and reconstruction of the Polish Government. If the Poles meant business they should clearly and openly accept the Curzon line, and he for his part would not tolerate any further demands from the Ukrainians or White Russians. He dismissed the Polish contention that it was impossible for them to make such a declaration at present. If the Government were to be reconstructed there could be no question of waiting until the recapture of Warsaw. But if a quick re-shuffle were effected and genuine democratic elements were brought into the administration this would help. (At this point the bogey of Sosnkowski stalked across the stage again.) But there arose the question of who would enter into a reconstructed Government, and here, to my surprise, he took up the old Molotov proposal to do some recruiting in America and in this country. About America I used the now well worn arguments which he finally admitted had some force, but not until he had tried to persuade me that dual citizenship was possible — witness ex-President Moscicki who was both Polish and Swiss.

7. He then suggested, if citizenship were a bar, a couple of Polish Americans — for instance Professor Lange and Orlemanski (a Catholic priest) might come to Moscow to see what was going on here and advise on the choice of appropriate Poles. He did not know either of them, but he understood that they were "good men, non-party men and not Communists". He said that he would like also to see some recruits from this country but he could not name any at the moment. He would not admit that all this presented any serious difficulty and he assumed that United States Government would put no obstacles in the way of its citizens coming to the Soviet Union. But it seemed to him that the Polish Government in London with its Sosnkowskis and its Kots and their agents in United States and Canada was too firmly established to be shaken.

8. This dreary and exasperating conversation lasted for well over an hour. No argument was of any avail.

9. When he has consulted his Government Stalin will be telegraphing his reply direct to the Prime Minister.[4]

4. Stalin made the same points as in this conversation in an interview with Harriman on 3 March (F.R.U.S. 1944, III, pp. 1264–6). He also denied that the London government controlled an underground of any size and belittled Harriman's fears of civil war.

No. 89

Marshal Stalin to Mr. Churchill: Letter
MOSCOW, 3 March 1944
Stalin Correspondence, I, No. 249

Both messages of February 20 on the Polish question reached me through Mr. Kerr on February 27.

Now that I have read the detailed record of you conversations with the leaders of the Polish émigré Government, I am more convinced than ever that men of their type are incapable of establishing normal relations with the U.S.S.R. Suffice it to point out that they, far from being ready to recognise the Curzon Line, claim both Lvov and Vilna. As regards the desire to place certain Soviet territories under foreign control, we cannot agree to discuss such encroachments, for, as we see it, the mere posing of the question is an affront to the Soviet Union.

I have already written to the President that the time is not yet ripe for a solution of the problem of Soviet-Polish relations. I am compelled to reaffirm the soundness of this conclusion.

No. 90

Mr. Churchill to Marshal Stalin: Letter[1]
LONDON, 7 March 1944
Stalin Correspondence, I, No. 250

I thank you for your message of March 3rd about the Polish question.

2. I made it clear to the Poles that they would not get either Lvov or Vilna and references to these places as my message shows merely suggested a way in those areas in which Poles thought they could help the common cause. They were certainly not intended to be insulting either by the Poles or by me. However, since you find them an obstacle, pray consider them withdrawn and expunged from the message.

3. Proposals I submitted to you make the occupation by Russia of the Curzon Line *de facto* reality in the agreement with the Poles from the moment your armies reach it and I have told you that provided the settlement you and we have outlined in our talks and correspondence was brought into being, His Britanic Majesty's Government would support it at the armistice or

1. In submitting this letter to Stalin, Clark-Kerr was instructed to stress the danger which a divergence of policy over Poland held for the relations between Russia and her western allies. Stalin was also adjured to observe the spirit of the British proposals (F.O. 371. C3289/8/55). At the same time, Churchill cabled Roosevelt that he now saw no reason why Mikołajczyk should not visit the United States, a course he had previously discourage 'It may, at any rate, make the Russians more careful if they see that Poland is not entirely without friends' (F.O. 371. C3046/8/55). Indeed, the War Cabinet had even considered or 6 March making a purely formal reply to Stalin. It was decided however that the Russians might take this as an indication that the British had washed their hands of the affair and that such a course was inconsistent with British obligations to Poland (W.M.(44)28.1.C.A.

peace conferences. I have no doubt that it would be equally supported by the United States. Therefore you would have the Curzon Line *de facto* with the assent of the Poles as soon as you get there, and with the blessing of your Western Allies at the general settlement.

4. Force can achieve much but force supported by the good will of the world can achieve more.[2] I earnestly hope that you will not close the door finally to a working arrangement with the Poles which will help the common cause during the war and give you all you require at the peace. If nothing can be arranged and you are unable to have any relations with the Polish Government which we shall continue to recognise as the government of the ally for whom we declared war upon Hitler, I should be very sorry indeed. The War Cabinet ask me to say that they would share this regret. Our only comfort will be that we have tried our very best.

5. You spoke to Ambassador Clark-Kerr of the danger of the Polish question making a rift between you and me. I shall try earnestly to prevent this. All my hopes for the future of the world are based upon the friendship and cooperation of the Western democracies and Soviet Russia.

2. Clark-Kerr suggested that this sentence be dropped, but Churchill insisted on its retention. 'Appeasement', he claimed 'has had a good run' (F.O. 371. C3312/8/55).

No. 91

Marshal Stalin to Mr. Churchill: Letter
MOSCOW, 23 March 1944
Stalin Correspondence, I, No. 257

I have lately received two messages from you on the Polish question[1] and have read the statement made by Mr. Kerr on the question to V. M. Molotov on instructions from you.[2] I have not been able to reply earlier as front affairs often keep me away from non-military matters.

I shall now answer point by point.

I was struck by the fact that both your messages and particularly Kerr's statement bristle with threats against the Soviet Union. I should like to call your attention to this circumstance because threats as a method are not only out of place in relations between Allies, but also harmful, for they may lead

1. The second message, sent on 21 March (Stalin Correspondence, I, No. 256) replied to Stalin's allegations that the British were responsible for a leak of the correspondence and also stated Churchill's intention shortly to make a speech in the House of Commons. This would state that the British attempts to mediate had failed and that the British would continue to recognize the Polish government and in the meantime could not recognize any 'forcible transferences of territory'.
2. Clark-Kerr had seen Molotov on 19 March. The British Ambassador while making the points he had been instructed to, stressed that 'heart and policy remained unchanged'. Molotov said little and commented that the Soviets regarded their acceptance of the Curzon line as a 'concession' which had been resented by the Ukrainians (F.O. 371. C3993/8/55).

to opposite results.

The Soviet Union's efforts to uphold and implement the Curzon Line are referred to in one of your messages as a policy of force. This implies that you are now trying to describe the Curzon Line as unlawful and the struggle for it as unjust. I totally disagree with you. I must point out that at Tehran you, the President and myself were agreed that the Curzon Line was lawful. At that time you considered the Soviet Government's stand on the issue quite correct, and said it would be crazy for representatives of the Polish émigré Government to reject the Curzon Line. But now you maintain something to the contrary.

Does this mean that you no longer recognise what we agreed on in Tehran and are ready to violate the Tehran agreement? I have no doubt that had you persevered in your Tehran stand the conflict with the Polish émigré Government could have been settled. As for me and the Soviet Government, we still adhere to the Tehran standpoint, and we have no intention of going back on it, for we believe implementation of the Curzon Line to be evidence, not of a policy of force, but of a policy of re-establishing the Soviet Union's legitimate right to those territories, which even Curzon and the Supreme Council of the Allied Powers recognised as non-Polish in 1919.

You say in your message of March 7 that the problem of the Soviet-Polish frontier will have to be put off till the armistice conference is convened. I think there is a misunderstanding here. The Soviet Union is not waging nor does it intend to wage war against Poland. It has no conflict with the Polish people and considers itself an ally of Poland and the Polish people. That is why it is shedding its blood to free Poland from German oppression. It would be strange, therefore, to speak of an armistice between the U.S.S.R. and Poland. But the Soviet Union is in conflict with the Polish émigré Government which does not represent the interests of the Polish people or express their aspirations. It would be stranger still to identify Poland with the Polish émigré Government in London, a government isolated from Poland. I even find it hard to tell the difference between Poland's émigré Government and the Yugoslav émigré Government, which is akin to it, or between certain generals of the Polish émigré Government and the Serb General Mihajlović.

In your message of March 21 you tell me of your intention to make a statement in the House of Commons to the effect that all territorial questions must await the armistice or peace conferences of the victorious Powers and that in the meantime you cannot recognise any *forcible* transferences of territory. As I see it you make the Soviet Union appear as being hostile to Poland, and virtually deny the liberation nature of the war waged by the Soviet Union against German aggression. That is tantamount to attributing to the Soviet Union something which is non-existent, and, thereby, discrediting it. I have no doubt that the peoples of the Soviet Union and world public opinion will evaluate your statement as a gratuitous insult to the Soviet Union.

To be sure you are free to make any statement you like in the House of Commons — that is your business. But should you make a statement of this nature I shall consider that you have committed an unjust and unfriendly act in relation to the Soviet Union.

In your message you express the hope that the breakdown over the Polish question will not affect our cooperation in other spheres. As far as I am concerned, I have been, and still am, for cooperation. But I fear that the method of intimidation and defamation, if continued, will not benefit our cooperation.

No. 92

Minute by Frank Roberts, Head of the Central Department (Extracts)[1]
LONDON, 27 March 1944
F.O. 371. C4302/8/55

. . . Quite apart from the immediate reply to Stalin, the moment would seem to have come to reconsider our position in the Polish-Soviet dispute from the point of view of our general interests. The moment has perhaps come to draft a paper on this. The Department have had no time to do this yet but would submit the following brief resumé of points for consideration.

1. It is neither in our own nor in Polish interests to quarrel with Russia over Poland.

2. The policy of the present Russian Government is increasingly actuated by considerations of historical Russian policy. Soviet-Polish hostility is unfortunately one of the main elements in traditional Russian policy. Since the relative weakening of Poland at the end of the seventeenth century the Russians have mainly seen in Poland an ally and puppet of the enemies of Russia (usually, in the past, of France). It is surely most important that we should not, in the eyes of the Russians be cast for the role played so long and so unhappily for Poland by France. Apart from this vital consideration, the Russians have often, e.g. under Peter the Great and under Alexander, been ready to prefer an independent Poland, admittedly under strong Soviet influence, to a Poland actually incorporated within the Soviet Union. It is submitted that this is probably still Stalin's policy today, if he can get it.

3. Despite Polish arguments to the contrary, there is nothing inconsistent with British interests in the existence of such a Poland under strong Soviet influence, provided there is some reality of independence and the Russians

1. In the introductory sections of this paper, Roberts criticized the misstatements in Stalin's letter, but conceded that Stalin was probably correct in claiming that the British had accepted the Curzon line at Teheran. Throughout the negotiations he had been entirely consistent in claiming the Curzon line and a reconstruction of the Polish government. Eden commented, however, on 6 April that 'our acceptance of Curzon Line and indeed any agreement on Polish-Russian affairs was based upon recognition by Soviets of Polish Government here. This the Russians have refused to do' (F.O. 371. C4657/8/55).

behave themselves in Poland.

4. We have, however, moral obligations to the Poles. Although Poland is not really a good test case of Soviet relations with the outside world, it is nevertheless essential that the Russians avoid major clashes in Poland and avoid imposing a solution which would appear too obviously to be a puppet Soviet administration. In fact, the Russians must 'save our face' in the hope that the Polish-Soviet relations might then develop sufficiently equably to prevent an outburst of public indignation in the outside world.

5. Our moral obligations demand continued recognition of the Polish Government at all events, until an alternative Government exists in Warsaw. We also have the practical obligation of keeping the Polish armed forces in good fighting trim and seeing that they are not eventually let down.

6. The Russians probably resent our intervention and would prefer, for good as well as bad reasons, to deal direct with the Poles.

7. We have made our attitude crystal clear to the Russians in the recent exchange and although we have failed to secure a working agreement we may well have succeeded in impressing upon Stalin the need for restrained Soviet behaviour and for an eventual arrangement which would at least prevent an explosion of public indignation.

8. There would be no advantage to Poland or to ourselves in continuing our mediation at the present stage. If things eventually go wrong in Poland it would be preferable that we could not be held responsible. If they go right, then our intervention is not necessary.

9. There is, in fact, practical advantage in holding up further exchange for the time being since (a) nothing will in fact be settled until the Russians are in Poland proper, and (b) the position will be much easier in regard to the Polish armed forces later in the year if, as we hope, the war is then much nearer to a conclusion.[2]

10. While we are clearly bound to do our best to get the Polish troops back to Poland or, failing this, to find homes for them in British territory, and while we must do our best to see that an independent Poland emerges from the war, we are not morally or actually bound to preserving the present Polish Government for ever. We shall be in a better position to consider our attitude on this point when we know what sort of a Polish administration emerges on the spot after the liberation of Warsaw.

11. A tentative conclusion would be that after the Prime Minister's reply to Stalin's present message we should drop the matter completely for the time being, maintaining our general attitude of support for the present Polish Government but without taking any steps which might appear to commit

2. Churchill agreed with this. He wrote to Eden on 1 April that the correct course would be 'to relapse into a moody silence so far as Stalin is concerned both by my personal telegrams and by all Foreign Office contacts through Ambassador Clark-Kerr' (F.O. 371. N2128/8/55). At the same he wrote to Roosevelt that 'I have a feeling that the Soviet bark may be worse than its bite and that they have a great desire not to separate themselves from their British and American Allies' (F.O. 371. C4562/8/55).

us to backing them through thick and thin against the Russians.

No. 93

Mr. Churchill to Sir Archibald Clark-Kerr: Draft Telegram (Extract)
1 April 1944
Roosevelt Papers, Polish-Russian relations

Please inform M. Molotov that the Prime Minister thought it necessary to refer Marshal Stalin's message of March 23rd about Poland to the War Cbinet whose considered views are set out below for communication to the Soviet Government.[1]

2. Marshal Stalin's references to power politics and threats are not understood here. The Prime Minister had only thought it necessary to say what he would have to do to make the position of His Majesty's Government quite clear to the British Parliament and public if no settlement of the Polish problem could be agreed now. He felt that his personal relations with Marshal Stalin and Anglo-Soviet relations in general demanded that degree of frankness. It is regretted that Marshal Stalin should characterise this as a threat.

3. To avoid any possible misunderstanding the Soviet Government should be informed that the Prime Minister has not departed in any way from what he regarded as just and reasonable at Tehran. His attitude has the approval of the War Cabinet. The Prime Minister has never suggested that the Poles should refuse to accept the Curzon Line. On the contrary, he has most strongly urged them to do so. His exchange of messages with Marshal Stalin related, however, to what he had been able to do in mediating between the Soviet Government and the Polish Government in London. In his message of February 21 he explained in particular why it was difficult for a Government, and especially a Government in exile, to agree publicly to the Curzon Line in isolation from other important issues concerning the future of Poland, which cannot be finally settled now. He had therefore proposed a de facto working arrangement to get round this difficulty. This was as far as he had been able to bring

. The War Cabinet had discussed Stalin's letter of 23 March on the 27th, when the Prime Minister had stressed that 'all other considerations must be subordinated to winning the war.' He welcomed Stalin's definite acceptance of the Curzon Line as the Polish eastern frontier. It was decided to postpone sending a reply to Stalin for a fortnight, and then to send it from the War Cabinet rather than the Prime Minister (W.M.(44)40.1.C.A.). The draft telegram was communicated to Roosevelt on 1 April, who replied that he agreed with its contents and that 'the essential consideration in the Polish-Russian controversy at the present time is to get the Polish military power, including the underground, into effective action against the Nazis' (Roosevelt Papers, President's Secretary's file). In general the Americans had been less prepared to make concessions at this stage than the British. In a telegram to Churchill, drafted on 16 March but not sent, Roosevelt had argued that 'the final determination of matters like boundaries can well be laid aside by the Russians by the Polish Government and by your Government.' He also stressed the importance of establishing contact between the Red Army and the Polish underground (Roosevelt Papers, President's Secretary's File). Similar arguments were presented in Stettinius' memorandum of 15 March (F.R.U.S. 1944, III, pp. 1267–8).

the Poles and he had hoped that it might have been considered acceptable to the Soviet Government.

4. His Majesty's Government felt very strongly that it was of the utmost importance, more particularly in order that means might be found to ensure the full co-operation of the Polish Underground Movement, controlled by the Polish Government in London, in the common struggle against the Germans, to find some working arrangement for the purposes and for the duration of th war. They still considered the co-ordination of the Polish Underground Movement with the advancing Soviet forces would be of immediate value to the war effort and a real advantage to future relations between Poland and the U.S.S.R.

5. The Prime Minister and the War Cabinet therefore deeply regret Marshal Stalin's inability to accept the proposals of February 21.

6. His Majesty's Government welcome Marshal Stalin's statement that the Soviet Union considers itself the ally of Poland and the Polish people and they trust that means can still be found providing for the active co-operation of the Soviet forces and the Polish population in the liberation of Poland from German oppression. It had never, of course, been the Prime Minister's intention to suggest that any war was being waged between the Soviet Union and Poland or that there was any need for a peace between the two countries. He had only referred to the practical difficulties which are likely to arise in th absence of a working arrangement on the lines suggested in his message of February 21. His reference to the peace conference was, of course, based upon the fact that all the future territorial arrangements in Europe, and not only the frontiers between enemy states, will eventually require the formal ratification and sanction of the victorious powers. His Majesty's Government would have preferred to reach some de facto understanding on this question now, but, in view of the Soviet Government's inability to accept a working arrangement now, the formal settlement, so far as His Majesty's Government are concerned, must clearly await ratification and agreement at the peace conference. Meanwhile, His Majesty's Government can only maintain the attitude they have hitherto consistently adopted and publicly stated in regard to the non-recognition of territorial changes effected since the war other than by agreement between the parties concerned.

7. In the present circumstances, His Majesty's Government must continue to regard the Polish Government in London as the legitimate Government of Poland, with whom their relations have never been interrupted since the Germans attacked Poland in 1939 and so brought this country into the war. Quite apart from this consideration, the Polish Government controls importar armed forces now actively engaged with us in the struggle against our commor enemy. These are, in themselves, sufficient reasons for our continued recognition of and co-operation with the Polish Government. Furthermore, our information goes to show that it is they who control the general resistance in Poland to the German oppressor and more particularly that of the organise

Underground Movement.

3. If, as His Majesty's Government now understand, the Soviet Government see no prospect of further discussion between them leading to a settlement, His Majesty's Government can only retire from the ungrateful role of mediator and announce their failure. In any statement the Prime Minister will make it plain that he had not departed from the views he has hitherto held regarding the proper settlement of this question. . .

No. 94

War Cabinet Minutes (Extract)
LONDON, 11 April 1944
W.M.(44)47.2.C.A.

. . . THE PRIME MINISTER acquainted the War Cabinet with the latest development in the Russo-Polish situation. He was informed by the Prime Minister of Poland that a much better situation had supervened in relation to the underground movement.[1] In obedience to the instructions of the Polish Government in London, that movement, despite certain unfortunate incidents in the early stages, had continued to co-operate with the advancing Russians who, as they moved further west, became increasingly conscious of its wide-spread character, reality and power. An agreement had now been reached between the Russian armies, with the approval of the Soviet Goverment, and the underground Polish leaders, with the approval of the Polish Government in London. That agreement (the text of which the Prime Minister read to the War Cabinet),[2] while providing for the operational subordination of the underground movement to the Soviet, also contained provisions which recognised the existence of the Polish authorities in Warsaw and in London, and recorded their approval of the arrangements now reached. The Prime Minister regarded this development as full of hope.[3] He had no doubt that this attitude which His Majesty's Government had adopted and the stiff terms of the latest communication which he had made to Premier Stalin, had had their influence on the Russian attitude, and he was confirmed in the view he had expressed at an earlier stage that, in spite of the somewhat intransigent tone adopted by the Russians in their diplomatic correspondence with us, they might in practice prove much more accommodating than they were anxious

1. On 7 April Raczyński had communicated to the Foreign Office a memorandum describing this cooperation (D.O.P.S.R.II, No. 123; F.O. 371. C4959/8/55). On 9 April, Mikołajczyk had told Churchill, Winant and Stettinius of the new development D.O.P.S.R.II, No. 124; S.D. 760c. 61/2267).
2. For this see the memorandum of 7 April.
3. The Prime Minister was even moved to press for the removal of General Sosnkowski, and told Mikołajczyk on 9 April that Sosnkowski should be dismissed. The Foreign Office felt, however, that too strong pressure in this direction was undesirable. Nevertheless, the message of 1 April was not despatched, and Churchill delayed his statement on the Polish question until 24 May when he went out of his way to calm Soviet anxieties (H. of C. Deb. 400, vols. 778–9).

to allow us to anticipate. . .

No. 95

Rudolf Schonfield to Cordell Hull: Telegram
LONDON, 12 May 1944
F.R.U.S. 1944, IV, p. 1363

Mikołajczyk tells me that a recent report from the Polish underground
indicates that the working arrangement between the underground and the
Soviet Commander in Volhynia . . . was not fulfilling initial hopes.

Cooperation between the Polish underground forces and the Soviet
Military continues on the fighting front but relations with the Soviet civil
authorities behind the lines are bad. The Soviet authorities are also compelling
Poles to join the Berling armies.

Mikolajczyk states he believes the arrangement will continue to operate
where there is active fighting; i.e., both at the front and in the areas behind
the German lines where Soviet parachutists have been dropped. The latter
particularly need the assistance of the underground. But he indicated doubt
as to the eventual outcome of the arrangement and mentioned that Moscow
had still not publicly affirmed or denied the arrangement.

No. 96

Sir Archibald Clark-Kerr to Anthony Eden: Telegram (Extracts)[1]
18 May 1944
F.O. 371. C6692/8/55

As a result of number of talks with members of the Union of Polish
Patriots Lange had formed the opinion that they were respectable body of
persons representative of Polish opinion in U.S.S.R. and standing well with
the Soviet Government (this differs from Orlemanski's view) who did not
however appear to regard them as suitable nucleus for a new Polish Government. Lange spoke of Witos as a good sincere man and thought that he and

---

1. On 21 February, Gromyko, the Soviet Ambassador in Washington, had asked Roosev
to facilitate the journey to the Soviet Union of Rev. Stanislaw Orlemanski, Chairman of
the Kościuszko Polish Patriotic League and Professor Oskar Lange, Professor of Economic
at Chicago University. Both were known for their opposition to the policies of the Polish
Government. The President had acceded to this request in spite of the objections of the
State Department and the two men spent nearly a month in the Soviet Union between 2
April and 20 May. For Lange's report on his visit, see Roosevelt papers, Lange-Orlemansh
File. Lange's account of his interview with Stalin on 17 May (See below No. 97) is also
printed in D.O.P.S.R.II, No. 132, and the account of it which he gave to Hamilton, the
American chargé d'affaires in Moscow is in F.R.U.S. 1944, III, 1409–11. Lange also met
Mikołajczyk during his visit to Washington and told him of his experiences (D.O.P.S.R.II
No. 143). For the memorandum by Elbridge Durbrow, Assistant Chief of the European
Affairs Department in the State Department on Lange's report, see F.R.U.S. 1944, III,
1418–22.

one or two others might be fitted for inclusion in a reconstructed émigré Government. . .

3. Lange had incidentally found that the Union of Polish Patriots was consumed with curiosity about the Polish National Committee's[2] eagerness to enter into contact with it, but apparently in complete ignorance as to its standing and activities. He was persuaded that the Soviet Government had had nothing to do with setting it up and that it was spontaneous movement from within Poland. Like Lange many members of the Union feared that when the Red Army entered Poland it would be found that there was nothing left but a vacuum and that all the responsible elements capable of future leadership had already been done away with.

2. On 22 January 1944, pro-Soviet elements in Poland had established a Polish National Committee, headed by Bolesław Bierut, Secretary-General of the Polish Workers Party and a former Comintern agent.

No. 97

Sir Archibald Clark-Kerr to Anthony Eden: Telegram (Extracts)
MOSCOW, 19 May 1944
F.O. 371. C6755, 6758, 6764, 6765/8/55

Lange has now been received by Marshal Stalin in the presence of Mr. Molotov.[1] He called on me yesterday as already arranged. Whilst readily replying to whatever question I put to him he was evidently anxious to reserve final judgment on all he had seen and heard during his visit here until his return home when he intended to sort out his impressions and submit a full report to the State Department. Both I and his Majesty's Minister who was present at the interview were much struck by his quiet good sense. The following information of his reception by M. Stalin emerged during the course of the two hours discursive talk.

Lange had found both Stalin and Molotov disappointed at the most recent public statement by Mikolajczyk (I have not seen the text) in which he apparently made it plain that he did not regard the enlargement of Poland in the west as adequate compensation for the losses in the east and also declared that 90% of the Poles supported him. Stalin had sardonically commented on this estimate, remarking with a chuckle that even he himself could not guarantee that he enjoyed the support of 90% of the Soviet people and that M. Molotov for his part was obviously in no position to assert exactly how the matter stood in Poland.

Lange gained the impressions that Stalin looked upon M. as well intentioned but ill-informed by the organisation in charge of the underground agents in Poland. (Lange himself was convinced from all he had heard before his visit here that this organisation gave a biased slant to the material which it submitted to the Polish Government).

1. This meeting took place on 17 May.

Notwithstanding his dissatisfaction with Mikolajczyk Stalin when asked by Lange how he viewed the possibility of arriving at a settlement with the existin Polish Government remarked without hesitation 'the door to an understandin is never closed'. Although Stalin did not apparently develop his ideas on this head Lange was convinced that he had by no means ruled out future dealings with Mikolajczyk and other like minded émigré Poles. At the same time Stalin' attitude was that of a man who was quietly confident that the odds were all o his side and Lange thought that if Mikolajczyk and his friends did not before long bestir themselves to arrive at a basis of understanding they would run the risk of being left out in the cold by the march of the Treaty negotiations. Thus Stalin said that there would be no Amgot in Poland implying that the Red Army would give General Berling[2] a free hand to turn over the administration to well disposed Poles as the campaign of liberation proceeded. Stalin also referred to the growing strength of Berling's army and remarked that he had little doubt that recruits would flow to it as it advanced in Poland and that with the equipment which the Soviet Union could supply it might number as many as a million men by the time it reached Warsaw.

Both Stalin and Molotov incidentally assured Lange that a large number of Poles belonging to the underground movement had of late come over to the rank and file of the Soviet lines and enlisted in Berling's army. They said that the arrival of these people had followed hard upon the recent appearance of the underground movement leaders at the Soviet Army Headquarters at the front. These leaders had discussed the possibility of co-operation but after it had been made clear to them that they must accept control by the Red Army they had gone away and had not yet returned.[3]

In general Lange gained the firm impression that Stalin had as yet come to no definite conclusion as to the particular individual Poles whom he wished t include in a future Polish Government. But of his wish to see a strong independent Poland under the control of responsible Poles there could be no question.

Whole tenour of Marshal Stalin's remarks both in relation to Poland and German problem led Lange. . . to infer that he approached question of Polan future strictly from standpoint of Soviet security. He was determined that Germany should be permanently helpless. (Stalin told Lange . . . about Teheran talks regarding compensation for Poland at Germany's expense. As a good Liberal Lange . . . had been somewhat shocked to discover that this compensation extended as far as Stettin).[4] Poland on the other hand

2. Head of the Soviet sponsored Polish army which had grown out of the Kościuszko Division. See above, No. 58 and note 1.
3. This is a reference to the Voihynia incident. See above, Nos. 94, 95.
4. In his report to the State Department, Lange stated that Stalin said that he was 'not yet sure whether the Poles should get Breslau or not' (D.O.P.S.R.II, No. 132). According to Ciechanowski's account of Lange's conversation with Mikołajczyk on June 13, the new Polish frontier was to reach 'as far as the Oder, up to Wrocław, this city being excluded' (D.O.P.S.R.II, No. 143).

should be strong and independent. It was quite evident that whilst Stalin wished to see permanently friendly Polish relations with the Soviet Union he had no intention of burdening his own country by absorbing Poland into it. Frequently he remarked that he had no intention of interfering in the domestic affairs of Poland.[5] He would be much too busy at home. It was also clear that he did not believe that Communism would work in Poland and that he considered that its future structure should conform to its national characteristics and Catholic outlook. Even when expressing the view that Polish heavy industry should be nationalized Stalin had based his opinion not upon the grounds of Socialist well-being but on the argument that such a reform would contribute to the stability of national economy and efficiency of Government. Lange . . . had been surprised to find a strong conservative strain in Stalin's make-up.

Lwow.   Stalin had lent an attentive ear when Lange . . . had described to him wishes of Polish soldiers in the U.S.S.R. that Lwow should remain Polish but had afterwards drily remarked 'the Ukrainians would be ready to go to war for its possession'. Lange. . . gained the impression, that although chances of Lwow remaining Polish were slender, all prospect of such an arrangement had not yet vanished. . .

Germany. . . Stalin had made it plain that Germany must be kept permanently powerless. When Lange. . . had remarked that this policy postulated a continued understanding between U.S.S.R., Great Britain and United States, Stalin replied 'our relations are established on a basis of mutual self-interest and they will endure'. . .

. . . Lange then spontaneously enquired whether I thought that it would help if, after he had made his report to Mr. Hull, he were to visit England to see Mikolajczyk in person and possibly also members of His Majesty's Government. I undertook to pass on this suggestion and am indeed convinced that nothing but good could come from such a visit by a patently sincere and level-headed observer who has been able to gain clear insight into the situation as it looks from here. If you approve idea of the visit, the matter could presumably be pursued through His Majesty's Ambassador at Washington. . .[6]

5. In a conversation with Churchill on 22 June, Mikołajczyk claimed that Stalin had told Lange, 'I am not interested in the political structure of Poland, provided it is democratic, but I am interested in Poland's foreign policy, in respect to which I shall always try to exert my influence' (F.O. 371. C8588/119/55).
6. Stalin had in fact suggested that Lange unofficially get into contact with Mikołajczyk and other members of his government and even with Sosnkowski (D.O.P.S.R.II, No. 132).

No. 98

Cordell Hull to Averell Harriman: Telegram (Extracts)
WASHINGTON, 17 June 1944
F.R.U.S. 1944, III, pp. 1285–9

For your private and confidential information there is given below a summary of the talks that Premier Mikołajczyk had while in Washington for 9 days.[1]

During his stay Mikołajczyk had four talks with the President and several lengthy discussions with the Acting Secretary, other officials of the Department, and called on the Secretary after the latter's return from his holiday. Mikołajczyk made a very favorable impression on all who talked with him as being very reasonable, understanding and quite objective in his approach to the many problems facing his country.

He brought no concrete plan for the solution of the Polish-Soviet question and no detailed plans were discussed with him. No binding commitments made.

The following are the principal specific points that he raised:

1. He reiterated his firm desire to establish friendly relations with the Soviet Union on a mutually satisfactory and permanent basis. He felt, however, that this could not be attained if the settlement should leave the people of Poland with a sense of injustice.

The Prime Minister stated that he had the feeling, without being in a position to give positive proofs thereof, that the possibilities of reestablishing relations with the Soviet Government were more propitious today than heretofore.[2] He indicated that his feeling was based upon the fact that the Soviet Government, having tried by various methods to build up, without success, strong pro-Soviet support inside Poland, was more disposed to consider the resumption of relations with the Polish Government-in-Exile as the first step. Mikołajczyk added that while he had this feeling, he did not know what conditions the Soviet Government might make in order to re-establish relations.

In this connection, he gave details of an informal Soviet-Polish contact made in London just before his departure. According to the Prime Minister, the informal Soviet representative, who apparently was not acting on specific instructions from Moscow, broached the question of reestablishment of relations but made the unacceptable conditions that the Polish Government-in-Exile be reorganized by removing the President, Commander-in-Chief, and

1. For the Polish version of these talks see D.O.P.S.R.II, No. 141; F.O. 371. C8482/8/55 In submitting this report, Romer stated . . . 'in our view the principle object of M. Mikołajczyk's visit to the United States was to increase the external authority of the Polish Government on the eve of the important international event for which it is now making preparation.'

2. This was also the view of the Foreign Office. In a telegram sent to Halifax at the time of Mikołajczyk's visit to inform him of recent developments in Polish-Soviet relations, it was argued that 'developments during the past two months have . . . not been too discouraging.' The worst fears of the Polish Government about the behaviour of the Red Army had not been fulfilled. The Poles in London were also more prepared to compromise and it was proposed to replace Sosnkowski as successor-designate to the President while allowing him to remain Commander-in-chief. The main difficulties remained Vilna and Lwów especially the latter and the 'maintenance of real Polish independence.' Direct intervention by Britain or the United States was to be avoided as it tended to be counter-productive (F.O. 371. C7698/8/55).

the Ministers of War and Information.[3]

The Prime Minister insisted that any settlement would have to be based upon as concrete assurances as possible that there would be no interference in the internal affairs of Poland. He insisted that the so-called National Council of Poland, whose representatives are now in Moscow, has at the most a very small following in the country, and he felt that it represented a new and again unsuccessful effort on the part of the Soviets to build up a rival government organization in Poland.

In regard to the question of the President-designate, the Prime Minister stated in confidence that the Deputy Prime Minister and head of the Polish Underground Government in the country had been asked if he would be willing to take Sosnkowski's place. If he accepts, he will be brought to London and his appointment will then be announced. If he should not accept, the Polish Underground has been asked to name another prominent person in the country who could be brought to London to fill this post.

2. On the territorial questions, he stated that he felt that no final settlements should be made until after the termination of hostilities. He admitted that in such final settlement territorial adjustments in the East might be made. He again brought up the question of establishing at this time a temporary demarcation line in eastern Poland which would run east of Vilna and Lwow with the territory west of this line to be under the administration of the Polish Government-in-Exile and the territory in the east to be under Soviet administration.

He stated that he felt that, for the future peace of Europe, and not as compensation for lost territory in the East, Poland should acquire East Prussia and Silesia. His basic reasons for desiring East Prussia were to eliminate the question of the Polish Corridor as well as the German springboard on the flank of Poland, and in regard to Silesia, to deprive Germany of an industrial area which she might use as an armament center for any future war. His government has no desire to acquire any other German territories.

3. The Prime Minister expressed a strong desire to reach an agreement for permanent collaboration during the war between the Polish Underground and the Red Army in order that the full weight of the combined forces could be brought to bear against the Germans, and thus assist the Russians as well as be of an indirect assistance to the Anglo-American forces in the West. He described in some detail his version of the successful contact made between these Polish and Soviet forces in eastern Poland and explained that, although the contacts had been broken off by a German counter-attack, he hoped that they could be renewed, not on a local basis, but on the basis of coordinated activities by the central military leaders of both groups. Despite the breaking off of direct contact with the Red Army, Mikolajczyk stated that the Polish Underground was nevertheless collaborating with Soviet Partisan paratroopers in the Lwow area.

3. See below No. 99.

In order to bring the full weight of the Polish Underground to bear against the Nazis, the Premier made a strong plea for American financial and material assistance to them. . .

4. The Prime Minister asserted that he favored a general European economic federation in order to raise the standard of living of the people of all countries.

6. Mikolajczyk also indicated that his Government felt that they, at the present time, are somewhat isolated and that matters which they consider to be of direct concern to Poland were being discussed by 'the big three' without Polish participation. He therefore expressed the hope that arrangements could be made for consultation with his Government when matters affecting his country were under consideration.

The President apparently found Mikolajczyk's approach to the many problems discussed to be objective and indicated to him that he could count upon the moral support of the United States Government in any efforts that the Premier might make to reach a mutually satisfactory understanding with the Soviet authorities. The President explained that he had outlined to Stalin at Tehran the reasons why he could not at this time enter into any detailed discussion on the Polish question. The President apparently intimated to Mikolajczyk that he might be able to be of further assistance later on. Mikolajczyk stated that he understood the President's position and did not wish to do anything which would be embarrasing to him. The President expressed the hope that Mikolajczyk might be able, as a minimum achievement, to work out a satisfactory arrangement which would bring about full cooperation between the Polish Underground and the Red Army and indicated in this connection that he would be willing to give consideration to furnishing supplies and funds to the Underground Army so that it might effectively carry on the fight against the Germans.

The President, in referring to the plans of the other exiled governments to return to their countries as soon as possible, suggested that it would be advisable for Premier Mikolajczyk to make similar plans but that, in order to assure success of such plans, he felt it was important for Mikolajczyk to bring about the reconstruction of his Government by eliminating the four persons who the Soviet Government felt are not friendly to it. Mikolajczyk indicated that he could not agree with this, stating that it would be misunderstood, particularly since one of them is the President of the Republic. He added that the Polish Government had declared on several occasions that it was their firm intention to hold elections as soon as possible after liberation in order that the people in the country could choose their own government. The President suggested that he publicly reiterate this plan.

The President expressed the conviction that Stalin did not wish to 'Sovietize' Poland and urged Mikolajczyk to have faith in the good intentions of Stalin. In this connection the President suggested that it might be advisable if Mikolajczyk himself should go to Moscow to discuss various problems with Stalin.[4] The President added that, although he did not feel that he could make this direct suggestion, he might be willing to intimate to Stalin that Mikolajczyk was inclined to carry through such a plan. Mikolajczyk, while not committing himself definitely on this point, indicated that he felt that it might be advisable for him to see Stalin provided no prior conditions were laid down for the meeting.

The President indicated he felt that if other matters could be worked out, Stalin would be reasonable in regard to the territorial question.[5] He urged Mikolajczyk to make every effort possible now to reach a mutually satisfactory solution with the Soviets.

The Secretary, in his discussion with Mikolajczyk, urged that an effort be made to establish contact between Polish and Soviet representatives in order to reach a satisfactory solution with the Soviets.

The Secretary, in his discussion with Mikolajczyk, urged that an effort be made to establish contact between Polish and Soviet representatives in order to reach a satisfactory friendly solution.

In conformity with his desire to find a solution to the Polish-Soviet difficulties, Mikolajczyk had a long talk with Professor Lange. It is understood that Mikolajczyk found his talk with Lange to be very interesting, particularly in regard to the purely Polish sentiments expressed by the members of Berling's Army. The Premier is reported to have been non-committal in his talk with Lange. . .

4. Roosevelt wrote to Stalin on 17 June. After stating his belief that Mikołajczyk was 'a very sincere and reasonable man' and stressing the importance of establishing effective collaboration between the A.K. and the Red Army, he suggested that Stalin invite Mikołajczyk to Moscow for discussions (Stalin Correspondence, II, No. 203). Stalin replied on 24 June, 'I must say . . . that Mr. Mikołajczyk's Washington statement makes it appear that he has not made a step forward on this point [the reconstruction of the Polish government and the acceptance of the Curzon line]. Hence at the moment I find it hard to express an opinion about a visit to Moscow by Mikolajczyk' (Stalin Correspondence, II, No. 206).
5. In a conversation on 12 June, Roosevelt claimed that . . . 'he did not agree on the formula based upon the old Curzon Line. He did not feel the Russians would insist upon this. Further, the President stated, he did not feel that Stalin would insist on Königsberg, and that he felt Stalin would be willing to have Königsberg as a "shrine for the world" inasmuch as the city controlled Danzig and was an important locality' (F.R.U.S. 1944, III, p. 1281). According to the Polish record of this conversation, the President assured Mikołajczyk that, 'at the appropriate time he would help Poland to retain Lwów, Drobobycz and Tarnopol and to obtain East Prussia, including Königsberg as well as Silesia' (D.O.P.S.R. II, No. 141). These promises, as well as the general encouragement given to Mikołajczyk, led Eden to write on 23 June, 'The President will do nothing for the Poles, any more than Mr. Hull did at Moscow or the President did at Teheran. The Poles are sadly deluding themselves if they place any faith in these vague and generous promises. The President will not be embarrassed by them hereafter any more than by the specific undertaking he has given to restore the French Empire' (F.O. 371. C8482/8/55).

No. 99

Anthony Eden to Sir Archibald Clark-Kerr: Telegram (Extracts)
LONDON, 8 July 1944
F.O. 371. C8860/8/55.

First meeting referred to in paragraph 3 of my telegram No. 1538 [of 23rd May] [1] was followed by a second on 31st May. These conversations were conducted between M. Lebedev, the Soviet Ambassador to the Allied Governments in London, and M. Grabski, the President of the Polish National Council. On 31st May the latter put forward, with the knowledge of the Polish Prime Minister and Minister for Foreign Affairs, the following proposals.

(1) The Polish Prime Minister would make a broadcast reaffirming the readiness of the Polish Secret Army to co-operate with the Soviet armies and declaring that German propaganda accusing the Soviet Government of responsibility for Katyn had completely failed in its purpose of weakening the assistance rendered to the Soviet armies by the Polish Secret Army through action against the Germans.

(2)   Marshal Stalin would issue an order stating that he was entering Polish territory in order to fight with the Polish Nation against the Germans.

(3)   A special delegation headed by the Polish Prime Minister should proceed to Moscow to conclude a treaty supplementing the agreement of July 1941 and settling the question of collaboration between the Polish underground organisation and Secret Army with the Soviet armies. The delegation would also discuss post-war Polish-Soviet relations and the question of territories and population.

(4)   Simultaneously with the conclusion of this treaty diplomatic relations would be resumed.

2. In the course of this meeting M. Lebedev agreed that the 1941 agreement had not been abrogated but only suspended and said that he was personally convinced that diplomatic relations would be resumed. He stated that the Poles need have no fear that the Russians would impose their authorities upon the Allied Polish nation. On the basis of M. Grabski's proposals M. Lebedev proposed a meeting with M. Mikolajczyk.

3. Before this meeting was arranged M. Mikolajczyk received a call from Dr. Benes who explained that he had been asked to communicate the Soviet Government's views on certain questions which the latter felt it difficult to raise with the Poles themselves. [2] He said:— (1) Moscow had full confidence in M. Mikolajczyk and sincerely intended to reach an agreement before the offensive was resumed on the Eastern front. (2) While recognising that it was an internal Polish problem, Moscow had reservations as to the persons

1. F.O. 371. C8860/8/55. At this meeting Lebedev had asked the Poles to make proposals with a view to resuming relations. For the full transcript of these talks see F.O. 371. C8836/8/55. Mikołajczyk also gave Schoenfield an account of these talks (F.R.U.S. 1944, III, pp. 1292–6).
2. This meeting took place on 2 June.

Sosnkowski, Kukiel, Kot and Raczkiewicz. (3) The problem of administration in Poland and co-operation between the Polish and Soviet forces would be settled immediately but the frontier question would be dealt with later. (4) The Union of Polish Patriots and the Polish Communists would present no obstacle.[3]

4. M. Mikolajczyk left immediately after this conversation for Washington. His meeting with M. Lebedev took place on 20th June on his return. M. Mikolajczyk stated that before Cabinet changes were made and before he went to Moscow agreement should be reached upon the principles of Polish-Soviet collaboration. In his view these were (1) resumption of diplomatic relations; (2) common plan of action for the Polish secret Army and the Soviet armies; (3) administrative co-operation between the Polish Government authorities in Poland and the incoming Soviet military authorities; (4) possible frontier changes to be postponed until the end of the war. M. Lebedev undertook to refer to Moscow and expressed the view that it would be advisable to make certain changes in the Polish Government before M. Mikolajczyk visited Moscow.

5. At a further meeting on 22nd June M. Lebedev said that he foresaw no difficulties in regard to the resumption of diplomatic relations or agreement concerning administration on Polish territories. He drew attention to the recent Russian agreement with Czechoslovakia and expressed the conviction that a similar agreement with Poland would be no less advantageous to her. He asked however, for elucidation of M. Mikolajczyk's point (4). M. Mikolajczyk explained that the Polish Government could not agree to any diminution of Poland's territories. They had, however, already declared their readiness to discuss the frontier problem as part of the whole question of the future territory of Poland. For the present, however, a demarcation line should be established to the west of which Polish administration would be set up. In order to ensure the maximum war effort on the part of the Polish nation this demarcation line should leave under Polish administration those territories in which the greatest agglomerations of Poles were to be found. The demarcation line must be treated as separate and different from the future frontier.[4] M. Lebedev made it clear that the Soviet Government in principle still regarded the Curzon Line as the only possible frontier but he indicated that this need not prejudice further exchange of view.

6. Up to this stage the conversations had been friendly and even cordial and M. Lebedev had showed every desire to reach agreement and confidence that this would be possible. At a further meeting on 23rd June, however, his

3. Churchill's comment at this stage of the negotiations was 'This story is almost too good to be true, but I have good hopes that the Second Front will bring about better relations between Russia and her western allies than has ever been possible before' (F.O. 371. C8479/8/55).
4. The detailed transcript makes it clear that the Poles were not prepared to accept the Curzon Line as this line of demarcation but wanted something between this and the Riga frontier. This was to be treated as separate and different from the final frontier.

tone completely changed. He stated that before the resumption of diplomatic relations the Soviet Government must demand (1) the resignation of Raczkiewicz, Sosnkowski, Kukiel and Kot; (2) the wholesale reconstruction of the Government to include representatives of the democratic Poles from the United Kingdom, the United States of America and the U.S.S.R. and the 'National Council' in Poland; (3) the Government thus reconstructed would condemn the previous Polish Government for their mistake over Katyn; (4) the Curzon Line should be the new frontier. These terms were presented on a 'take it or leave it' basis and M. Mikolajczyk stated that in these circumstances he had nothing more to say.[5]

7. There have been no further contacts or developments. The Polish Ministers are at a loss to account for the sudden change in the Soviet attitude (which coincided with the resumption of the Soviet offensive and was clearly the result of fresh instructions from Moscow). I had feared that the Russians might have been indisposed by some American intervention after M. Mikolajczyk's message to Marshal Stalin on that occasion and I do not see how any exception could have been taken to it.

8. Foregoing is based upon a full account furnished to me in strictest confidence by the Polish Minister for Foreign Affairs and is for your own information only. Story is known only to Polish Prime Minister and Minister for Foreign Affairs and it is important that Soviet Government should receive no hint that the Poles have taken us into their confidence.

9. In the circumstances there seems little His Majesty's Government can usefully do and I consider that our best policy is not to intervene in any way at this stage. I am, of course, maintaining pressure on Polish Ministers to hasten forward with conciliatory gestures such as (a) replacement of General Sosnkowski as President Designate by a candidate more acceptable to the Russians and (b) measures to amend Polish constitutional position so as to bring the Commander-in-Chief in theory as well as in practice under the control of the Government. M. Mikolajczyk has assured me that favourable decisions in principle have been reached on both points and he does not anticipate much further delay. One difficulty is to secure the right person for (a), who is to be someone from Poland with the requisite authority but who can be spared and got out of the country. Polish Prime Minister has also assured me (i) that he is repeating instructions to Polish Underground authorities and army to co-operate with advancing Soviet forces and (ii) that he will maintain a conciliatory tone in official Polish public statements. This assurance was fully observed by the President and M. Romer, as well as by M. Mikolajczyk himself, in their recent speeches on the anniversary of General Sikorski's death.

5. When the news of the breakdown of negotiations reached him Eden minuted 'I fear that the P.M.'s judgment has been proved correct. They opened their mouths too wide and Russia has turned tough. It is fantastic that Poles should suppose Russians would agree to their administering Vilna' (F.O. 371. C9096/8/55).

No. 100

Averell Harriman to Cordell Hull: Telegram (Extracts)
MOSCOW, 5 July 1944
F.R.U.S. 1944, III, pp. 1423–4

At lunch yesterday I asked Molotov for his further impressions regarding the four delegates and the Polish National Council they represent.[1] He said that he did not believe the Council had so far developed a large organisation throughout Poland but that he believed that it represented the majority of the Polish people. The delegates during their visit to Russia had found that they talked the same language as the Union of Polish Patriots and the Polish Army here and had come to an understanding with them. He realized that the traditional suspicion of Russia by Poles was a factor that would have to be taken into account but he believed that when Poland was liberated and the Polish Army came into Poland the overwhelming majority of the Poles would be convinced of the Soviet Union's friendly intents.

Molotov told me that they intended to supply the Partisans of the Council with arms in so far as they were able to get them through considering all the difficulties.

In discussing the personalities in the Government in London he thought that if Mikolajczyk and the democratic members of the Government returned to Poland and they would be welcomed by the Poles to take part in the development of a government.[3] He said again that he hoped some Poles from the United States would return to assist as well. I asked him whether Dr. Lange had been persuaded to do this. In reply he said that was entirely Dr. Lange's personal affair but that he thought Dr. Lange was a Polish patriot at heart. . .

I found nothing in Molotov's comments to substantiate Mikolajczyk's hope as expressed in Department's 1512 June 17, 10 p.m.,[2] that 'the possibilities of reestablishing relations with the Soviet Government were more propitious today than heretofore' based upon the fact that the Soviet Government having tried by various methods to build up without success strong pro-Soviet support inside Poland was more disposed to consider the resumption of relations with the Polish Government in exile as the first step'.

Throughout the conversation Molotov talked with less of the usual Soviet reserve. He made it clear that he was reserving judgment as to just how things would develop and that the Soviet Government was not at present time committed to the final support of any particular group. He gave me the impression that the Soviet Government was hopeful that by bringing all

1. The four delegates, led by the committee's deputy chairman, Edward Osóbká-Morawski had been in Moscow for talks with the Soviet government and had met both the British and American ambassadors. For Clark-Kerr's account of his meeting with them, see S.D. 860. C.01/744. For Harriman's account see F.R.U.S. 1944, III, pp. 1417–8.
2. See above, No. 98, p. 200.
3. The delegation expressed similar views to Clark-Kerr on 15 June (F.O. 371. C8104/8/55).

democratic minded Poles together and allowing them a free hand the situation would be worked out satisfactorily. It appeared his present feeling that the Council might well form the nucleus of the future Government of Poland.

No. 101

Marshal Stalin to Mr. Churchill: Letter
MOSCOW, 23 July 1944
Stalin Correspondence, I, No. 301

Your message of July 20 received.[1] I am now writing to you on the Polish question only.

Events on our front are going forward at a very rapid pace. Lublin, one of Poland's major towns, was taken today by our troops, who continue their advance.

In this situation we find ourselves confronted with the practical problem of administration on Polish territory. We do not want to, nor shall we, set up our own administration on Polish soil, for we do not wish to interfere in Poland's internal affairs. That is for the Poles themselves to do. We have, therefore, seen fit to get in touch with the Polish Committee of National Liberation, recently set up by the National Council of Poland, which was formed in Warsaw at the end of last year, and consisting of representatives of democratic parties and groups, as you must have been informed by your Ambassador in Moscow. The Polish Committee of National Liberation intends to set up an administration on Polish territory, and I hope this will be done. We have not found in Poland other forces capable of establishing a Polish administration. The so-called underground organisations, led by the Polish Government in London, have turned out to be ephemeral and lacking influence. As to the Polish Committee, I cannot consider it a Polish Government, but it may be that later on it will constitute the core of a Provisional Polish Government made up of democratic forces.[2]

As for Mikolajczyk, I shall certainly not refuse to see him.[3] It would be better, however, if he were to approach the Polish National Committee, who are favourably disposed towards him.

1. In this, Churchill had responded to a request of Romer's on 11 July (F.O. 371. C9192/8/55), and had asked Stalin if he would invite Mikołajczyk to come to Moscow for talks (Stalin Correspondence, I, No. 299).
2. Already on 21 July the National Council of Poland had issued a decree in Chełm, the first town west of the Curzon Line, to be liberated establishing a 'Provisional Committee of National Liberation', (PCNL) which had assumed authority over the Union of Polish Patriots and the Polish Army in the Soviet Union (F.O. 371. C9792/8/55). On 25 July, *Pravda* stated that the Soviet government had decided to recognize this committee as 'the only lawful temporary organ of executive power' and on the 27th signed an agreement with it regulating relations between the Polish authority and the Red Army, similar in character to the Soviet-Czechoslovak agreement of 30 April 1944.
3. The establishment of the P.C.N.L. at first led Mikołajczyk to refuse to go to Moscow but under strong British pressure, he agreed to go on 26 July. After his departure,

Churchill wrote to Stalin

'I am sure M. Mikolajczyk is most anxious to help a general fusion of all Poles on the lines on which you and I and the President are, I believe, agreed. I believe that the Poles who are friendly to Russia should join with the Poles who are friendly to Britain and the United States in order to establish a strong, free, independent Poland, the good neighbour of Russia, and an important barrier between you and another German outrage. We will all three take good care that there are other barriers also.

'2. It would be a great pity and even a disaster if the Western democracies find themselves recognising one body of Poles and you recognising another. It would lead to constant friction and might even hamper the great business which we have to do the wide world over. Please, therefore, receive these few sentences in the spirit in which they are sent, which is one of sincere friendship and our twenty-years' alliance' (Stalin Correspondence, I, No. 305).

No. 102

The Moscow talks of August 1944

1. Sir Archibald Clark-Kerr to Anthony Eden: Telegram
MOSCOW, 4 August 1944
F.O. 371. C10240/8/55

1. M. Romer has given me some account of meeting last night between Mikolajczyk and Stalin at which he and M. Grabski were present.[1] It lasted two and a half hours. Although from time to time the talk was lively and direct, the atmosphere throughout was friendly. Molotov's contributions were few but helpful. There were no recriminations from the Russian side, no mention of the Polish Government in London or of names of any of its members.

2. The Poles were impressed by the great 'wisdom' and apparent willingness of Stalin and his readiness to listen.[2] They felt that he in his turn was impressed and even surprised by the simplicity and liberalism of Mikolajczyk.

3. Stalin began by saying that he was receiving Mikolajczyk in order to redeem a promise he had made to Churchill and he expressed the hope that common ground would be reached.

4. Three main subjects discussed were (1) relations between Polish armed forces in Poland and the Red Army (2) frontiers and (3) relations between Polish Government and Polish Committee of National Liberation.

5. Poles got the impression that Stalin was ill-informed about military contribution which their people in Poland were able to give. He tended to belittle it because Polish forces were without aircraft artillary and tanks. But he listened carefully to Mikolajczyk's claims that these forces were nevertheless of great value and he seemed to recognize it. He admitted that the Red Army was in touch with them but he deprecated the orders that had

1. This meeting took place on 3 August. For a fuller account of the discussions, see D.O.P.S.R. II, No. 180; for Harriman's description see F.R.U.S. 1944, III, pp. 1305–6.
2. This was in contrast to the pessimism Mikołajczyk had expressed to Harriman on his arrival in Moscow (F.R.U.S. 1944, III, p. 1202–3).

been given for a general mobilization. This would cause embarrassment, to the Red Army which as it advanced need complete quiet in its rear. General mobilization would have the effect too of preventing people in liberated areas from settling down to the work of restoration. It would be bad for Poland. It had been necessary at one place to arrest a Polish officer who had insisted, in defiance of the wishes of the Polish Committee, on issuing written orders for mobilisation. I gathered in this matter the Poles were disposed to take the same view as Stalin.

6. About frontiers they found Stalin resolved on the Curzon Line on the ground that it had been drawn by a group of completely objective people. It must therefore be as fair as any frontier could be made. He said the Poles could not claim that the Russians had had a hand in it. Nevertheless they were ready to abide by it. At this point the Poles called in the persuasive eloquence of Grabski who had been cupping his deaf ears from across the table in order to follow what was passing. Grabski addressed Stalin in Russian but could not hear his replies. Undaunted he went round the table and sat himself down next to Stalin. He made an impassioned appeal for Vilna and Lemberg using all his limbs and even banging the table to drive his arguments home.

7. Stalin listened with complete good humour but asserted that with East Prussia (excepting Konigsberg which he proposed to keep for himself) and a frontier on the Oder with Stettin as a port, a sizeable and strong Poland would emerge. Surely a Breslau was worth a Lwow? Poles were somewhat taken aback by the mention of Stettin and (though less so) of Breslau. Then as M. Grabski had the air of beginning again. Stalin said that the question of frontiers was not an immediate one. It could be reverted to when M. Mikolajczyk had come to terms with the Polish Committee. And turning to M. Grabski he said 'you are a first-class propagandist'. Poles got the impression that about Lwow at any rate M. Grabski had shaken him a little.

8. Here the talk turned on a meeting between M. Mikolajczyk and the Committee and Stalin.seemed surprised and pleased that M. Mikolajczyk made no difficulties. Stalin said that an agreement with the Committee was the most important thing of all. He had some observations to make about the tendency of the peoples, more particularly where they had been over-run by the Germans, to move towards the left, and he warned M. Mikolajczyk to be prepared for this in Poland. M. Mikolajczyk retorted by reminding Stalin of his humble origins and his liberal background. Stalin went on to say that finding of common ground by M. Mikolajczyk and the Committee was a purely Polish affair in which he did not wish to intervene. Indeed he did not mean to interfere with any internal Polish matters. M. Mikolajczyk said he was willing to go to Poland to meet the Committee but Stalin thought it better to call representatives to Moscow and said he would do so.

2. Averell Harriman to Cordell Hull: Telegram
MOSCOW, 10 August 1944
F.R.U.S. 1944, III, p. 1308–10

Mikolajczyk and his party left Moscow early this morning. Mikolajczyk accompanied by Romer called on me late yesterday afternoon and I saw him again after midnight. In the meantime he had had his final talk with Stalin.[1]

Mikolajczyk leaves Moscow much more hopeful of the possibility of settlement than when he arrived. He was impressed by his cordial reception and his frank discussions with Stalin and Molotov. At the meeting last night Stalin agreed to undertake to drop arms in Warsaw for the underground forces. A communications officer will first be parachuted to the Polish head-quarters with ciphers in order to establish direct communication to facilitate this operation. Stalin at last admitted that his information agreed with Mikolajczyk's that all Poles were united for resistance in Warsaw under the leadership of the commanding general of the underground forces at whose headquarters there is now a Red Army observer.[2] Stalin told him that he had expected to take Warsaw on August 6 but that because the Germans had brought in four new Panzer divisions and two other divisions to hold the bridgehead, the taking of the city had been delayed but he was confident that the new difficulties could be overcome.

Mikolajczyk is at least partially convinced that it is not the objective of the Soviet Government to communize Poland.[3] He is however still suspicious that this is the objective of the majority of the members of the Council of Liberation.[4] He believes that the Soviets realize that they cannot attain their objective in having a united Polish people behind the Red Army without the

1. Mikolajczyk had had three sessions with the Polish Committee of National Liberation on 6, 7 and 8 August. His meeting with Stalin took place on 9 August. For the Polish record of these conversations see D.O.P.S.R.II, No. 186, 187; for the British account, F.O. 371. C10439, 10460, 10461, 10483/8/55; for Harriman's further observations, F.R.U.S., 1944, III, pp. 1313–5.
2. Stalin's statement was confirmed by Molotov (F.R.U.S. 1944, III, pp. 1313–5). The uprising in Warsaw had commenced on 31 July. Already on 4 August, Churchill had cabled Stalin requesting him to assist the insurgents (Stalin Correspondence, I, No. 311). On 5 August, Stalin replied that the information from Warsaw was probably greatly exaggerated and unreliable (Stalin Correspondence, I, No. 313).
3. At the final meeting with Stalin, the Soviet leader had told Mikołajczyk that while Poland needed an alliance with the Soviet Union, she should also have alliances with Great Britain, the United States and France. Mikołajczyk was also impressed by Stalin's hostility to Germany and by his statement that communism was 'no more fit for Germany than a saddle for a cow' (F.O. 371. C10483/8/55).
4. At a private meeting, General Rola-Żymerski, head of the department of national defence of the P.C.N.L., had adjured Mikołajczyk to go to Poland as soon as possible. 'If he did not, the Committee would act without him and the result would be the setting up of a Communist Government, whereas if he were to go to Warsaw control would be in his hands' (F.O. 371. C10461/8/55). This was also the view of the Foreign Office who cabled Clark-Kerr that 'we have grave doubts as to whether Mikolajczyk is wise to come back here' (F.O. 371. C10461/8/55).

cooperation of Mikolajczyk and his government.

He believes further that the Committee for Liberation has found that they are not getting the full support of the Polish people and that they realize that they cannot set up competent governmental machinery without the cooperation of himself and the leaders in his government. This situation gives him confidence that some arrangements can be worked out through which all factions can unite. He has however not been able to agree with the Committee on a plan.

The Committee proposed that Mikolajczyk and three members of his government come to Warsaw and join the Committee in establishing a government, Mikolajczyk to head this new government, under the authority of the Polish National Council in Warsaw. This new government would have 18 members of which 14 would be drawn from the present Committee of Liberation or those associated with the Council. The 1935 Constitution would be repudiated and the 1921 Constitution accepted. Mikolajczyk pointed out that this government would have no constitutional basis. He proposed that they continue to work under the 1935 Constitution, much as he himself disliked its provisions. The President should be retained and a new Cabinet formed consisting of the representatives of the four established democratic parties (eliminating the Sanacja[5]) and adding representatives of the Workers Party and, if desired, of the Communists.

After lengthy arguments between the Poles, a meeting was held at which Molotov presided. Molotov listened to the arguments of both sides. It was Mikolajczyk's feeling that Molotov was impressed with his position and appreciated lack of clarity and practicability of the approach of the Committee. Mikolajczyk hopes that he can work out some plan with his colleagues when he returns to London, perhaps finding a way to install a new individual as President. He intends to submit this proposal to Moscow by telegraph and hopes that it will become a basis for discussion which will permit him and some of his associates to return to Warsaw, when taken, to work out the details, including the reaching of an agreement on individuals to be selected to make up the new Cabinet. His primary interest is to join all factions at this time in a government which will have a legal basis and which can hold the country together until such time as a truly free general election can be held to establish a new constitution and government. He is satisfied that the Committee of Liberation has not the standing with the Polish people to take control of Poland without the force of the Red Army, but is fearful that if it once gets control, there will not be a free election.

He was much impressed with the ability of this mysterious figure, Bierut.[6] He cannot figure out who he is or his background. Bierut talks sensibly about the social and economic program for Poland, but admits he has had no experience in politics and wants to leave that to Mikolajczyk. Bierut is impatient with Mikolajczyk when the latter speaks of the necessity of bringing in the party leaders, saying that parties are a thing of the past and that he and his associates represent the Polish masses. His governmental ideas are revolutionary and the question of the authority of the new government does not bother him. Mikolajczyk, on the other hand, lays first importance on the development of a basis for authority of the government and is unwilling to dissociate himself from the constitutional basis of his present government, although he is willing to have complete reorganization of the membership of the government in any reasonable way to meet the wishes of the Committee.[7]

An unsuccessful attempt was made among the Poles to agree on a joint communiqué, but it was verbally agreed that public recriminations should cease. Mikolajczyk doubts that the Committee will live up to this. . .

5. The pre-war governing group.
6. Bierut had been an important member of the underground Communist party of Poland, although not of the inner leadership. For his activities, he was imprisoned (1933–9) by the Polish authorities. He was thus not affected by Stalin's purge of Polish Communists which had culminated in the dissolution of the K.P.P. in 1938 and the death of most of its leaders. In 1943, he had been flown back from Russia to reorganize the communist-controlled Polish Workers' Party formed in January 1942 and he remained on its central committee throughout the war.
7. After Mikołajczyk's talks with the P.C.N.L. but before his final meeting with Stalin, the Soviet leader had written to Churchill that he was convinced that Mikołajczyk had 'inadequate information about the situation in Poland. At the same time, I had the impression that Mikolajczyk is not against ways being found to unite the Poles.' He reaffirmed the offer of the P.C.N.L. to Mikołajczyk of 4 portfolios, including that of premier in a reformed government. Although Mikołajczyk had rejected these terms, he 'hoped things will improve' (Stalin Correspondence, I, No. 315). He wrote in identical terms to Roosevelt on 9 August with a final paragraph asking if Lange, an American citizen, could be allowed to join the P.C.N.L. (Stalin Correspondence, II, No. 218). Churchill replied on 10 August agreeing that some progress had been made and expressing the hope that 'the business will go better in future' (Stalin Correspondence, I, No. 316). In conversation with Harriman, Molotov had also expressed reasonably optimistic views of the situation (F.R.U.S. 1944, III, 1311–3). He felt that agreement could be reached on the distribution of portfolios between the two groups of Poles, but warned that the Poles had always been late:– 'Now they must make up their minds quickly or it will be too late.'

No. 103

Tass communiqué
MOSCOW, 12 August 1944
D.O.P.S.R.II, No. 192

Recently reports have appeared in the foreign Press referring to reports in the newspapers and radio of the Polish émigré Government on the uprising and fighting started in Warsaw on August 1 by order of the Polish émigré Government in London, and which continue up to the present time. At the same time the newspapers and radio of the Polish émigré Government in London hint that they who rose up in Warsaw were allegedly in contact with the Soviet Command, that the latter did not render the necessary assistance. TASS is authorized to declare these statements and hints in the foreign Press either the result of a misunderstanding, or else the manifestation of slander against the Soviet Command.

It is known to TASS that on the side of the Polish London circles who are responsible for what is happening in Warsaw, no attempt was made to inform before-hand the Soviet Military Command, or to coordinate with the Soviet Military Command any kind of action in Warsaw. In view of this, the responsibility for all that is taking place in Warsaw falls exclusively on the Polish émigré circles in London.

No. 104

Mr. Churchill to Marshal Stalin: Letter
LONDON, 12 August 1944
Stalin Correspondence, I, No. 317

I have seen a distressing message from the Poles in Warsaw, who after ten days are still fighting against considerable German forces which have cut the city into three. They implore machine-guns and ammunition. Can you not give them some further help, as the distance from Italy is so very great?

No. 105

Marshal Stalin to Mr. Churchill: Letter (Extract)
MOSCOW, 16 August 1944
Stalin Correspondence, I, No. 321

After a talk with Mr Mikolajczyk I instructed the Red Army Command to drop munitions intensively into the Warsaw area. A liaison officer was parachuted, but headquarters report that he did not reach his objective, being killed by the Germans.

Now, after probing more deeply into the Warsaw affair, I have come to the conclusion that the Warsaw cation is a reckless and fearful gamble, taking a heavy toll of the population. This would not have been the case had Soviet headquarters been informed beforehand about the Warsaw action and had the Poles maintained contact with them.[1]

Things being what they are, Soviet headquarters have decided that they must dissociate themselves from the Warsaw adventure since they cannot assume either direct or indirect responsibility for it. . .[2]

1. Stalin also sent a similar message to Mikołajczyk, who replied in conciliatory language pleading with Stalin to allow the American mission to go ahead (F.R.U.S. 1944, III, pp. 1379–81).
2. On the receipt of this message, Eden summoned Gusev, the Soviet Ambassador on 18 August and informed him of the extreme disquiet of the British at the Soviet position (F.O. 371. C10926/61/55).

No. 106

Andrei Vyshinsky to Averell Harriman: Letter
MOSCOW, 15 August 1944
F.O. 371. C1073/8/55

In connexion with your letter of August 14th addressed to the People's Commissar for Foreign Affairs, V.M. Molotov, stating that a unit of American Air Forces has received an urgent directive to clear with Air Forces of Red Army the question of the possibility of carrying out a shuttle flight from England so that the bombers and fighters should proceed across to bases in the Soviet Union and also a proposal regarding the necessity of concerting with Soviet Air Forces of a similar attempt to drop arms in Warsaw if such an operation should be undertaken on that day from the Soviet side, I am instructed by People's Commissar to state that the Soviet Government cannot go along with this. The outbreak in Warsaw into which Warsaw population has been drawn is purely the work of adventurers and the Soviet Government cannot lend its hand to it. Marshal I. V. Stalin on the fifth of August informed Mr. W. Churchill[1] that it could not be supposed that a few Polish detachments, the so called National Army, could take Warsaw when it does not possess artillery, aviation or tanks at a time when the Germans had assigned for defence of Warsaw four tank divisions.[2]

1. See above No. 102, doc. 2, note 3.
2. On receipt of this letter, Harriman and Clark-Kerr decided to make a joint approach to Molotov. Because of his alleged absence, they were received by Vyshinsky. They stated that they regarded the decision of the Soviet Union as a 'grave mistake' and stressed that no Soviet participation in arms drops was being requested. Vyshinsky refused to modify his position and reiterated that the Soviet Government did not wish to encourage 'adventuristic actions' (F.R.U.S. 1944, III, pp. 1375–6; F. O. 371. C10730/8/55). The Soviet action led Harriman to cable Hull,
   'For the first time since coming to Moscow I am gravely concerned by the attitude of the Soviet Government in its refusal to permit us to assist the Poles in Warsaw as well as in its own policy of apparent inactivity. If Vyshinski correctly reflects the position of the Soviet Government, its refusal is based not on operational difficulties or denial that the resistance exists but on ruthless political considerations' (F.R.U.S. 1944, III, pp. 1376–7).

No. 107

Averell Harriman to Cordell Hull and the President: Telegram
MOSCOW, 17 August 1944
Roosevelt Papers, President's Secretary's File, Poland

The British Ambassador requested an appointment with Stalin for himself and me.[1] As Stalin was said to be too busy Molotov received us tonight at

1. For a more detailed account by Harriman, see F.R.U.S. 1944, III, pp. 1386–9, for both Clark-Kerr's account, F.O. 371. C10909/61/55. Harriman's instructions are printed in F.R.U.S. 1944, III, pp. 1378–9, Clark-Kerr's instructions are in F.O. 371. C10730/61/55.

10 o'clock.

During the three hours of argument in which the British Ambassador presented the views of his government and I explained the unfortunate reaction that would result in the United States if the Soviets adhered to their position of refusing aid to the Poles fighting in Warsaw Molotov adamantly maintained the position that they were adventurers antagonistic to the Soviet Union and that the Soviet Government could not lend its support to them directly or indirectly. The decision of the Soviet Government could not be reconsidered and the Soviet Government would know its friends by those who accepted its position.

Molotov admitted that August 9 Marshal Stalin had promised Mikolajczyk that he would give aid but explained that because of the newspaper and radio statements emanating from Polish emigre government sources in London it was evident by the twelfth of August that the movement was inspired by men antagonistic to the Soviet Union and therefore the Soviet Government could no longer countenance any association with the uprising.

In order that there could be no misunderstanding I questioned Molotov persistently to ascertain whether the Soviets had received any information from Warsaw which had influenced their decision but after first being vague he finally admitted unequivocally that their decision to abandon the Poles in Warsaw was based on the publicly known newspaper and radio criticisms of the good faith of the Red Army operations attacking Warsaw and of the Soviet Government's motivation generally towards the Poles.

Molotov was obviously following the line of his instructions and it was futile to reason with him.

As you know, I have been consistently optimistic and patient in dealing with our various difficulties with the Soviet Government. My recent conversations with Vyshinski and particularly with Molotov tonight lead me to the opinion that these men are bloated with power and expect that they can force their will on us and all countries to accept their decisions without questions.[2]

From Clark-Kerr's cables it appears to be the British Government's view that if Stalin goes back on his promise to Mikolajczyk to aid the Poles in Warsaw there is little hope for a Polish settlement.[3] From here this conclusion seems unavoidable.

I am still hopeful that if this subject with all its implications can be presented to Stalin a reconsideration of the Soviet position can be obtained. I recommend that I be instructed to press for an interview with Stalin. I assume of course that I will be receiving your views.

2. On August 17, Harriman had again unsuccessfully approach Vyshinsky for permission for a shuttle bombing mission which would drop supplies on Warsaw (Roosevelt papers, President's Secretary's File, Poland).
3. The relevant paragraph in Clark-Kerr instructions read
    '4. What is, however, equally important is the effect of the latest Soviet attitude upon M. Mikolajczyk's position and therefore upon the prospect of an eventual satisfactory

solution of the Polish problems. It is clear from his own account of his talks in Moscow that M. Mikolajczyk has returned with the determination to base his future policy upon faith in Soviet good intentions. He is prepared to go very far with his colleagues here to bring about a solution in the sense desired by the Soviet Government. His main trump card in playing his difficult hand was Marshal Stalin's undertaking to send help to Warsaw. He has no doubt already made much of this and it is a matter to which the Polish troops now fighting so effectively in Italy, Normandy and elsewhere naturally attribute the highest importance. If the present Soviet attitude is maintained I fear M. Mikolajczyk's personal position will be fatally harmed. At the best, he will be unable to proceed at this stage with the efforts he is now making to unite Polish political forces behind a policy of friendship with the Soviet Union. At the worst, the possibility of such a settlement may be irretrievably compromised' (F.O. 371. C10730/61/55).

The British had reached this conclusion on the basis of a conversation between Eden and Mikołajczyk on 14 August (F.O. 371. C10768/8/55). The failure to secure effective help for the Warsaw insurgents did indeed seriously undermine Mikołajczyk's position and on September 5, he had told Eden, to the latter's great dismay, that he was on the point of resignation (F.O. 371. C11843/8/55).

No. 108

Mr. Churchill and President Roosevelt to Marshal Stalin: Letter[1]
LONDON AND WASHINGTON, 20 August 1944
Roosevelt Papers, President's Secretary's File, Poland

We are thinking of world opinion if the anti-Nazis in Warsaw are in effect abandoned. We believe that all three of us should do the utmost to save as many of the patriots there as possible. We hope that you will drop immediate supplies and munitions to the patriot Poles in Warsaw, or you will agree to help our planes in doing it very quickly. We hope you will approve. The time element is of extreme importance.

1. This joint approach was proposed by Churchill after an appeal by Mikołajczyk (Roosevelt papers, President's Secretary's File, Poland). In general, as Hull cabled Harriman on 19 August, the Americans were not prepared to go as far as the British in putting pressure on the Soviets for fear of imperilling their shuttle bombing arrangement in the U.S.S.R. (F.R.U.S. 1944, III, pp. 1381–2).

No. 109

Marshal Stalin to President Roosevelt and Mr. Churchill: Letter
MOSCOW, 22 August 1944
Stalin Correspondence, I, No. 323

The message from you and Mr Roosevelt about Warsaw has reached me. I should like to state my views.

Sooner or later the truth about the handful of power-seeking criminals who launched the Warsaw adventure will out. Those elements, playing on the credulity of the inhabitants of Warsaw, exposed practically unarmed people to German guns, armour and aircraft. The result is a situation in which every day is used, not by the Poles for freeing Warsaw, but by the Hitlerites, who are cruelly exterminating the civil population.

From the military point of view the situation, which keeps German attention riveted to Warsaw, is highly unfavourable both to the Red Army and to the Poles. Nevertheless, the Soviet troops, who of late have had to face renewed German counter-attacks, are doing all they can to repulse the Hitlerite sallies and go over to a new large-scale offensive near Warsaw, I can assure you that the Red Army will stint no effort to crush the Germans at Warsaw and liberate it for the Poles. That will be the best, really effective, help to the anti-Nazi Poles.[1]

1. The response to this letter illustrated very closely the difference between the British and American positions on aid to Poland. Churchill after consulting Eden, who was even in favour of American aircraft 'gate-crashing' Russian airfields, suggested to Roosevelt that another joint letter should be sent (F.O. 371. C11637/8/55). Roosevelt replied that he was not opposed to the Prime Minister making a further approach, but that in view of current American conversations 'in regard to the subsequent use of other Soviet bases, I do not consider it advantageous to the long range general war prospect for me to join with you in the proposed message to Uncle J' (F.O. 371. C11362/61/55). Roosevelt even cabled Churchill on 5 September with obvious relief, after receiving a false report that the rising had collapsed,
    'The problem of relief for the Poles in Warsaw has therefore unfortunately been solved by delay and by German action and there now appears to be nothing we can do to assist them' (Roosevelt papers, President's Secretary's File).
    In these conditions, the War Cabinet as a whole sent a message to the Soviet Government (See below, No. 110).

No. 110

His Majesty's Government to Mr. Molotov: Message
LONDON, 4 September 1944
Roosevelt Papers, President's Secretary's File, Poland

The War Cabinet at their meeting to-day considered the latest reports of the situation in Warsaw which show that the Poles fighting against the Germans there are in desperate straits.

2. The War Cabinet wish the Soviet Government to know that the public opinion in this country is deeply moved by the events in Warsaw and by the terrible sufferings of the Poles there. Whatever the rights and wrongs about the beginnings of the Warsaw rising, the people of Warsaw themselves cannot be held responsible for the decision taken. Our people cannot understand why no material help has been sent from outside to the Poles in Warsaw. The fact that such help could not be sent on account of your Government's refusal to allow United States aircraft to land on Aerodromes in Russian hands is now becoming publicly known. If on top of all this the Poles in Warsaw should now be overwhelmed by the Germans, as we are told they must be within two or three days, the shock to public opinion here will be incalculable. The War Cabinet themselves find it hard to understand your Government's refusal to take account of the obligations of the British and American Governments to help the Poles in Warsaw. Your Government's action in preventing this help

being sent seems to us a variance with the spirit of Allied co-operation to which you and we attach so much importance both for the present and the future.

3. Out of regard for Marshal Stalin and for the Soviet peoples, with whom it is our earnest desire to work in future years, the War Cabinet have asked me to make this further appeal to the Soviet Government to give whatever help may be in their power, and above all to provide facilities for United States aircraft to land on your airfields for this purpose.

No. 111

Mr. Molotov to His Majesty's Government: Message (Extract)
MOSCOW, 9 September 1944
Roosevelt Papers, President's Secretary's File, Poland

The Soviet Government on September 5th received a message from British Government on the question of Warsaw.

The Soviet Government has already informed the British Government of their opinion that members of Polish Émigré Government in London are responsible for Warsaw adventure undertaken without the knowledge of Soviet Military Command, and in violation of the latter's operational plans.

The Soviet Government would like an unprejudiced commission to be organised with the object of ascertaining exactly by whose order the rising in Warsaw was undertaken and who was to blame for the fact that Soviet Military Command was not informed thereof in advance. . .

Nobody will be able to reproach Soviet Government with the allegation that they rendered inadequate aid to the Polish people including Warsaw. The most practical form of help is active military operation of the Soviet troops against the German invaders of Poland and the liberation of more than one fourth of Poland. All this is the work of the Soviet troops and of the Soviet troops only who are shedding their blood for the liberation of Poland. There is again the hardly effective form of help to Warsaw people namely the dropping of weapons, medical stores and food from aircraft. We have several times dropped both weapons and food for Warsaw insurgents but we have each time received information that the load dropped had fallen into the hands of the Germans. However, if you are so firmly convinced of the efficacy of this form of assistance and insist upon Soviet Command organising jointly with British and Americans such aid, the Soviet Government are prepared to agree to it. However it is necessary to render this aid in accordance with a pre-arranged plan.

As regards your attempt to make Soviet Government in any degree responsible for Warsaw adventure and for the sacrifices of the Warsaw people, the Soviet Government cannot regard this otherwise than as a wish to shift responsibility "from a sick head to a clear one". The same must be said on the point that the Soviet Governments position in the Warsaw question is apparently contrary to the spirit of Allied co-operation. There can be no doubt that if the British Government had taken steps to see that the Soviet Command had been warned of proposed Warsaw rising in good time, then events in Warsaw would have taken a totally different turn. . .

As regards public opinion in various countries the Soviet Government express their complete confidence in the fact that true statement of the facts regarding events in Warsaw will give public opinion every reason uncondition- ally to condemn the authors of Warsaw adventure and correctly to understand the position of the Soviet Government. It would only be necessary to try to enlighten public opinion thoroughly about the truth of events in Warsaw.[1]

1. The British Government were greatly encouraged by this change in the Soviet position. Churchill wrote to Eden, 'This is really a great triumph for our persistence in hammering at the Russians where we had a good case' (F.O. 371. C12788/1077/55). He thought that the time was ripe 'to push ahead with the Russo-Polish business' and informed Eden that he was going to press Mikołajczyk to drop Sosnkowski and resume his contacts with the Soviets through Lebedev. Eden agreed with this line of policy. When he saw Mikołajczyk on 13 and 19 September, he tried to persuade him to remove Sosnkowski and undertake a trip to Moscow (F.O. 371. C12010/1077/55, C12658/8/55). On 28 September, after strong British pressure, President Raczkiewicz did finally agree to relieve Sosnkowski of his post. He was replaced by General Bor-Komorowski, Commander of the Polish forces in Warsaw (who was shortly afterwards taken captive by the Germans), an appointment violently attacked by the Soviets and the P.C.N.L. Supply flights to Warsaw were delayed by bad weather, but a big American shuttle operation took place on 18 September. Permission for a second large drop was refused by the Soviets. On 4 October, the insurgents in Warsaw finally surrendered.

No. 112

The Moscow talks of October 1944

1. Anthony Eden to Sir Orme Sargent: Telegram (Extract)
MOSCOW, 12 October 1944
F.O. 371. C14115/8/55

In conversation after dinner at the Embassy last night Marshal Stalin was at great pains to assure the Prime Minister that failure to relieve Warsaw had not been due to any lack of efforts by the Red Army. The failure was due entirely to the enemy's strength and difficulties of terrain. Marshal Stalin could not admit this failure before the world. Exactly the same situation had arisen at Kiev which in the end had only been liberated by outflanking movement. The Prime Minister said he accepted this view absolutely and he assured Marshal Stalin that no serious persons in the United Kingdom had credited reports that failure had been deliberate. Criticism had only referred to the apparent unwillingness of the Soviet Government to send aeroplanes. Mr. Harriman who was present said that the same was true of the people in America.

2. The Prime Minister and I then sought to impress on Marshal Stalin how essential it was in the interests of Anglo-Soviet relations that the Polish

question should now be settled on a basis which would seem reasonable to the British people.[1] The Prime Minister emphasised how we had entered the war for the sake of Poland although we had no sordid or material interest in that country. The British people would not understand that she should be let down. The London Poles and Lublin Poles must now be told that they must agree together. If they refused or were unable to agree then the British and Soviet Governments, the two great Allies, must themselves impose a reasonable settlement.

3. Later in the evening I had a long conversation with M. Molotov on the same subject. Mr. Harriman also took part. M. Molotov spoke well of Mikolajczyk but said that on his previous visit he had given the impression of being willing but weak. I said this time we must ensure that he did not return to London but that he should form a new Government here on the basis of his proposals and should proceed to Lublin. M. Molotov said that he had regretted M. Mikolajczyk's departure last time. If he had said no they would have been sorry but they would have understood. If he had said yes they would have been very glad. He said neither no nor yes but simply disappeared. They could not stop him going. M. Molotov spoke of 1935 constitution as symbol of Fascist past which only aroused memories of Marshal Pilsudski and Colonel Beck. I maintained that the constitutional issue was now only of secondary interest since our aim should be fusion of the two parties with a view to election in Warsaw for a new constituent assembly. . .

1. On 9 October, Churchill and Eden had induced Stalin to invite Mikołajczyk to come to Moscow. After some hesitation Mikołajczyk, Romer and Grabski left for Moscow on the night of 10–11 October.
    Churchill's arguments to Stalin followed the line of reasoning set out in a memorandum for the Secretary of State by Frank Roberts dated 4 October. Roberts claimed that the main issue was no longer the frontier problem but the 'internal organization of the new Poland', and the different interpretation which the British and Soviets placed on concepts like 'independence' or 'friendship'. In this respect, he argued, the British position was fundamentally weak, since the Soviets could find many pretexts for objecting to the Polish government-in-exile. He thus concluded that 'our only hope of achieving our prupose of an early and definite solution by a fusion of the two Polish organizations and M. Mikołajczyk's return to Moscow would seem to be to persuade the Russians that the future of Anglo-Soviet cooperation is really dependent on this' (F.O. 371. C1410/8/55).

2. Sir Alexander Cadogan to Viscount Halifax: Telegram
    LONDON, 21 October 1944
    F.O. 371. C14452/8/55

Following is summary for your confidential background information of negotiations which have been taking place in Moscow regarding Poland.[1]

1. On 13th October full meeting with Poles took place when Marshal

1. For the full British record, F.O. 371. C14300, 14874, 14222, 14875, 14223, 14281, 14551, 14553/8/55; for the Polish record, D.O.P.S.R. II, Nos. 237–46; for Harriman's account, F.R.U.S. 1944, III, pp. 1322–6; F.R.U.S. Yalta, pp. 204–5.

Stalin, Molotov, the Prime Minister and Secretary of State saw Messrs. Mikolajczyk, Romer and Grabski. Sir A. Clark-Kerr and Mr. Harriman were also present. M. Mikolajczyk went through point by point his memorandum of 20th August and M. Grabski gave an account of his conversation with M. Lebedev when communicating the memorandum to him.[2] Marshal Stalin observed that the memorandum ignored the existence of the Polish Committee of National Liberation and did not provide a solution of the eastern frontier question: with regard to the latter, Stalin insisted on the Curzon Line. Prime Minister urged M. Mikolajczyk to realise that United Kingdom Government fully supported the Soviet attitude on this because a solution on this basis would provide the best guarantee for the future of Poland.

2. Later on 13th October a similar meeting was held with M. Berut, M. Morawski and General Zymierski. They were told of the earlier meeting with the Polish Government and Prime Minister stressed the paramount need for all Poles to sink their differences and unite against the Germans. M. Berut, supported by M. Morawski, embarked upon a long catalogue of grievances against M. Mikolajczyk and his Government and did not make a good impression. Prime Minister chided them for being cantankerous and un-cooperative, while Marshal Stalin appeared to be chiefly concerned with the acceptance of the Curzon Line and to care little about the Committee's domestic ambitions and bickerings.

3. On 14th October the Prime Minister and the Secretary of State had an informal meeting with Messrs. Mikolajczyk, Romer and Grabski at which Prime Minister emphasised the supreme importance of agreeing to the Curzon Line, in return for which Poland would enjoy our full support and a British Ambassador would be accredited to M.Mikolajczyk's Goverment in that country. M. Mikolajczyk urged that if the Curzon Line were insisted upon

2. This memorandum was first presented to O'Malley on 25 August (F.O. 371. C11344/8/55) and a revised version was given to him on 31 August (F.O. 371. C11598/8/55; D.O.P.S.R. II, No. 214). It argued that after the liberation of Warsaw, the Polish Governmen should be reconstructed and should be composed in equal strength of the Peasant Party, the National-Democratic Party, the Polish Socialist Party, the Christian Democratic Labour Party and the Polish Workers Party. The participation in the government of 'Fascist-minded and non-democratic political groups' as well as those 'responsible for the pre-September 1939 system of government' was precluded. The new government was to conclude an 'agreement with the Soviet Government with the view to the joint prosecution of the war against Germany and the laying of foundations for a desirable Polish-Soviet friendship after the war based on a Polish-Soviet Alliance. . .' On the territorial question, the manifesto affirmed that Poland could not emerge from this war diminished in territory. 'In the East, the main centres of Polish cultural life and the sources of raw materials indispensable to the economic life of the country shall remain within Polish boundaries.'
    When O'Malley pointed out that these terms would be totally unacceptable to the Soviets, Romer stated that he and Mikolajczyk saw the programme as 'a basis for further discussion' and made a number of glosses on the text. He stated firstly that Mikołajczyk was prepared for the P.C.N.L. to have considerably more than 20% of the portfolios in the new government, since it included members of parties apart from the Polish Workers Party. He also stated that Raczkiewcz could be replaced as President and a new constituion could be discussed. Frontiers were also certainly negotiable.

Poland would have to be given territories in the west. A draft formula was prepared to cover these points and at a private meeting with Prime Minister Marshal Stalin agreed in principle to a solution on the lines proposed.[3]

4. On 16th October Prime Minister and the Poles discussed the draft formula, but the latter insisted on an amendment to specify that the Curzon Line in its southern section should be so drawn as to leave Lwow in Poland. Prime Minister and Secretary of State pointed out that this would clearly be unacceptable to Marshal Stalin and urged M. Mikolajczyk not to wreck the negotiations on this issue. On M. Mikolajczyk's insistence, however, Prime Minister referred the point to Marshal Stalin, who listened attentively but was adamant on retaining Lwow for Russia, as being in the midst of Ukranian territories.

5. On 16th October the Secretary of State gave the Poles an account of the conversation with Marshal Stalin, explaining that the latter appeared genuinely anxious to reach a settlement but would clearly insist on retaining Lwow. The Polish Prime Minister seemed to have formed a fair assessment of the position and further amendments were accordingly made in the draft declaration referred to in paragraph 3 above; the most important accepted the Curzon Line as a line of demarcation but not as a final agreed frontier.[4] Prime Minister thereupon showed Marshal Stalin the latest revised draft of the declaration, but the latter would not accept its wording, insisting that the Poles should agree to the Curzon Line 'as the basis of the frontier between Russia and Poland', not merely 'as the line of demarcation' between the two countries. M. Mikolajczyk, however, maintained that he could not fall in with Marshal Stalin's wishes without losing control not only of his followe s in London but of the troops and people in Poland itself. He expressed his anxiety, on the other hand, to see Berut before leaving Moscow and attempt to reach with him some agreement on the other outstanding issues, such as the composition of the new United Polish Government and the problem of the Presidency. He also considered it important to see Stalin and make clear to him his anxiety to reach agreement and exchange ideas about the possible constitution of the new Polish Government. If successful in this field, he would have something to show to his followers as a palliative for accepting the Curzon Line. He would then return to London, if only for a brief visit for necessary consultation. Prime Minister agreed with his proposed action and has prepared the way with the Russians.

6. Both Marshal Stalin and Prime Minister felt that it was not desirable to proceed with an attempt to form a United Polish Government without the frontier question being agreed. Had this been settled Stalin was quite willing

3. Following his meeting with Stalin, Churchill had another meeting with the Poles at which the draft declaration was revised on suggestions from the Poles to make clear that the British government took full responsibility for the settlement and that the Poles had only accepted it in response to strong pressure. More emphasis was also laid on Poland's gains in the west (for the draft declaration, see below, No. 112, doc. 3).

4. For these amendments, see below No. 112, doc. 4.

that M. Mikolajczyk should be head of the new government. Prime Minister felt that difficulties no less obstinate would arise in discussions for the merger of the Polish Government with the Lublin Poles, who had made the worst possible impression upon both him and the Foreign Secretary. In the circumstances the best course would be for the two Polish delegations to return whence they came though only M. Mikolajczyk and his Ministers would know what had passed and the state of the negotiations.

7. Marshal Stalin received M. Mikolajczyk alone on 18th October. Latter had recently had a long conversation with M. Berut who gave the impression that he was not confident of his ability to deal with difficulties confronting him. Berut was accommodating on the constitutional issue and willing to discuss formation of a united Government, though holding out for an absolute majority of seats. Encouraged by this interview M. Mikolajczyk explained to Marshal Stalin his willingness to form a united and friendly government prepared to cooperate with Russians. He mentioned some names which he had in mind and Stalin did not dissent. M. Mikolajczyk had formed the impression that Stalin would agree in principle to his proposal for five major political parties including the National Democrats being represented in the new government. He found Stalin friendly and receptive and apparently anxious for Mikolajczyk to return to Poland soon. He is returning to London very shortly to discuss position further with his colleagues here.[5]

5. After the meeting with Stalin, Mikołajczyk told Eden that he was flying back to London at once 'in order to win over his followers to support his plan including acceptance of Curzon Line frontier' (F.O. 371. C14453/8/55). At a dinner after Mikołajczyk's departure Stalin at first told Churchill that he would be prepared to let Mikołajczyk's followers have 50% of the portfolios in a new government but 'rapidly corrected himself to a worse figure' (F.R.U.S. Yalta, p. 206; F. O. 371. C14877/8/55).

3. Draft declaration submitted by the British to the Polish delegation
MOSCOW, 15 October 1944
F.O. 371. C14222/8/55

The British and Soviet Governments, upon the conclusion of discussions at Moscow in October 1944 between themselves and with Polish Government have reached the following agreement:

Upon unconditional surrender of Germany the territory of Poland in the West will include the Free City of Danzig, regions of West Prussia West and South of Konigsberg, administrative district of Oppeln-in-Silesia and lands desired by Poland [1] to the East of line of the Oder. It is further agreed that possession of these territories shall be guaranteed to Poland by Soviet and British Governments. It is understood that the Germans in the said regions shall be repatriated to Germany and that all Poles in Germany shall at their wish be repatriated to Poland.

1. This phrase was inserted at the request of the Poles in place of 'as may subsequently pass to Poland.'

In consideration of the foregoing agreement, and upon the urgent advice of His Majesty's Government, the Polish Government are forced to submit to the necessity of accepting the Curzon Line[2] as the basis of future Polish-Russian frontiers, and undertake to recommend such a settlement to their Parliament. It is agreed that necessary measures will be taken for transfer of all persons of both countries desiring to change their allegiance in accordance with their freely expressed wishes.

Separate Soviet-Polish agreements will regulate reciprocal transfer and repatriation of population of both Countries, and release of persons detained.[3]

It is agreed that a Polish Government of National United under Prime Minister Mikolajczyk will be set up at once in territory already liberated by Russian arms.

The Soviet Government take this occasion to reaffirm their unchanging policy of supporting the establishment within the territorial limits set forth, of a sovereign independent Poland, free in every way to manage its own affairs, and their intention to make a treaty of durable friendship and mutual aid with the Polish Government which, it is understood, will be established on an anti-fascist and democratic basis.

The treaties and relationships existing between Poland and other countries will be unaffected by this settlement, the parties to which declare again their implacable resolve to wage war against Nazi tyranny until it has surrendered unconditionally.

2. The text here printed is that cabled back to the Foreign Office on 15 October. It differs from that in the parallel set of drafts assembled by D. Allen under F. O. 371. C14869/8/55. This reads 'the Polish Government are prepared to admit the necessity of accepting the Curzon Line. . .'
3. This sentence was inserted at the request of the Poles. It is not in the final draft of the Allen file, but is in the text telegraphed on 18 October (F.R.U.S. 1944, III, pp. 1327–8).

4. Suggested amendment to draft declaration
MOSCOW, 16 October 1944
F.O. 371. C14281/8/55

Paragraph 3 to read:—

In consideration of the foregoing agreement, the Polish Government accept Curzon Line as the line of demarcation between Poland and U.S.S.R.

Separate Soviet-Polish agreement will regulate reciprocal transfer and repatriation of the population of both countries and the release of persons detained. It is agreed that the necessary measures will be taken for the transfer of all persons of both countries desiring to change their allegiance in accordance with their freely expressed wishes.[1]

1. Stalin made two changes in this amended draft before accepting it:—
    1. In paragraph 3 for 'line of demarcation' substitute 'basis for frontier'.
    2. Paragraph 5 should read, 'It is agreed that a Polish Government of National Unity

in accordance with agreement (or understanding) reached between the Polish Government in London and Polish Committee of National Liberation in Lublin will be set up in territory already liberated by Russian armies.'

In proposing this amendment, Stalin stated that 'he agreed that M. Mikołajczyk should be Prime Minister' (F.O. 371. C14452/8/55).

No. 113

Sir Alexander Cadogan to Tadeusz Romer: Letter
LONDON, 2 November 1944
D.O.P.S.R. II, No. 256

I DULY reported to the Prime Minister the conversation which I had with your Excellency and the Polish Ambassador on the 31st October, in the course of which you put to me three questions for the consideration of His Majesty's Government.[1]

2. The Prime Minister, after consultation with the Cabinet,[2] has now directed me to give you the following replies.

3. You asked in the first place whether, even in the event of the United States Government finding themselves unable to agree to the changes in the western frontier of Poland foreshadowed in the recent conversations in Moscow, His Majesty's Government would still advocate these changes at the Peace Settlement. The answer of His Majesty's Government to this question is in the affirmative.

4. Secondly, you enquired whether His Majesty's Government were definitely in favour of advancing the Polish frontier up to the line of the Oder, to include the port of Stettin. The answer is that His Majesty's Government do consider that Poland should have the right to extend her territory to this extent.

5. Finally, you enquired whether His Majesty's Government would guarantee the independence and integrity of the new Poland. To this the answer is that His Majesty's Government are prepared to give such a guarantee jointly with the Soviet Government. If the United States Government could see their way to join also, that would plainly be of the greatest advantage though His Majesty's Government would not make this a condition of their own guarantee in conjunction with that of the Soviet Government. This Anglo-Soviet guarantee would, in the view of His Majesty's Government, remain valid until effectively merged in the general guarantee which it is hoped may be afforded by the projected World Organisation.

6. With regard to what you said in regard to anticipated difficulties in the way of negotiations in Moscow for a reformation of the Polish Govern-

1. Mikołajczyk found much greater difficulty than he had anticipated in persuading his cabinet colleagues to accept his policy. Already on 26 October, he told Churchill that he did not know whether he would be able to get his views accepted (F.O. 371. C14877/8/55; D.O.P.S.R. II, No. 50).
2. These questions were discussed in the cabinet on 1 November (WM.(44)143.C.A.).1

ment, the Prime Minister observes that the success of these negotiations must depend on a solution of the frontier question. It is impossible to ignore the possibility that agreement might be reached on the frontier question and that it might nevertheless prove impossible to reach agreement on the other matter. That would, of course, be most unfortunate, but the Polish Government would be in a much better position if negotiations broke down on this point, on which they would have the support of His Majesty's Government and probably of the United States Government, than on the frontier question.[3]

3. These answers did not satisfy the Polish Council of Ministers which voted on 3 November against Mikołajczyk's policy. Mikołajczyk hesitated to inform the British of this (he had been subjected to a blistering attack by Churchill on 2 November, F.O. 371. C15255/8/55; D.O.P.S.R.II, No. 257), and, in a further attempt to win over his cabinet, instructed his ambassador in the United States on 6 November to ask the Americans a series of questions (See below No. 114, also D.O.P.S.R.II, No. 262). In addition, the Poles attempted to obtain clearer guarantees from the British and a renewal of the Anglo-Polish alliance (F.O. 371. C15747/62/55). Churchill wrote to Stalin on 5 November that 'he had not been idle' in relation to the Poles who were waiting for the U.S. reply to their queries. (Stalin Correspondence I, No. 344). Stalin replied on 9 November that 'Mr. Mikolajczyk, to the detriment of his own chances, is wasting much valuable time' (Stalin Correspondence, I, No. 347).

No. 114

President Roosevelt to Mr. Mikołajczyk: Letter
WASHINGTON, 17 November 1944
F.R.U.S. 1944, III, pp. 1334–5

I have had constantly in mind the problems you are facing in your endeavors to bring about an equitable and permanent solution of the Polish-Soviet difficulties and particularly the questions which you raised in your message of October 26.[1] I have asked Ambassador Harriman, who will bring you this letter, to discuss with you the question of Lwow.[2]

While I would have preferred to postpone the entire question of this Government's attitude until the general postwar settlement in Europe, I fully realize your urgent desire to receive some indication of the position of the United States Government with the least possible delay. Therefore, I am giving below in broad outline the general position of this Government in the hope that it may be of some assistance to you in your difficult task.[3]

1. D.O.P.S.R. II, No. 249. In this letter Mikołajczyk appealed to Roosevelt to intervene to secure Lwow and the East Galician oilfields for Poland.
2. Harriman told Mikołajczyk on 22 November that Roosevelt had instructed him to intervene with Stalin over the question of Lwów and the oil district if the Polish Government desired this. He also stated that his own belief was that this intervention would be fruitless (D.O.P.S.R. II, No. 269).
3. Ciechanowski had been instructed to consult the American Government on the following issues:
   1. Would the U.S. support the westward extension of the Polish frontier?
   2. Would the U.S. advocate and support the 'real independence' of Poland in her new frontiers?
   3. Would the U.S. be prepared to provide large-scale U.S. aid for Poland? (D.O.P.S.R.II, No. 262).

1. The United States Government stands unequivocally for a strong, free and independent Polish state with the untrammeled rights of the Polish people to order their internal existence as they see fit.

2. In regard to the future frontiers of Poland, if a mutual agreement on this subject including the proposed compensation for Poland from Germany is reached between the Polish, Soviet and British Governments, this Government would offer no objection. In so far as the United States guarantee of any specific frontiers is concerned I am sure you will understand that this Government, in accordance with its traditional policy, cannot give a guarantee for any specific frontiers. As you know, the United States Government is working for the establishment of a world security organization through which the United States together with the other member states will assume responsibility for general security which, of course, includes the inviolability of agreed frontiers.

3. If the Polish Government and people desire in connection with the new frontiers of the Polish state to bring about the transfer to and from the territory of Poland of national minorities, the United States Government will raise no objection and as far as practicable will facilitate such transfer.

4. The United States Government is prepared, subject to legislative authority, to assist in so far as practicable in the postwar economic reconstruction of the Polish state.[4]

4. Romer told O'Malley on 24 November that the Polish Government had 'found Mr. Roosevelt's letter less non-committed and unhelpful than they had feared, while falling far short of what they would have liked to receive' (F.O. 371. C16359/8/55).

No. 115

Averell Harriman to President Roosevelt and Edward Stettinius: Telegram
23 November 1944
F.R.U.S. 1944, III, pp. 1335–6

I lunched with Mikolajczyk and Romer today.[1] Mikolajczyk told me that since receipt of your letter, he had had discussions with his associates in his Government. He is now convinced that he can not get any support for his program for reconciliation with the Soviets and the Lublin Poles.

He has obtained from the Peasant Party leaders within Poland complete support and authority to act but the leaders of the other three parties in his Government are all definitely opposed to settlement at the present time. Under the circumstances he cannot now in fairness ask you to intervene with Stalin in an attempt to obtain a more favorable settlement of the boundary to include the Lwow area, since, even if Stalin would agree to inclusion of Lwow within Poland, he could not obtain the consent of his associates to any boundary settlement now. Therefore, unless you instruct me otherwise, I

1. For Romer's version of this conversation, see D.O.P.S.R. II, No. 269.

will not discuss the question of Lwow at this time with Stalin.

Mikolajczyk is very grateful to you for your letter and for your sympathetic consideration of the Polish problems. He will so communicate to you direct. He asked me to express to you his apologies for having asked you to intervene at a time when it develops he cannot obtain the support of his associates in attempting to reach a realistic settlement with the Russians.

Mikolajczyk said his associates were convinced what [that] the Soviet policy was to communize Poland, and that they intended to wait until Poland was liberated, to retain within Poland a resistance to Russian domination, and to hope that at some future time the influence of Great Britain and the United States might be brought to bear on Russia to induce her to give the Polish people a free right of choice of their Government. Mikolajczyk personally does not agree with this policy and deeply regrets that he cannot get his associates to join him in making an earnest attempt now to find a solution.[2]

Under these circumstances, it is Mikolajczyk's intention, after a further talk with Churchill and Eden, to resign. He feels that if he remains Prime Minister, he will be involved in recriminations and counterrecriminations with the Russians, that no good will come from it and that his usefulness in the future to his people will be destroyed.

I am waiting over one more day to see Churchill and Eden and will report to you their reaction to these developments.[3]

Mikolajczyk told me further that the Communist influence in the Lublin Committee was increasing[;] that several of the more independent individuals had been forced out or had resigned; and that he is fearful terrorism and counterterrorism will result. He is very pessimistic over the developments in London and Lublin and feels that his best course is to withdraw, keeping himself available to be of use if the moment arises in the future. He does not believe that the Lublin Committee, even with full Soviet support, can control Polish sentiment and that some day some compromise may be found which will give a chance for expression of Polish nationalism.

2. Romer told O'Malley on 24 November when informing him of Mikołajczyk's intention to resign, that Mikołajczyk and he, while seeing some force in the arguments of the opposition, felt that attempts to achieve a negotiated settlement should be continued. They fully realised the immense risks of such a course, but preferred it to what they foresee as the alternative, namely the mass deportation to Siberia by the Soviet Government of the best elements of the Polish population and the destruction, by this and comparable means, of the spirit of the Polish nation' (F.O. 371. C16359/8/55). Mikołajczyk resigned on the same day.

3. Mikołajczyk saw Eden on 27 November to explain the reasons for his resignation D.O.P.S.R. II, No. 274, F.O. 371. C16409/8/55). Eden informed the War Cabinet of the situation on the same day (WM(44)57 C.A.).

CHAPTER FIVE

FROM DECEMBER 1944 TO THE POTSDAM CONFERENCE

No. 116

Mr. Churchill to Marshal Stalin: Letter
LONDON, 3 December 1944
Stalin Correspondence, I, No. 362

I have seen Mr. Mikolajczyk, who has explained to me the reason for his resignation. Briefly, the position is that he could not count on the support of important sections of his cabinet for his policy and was, therefore, unable at this stage to conclude an agreement on the basis of the discussions between us at our recent Moscow meeting.

2. Attempts are now being made to form an alternative Polish Government in which Mr Mikolajczyk, Mr Romer and the Ambassador, Mr Raczynski, have refused to participate. A change of Prime Ministers does not affect the formal relations between States.[2] The desire of His Majesty's Government for the reconstitution of a strong and independent Poland, friendly to Russia, remains unalterable. We have practical matters to handle with the Polish Government, and more especially the control of the considerable Polish armed forces, over 80,000 excellent fighting men, under our operational command. These are now making an appreciable contribution to the United Nations' war effort in Italy, Holland and elsewhere. Our attitude towards any new Polish Government must therefore be correct, though it will certainly be cold. We cannot of course have the same close relations of confidence with such a government as we have had with Mr Mikolajczyk or with his predecessor, the late General Sikorski, and we shall do all in our power to ensure that its activities do not endanger the unity between the Allies.

1. After some difficulty, a new Polish government was formed under the veteran socialist Tomasz Arciszewski on 29 November.
2. Churchill rejected the Clark-Kerr's view that British recognition of this new governme would mean 'a head-on collision with Stalin' (F.O. 371. C16310/8/55). He cabled to Moscow 'One does not cease to recognize a State every time the Prime Minister changes' (F.O. 371. C16777/8/55). He at first also rejected the advice of Clark-Kerr and also of the Foreign Office that he should send a message to Stalin, but decided after his meeting with Mikołajczyk on 28 November to dispatch the letter here printed. On this occasion, also told Mikołajczyk that his decision to resign was 'wise' and that 'if no alternative Poli Government was successful M. Mikołajczyk would return to power in a much stronger position than he had ever enjoyed' (F.O. 371. C16467/8/55). In his speech to the House Commons on 15 December, he again outlined the British position in familiar terms and expressed his regret that no agreement had been reached on the basis of the Moscow conversations (H. of C. Debates, vol. 406, cols. 1478–89).

3. It is not thought that such a government, even when formed, will have a long life. Indeed, after my conversations with Mr Mikolajczyk, I should not be surprised to see him back in office before long with increased prestige and with the necessary powers to carry through the programme discussed between us in Moscow. This outcome would be all the more propitious because he would by his resignation have proclaimed himself and his friends in the most convincing way as a champion of Poland's good relations with Russia.

4. I trust, therefore, that you will agree that our respective influence should be used with the Poles here and with those at Lublin to prevent any steps on either side which might increase the tension between them and so render more difficult Mr Mikolajczyk's task when, as I hope, he takes it up again in the not far distant future. He is himself in good heart and remains anxious, as ever, for a satisfactory settlement. I see no reason why he should not emerge from this crisis as an even more necessary factor than before for the reconstruction of Poland.

No. 117

Marshal Stalin to Mr. Churchill: Letter
9 December 1944
Stalin Correspondence, I, No. 317

Your message on Mikolajczyk received.

It has become obvious since my last meeting with Mr Mikolajczyk in Moscow that he is incapable of helping a Polish settlement. Indeed, his negative role has been revealed. It is now evident that his negotiations with the Polish National Committee are designed to cover up those who, behind his back, engaged in criminal terror acts against Soviet officers and Soviet people generally on Polish territory. We cannot tolerate this state of affairs. We cannot tolerate terrorists, instigated by the Polish émigrés, assassinating our people in Poland and waging a criminal struggle against the Soviet forces liberating Poland. We look on these people as allies of our common enemy, and as to their radio correspondence with Mr Mikolajczyk, which we found on émigré agents arrested on Polish territory, it not only exposes their treacherous designs, it also casts a shadow on Mr Mikolajczyk and his men.

Ministerial changes in the émigré Government no longer deserve serious attention. For these elements, who have lost touch with the national soil and have no contact with their people, are merely marking time. Meanwhile the Polish Committee of National Liberation has made substantial progress in consolidating its national, democratic organisations on Polish soil, in implementing a land reform in favour of the peasants and in expanding its armed forces, and enjoys great prestige among the population.

I think that our task now is to support the National Committee in Lublin and all who want to cooperate and are capable of cooperating with it. This is particularly important to the Allies in view of the need for accelerating the defeat of the Germans.[1]

1. Churchill replied briefly on 10 December that 'We must make sure that our permanent and loyal relations are not disturbed by awkward moves of subordinate events' (Stalin Correspondence, I, No. 369).

No. 118

Press Release issued by the Department of State[1]
WASHINGTON, 18 December 1944
F.R.U.S. 1944, III, pp. 1346–7

The United States Government stands unequivocally for a strong, free, and independent Polish state with the untrammeled right of the Polish people to order their internal existence as they see fit.

2. It has been the consistently held policy of the United States Government that questions relating to boundaries should be left in abeyance until the termination of hostilities. As Secretary Hull stated in his address of April 9, 1944,[2] 'This does not mean that certain questions may not and should not in the meantime be settled by friendly conference and agreement.' In the case of the future frontiers of Poland, if a mutual agreement is reached by the United Nations directly concerned, this Government would have no objections to such an agreement which could make an essential contribution to the prosecution of the war against the common enemy. If, as a result of such agreement, the Government and people of Poland decide that it would be in the interests of the Polish state to transfer national groups, the United States Government in cooperation with other governments will assist Poland, in so far as practicable, in such transfers. The United States Government continues

1. This statement was provoked by a passage in Churchill's speech to the House of Commons on 15 December (see above No. 116, note 2). When discussing the proposed territorial compensation of Poland in the North and West, Churchill, while claiming that the U.S. was in general agreement with U.K. policy, regretted that 'the attitude of the United States has not been defined with the precision which the British Government have thought it wise to use' (H. of C. Deb. vol. 406, col. 1486). In sending this message to Stalin, Roosevelt explained that Churchill's speech had placed the U.S. government under 'strong pressure' to make known its position. He also appealed to Stalin not to recognize the Lublin committee as the provisional government of Poland before a meeting of the Big Three (Stalin Correspondence, II, No. 248).

The statement as finally issued watered down somewhat the commitment of the U.S. to compensating Poland at the expense of Germany. (For the original statement, see F.R.U.S. Yalta, pp. 217–8). This rather distressed the British, and on 17 December Halifax, on War Cabinet instructions, intervened unavailingly to have the second paragraph of the declaration modified. He did manage to induce the Americans to change one sentence in the second section (that beginning 'In the case of the future frontiers . . . ') to make clear U.S. support for an immediate solution (W.M.(44)170.6 C.A.; F.O. 371. C17585/8/55).
2. In a broadcast on C.B.S.

to adhere to its traditional policy of declining to give guarantees for any specific frontiers. The United States Government is working for the establishment of a world security organization through which the United States together with other member states would assume responsibility for the preservation of general security.

3. It is the announced aim of the United States Government, subject to legislative authority, to assist the countries liberated from the enemy in repairing the devastation of war and thus to bring to their peoples the opportunity to join as full partners in the task of building a more prosperous and secure life for all men and women. This applies to Poland as well as the other United Nations.

The policy of the United States Government regarding Poland outlined above has as its objective the attainment of the announced basic principles of United States foreign policy.

No. 119

Marshal Stalin to President Roosevelt: Letter
MOSCOW, 27 December 1944
Stalin Correspondence, I, No. 254

Your message on Polish affairs reached me on December 20.

As to Mr Stettinius' statement of December 18, I should prefer to comment on it when we meet. At any rate events in Poland have already gone far beyond that which is reflected in the said statement.

A number of things that have taken place since Mr Mikolajczyk's last visit to Moscow, in particular the wireless correspondence with the Mikolajczyk Government, which we found on terrorists arrested in Poland — underground agents of the émigré Government — demonstrate beyond all doubt that Mr Mikolajczyk's talks with the Polish National Committee served to cover up those elements who, behind Mr Mikolajczyk's back, had been engaged in terror against Soviet officers and soldiers in Poland. We cannot tolerate a situation in which terrorists, instigated by Polish émigrés, assassinate Red Army soldiers and officers in Poland, wage a criminal struggle against the Soviet forces engaged in liberating Poland and directly aid our enemies, with whom they are virtually in league.[1] The substitution of Arciszewski for Mikolajczyk and the ministerial changes in the émigré Government in general have aggravated the situation and have resulted in a deep rift between Poland and the émigré Government.

Meanwhile the National Committee has made notable progress in consolidating the Polish state and the machinery of state power on Polish soil, in

---

1. According to Litauer, Stalin had made similar claims to Bierut and Jakub Berman during their visit to Moscow in December. He had also stated that 'they could henceforth dismiss any idea of a compromise with Mikolajczyk whom he (the Marshal) was no longer prepared to allow into Poland' (F.O. 371. C17792/8/55).

expanding and strengthening the Polish Army, in implementing a number of important government measures, primarily the land reform in favour of the peasants. These developments have resulted in the consolidation of the democratic forces in Poland and in an appreciable increase in the prestige of the National Committee among the Polish people and large sections of the Poles abroad.

As I see it, we must now be interested in supporting the National Committee and all who are willing to cooperate and who are capable of cooperating with it, which is of special moment for the Allies and for fulfilment of our common task — accelerating the defeat of Hitler Germany. For the Soviet Union, which is bearing the whole burden of the struggle for freeing Poland from the German invaders, the problem of relations with Poland is, in present circumstances, a matter of everyday, close and friendly relations with an authority brought into being by the Polish people on their own soil, an authority which has already grown strong and has armed forces of its own, which, together with the Red Army, are fighting the Germans.

I must say frankly that in the event of the Polish Committee of National Liberation becoming a Provisional Polish Government, the Soviet Government will, in view of the foregoing, have no serious reasons for postponing its recognition.[2] It should be borne in mind that the Soviet Union, more than any other Power, has a stake in strengthening a pro-Ally and democratic Poland, not only because it is bearing the brunt of the struggle for Poland's liberation, but also because Poland borders on the Soviet Union and because the Polish problem is inseparable from that of the security of the Soviet Union. To this I should add that the Red Army's success in fighting the Germans in Poland largely depends on a tranquil and reliable rear in Poland, and the Polish National Committee is fully cognisant of this circumstance, whereas the émigré Government and its underground agents by their acts of terror threaten civil war in the rear of the Red Army and counter its successes.

On the other hand, in the conditions now prevailing in Poland there are no

---

2 . On receiving this letter Roosevelt replied to Stalin that he 'was disturbed and deeply disappointed at Stalin's refusal to postpone the recognition of the Lublin committee until a meeting of the three heads of government (Stalin Correspondence, II, No. 255). The British were informed on 30 December of Stalin's intentions and the War Cabinet decided to continue 'to press Premier Stalin not to recognise the Lublin Government'. Churchill also argued that 'we should reconsider the existing arrangements under which Poles in the Polish forces in our armies in Italy were allowed to conduct flights which, in present circumstances, passed over Russian territory with a view to dropping arms, supplies etc. to the Underground Movement in Poland' (W.M. (44) 176 C.A.).

On 31 December the Soviet government announced that the Polish National Committee had transformed itself into a provisional government and that the Soviet government would recognize it. Stalin wrote back to Roosevelt on 1 January regretting that 'I have not succeeded in convincing you of the correctness of the Soviet Government's stand. . .' (Stalin Correspondence, II, No. 256). He sent a similar message to Churchill on 30 January (Stalin Correspondence, I, No. 381) to which Churchill replied on the 5th, stressing the importance of a meeting of the three heads of governments (Stalin Correspondence, I, No.38

grounds for continuing to support the émigré Government, which has completely forfeited the trust of the population inside the country and which, moreover, threatens civil war in the rear of the Red Army, thereby injuring our common interest in the success of the struggle we are waging against the Germans. I think it would be only natural, fair and beneficial to our common cause if the Governments of the Allied Powers agreed as a first step exchange representatives at this juncture with the National Committee with a view to its later recognition as the lawful government of Poland, after it has proclaimed itself the Provisional Government of Poland. Unless this is done I fear that the Polish people's trust in the Allied Powers may diminish. I think we should not countenance a situation in which Poles can say that we are sacrificing the interests of Poland to those of a handful of emigres in London.

No. 120

Foreign Office brief on Poland for Yalta Conference[1] (Extracts)[2]
LONDON, 27 January 1945
F.O. 371. N1038/6/55

... 9. Our own ultimate objective must clearly be to secure eventual free elections in Poland. To do this, it is necessary first to ensure that we and the U.S. Govt. are not now cut off from all contact with Poland, but on the contrary have representatives there to report to us and influence the situation so far as possible in accordance with our views. Secondly, we must try to reach agreement with the Soviet Govt. upon an interim régime in Poland of a nature to reduce the danger of civil war and of Soviet or Lublin excesses and to prevent the eventual free elections being rendered futile in advance by the suppression of free expression of opinion. It seems quite unrealistic to suppose that any Polish Govt. in London or any Poles that remain here can have any further influence on the situation in Poland, save to increase the likelihood of hopeless armed resistance to the Russians or, alternatively the severity of Russian and Lublin measures against the inhabitants of Poland.[3] There seems no doubt that the chances of our reaching a satisfactory agreement with the Soviet Govt. about Poland are slender so long as we maintain our decision to go on recognising the London Govt. indefinitely; nor does it seem possible to have represenatives on a satisfactory basis in Poland without recognition of a Govt. there. Our aim, therefore, must be to reach some arrangement by which a sufficiently respectable and satisfactory Govt. is established in Poland to enable us and the U.S. Govt. to transfer recognition to them without shocking public opinion here and in the States and without losing the loyalty of the Polish forces fighting with us. We should work, therefore, to secure Soviet agreement to the setting up in Poland of a Govt. containing adequate representatives of the three Centre and Left Wing Parties in Poland. It seems hopeless to think of securing representation for the National Democrats, the Right Wing, nationalist reactionary and predominantly anti-Russian party. It will also be desirable, if only for the sake of public opinion here and in the U.S., to secure the inclusion of at least M. Mikolajczyk and, if possible, one or two other representative London Poles.

10. If the Soviet Govt. prove willing to agree to a remodelling of the Lublin Govt. on these lines, they will almost certainly want the new Polish Govt. to accept the 1921 constitution. . .

11. A further condition of Soviet and Lublin agreement to the formation of a representative Govt. in Poland would almost certainly be the agreement of those introduced into the new Govt. to recognise the Curzon Line and Line A finally as the Eastern frontier of Poland. As stated above, M. Romer has expressed the view that it will be necessary that this should be imposed on the Poles by the three Allied Govts. . .[4]

12. Our proposal might be put to Marshal Stalin in the following way. H.M. Govt. and the U.S. Govt. cannot recognise the Lublin Provisional Govt., who are regarded by British and American public opinion as completely unrepresentative, a view which H.M.G. cannot but share. H.M.G. have no choice but to continue to recognise the London Govt., to whom the Polish forces under our command owe allegiance. We recognise, however, that, cut off from liberated Poland, they will become less and less representative. We know that Marshal Stalin wants a strong and independent Poland with a democratic Govt. in good relations with Russia and the Western Allies. Neither the Lublin nor the London Govt. fill this bill. It should now be possible to form a representative Govt. which would secure acceptance from the majority of Poles in Poland and from British and American public opinion and consisting of persons known to desire to good relations with Russia. Such a Govt. could ensure the cooperation of Poland in the effort of the Red Army against Germany in a way that cannot for a moment be expected under the present Lublin administration; they could be recognised by H.M.G. and (we hope) by the U.S. Govt. and would prepare the way for free elections to be held at a suitable moment. There are now available in Poland at the present time respected and influential leaders of the Peasant and Socialist Parties who are believed to have been consistently in favour of wholehearted collaboration with Russia; viz: M. Witos and M. Zuławski. These should be invited to cooperate in a new Polish Govt. together with representatives of Lublin and M. Mikolajczyk and other suitable London Poles who would be representative of Polish opinion outside Poland at the present time and whose name commands respect in the British Commonwealth and the United States. (If Marshal Stalin brings up against M. Mikolajczyk the accusation made in his message to the Prime Minister of the 9th December[5] that messages to M. Mikolajczyk from Poland regarding anti-Soviet underground measures have been intercepted, we can reply that we have reason to know that M. Mikolajczyk did not see and approve by any means all messages that passed between his government and Poland.)

13. As regards the *modus operandi* of securing the establishment of such a Polish Government, there seem to be three possible lines of approach:

(1) the establishment by agreement between the Three Great Powers of an interim international authority in Poland;

(2) M. Romer's proposal that a meeting of Party leaders should be held under the Chairmanship of some suitable Polish personality e.g. Prince Sapieha;[7]

(3) M. Mikolajczyk's more detailed proposal that a 'presidential council' of outstanding personalities should be formed and summon a conference which would determine what parties should be represented in a new Government and in what proportion and could designate a Prime Minister who would form a Cabinet to be nominated by the 'presidential council';[8]

(4) that the Three Powers having agreed as to the composition of the new Government, it should be left to the Soviet Government to arrange for its establishment.

14. Of these, (1) is in line with the present Polish Government's proposal and that of Mr. Bohlen referred to above. Some such proposal for international supervision would no doubt be the best solution. But Marshal Stalin will have to be pressed very hard if he is even to consider it. In my opinion he should be so pressed.

15. (2) above would be the next best solution if Soviet agreement could be secured and a suitable personality or personalities found. . .   But here again it is very doubtful whether Stalin and the Lublin Government would be willing to give so much authority and power to a comparatively unknown man of the Archbishop's rank and calling [Prince Sapieha] both of which must make him suspect in their eyes. . .

16. M. Mikolajczyk's proposal (3) above, has the disadvantage of being slow and over-elaborate. . . A further disadvantage . . . is the exclusion in the first stage at least of all Poles from outside Poland including M. Mikolajczyk himself. . .

17. In my judgement (4) above cannot be accepted, however difficult the Russians are unless accompanied by full facilities to Americans and ourselves to see what goes on in Poland and unless elections are held in due course under Allied supervision. It would then be necessary to agree with the Russians as regards the personalities in the new Government. Of those available in Western Poland, M. Witos, the acknowledged leader of the Peasant Party, should certainly be included. . . M. Zuławski was one of the leaders of the Polish Socialist Party before the war; he is understood always to have been in favour of territorial concessions to Russia and is reported to have advocated the mass organisation of the urban workers in Poland for direct action against the Germans. It is probable that a representative of the Christian Democrat Party should be included. . .

18. In order to secure Russian agreement, no doubt the fewer Poles from London that are suggested for inclusion in a new Polish Government

the better, but public opinion here and in America would expect to see
M. Mikolajczyk a member of the new government. . .

Further information regarding other possible candidates for the new
government is being collected and the details will be embodied in a separate
paper.

19. Under either (2), (3) or (4) above, it would clearly be most important
to recognise a Government in Poland at the earliest possible moment, in order
to have an Embassy there to watch and, if possible, influence events and keep
H.M.G. informed.

1. This brief was written by Christopher Warner, head of the Northern Department.
Eden, who made a number of modifications in its wording, minuted on 27 January,
'This is very well done by Dept. . . . . Copy should certainly go to P.M. soon and we take
one with us.'
2. The first section of the brief described the general evolution of the situation in
Poland, the second went into some detail on the various Polish proposals made in
London to deal with the problem.
3. It is interesting to note that the Foreign Office rejected a proposal by Cripps and
Retinger in early January for a conference in London to establish a more representative
London government. A similar scheme had aroused the interest of the State Department
((F.O. 371. N198/6/55). The Foreign Office held that these proposals were ill-advised,
since, as Eden wrote in a draft minute for the Prime Minister on 12 January (which was
not sent since Eden discussed this matter personally with Churchill),
    We clearly do not want to give the appearance of challenging Stalin by going out of
    our way to build up a new Polish Govt. in London as a rival to the Lublin Govt. If
    the Poles in London decide to strengthen their government well and good, but even
    so it is doubtful whether things have not gone too far now for it to be possible to
    bring about an agreement between the Polish Govt. in London, however represen-
    tative they claim to be, and the Polish Govt. in Lublin. I sometimes wonder whether,
    instead of relying upon a representative Government in London, the better course
    would not be to try to "penetrate" the Lublin Govt. by arranging for Mikolajczyk
    and other political leaders and groups who want to work for a Polish-Russian
    entente to go to Lublin while the Lublin people are still prepared to welcome them
    on account of the knowledge, experience and influence which they can contribute.
4. Mikołajczyk expressed the same view to Eden on 26 January (F.O. 371. N1104/6/55).
5. See above, Nos. 117, 119.
6. This should read 'four'.
7. Romer had outlined his views to Sir Owen O'Malley on 27 January (F.O. 371.
N1038/6/55). His plan involved the establishment of a Regency or Regency council on
the Greek model which would call a conference in Poland in order to establish a
government made up of representatives of the Lublin and London governments and
independent personalities in Poland.
8. Mikołajczyk's views had been outlined to Cadogan on 24 January (F.O. 371.
N892/6/55) and were embodied in a long memorandum presented to the Foreign Office
on 26 January (F.O. 371. N996/8/55; F.R.U.S. 1945, V, pp. 115–21). His main
proposal was for the immediate appointment of a 'presidential council' composed of
well-known figures from political scene and the church. This would summon a conference of representatives of the Lublin government, the Polish underground government
and other political leaders in Poland. At this conference, in the presence of representatives
of the Great Powers, a new government would be established. Mikołajczyk argued that
Poles from outside Poland would not be safe at such a conference and that the
representation of the Lublin government in the new cabinet should be less than 50%.

No. 121

War Cabinet Minutes (Extracts)
LONDON, 26 January 1945
W.M. (45) 10.1 C.A.

The War Cabinet had before them a Memorandum (W.P.(45) 48) by the Secretary of State for Foreign Affairs on the Western Frontier of Poland.[1] The Memorandum reviewed the undertakings given to the Polish Government in the past in regard to their Western Frontiers, and recorded that they had been given as part of our endeavours to induce the Polish Government to accept the Curzon Line as the basis of a settlement with Soviet Russia in the East.

If, as now seemed more probable, we had to deal with the claims of the Lublin Poles who were ready to accept the Curzon Line anyhow, there was no longer any need for H.M. Government to support any more extensive transfers of territory than we thought convenient and proper on other grounds.

The present indications were that the Lublin Poles were anxious that the frontier should follow the line of the River Oder up to the Görlitzer Neisse (the more westerly of two tributaries of this name).

While we should not commit ourselves in such a way as to prejudge the future settlement, the Memorandum suggested that the time had come to make clear to our principal Allies that we had doubts on the subject and must not be regarded as committed to the support of any annexation by Poland beyond those of East Prussia, Danzig and the Oppeln District.

Our line might be that H.M. Government must not be considered as having accepted any definite line as a Western Frontier of Poland; but we considered that the matter, affecting as it did other aspects of long-term policy towards Germany, was a suitable one for examination by the European Advisory Commission

THE FOREIGN SECRETARY said . . . a frontier represented by the Western Neisse would go far beyond any commitment which had ever been made either by the Prime Minister or by himself.

THE PRIME MINISTER said that he entirely agreed with the Foreign Secretary's view that we should oppose a Western Neisse boundary. It would be no small matter to arrange for the removal of 5 to 6 million Germans from the territories which we were in any event prepared to see Poland acquire if she so desired. But a total figure of 8 or 9 millions would, in his judgment, be quite unmanageable. Nor could we be certain that the reduced Germany would be able to absorb so large a figure.

The War Cabinet took note of the statement by the Foreign Secretary and agreed with the view expressed by the Prime Minister at "A".[2]

A discussion followed on the general Polish position.

1. For this memorandum, dated 23 January 1945, see W.P. (45) 48.
2. I.e. the sentence, 'The Prime Minister said . . . a Western Neisse boundary.'

THE PRIME MINISTER said that it must be expected, now that the Germans had been practically driven out of the whole of Poland, that the Lublin Committee, with the Russian Government behind them, would grow very rapidly in power. He anticipated that the Soviet representatives at the forthcoming meetings of Heads of Governments would demand the recognition of the Lublin Committee as the Government of Poland. We must bear in mind that recognition was the one counter which remained in our hands, and that we should not give it up save in return for something worth having. In general, our attitude would be, if the War Cabinet approved, to continue to advise the Poles to compromise as regards the Eastern frontier, and to remain adamant on the question of ensuring a free, sovereign and independent Poland, coupled with arrangements for free elections.

THE FOREIGN SECRETARY expressed his agreement with the Prime Minister's view. The Soviet Government had the chance, now that Poland had been so largely liberated, to make the Lublin Committee much more representative and to bring in personalities such as M. Mikolajczyk and M. Witos. It was important that the parts of Western Poland now being liberated were the least anti-Russian and the most anti-German. . .

The War Cabinet took note of the statements by the Prime Minister and the Foreign Secretary, and approved the general line proposed by the Prime Minister at "Y".[3]

3. I.e. the sentence, 'In general, our attitude . . . coupled with arrangements for free elections.'

No. 122

Anthony Eden to Winston Churchill
MALTA, 1 February 1945
F.R.U.S. Yalta, pp. 508–9

CONVERSATIONS WITH MR. STETTINIUS[1]
POLAND

We found that we were in broad agreement on the necessity for finding a solution and that it was impossible for our Governments to recognise the Lublin Government. Mr. Stettinius stressed that failure to find a solution would greatly disturb American public opinion, and might prejudice the whole question of American participation in the World Organisation.

2. I agreed that a "Russian" solution of the question would be very likely to produce the latter result.

1. For the British record of these conversations, W.P. (45) 157, pp. 4, 7; for the U.S. record, F.R.U.S., Yalta, pp. 499–500, 505. During the conversations, each delegation agreed to submit to the Prime Minister and President notes reflecting the substance of the discussion. Eden's note for Churchill is printed here. For Stettinius' note to Roosevelt which follows closely the form of Eden's, see F.R.U.S. Yalta, pp. 510–11.

3. We found that we had very similar ideas on the lines of a possible solution. We should have to stress to Marshal Stalin the unsatisfactory nature of the present state of affairs, with the Soviet recognising one Government in Lublin and ourselves another Government in London. (We, of course, ourselves have the added problem of the Polish forces, acting with ours, who owe allegiance to the London Government). There would be apparent to the world a definite divergence of view on a point of first-rate importance. This would give rise to uneasiness amongst our peoples and would afford valuable material to enemy propaganda.

4. The time has probably gone by for a 'fusion' of London and Lublin, and the only remedy that we can see is the creation of a *new* interim Government, in Poland, pledged to hold free elections as soon as conditions permit. This would be representative of all Polish political parties and would no doubt include elements from the Lublin Government, from Poles in Poland, and from Poles abroad. There are no good candidates from the Government in London, but if M. Mikolajczyk and, perhaps, M. Romer and others such as M. Grabski could be included, that would make it much easier for us to recognize the new Government, which should be far more representative of Poland as a whole than as the Lublin Government.

5. If it would facilitate the realisation of this plan, we should be ready to see the adoption of M. Mikolajczyk's idea of a 'Presidential Council' consisting of such men as the former Prime Minister, M. Witos, Archbishop Sapieha, M. Zulawski and M.Bierut. Such a Council could appoint the new Government.

6. If the Russians persist in their present policy, that would only neutralise the efforts of all those in our two countries most anxious to work with Russia.

7. There remains the territorial problem. As regards Poland's eastern frontier, H.M.G. have already agreed with the Russians and announced publicly that this should be the Curzon Line, giving Lwow to the U.S.S.R. The Americans may however still wish to press the Russians to leave Lwow to Poland. As regards Poland's western frontier, we and the Americans agreed that Poland should certainly have East Prussia south and west of Konigsberg, Danzig, the eastern tip of Pomerania and the whole of Upper Silesia. The Lublin Poles, no doubt with Soviet approval, are however also claiming not only the Oder line frontier, including Stettin and Breslau, but also the western Neisse frontier.

8. The cessions upon which we and the Americans are agreed would involved the transfer of some 2½ million Germans. The Oder frontier, without Breslau and Stettin would involve a further 2¼ millions. The western Neisse frontier with Breslau and Stettin would involve an additional 3¼ millions making 8 millions in all.

9. We were prepared last October in Moscow to let M. Mikolajczyk's Government have any territories they chose to claim up to the Oder, but this was conditional upon agreement then being reached between him and the Russians and there was no question of our agreeing to the western Neisse

frontier. It was agreed before we left London that we should oppose the western Neisse frontier. I also think that we should keep the position fluid as regards the Oder line frontier, and take the line that H. M. G. cannot be considered as having accepted any definite line for the western frontier of Poland, since we need not make the same concessions to the Lublin Poles which we were prepared to make to M. Mikolajczyk in order to obtain a solution of the Polish problem. Even the Oder line frontier would severely tax the Polish capacity for absorption and would increase the formidable difficulties involved in the transfer of millions of Germans. We agreed with the Americans that in any event these transfers should be gradual and not precipitate.

10. If the Russians refuse to accept any solution such as that outlined above, the present deadlock must continue. That would be bad, but a simple recognition of the Lublin Government would be even worse.

The Polish Question at the Yalta Conference

No. 123

President Roosevelt to Marshal Stalin: Letter (Extracts)
KOREIZ, the Crimea, 6 February, 1945
Stalin Correspondence, II, No. 265

My dear Marshal Stalin,

I have been giving a great deal of thought to our meeting this afternoon,[1] and I want to tell you in all frankness what is on my mind.

In so far as the Polish Government is concerned, I am greatly disturbed that the three Great Powers do not have a meeting of minds about the political set up in Poland. It seems to me that it puts all of us in a bad light throughout the world to have you recognizing one government while we and the British are recognizing another in London. I am sure this state of affairs should not continue and that if it does it can only lead our people to think there is a breach between us, which is not the case. I am determined that there shall be no breach between ourselves and the Soviet Union. Surely there is a way to reconcile our differences.

I was very much impressed with some of the things you said today, particularly your determination that your rear must be safeguarded as your

1. The second plenary session (American numbering third) of the conference. For the British minutes, W.P. (45) 157, pp. 28–32; for the U.S. minutes, F.R.U.S. Yalta, pp. 667–71, 677–81; for the Soviet minutes, Soviet Protocols, pp. 84–91. On this occasion the three heads of governments outlined their positions along familiar lines. In particular, Stalin refused to budge on Lwów and advocated the Oder-western Neisse frontier line. He suggested calling to Yalta representatives of the Lublin government (which had now moved to Warsaw) and stated that its members would accept Grabski and Żeligowski in a reformed cabinet but 'would not hear of Mikołajczyk becoming Prime Minister.' Both Churchill and Roosevelt stressed that the character of the future Polish government was of more importance than the frontier question.

army moves into Berlin. . .

You must believe me when I tell you that our people at home look with a critical eye on what they consider a disagreement between us at this vital stage of the war. They, in effect, say that if we cannot get a meeting of minds now when our armies are converging on the common enemy, how can we get an understanding on even more vital things in the future.

I have had to make it clear to you that we cannot recognize the Lublin Government as now composed, and the world would regard it as a lamentable outcome of our work here if we parted with an open and obvious divergence between us on this issue.

You said today that you would be prepared to support any suggestions for the solution of this problem which offered a fair chance of success, and you also mentioned the possibility of bringing some members of the Lublin Government here.

Realizing that we all have the same anxiety in getting this matter settled, I would like to develop your proposal a little and suggest that we invite here to Yalta at once Mr. Bierut and Mr. Osubka Morawski from the Lublin Government and also two or three from the following list of Poles, which according to our information would be desirable as representatives of the other elements of the Polish people in the development of a new temporary government which all three of us could recognize and support: Bishop Sapieha of Cracow, Vincente Witos, Mr Zurlowski,[2] Professor Buyak,[3] and Professor Kutzeba.[4] If, as a result of the presence of these Polish leaders here, we could jointly agree with them on a provisional government in Poland which should no doubt include some Polish leaders from abroad such as Mr. Mikolajczyk, Mr. Grabski and Mr. Romer, the United States Government, and I feel sure the British Government as well, would then be prepared to examine with you conditions in which they would dissociate themselves from the London government and transfer their recognition to the new provisional government.

I hope I do not have to assure you that the United States will never lend its support in any way to any provisional government in Poland that would be inimical to your interests.

It goes without saying that any interim government which could be formed as a result of our conference with the Poles here would be pledged to the holding of free elections in Poland at the earliest possible date. I know this is completely consistent with your desire to see a new free and democratic Poland emerge from the welter of this war.

2. Zuławski.
3. Bujak.
4. Kutrzeba.

No. 124

Proposal submitted by Mr. Molotov at the third plenary meeting (U.S. Fourth) of the Yalta conference[1]
7 February 1945
W.M. (45) 157, pp. 44—5

1. It was agreed that the Curzon Line should be the Eastern frontier of Poland with adjustments in some regions of 5—8 kilometres in favour of Poland.

2. It was decided that the Western frontier of Poland should be drawn from the town of Stettin (Polish) and thence southwards along the River Oder and the Western Neisse.[2]

3. It was considered desirable to add to the Provisional Polish Government some democratic leaders from Polish *émigré* circles.[3]

4. It was considered desirable that the enlarged Provisional Polish Government should be recognised by the Allied Governments.

5. It was considered desirable that the Provisional Polish Government enlarged as suggested in paragraph 3, should as soon as possible call the population of Poland to the polls for the establishment by general vote of permanent organs of the Polish Government.

6. M. Molotov, Mr. Harriman and Sir A. Clark-Kerr were entrusted with the discussion of the question of enlarging the Provisional Polish Government and submitting their proposals for the consideration of the three Governments.

1. For the British minutes, W.M. (45) 157, pp. 44—5; for the U.S. minutes, F.R.U.S. Yalta, 711, 716—21. On this occasion, Roosevelt again stated that the key issue was not frontiers, but the character of the Polish government. Referring to the proposal in Roosevelt's letter of 6 February, both Stalin and Molotov stated that they had been unable to contact Bierut and Osóbka-Morawski.
2. While supporting the movement westward of Poland, Churchill said the Poles should not take more territory 'than they wished or could properly manage.'
3. In discussion both Roosevelt and Churchill objected to the term emigre. Churchill also suggested adding the phrase 'and from within Poland itself', which was accepted by Stalin.

No. 125

Proposal submitted by President Roosevelt at the fourth plenary meeting (U.S. fifth) of the Yalta conference[1]
8 February, 1945
F.R.U.S. Yalta, pp. 792—3

The proposals submitted by Mr. Molotov in regard to the Polish question in reply to the President's letter to Marshal Stalin dated February 6, 1945, have been given careful study.

In regard to the frontier question, no objection is perceived to point One

1. For the British minutes, W.P. (45) 157, pp. 55—60; for the U.S. minutes, F.R.U.S. Yalta, pp. 776—82; 786—790; for the Soviet minutes, Soviet protocols, pp. 103—8.

of the Soviet proposals, namely, that the eastern boundary of Poland should be the Curzon line with modifications in favor of Poland in some areas of from five to eight kilometers.

In regard to point Two, while agreeing that compensation should be given to Poland at the expense of Germany, including that portion of East Prussia south of the Koenigsberg line, Upper Silesia, and up to the line of the Oder, there would appear to be little justification to the extension of the western boundary of Poland up to the Western Neisse River.[2]

In regard to the proposals of the Soviet Government concerning the future Government of Poland, it is proposed that Mr. Molotov, Mr. Harriman and Sir Archibald Clark-Kerr be authorized on behalf of the three Governments to invite to Moscow Mr. Bierut, Mr. Osubka-Morawski, Bishop Sapieha, Mr. Vicente Witos, Mr. Mikolajczyk and Mr. Grabski to form a Polish Government of National Unity along the following lines:[3]

1. There will be formed a Presidential Committee of three, possibly consisting of Mr. Bierut, Mr. Grabski and Bishop Sapieha, to represent the Presidential office of the Polish Republic.[4]

2. This Presidential Committee will undertake the formation of a government consisting of representative leaders from the present Polish provisional government in Warsaw; from other democratic elements inside Poland, and from Polish democratic leaders abroad.[5]

3. This interim government, when formed, will pledge itself to the holding of free elections in Poland as soon as conditions permit for a constituent assembly to establish a new Polish constitution under which a permanent Government would be elected.[6]

4. When a Polish Government of National Unity is formed, the three Governments will then proceed to accord it recognition as the Provisional Government of Poland.[7]

2. In relation to these two paragraphs, Molotov stated that whereas there was now agreement on the Polish eastern frontier, this was not the case as regards the western frontier. The Poles could be asked their views, but he knew that the Lublin government favoured the Oder-Western Neisse frontier.
3. In discussion, Molotov accepted the proposal for talks in Moscow under the auspices of the three ambassadors. He thought the Lublin government would send Bierut, Osóbka-Morawski and Gen. Rola-Żymierski. He suggested that these three and two persons from the list suggested in the President's letter of 6 February should be invited. He also stated that 'the possibility could not be excluded that the Provisional Government would refuse to talk with some people, for instance with M. Mikolajczyk' (W.P. (45) 157, p. 57).
4. Molotov rejected the creation of a Presidential council as too complicated and suggested rather the enlargement of the National Council in Poland. Stalin stated that the Lublin Poles might agree to a Presidential council, but would have to be consulted.
5. Both Molotov and Stalin stressed in discussion that the Soviet position envisaged that any new government would have to take as its basis the existing Provisional Government which should be enlarged. This government, they claimed, enjoyed great popularity becasue it had participated in the liberation of Poland and had enacted a land reform. Churchill denied this and asserted that 'If they gave up the Polish Government in London a new start should be made from both sides on more or less equal terms' (W.P. (45) 157, p. 50).

6. Both Roosevelt and Churchill stressed the importance of free elections. In reply, Stalin stated that elections could be held within a month, but that until then one would have to deal with the Provisional government, which had as much moral justification to hold its position as General de Gaulle.

7. Molotov asked whether, when the Provisional Government of National Unity had been established, the Polish Government would cease to be recognised. Churchill and Roosevelt agreed that this was the case.

No. 126

Proposal submitted by Winston Churchill at the fourth plenary meeting of the Yalta conference[1]
8 February 1945
F.R.U.S. Yalta, pp. 869–70

1. It was agreed that the Curzon Line should be the eastern frontier of Poland with adjustments in some regions of 5 to 8 kilometres in favour of Poland.

2. It was decided that the territory of Poland in the west should include the free city of Danzig, the regions of East Prussia west and wouth of Konigsberg, the administrative district of Oppeln in Silesia and the lands desired by Poland to the east of the line of the Oder. It was understood that the Germans in the said regions should be repatriated to Germany and that all Poles in Germany should at their wish be repatriated to Poland.

3. Having regard to the recent liberation of western Poland by the Soviet armies it was deemed desirable to facilitate the establishment of a fully representative Provisional Polish Government based upon all the democratic and anti-Fascist forces in Poland and including democratic leaders from Poles abroad. That Government should be so constituted as to command recognition by the three Allied Governments.

4. It was agreed that the establishment of such a Provisional Government was the primary responsibility of the Polish people, and that, pending the possibility of free elections, representative Polish leaders should consult together on the composition of this Provisional Government. M. Molotov, Mr. Harriman and Sir Archibald Clark-Kerr were entrusted with the task of approaching such leaders and submitting their proposals to the consideration of the three Allied Governments.

5. It was deemed desirable that the Provisional Polish Government, thus established, should as soon as possible hold free and unfettered elections on the basis of universal suffrage and secret ballot, in which all democratic parties should have the right to participate and to promote candidates, in order to ensure the establishment of a Government truly representative of the will of the Polish people.

1. In presenting this proposal, Churchill stated that since discussion had begun on the President's draft, the British would not discuss their own suggestions until agreement had been reached in principle.

No. 127

Proposal submitted by Edward Stettinius to a meeting of Foreign Ministers at the Yalta conference[1]
9 February 1945
F.R.U.S. Yalta, pp. 803—4

After further consideration I agree with M. Molotov's statement that the question of the creation of a Presidential Committee should be dropped and am therefore prepared to withdraw our suggestion on that point.

I believe that, with this change, our three positions are not far apart on the substance of the governmental question. M. Molotov spoke of the reorganisation of the Polish Government. The British formula suggests the establishment of a fully representative 'Provisional Polish Government' and we speak of the formation of a 'Government of National Unity'. All three agree that only the Poles themselves can definitely decide this. All three agree that this Government should be composed of members of the present Polish Provisional Government and in addition representatives of other democratic elements inside Poland and some Polish democratic leaders from abroad.

The following formula might therefore be considered:—

That the present Polish Provisional Government be reorganised into a fully representative Government based on all democratic forces in Poland and including democratic leaders from Poland abroad, to be termed 'The Provisional Goverment of National Unity',[2] M. Molotov, Mr. Harriman and Sir Archibald Clark Kerr to be authorised to consult in the first instance in Moscow with members of the present Provisional Government and other democratic leaders from within Poland and from abroad with a view to the reorganisation of the present Government along the above lines. This 'Government of National Unity' would be pledged to the holding of free and unfettered elections as soon as possible on the basis of universal suffrage and secret ballot in which all democratic parties would have the right to

1. For the U.K. minutes of this meeting, see W.P. (45) 157, pp. 62—7; for the U.S. minutes, see F.R.U.S. Yalta, pp.803—7. There are no printed Soviet minutes.
2. Eden stated his reservations about this section of Stettinius' proposals. The British did not regard the Lublin government as representative and accordingly, the proposal they had presented on 8 February (see above, No. 126) had called for the establishment of a new government and had not mentioned the Lublin government. He stressed that the British regarded the participation of Mikołajczyk in any future government as vital. He also read out a proposed British amendment to the U.S. proposal (See below No. 128). Molotov repeated Stalin's argument that the rapid holding of elections would resolve the problem and claimed that the Poles would have to decide on Mikołajczyk, but that his position 'might prove to be not so acute'. He also suggested a formula on the lines 'that a new Government was being created on the basis of the present by adding democratic forces from within and abroad.' Stettinius approved Eden's amendement, which was rejected by Molotov because it failed to 'mention that the new Government would be formed on the basis of the present Government.' No harmony was reached on this fundamental point, and the foreign ministers therefore reported to the 5th plenary meeting (U.S. sixth) that no agreement had been reached but that Molotov wished to present to Stalin certain considerations advanced in the American memorandum before making a final statement (W.P. (45) 157, p. 70).

participate and to put forward candidates.

When a 'Polish Government of National Unity' is satisfactorily formed, the three Governments will then proceed to accord it recognition. The Ambassadors of the three Powers in Warsaw following such recognition would be charged with the responsibility of observing and reporting to their respective Governments on the carrying out of the pledge in regard to free and unfettered elections.

No. 128

Proposal submitted by Anthony Eden at a meeting of Foreign Ministers at the Yalta conference
9 February 1945
W.P. (45) 157, p. 67

The three Governments consider that a new situation has been created by the complete liberation of Poland by the Red Army. This calls for the establishment of a fully representative Provisional Polish Government which can now be more broadly based than was possible before the recent liberation of western Poland. This Government should comprise members of the present Provisional Government at Warsaw and other democratic Polish leaders from within Poland and from Poles abroad. The new Government, thus established, should be termed 'the Provisional Government of National Unity.' M. Molotov, Mr. Harriman, Sir A. Clark Kerr, &c.

No. 129

Amendments proposed by Mr. Molotov to the American draft at the fifth Plenary meeting (U.S. sixth) of the Yalta conference[1]
9 February 1945
W.P. (45) 157, pp. 71–2

M. MOLOTOV said that the Russians would like to reach agreement on the basis of the United States document subject to some amendments. These were as follows:—

They would like the first sentence of the formula to read as follows:—

'That the present Provisional Government of Poland[2] should be re-organized on a wider democratic basis with the inclusion of democratic leaders from Poland itself and also from those living abroad. This Government would be called the National Provisional Government of Poland.'

He had withdrawn his former paragraph, in which he had stated that the

1. For the U.K. minutes of this meeting, see W. P. (45) 157, pp. 70–2, 74–6; for the U.S. minutes, F.R.U.S. Yalta, pp. 842–3, 846–8, 850–4; for the Soviet minutes, Soviet protocols, pp. 108–9, 113–7.
2. Roosevelt objected to this phrase but Molotov pointed out that it came from the U.S. draft. Roosevelt claimed his suggestion was 'the Polish Government now functioning in Poland' which was accepted by Stalin at the end of the discussion.

reorganisation of the Provisional Government would proceed on the basis of the existing Government.

No alternations were proposed in the next two sentences. He wished, however, to delete the last line and a half of the paragraph after the words 'secret ballot' and to substitute for the rest of the sentence the following:—

.... 'In these elections all non-Fascist and anti-Fascist[3] democratic parties should have the right to take part and put forward candidates.'

M. MOLOTOV proposed the last paragraph should read as follows:—

'When a Polish Government of National Unity has been formed on the lines laid down above, the three Governments will proceed to recognise it.'

He wanted to omit the final sentence which referred to the Ambassadors of the three Powers being charged with the responsibility for observing and reporting to their Governments on the carrying-out of the elections. This sentence would hurt the *amour propre* of the Poles.[4]

3. Churchill objected to the phrase 'anti-fascist' as too vague and proposed the phrase 'democratic forces.'
4. Both Roosevelt and Churchill refused to accept this omission and stressed the importance of free elections. Churchill also appealed to Stalin to allow U.K. and U.S. observers to go to Poland. In view, however, of the progress which had been made it was decided that the foreign ministers should meet to see if agreement on a draft could be reached.

No. 130

Communique issued at the end of the Yalta Conference (Extract)
11 February 1945
F.R.U.S. Yalta, pp. 973–4

VI
POLAND

We came to the Crimea Conference resolved to settle our differences about Poland.[1] We discussed fully all aspects of the question. We reaffirm our common desire to see established a strong, free, independent and democratic Poland. As a result of our discussions we have agreed on the conditions in which a new Polish Provisional Government of National Unity may be formed in such a manner as to command recognition by the three major powers.

The agreement reached is as follows:

A new situation has been created in Poland as a result of her complete liberation by the Red Army. This calls for the establishment of a Polish Provisional Government which can be more broadly based than was possible before the recent liberation of western Poland. The Provisional Government

1. At the eighth plenary meeting on 11 February (W.P. (45) 157, p. 104; F.R.U.S. Yalta, pp. 927–8, Yalta Protocols, p. 124–5) this first sentence was substituted for one reading: 'We were impressed by the dangers inherent in the failure of the major allies to agree on the recognition of the Polish Government' (W.P. (45) 157, p. 104).

which is now functioning in Poland should therefore be reorganized on a broader democratic basis with the inclusion of democratic leaders from Poland itself and from Poles abroad.[2]   This new Government should then be called the Polish Provisional Government of National Unity.

M. Molotov, Mr. Harriman and Sir A. Clark Kerr are authorized as a Commission to consult in the first instance in Moscow with members of the present Provisional Government and with other Polish democratic leaders from within Poland and from abroad, with a view to the reorganization of the present Government along the above lines. This Polish Provisional Government of National Unity shall be pledged to the holding of free and unfettered elections as soon as possible on the basis of universal suffrage and secret ballot. In these elections all democratic and anti-Nazi parties[3] shall have the right to take part and to put forward candidates.

When a Polish Provisional Government of National Unity has been properly formed in conformity with the above,[4] the Government of the U.S.S.R., which now maintains diplomatic relations with the present Provisional Government of Poland, and the Government of the United Kingdom and the Government of the United States will establish diplomatic relations with the new Polish Provisional Government of National Unity, and will exchange Ambassadors by whose reports the respective Governments will be kept informed about the situation in Poland.[5]

The three Heads of Government consider that the eastern frontier of Poland should follow the Curzon Line with digressions from it in some regions of five to eight kilometres in favor of Poland. They recognize that Poland must receive substantial accessions of territory in the north and west. They feel that the opinion of the new Polish Provisional Government of National

2. The British revised proposal which had been presented at the meeting of foreign ministers on 9 February (W.P. (45) 157, pp. 80–2) had read, 'This Government should be based upon the Provisional Government now functioning in Poland and upon other democratic Polish leaders in Poland and from abroad' (W.P. (45) 157, p. 82).
3. The phrase 'anti-fascist' was thus avoided.
4. The U.K. revised draft proposed the phrase 'When a Polish Provisional Government of National Unity has been formed which the three Governments can regard as fully representative of the Polish people, the three Governments will accord it recognition' (W.P. (45) 157, p. 82). Molotov objected to this as likely to cause further dispute and also ruled out the insertion of the word 'satisfactorily' before 'formed' as offensive to the Poles.
5. The U.K. draft had a last sentence in this paragraph which read
    'The Ambassadors of the three Powers in Warsaw, following such recognition, would be charged with the responsibility of observing and reporting to their respective Governments on the carrying out of the pledge in regard to free and unfettered elections' (W.P. (45) 157, p. 82).
No agreement was reached on the 9th as to whether this should be omitted or not. At the foreign ministers' meeting of 10 February (W.P. (45) 157, pp. 84; F.R.U.S. Yalta, pp. 872–3) Stettinius agreed to omit the sentence provided it was understood that President Roosevelt could make a statement on the elections on the basis of his Ambassador's reports. Eden refused to accept this. The sentence as it finally appears was agreed at a meeting between Churchill, and Stalin on 10 February (W.P. (45) 157, p. 93). On this occasion, Stalin assured Churchill, that, subject to Polish consent, the U.K. ambassador would be able to move freely through Poland.

Unity should be sought in due course on the extent of these accessions and that the final delimitation of the western frontier of Poland should thereafter await the Peace Conference.[6]

6. This paragraph of frontiers was added at Churchill's suggestion at the Seventh plenary meeting on 10 February (W.P. (45) 157, pp. 96–7; F.R.U.S. Yalta, 897–9, 905–6, 907–8, 911; Soviet protocols, pp. 119–20, 122). The vagueness of the recommendation on the western frontier reflected the unease of the War Cabinet, expressed in a telegram on 9 February that Poland should not expand too far in the west (W.M. (45) 15 C.A.).

No. 131

War Cabinet Minutes (Extract)
LONDON, 19 February 1945
W.M. (43) 22.1 C.A.

. . . Sor far as *Premier Stalin* was concerned, he [Churchill] was quite sure that he meant well to the world and to Poland. He did not himself think that there would be any resentment on the part of Russia about the arrangements that had been made for free and fair elections in that country. . . In his discussions at the Crimea Conference he had been at pains at all times to press the policy that had been approved by the War Cabinet viz. a free and independent Poland, sovereign in her own territories; with a Government more broadly composed than it had been, and with the principles of free and fair elections maintained. Whatever criticisms there might be of the arrangements that had been reached, he felt no doubt that they were on any broad and statesmanlike view the best practicable, and that they were truly in the interest of Poland. Premier Stalin, at the beginning of their conversations on the Polish question, had said that Russia had committed many sins (the word was so translated, but the actual word used might have been crimes) against Poland, and that she had in the past joined in the partitions of Poland and in cruel oppression of her. It was not the intention of the Soviet Government to repeat that policy in the future. He felt no doubt whatever that in saying that Premier Stalin had been sincere.

No. 132

Anthony Eden to Sir Archibald Clark-Kerr: Telegram (Extracts)
LONDON, 18 February 1945
F.O. 371. N1745/6/55

From point of view of His Majesty's Government and United States Government crucial points of settlement are
   (1) that new Provisional Government of National Unity should contain adequate representation of different 'non-Lublin' sections of Polish opinion,
   (2) that these should be in a position to exercise real influence not only

over decisions of new Government, but also over their execution,

(3) that new Government should inspire maximum degree of confidence on anti-Lublin Poles inside and outside Poland (including of course Polish forces under our command) and on British, American and world opinion,

(4) that new Government so established should be assured of permanency pending holding of elections,

(5) that position in Poland should not be prejudiced to disadvantage of anti 'Lublin' Poles pending establishment of new Government.

2. We must expect M. Molotov to use his influence on Commission in favour of 'Lublin' Poles, and to work for retention of real power in their hands.

... we and Americans will have to stand up with greatest vigour from the start for principles that new regime must not only be 'properly formed' (vide paragraph 5 of Polish Section of Crimea Communiqué) but also be enable to function properly and freely. As at Yalta M. Molotov will no doubt take the line that Soviet Government can only act after consultation with Lublin. He will thus constitute himself from the start Counsel for 'Lublin' and Sir A. Clark Kerr (with we hope Mr. Harriman's support) need not hesitate openly to act as Counsel for other Poles inside and outside Poland.[1]

3. All will be prejudiced from the start unless functions of Commission are established on a proper basis. The first object must therefore be to secure agreement on method of work of Commission. Apart from other things it is clear that co-operation of representative Poles abroad and inside Poland will not be secured unless their natural fear that dice are heavy loaded against them can be allayed.[2] This can only be done by reassuring them regarding way in which Commission is to set about its task.

4. In our view Commission should not themselves select Poles to form new Government but should preside over discussions among representative Poles, Commission themselves acting more or less as a neutral 'Chairman'. Otherwise we run the risk that M. Molotov will be likely judging by Russian line at Crimea Conference, to start by enquiring what Poles from outside 'Lublin' should be included in reorganised 'Lublin' Government (perhaps suggesting a fixed number) and to consult 'Lublin' regarding names suggested and blackball those that do not suit Lublin book.

5. We should propose therefore that Commission should at once invite representatives of 'Lublin' and an unspecified number of representative Poles from inside and outside Poland to Moscow to discuss among themselves under Commission's auspices how representative Government can be formed, allocation of key posts, and how presidential functions should be performed

1. Grew, the acting Secretary of State disagreed with this position. In a memorandum to the President dated 3 March, he wrote that he was instructing Harriman 'that the Commission should act as a unit in all dealings with the various Polish factions' (SD. 860c 01/3–245).
2. Eden had been surprised at the scepticism which Mikołajczyk and Romer had expressed on 20 February over the workability of the Yalta agreements (F.O. 371. N1883/6/55).

pending elections. Representatives of 'Lublin' will no doubt select themselves.

6. As regards other Poles outside Poland we should hope provided procedure of Commission is settled in a satisfactory manner to be able to induce a number of representative Poles such as M. Mikolajczyk,[3] M. Grabski, M. Romer, and Socialist and Christian Democrat representatives to attend discussions with power to invite other Poles from inside or outside Poland to join the discussions. No-one suggested should be barred (save by unanimous vote of three members of Commission and on ground that they do not fulfil the qualifications of being Democratic and anti-Nazi).

7. Similarly, from inside Poland, one or two Poles whose names we knew Mr. Witos (who we note is reported by Reuter from Moscow to have been found), Prince Sapieha, M. Zulawski, etc. etc., should be invited to come with power to suggest others. It would be for Soviet authorities to instruct 'Lublin' administration to produce them. Here again blackballing should be barred.

8. It is clearly most desirable, if possible, that an immediate stop should be put to measures against anti 'Lublin' Poles and Polish underground leaders, movement and army. . .

9. The first step appears to be to secure United States agreement to above proposals. If Mr. Stettinius is still in Moscow His Majesty's Ambassador could show him this telegram and invite him to issue instructions to Mr. Harriman to concert with Sir A. Clark Kerr (a) in making the representations suggested in paragraph 8 above and (b) in proposing that the Commission on Poland should proceed along the lines proposed in paragraphs 4–7 above. We would simultaneously inform State Department through His Majesty's Ambassador at Washington that this was being done.[4]

10. It is no doubt important if possible to put these proposals to M. Molotov before he puts forward his own proposals for work of Commission.

3. Churchill told the War Cabinet on 21 February that the 'acid test' of Soviet sincerity would be whether they allowed Mikołajczyk to return to Poland (W.M. (45) 23.2 C.A.).
4. Grew cabled Harriman on 28 February that the State Department in general agreed with Clark-Kerr's instructions. In particular, Grew told Harriman that the Poles should be encouraged to form a government themselves, the commissioners acting as arbiters. Any Pole opposed by any of the commissioners should be eligible unless there was conclusive proof of his anti-democratic views. The Lublin government should also be urged to suspend legal proceedings and administrative measures against its political opponents save in the case of crimes against the Red Army (F.R.U.S. 1945, V, pp. 130–1).

No. 133

Winston Churchill to President Roosevelt: Letter (Extracts)
LONDON, 8 March 1945
F.R.U.S. 1945, V, pp. 147–9

. . . 4. The news from Moscow about Poland is also most disappointing. I must let you know that the government majorities here bear no relation to the

FROM DECEMBER 1944 TO THE POTSDAM CONFERENCE

strong undercurrent of opinion among all parties and classes and in our own hearts against a Soviet domination of Poland.

Labour men are as keen as conservatives, and Socialists as keen as Catholics. I have based myself in Parliament on the assumption that the words of the Yalta declaration will be carried out in the letter and the spirit.[1] Once it is seen that we have been deceived and that the well-known communist technique is being applied behind closed doors in Poland, either directly by the Russians or through their Lublin puppets, a very grave situation in British public opinion will be reached.

How would the matter go in the United States? I cannot think that you personally or they would be indifferent. Thus just at the time when everything military is going so well in Europe and when the Japanese policy is also satisfactorily arranged, there would come an open rift between us and Russia not at all confined, in this country at any rate, to government opinion, but running deep down through the masses of the people.

5. After a fairly promising start Molotov is now refusing to accept any interpretation of the Crimea proposals except his own extremely rigid and narrow one.[2] He is attempting to bar practically all our candidates for the consultations, is taking the line that he must base himself on the views of Bierut and his gang and has withdrawn his offer that we should send observers to Poland.[3]

1. The debate in the House of Commons, which began on 27 February showed a good deal of opposition to the Yalta settlement. Churchill had stressed the broad nature of the consultations which the Moscow commission was to undertake and underlined the importance of free elections (H. of C. deb. vol. 408, cols. 1267–1672).
2. At the first meeting of the Commission on 23 January, Molotov had been reasonably accommodating (F.O. 371. N1981/6/55; F.R.U.S. 1945, V, 123–5). He had accepted the three names from Poland suggested by Clark-Kerr and had proposed adding the two others mentioned in Roosevelt's letter of 6 February (See above, No. 123). But though he was prepared to invite Grabski and Romer he felt that the Warsaw Poles might object to Mikołajczyk. On his insistence, the commission cabled Warsaw for information and received the reply that Witos, Romer and Mikołajczyk were all unacceptable (F.O. 371. N2071/6/55). The second meeting of the commission on 27 February was therefore taken up with argument over the participation of Mikołajczyk (F.O. 371. N2090/6/55; F.R.U.S. 1945, V. 134). The basic disagreement at Yalta over whether the Warsaw government was to be the nucleus of the new government appeared in a new form when Molotov claimed that in the Russian text the first sentence of the second paragraph of the Yalta communique read '. . . to consult in Moscow, in the first instance with members of the present Provisional Government.' Harriman and Clark-Kerr agreed that if the Warsaw Poles could be brought to Moscow they could be informed that they had completely misunderstood the spirit of the Yalta agreement and they were accordingly invited. The Foreign Office disagreed with this view, and Clark-Kerr was accordingly instructed that their presence was to be kept secret and invitations dispatched to the other Poles. The next two meetings of the Commission on 1 and 5 March were also quite unproductive (F.O. 371. N2267/6/55, N2415/6/55; F.R.U.S. 1945, V. pp. 134–7, 142–4).
3. Molotov had offered to allow the U.K. and U.S. to send observers to Poland on 27 February, but withdrew this offer on 5 March, ostensibly because of the disparaging remarks he claimed Eden and Churchill made about the Warsaw Poles in the House of Commons debate, but perhaps because he was alarmed by the scope envisaged by the British for their Mission.

In other words, he clearly wants to make a farce of consultations with the "Non-Lublin" Poles — which means that the new government in Poland would be merely the present one dressed up to look more respectable to the ignorant and also wants to prevent us from seeing the liquidations and deportations that are going on and all the rest of the game of setting up a totalitarian regime before elections are held and even before a new government is set up. As to the upshot of all this, if we do not get things right now, it will soon be seen by the world that you and I by putting our signatures to the Crimea settlement have under-written a faudulent prospectus.

6. I am in any case pledged to Parliament to tell them if the business of setting up a new Polish government etc. cannot be carried out in the spirit of the Yalta declaration. I am sure the only way to stop Molotov's tactics is to send a personal message to Stalin and in that message I must make clear what are the essential things we must have in this business if I am to avoid telling Parliament that we have failed.

I think you will agree with me that far more than the case of Poland is involved. I feel that this is the test case between us and the Russians of the meaning which is to be attached to such terms as Democracy, Sovereignty, Independence, Representative Government and free and unfettered elections.

I therefore propose to send to Stalin a message on the lines set out below. It is as you will see based on the ideas in Eden's telegram to Halifax number 2078[4] which has been communicated to State Deaprtment. I hope you will be ready to send Stalin a similar message containing the same minimum requirements. I shall not send my message till I hear from you.[5]

4. Not printed.
5. Churchill's draft letter laid down five principles which the British felt should govern the working of the committee:—
  1. There was to be no prior right of consultation for the Warsaw government.
  2. A Pole could only be excluded from consultation by a unanimous vote of the three ambassadors.
  3. The Poles should aim at creating 'a government truly representative of the various sections of Polish opinion. . .'
  4. The Soviet government should put pressure on the Warsaw administration to prevent it taking any further legal or administrative action of a fundamental character affecting social, constitutional, economic or political conditions in Poland.
  5. U.K. and U.S. observers should be allowed to visit Poland.
The terms of this letter were felt both by the President and the State Department to be too harsh and Churchill accordingly decided not to send it.

No. 134

Averell Harriman to Vyacheslav Molotov: Memorandum (Extracts)[1]
MOSCOW, 19 March 1945
F.R.U.S. 1945, V, pp. 172—6

1. United States Government is concerned at the difficulties which the Moscow Commission has encountered in its first efforst to carry out the terms

of the Crimean decision of Poland. It is felt that a clear statement of the understanding of this Government not only as to the intent and purpose of the decision but also the role of the Commission itself would be of value in overcoming these difficulties which appear to be in large measure a question of interpretation.

The decision on Poland reached by the three heads of Government in the Crimea was based on the common declared policy of the three countries to facilitate in every way possible the emergence after this war of a strong, independent and democratic Poland with the free and unfettered right of the Polish people to choose for themselves the Government and institutions under which they are to live. This common objective was seriously prejudiced by the fact that there was a divergence in the policies of the United States and the United Kingdom on the one hand and the Soviet Union on the other as to what constituted the governmental authority of Poland. In addition the dangers to Allied unity inherent in such a situation were fully recognized by the three heads of Government at the Crimea. The problem confronting the three Governments at the Crimean Conference was thus related to the question of the provisional governmental authority of Poland during the interim period pending the establishment of conditions which would permit the holding of free elections inside Poland. The Crimean decision in the first place was designed to afford a practical solution of the problem of the provisional authority of Poland. The discussion in the Crimea made it obvious that neither the United States Government nor the British Government considered the provisional governmental authority now functioning in Poland as sufficiently representative to consider according it recognition as the Provisional Government of Poland. The Soviet Government for its part made it equally clear that it would not consider recognizing in that capacity the Polish Government in London. In the circumstances the only solution was the one reached, namely, that the three Governments would agree to assist in the formation of a new Polish Provisional Government of national unity 'which can be more broadly based than was possible before the recent liberation of Western Poland'. This new Government of national unity was to be made broadly representative of democratic elements of the Polish state by a reorganization of the existing provisional authority functioning in Poland with the inclusion of democratic leaders from Poland itself and Poles abroad. An essential feature of the Crimean decision was that this new provisional government should be formed in such a manner as to command recognition by the three larger powers. In order to facilitate the formation of this interim government the Commission in Moscow was created. It would appear obvious that the Commission could not discharge responsibility placed upon it nor could the basic objectives as set forth above of the Crimean decision be achieved if any one of the three groups of Polish democratic elements from which the reorganized government is to emerge were permitted to dictate to the Commission which individuals from the other groups were to be invited to Moscow for consultation. It would, therefore, appear logical that in the discharge of its responsibilities the Commission in Moscow should as a first step reach an agreement as to what Polish democratic leaders should come to Moscow to consult together with representatives of the Poliesh Provisional Government with a view to the formation of a new government of national unity. Agreement on this step would of course not involve any commitment on the actual composition of the new government.

In discussions which have already taken place in the Moscow Commission on Poland it has been suggested by the Soviet Government that terms of the Crimea Communiqué established for present Warsaw Administration a right to prior consultation. As British and United States representatives on Commission have already explained the text of the Crimea Communiqué cannot in the view of the United States Government bear this interpretation. . .

2. In the view of the United States Government all Poles nominated by any of the three Governments should be accepted for consultation unless conclusive evidence is produced to show that they do not represent the democratic elements in the country. It should be for the Commission alone and not for the Provisional Governmental authority now functioning in Warsaw to decide this matter. The United States Government would consider it contrary to the spirit of the Yalta meeting for any one of the Commissioners to exercise a veto and are confident that a unanimous decision of the three Commissioners will be possible. Every effort should be made to produce the Polish leaders whom they wish to consult at the earliest possible moment and the Commission should ensure to them the right to suggest to the Commission the names of other Poles who they think should be invited to any such proceedings. All Poles appearing before the Commission would by that very fact naturally enjoy the facilities necessary for communication and consultation among themselves in Moscow.

The United States Government wishes to repeat in this connection that it regards participation of Mr. Mikolajczyk in consultations as vital to the success of the work of the Commission. . .

3. It is the understanding of the United States Government that Polish leaders invited for consultation should discuss among themselves with a view to reaching agreement on the composition of a Government fully representative of the various democratic sections of Polish opinion. The Commission should follow these discussions in the impartial capacity of an arbitrator.

4. In as much as it was agreed in the Crimea communiqué that the new situation of Poland called for the establishment of a new and more broadly based Polish Provisional Government pledged to holding of free elections as soon as possible it follows in the view of the United States Government that any arrangements for measures affecting the future of the Polish state should await so far as possible the establishment of that Provisional Government and be subject to final confirmation after the elections. As provided in the communiqué it is the opinion of the United States Government that

there should be the maximum amount of political tranquility inside Poland during these political negotiations. The United States Government therefore assumes that no action will be taken by provisional authorities in Poland against any individuals or groups there or otherwise which might disturb the atmosphere in which the present negotiations are taking place and so prejudice their successful outcome. If as may be expected this is also the view of the Soviet Government the United States Government trusts this will be made clear to the Polish Provisional Government in Warsaw. For its part the United States Government will similarly use its good offices with the Polish Government in London.[2]

The United States Government wishes to revert to a suggestion first put forward by Mr. Molotov that British and American observers should visit Poland to report upon conditions there. . .

5. The United States Government believes that if in the first stage the Commission would adopt as a basis the considerations suggested above, the negotiations would begin in accordance with the spirit and intent of the Crimean decision. The execution of the agreement on Poland reached by the three heads of Government at the Crimea will be watched by the entire world as an indication of the reality of the unity there so successfully established between the three principal Allies.

1. This memorandum was drawn up by Sir Archibald Clark-Kerr and Averell Harriman on the basis of the Prime Minister's draft letter (see above, No. 133, note 5) and American views (S.D. 860 C.01/3–945). Churchill submitted the original draft to Roosevelt on 16 March (F.O. 371. N2906/6/55). The President accepted it with minor changes, the most important of which substituted the last clause of (2) as printed for the British insistence that only a unanimous decision should bar any Poles. On 19 March Clark-Kerr submitted to Molotov an identical note to that printed.
2. Roosevelt and the State Department originally favoured the concept of a 'political truce', but this was rejected by Churchill as likely to be exploited by the Soviets and the Warsaw administration (F.R.U.S. 1945, V, pp. 154–5; pp. 158–60; pp. 163–5; F.O. 371. N2906/6/55).

No. 135

Commissar Molotov to Sir Archibald Clark-Kerr: Note (Extracts)[1]
MOSCOW, 22 March 1945
F.O. 371. N3204/6/55

. . . The Crimea Conference agreed that 'Provisional Government which is functioning in Poland should be reorganised on broader democratic basis with the inclusion of democratic leaders from Poland itself and Poles from abroad'. Thus new reorganised Polish Government which will be called Polish

1. An identical note was presented to Harriman. A paraphrased version is printed in F.R.U.S. 1945, V, pp. 176–8. Molotov used this memorandum as the basis for his exposition at the meeting of the commission on 23 March (F.R.U.S. 1945, V, pp. 180–2; F.O. 371. N3228/6/55).

Provisional Government of National Unity must be formed on the basis of present Provisional Government functioning in Poland. Any other interpretation of the decisions of the Crimea Conference would be a violation of these decisions. It is therefore entirely natural that in decisions of the Crimea Conference the Polish emigrant Government should not be mentioned at all whereas present Provisional Government is considered in these decisions as the core of the above-mentioned Government of National Unity. In this the Soviet Government sees a recognition by British and United States Governments that only the present Provisional Government which exercises State authority over the whole territory of Poland and which has acquired great authority among the Polish people, can become with the inclusion of new democratic forces from Poland and abroad, a Government resting on a broader basis which was the aim of the three Allied Governments.

After this, to consider the present Provisional Government in Warsaw as only one of three groups of democratic Poland, as was done in the British Ambassador's letter of March 19th, would be entirely incorrect and a violation of the proposals cf the Crimea Conference to which the Soviet Government cannot give any degree of assent.

2. The first task of the Moscow Commission set up by the Crimea Conference, namely the conduct of consultations with Polish Provisional Government and other democratic leaders from Poland and abroad must be accomplished in accordance with the Conference's decisions. Yet the Commission has not succeeded in doing this in spite of the efforts of the representative of the Soviet Government.

As is known, in the published text of the decisions of the Crimea Conference the Commission is authorised 'to consult in Moscow in the first instance with members of the present Provisional Government and with other Polish democratic leaders from within Poland and from abroad'. It follows from this that the Commission must consult in the first instance with present Provisional Government. This was in fact done by Moscow Commission in its first decisions of February 24th and February 27th when it invited representatives of present Provisional Government immediately to come to Moscow for consultation but however cancelled [?gp. omitted] after a few days at the instance of the British representative. The obligation to consult in the first instance with the Provisional Polish Government follows from the very sense of decisions of the Crimea Conference, as the final aim of the consultation is to transform the present Polish Provisional Government into a Government of National Unity which, in accordance with decisions of the Crimea Conference, must be formed on the basis of the Provisional Government now functioning in Poland. Consultation with other democratic Polish leaders must be supplementary to consultation with Provisional Polish Government, with a view to reorganising this Government on a broader basis. Moreover, according to the Crimea Conference the Provisional Polish Government as such is to be invited for consultation together with such other Polish statesmen as can be counted democratic leaders. As members of the Moscow Commission must work as a Commission, justly settling the question of precisely which Polish statesmen can be invited for consultation, a decision must be reached which is accepted by all three members of the Commission according to the Crimea decisions.

The proposal of the British Ambassador's original letter of March 19th in a number of points departs from the Crimea decisions. Thus supporters of the emigrant Polish Government such as Arciszewski Anders Raczkiewicz and others who are openly hostile to the U.S.S.R. and Crimea decisions cannot be invited for consultation although they call themselves democrats. It is clear that other opponents too of these decisions, such as Mikolajczyk for example, are not to be included in the category of the Polish leaders consultation with whom could contribute towards fulfilment of the decisions of the Crimean Conference.

The Soviet Government expresses its confidence that the decisions accepted unanimously by all members of the Commission regarding conduct of the consultation, will ensure in largest possible measure fulfilment of the Crimea decisions.

3. The Soviet Government learnt with astonishment of the British Government's intention to send into Poland British and American observers, in-as-much as such a proposal might offend the feelings of national dignity of the Poles. Moreover in the decisions of the Crimea Conference this question was not even raised. In any event the British Government could clarify this question best if it were to address itself direct to the Provisional Polish Government.

4. The Soviet Government proposes that the following rules should be unanimously recognised:

(a) Commission should base its work on the fundamental rule of the Crimea Conference that Provisional Polish Government is basis for a new Provisional Polish Government of National Unity with the inclusion in its composition of democratic leaders from Poland and Poles from abroad.

(b) Commission should immediately begin consultation with which it has been charged, for which purpose in the first place representatives of the Provisional Polish Government should be summoned.

(c) Commission should also immediately summon for consultation those Polish democratic leaders from Poland and abroad with regard to whom there is already agreement on the part of all three members of the Commission.

(d) After this Commission should decide question of summoning of other Polish democratic leaders from Poland and abroad whom the Commission recognises it as desirable to consult.[2]

The Soviet Government considers that the execution of the foregoing proposals would secure fulfilment of decisions of the Crimea Conference on this questions of Provisional Polish Government of National Unity and free elections which are subsequently to be held, which is the obligation of the Moscow Commission and which corresponds to the interest of democratic Poland and also of the Allied Powers.

2. The U.S. and U.K. ambassadors agreed to present a redraft of these four rules on 26 March (for this, see F.R.U.S. 1945, V, p. 179). The Foreign Office and the Prime Minister were strongly against submitting any redraft as it was felt this would enable Molotov to avoid discussing the issues of substance in the memorandum of 19 March. Churchill explained the British position to Roosevelt in a telegram on 27 March (F.O. 371. N3404/6/55; F.R.U.S. 1945, V, pp. 185–8). He proposed a joint message to Stalin. The State Department and the President favoured however pushing on with the redraft of Molotov's four rules (F.O. 371. N3576/6/55; F.R.U.S. 1945, V, pp. 189–90). The President sent his proposed message to Stalin to Churchill on 29 March (see below, No. 136). The western redraft was presented to the meeting of the commission on 2 April and rejected by Molotov (F.R.U.S. 1945, V, pp. 196–8; F.O. 371. N3586/6/55). Harriman felt that on this occasion Molotov took a harder stance than before.

No. 136

President Roosevelt to Marshal Stalin: Letter (Extracts)[1]
WASHINGTON, 1 April 1945
F.R.U.S. 1945, V, pp. 194–6

I cannot conceal from you the concern with which I view the development of events of mutual interest since our fruitful meeting at Yalta. The decisions we reached there were good ones and have for the most part been welcomed with enthusiasm by the peoples of the world who saw in our ability to find a common basis of understanding the best pledge for a secure and peaceful world after this war. Precisely because of the hopes and expectations that these decisions raised, their fulfillment is being followed with the closest attention. We have no right to let them be disappointed. So far there has been a discouraging lack of progress made in the carrying out, which the world expects, of the political decisions which we reached at the Conference particularly those relating to the Polish question. I am frankly puzzled as to why this should be and must tell you that I do not fully understand in many respects the apparent indifferent attitude of your Government. Having understood each other so well at Yalta I am convinced that the three of us can and will clear away any obstacles which have developed since then. I intend, therefore, in this message to lay before you with complete frankness the problem as I see it. . .

. . . the part of our agreements at Yalta which has aroused the greatest popular interest and is the most urgent relates to the Polish question. You are aware of course that the Commission which we set up has made no progress.

1. Roosevelt sent this letter to Churchill on 29 March (F.O. 371. N3576/6/55). Churchill replied on the 30th suggesting some alterations which made clearer the western unwillingness to enter into discussion with the Warsaw administration before the other Poles arrived, and which underlined the western refusal to accept Molotov's right of veto over individual Poles (F.O. 371. N3577/1/55). Roosevelt accepted these suggestions. Churchill sent a similar message to Stalin on 1 April (F.O. 371. N3578/6/55).

I feel this is due to the interpretation which your Government is placing upon the Crimean decisions. In order that there shall be no misunderstanding I set forth below my interpretation of the points of the agreement which are pertinent to the difficulties encountered by the Commission in Moscow.

In the discussions that have taken place so far your Government appears to take the position that the new Polish Provisional Government of National Unity which we agreed should be formed should be little more than a continuation of the present Warsaw Government. I cannot reconcile this either with our agreement or our discussions. While it is true that the Lublin Government is to be reorganized and its members play a prominent role it is to be done in such a fashion as to bring into being a new Government. This point is clearly brought out in several places in the text of the agreement. I must make it quite plain to you that any such solution which would result in a thinly disguised continuance of the present Warsaw regime would be unacceptable and would cause the people of the United States to regard the Yalta agreement as having failed. It is equally apparent that for the same reason the Warsaw Government cannot under the agreement claim the right to select or reject what Poles are to be brought to Moscow by the Commission for consultation. Can we not agree that it is up to the Commission to select the Polish leaders to come to Moscow to consult in the first instance and invitations be sent our accordingly. If this could be done I see no great objection to having the Lublin group come first in order that they may be fully acquainted with the agreed interpretation of the Yalta decisions on this point. It is of course understood that if the Lublin group comes first no arrangements would be made independently with them before the arrival of the other Polish leaders called for consultation.[2] In order to facilitate the agreement the Commission might first of all select a small but representative group of Polish leaders who could suggest other names for the consideration of the Commission. We have not and would not bar or veto any candidate for consultation which Mr. Molotov might propose being confident that he would not suggest any Poles who would be inimical to the intent of the Crimean decision. I feel that it is not too much to ask that my Ambassador be accorded the same confidence and that any candidate for consultation presented by any one of the Commission be accepted by the others in good faith.[3] It is obvious to me that if the right of the Commission to select these Poles is limited or shared with the Warsaw Government the very foundation on which our agreement rests would be destroyed. While the foregoing are the immediate obstacles which in my opinion have prevented the Commission from making any progress in this vital matter there are two other suggestions which were not in the agreement but nevertheless have a very important bearing on the result we all seek. Neither of these suggestions has been as yet accepted by your Government. I refer to (1) that there should be the

2. This sentence was suggested by Churchill.
3. The clause '. . . and that . . . good faith' was suggested by Churchill.

maximum of political tranquility in Poland and that dissident groups should cease any measures and countermeasures against each other. That we should respectively use our influence to that end seems to me so eminently reasonable. (2) It would also seem entirely natural in view of the responsibilities placed upon them by the agreement that representatives of the American and British members of the Commission should be permitted to visit Poland. As you will recall Mr. Molotov himself suggested this at an early meeting of the Commission and only subsequently withdrew it.

... You are, I am sure, aware that genuine popular support in the United States is required to carry out any Government policy foreign or domestic. The American people make up their own mind and no Governmental action can change it. I mention this fact because the last sentence of your message about Mr. Molotov's attendance at San Francisco made me wonder whether you give full weight to this factor.[4]

4. This sentence reads: 'As to the different interpretations [of Molotov's absence] you will appreciate that they cannot determine the decisions to be taken' (Stalin Correspondence, II, No. 282).

No. 137

Marshal Stalin to President Roosevelt: Letter[1]
MOSCOW, 7 April 1945
Stalin Correspondence, II, No. 289

With reference to your message of April 1st I think I must make the following comments on the Polish question.

The Polish question has indeed reached an impasse.

What is the reason?

The reason is that the U.S. and British Ambassadors in Moscow — members of the Moscow Commission — have departed from the instructions of the Crimea Conference, introducing new elements not provided for by the Crimea Conference.

Namely:

(a) At the Crimea Conference the three of us regarded the Polish Provisional Government as the government now functioning in Poland and subject to reconstruction, as the government that should be the core of a new Government of National Unity. The U.S. and British Ambassadors in

1. Stalin sent a similar letter to Churchill on 7 April (Stalin Correspondence 1, No. 418). In it he stated that the unfriendly attitude of the British towards the provisional government explained the latter's unwillingness to accept U.K. observers. He also expressed his willingness to 'use my influence with the Provisional Polish government to make them withdraw their objections to Mikolajczyk', providing he made a public declaration accepting the Yalta decisions on Poland. Churchill thought that Mikołajczyk should respond to this statement and when he did so on 15 April, Churchill wrote to Stalin informing him of this (Stalin Correspondence, I, Nos. 425, 426, 429, 435).

Moscow, however, have departed from that thesis; they ignore the Polish Provisional Government, pay no heed to it and at best place individuals in Poland and London on a par with the Provisional Government. Furthermore, they hold that reconstruction of the Provisional Government should be understood in terms of its abolition and the establishment of an entirely new government. Things have gone so far that Mr Harriman declared in the Moscow Commission that it might be that not a single member of the Provisional Government would be included in the Polish Government of National Unity.[2]

Obviously this thesis of the U.S. and British Ambassadors cannot but be strongly resented by the Polish Provisional Government. As regards the Soviet Union, it certainly cannot accept a thesis that is tantamount to direct violation of the Crimea Conference decisions.

(b) At the Crimea Conference the three of us held that five people should be invited for consultation from Poland and three from London, not more. But the U.S. and British Ambassadors have abandoned that position and insist that each member of the Moscow Commission be entitled to invite an unlimited number from Poland and from London.

Clearly the Soviet Government could not agree to that, because, according to the Crimea decision, invitations should be sent not by individual members of the Commission, but by the Commission as a whole, as a body. The demand for no limit to the number invited for consultation runs counter to what was envisaged at the Crimea Conference.

(c) The Soviet Government proceeds from the assumption that, by virtue of the Crimea decisions, those invited for consultation should be in the first instance Polish leaders who recognise the decisions of the Crimea Conference, including the one on the Curzon Line, and, secondly who actually want friendly relations between Poland and the Soviet Union. The Soviet Government insists on this because the blood of Soviet soldiers, so freely shed in liberating Poland, and the fact that in the past 30 years the territory of Poland has twice been used by an enemy for invading Russia, oblige the Soviet Government to ensure friendly relations between the Soviet Union and Poland.

The U.S. and British Ambassadors in Moscow, however, ignore this and want to invite Polish leaders for consultation regardless of their attitude to the Crimea decisions and to the Soviet Union.

Such, to my mind, are the factors hindering a settlement of the Polish problem through mutual agreement.

In order to break the deadlock and reach an agreed decision, the following steps should, I think, be taken:

(1) Affirm that reconstruction of the Polish Provisional Government implies, not its abolition, but its reconstruction by enlarging it, it being under-

2. This incident occurred at the meeting of the commission on 23 March when Harriman pointed out that the word 'reorganize' in the Yalta protocol had a very wide meaning. Clark-Kerr regarded Stalin's objections as 'frivolous' (F.O. 371. C4050/6/55). For Harriman's own explanation, see F.R.U.S. 1945, V, p.214.

stood that the Provisional Government shall form the core of the future Polish Government of National Unity.

(2) Return to the provisions of the Crimea Conference and restrict the number of Polish leaders to be invited to eight persons, of whom five should be from Poland and three from London.

(3) Affirm that the representatives of the Polish Provisional Government shall be consulted in all circumstances, that they be consulted in the first place, since the Provisional Government is much stronger in Poland compared with the individuals to be invited from London and Poland whose influence among the population in no way compares with the tremendous prestige of the Provisional Government.

I draw your attention to this because, to my mind, any other decision on the point might be regarded in Poland as an affront to the people and as an attempt to impose a government without regard to Polish public opinion.

(4) Only those leaders should be summoned for consultation from Poland and from London who recognise the decisions of the Crimea Conference on Poland and who in practice want friendly relations between Poland and the Soviet Union.

(5) Reconstruction of the Provisional Government to be effected by replacing a number of Ministers of the Provisional Government by nominees among the Polish leaders who are not members of the Provisional Government.

As to the ratio of old and new Ministers in the Government of National Unity, it might be established more or less on the same lines as was done in the case of the Yugoslav Government. I think if these comments are taken into consideration the Polish question can be settled in a short time.[3]

3. Clark-Kerr and Harriman felt that Stalin's letter was an indication that the Soviets were not prepared to break with the western allies on this question. In particular, his preparedness to accept Mikołajczyk even though conditional, was held to be encouraging. Harriman felt however that the question should now be discussed at a 'high level' and that there was no point in the commission meeting until a firm agreement had been reached on the number and names of the persons to be invited for consultation (F.R.U.S. 1945, V, 213–8; F.O. 371. C4050/6/55). Another sign of Stalin's willingness to respond to pressure was the announcement that Molotov would after all attend the San Francisco conference.

No. 138

President Truman and Prime Minister Churchill to Marshal Stalin: Letter[1]
WASHINGTON AND LONDON, 18 April 1945
Stalin Correspondence, I, No. 430

1. This letter was drafted by Truman, Churchill approved of it, but the Foreign Office favoured a number of alterations in the original draft. As finally sent, the message omitted an explanation of Harriman's statement on 23 March (see above, No. 137) and specified four non-Lublin Poles from Poland of whom Stalin should select one.

The Foreign Office thought that, in view of the recommendations of Harriman and Clark-Kerr for standing firm and because discussions on the question were to take place in the U.S.A., the message should not be delivered. The Prime Minister disagreed and the letter was communicated on 18 April.

We are sending this joint reply to your messages of April 7th in regard to the Polish negotiations for the sake of greater clarity and in order that there will be no misunderstanding as to our position on this matter. The British and United States Governments have tried most earnestly to be constructive and fair in their approach and will continue to do so. Before putting before you the concrete and constructive suggestion which is the purpose of this message, we feel it necessary, however, to correct the completely erroneous impression which you have apparently received in regard to the position of the British and United States Governments as set forth by our Ambassadors under direct instructions during the negotiations. It is most surprising to have you state that the present government functioning in Warsaw has been in any way ignored during these negotiations. Such has never been our intention nor our position. You must be cognisant of the fact that our Ambassadors in Moscow have agreed without question that the three leaders of the Warsaw Government should be included in the list of Poles to be invited to come to Moscow for consultation with the Polish Commission. We have never denied that among the three elements from which the new Provisional Government of National Unity is to be formed the representatives of the present Warsaw Government will play, unquestionably, a prominent part. Nor can it be said with any justification that our Ambassadors are demanding the right to invite an unlimited number of Poles. The right to put forward and have accepted by the Commission individual representative Poles from abroad and from within Poland to be invited to Moscow for consultation cannot be interpreted in that sense. Indeed, in his message of April 1st President Roosevelt specifically said: "In order to facilitate agreement the Commission might first of all select a small but representative group of Polish leaders who could suggest other names for consideration by the Commission." The real issue between us is whether or not the Warsaw Government has the right to veto individual candidates for consultation. No such interpretation, in our considered opinion, can be found in the Crimea decision. It appears to us that you are reverting to the original position taken by the Soviet delegation at the Crimea, which was subsequently modified in the agreement. Let us keep clearly in mind that we are now speaking only of the group of Poles who are to be invited to Moscow for consultation.

You mention the desirability of inviting eight Poles — five from within Poland and three from London — to take part in these first consultations, and in your message to the Prime Minister you indicate that Mikolajczyk would be acceptable[2] if he issued a statement in support of the Crimea decision. We therefore submit the following proposals for your consideration in order to prevent a breakdown, with all its incalculable consequences, of our endeavours to settle the Polish question. We hope that you will give them

2. The Foreign Office thought that this sentence should read '. . . you indicate that you will do your best to arrange that Mikolajczyk will be accepted' (F.O. 371. N4091/6/55).

your most immediate and earnest consideration:

(1) That we instruct our representatives on the Commission to extend invitations immediately to the following Polish leaders to come to Moscow for consultation: Bierut, Osubka-Morawski, Rola-Zymerski, Bishop Sapieha, one representative Polish political party leader not connected with the present Warsaw Government (if any of the following were agreeable to you he would be agreeable to us — Witos, Zulawski, Chachinski, Jasiukowcz), and from London: Mikolajczyk, Grabski and Stanczyk.

(2) That once invitations to come for consultation have been issued by the Commission, the representatives of the Warsaw Provisional Government would arrive first if desired.

(3) That it be agreed that these Polish leaders called for consultation could suggest to the Commission the names of a certain number of other Polish leaders from within Poland or abroad who might be brought in for consultation in order that all the major Polish groups be represented in the discussions.

(4) We do not feel that we could commit ourselves to any formula for determining the composition of the new Government of National Unity in advance of consultation with the Polish leaders and we do not in any case consider the Yugoslav procedent to be applicable to Poland.

We ask you to read again carefully the American and British messages of April 1st since they set forth the larger considerations which we still have very much in mind and to which we must adhere.

No. 139

President Truman to Marshal Stalin: Note[1]
WASHINGTON, 23 April 1945
F.R.U.S. 1945, V, pp. 258–9

There was an agreement at Yalta in which President Roosevelt participated for the United States Government to reorganize the Provisional Government functioning in Warsaw in order to establish a new Government of National Unity in Poland by means of previous consultation between representatives of the Provisional Polish Government of Warsaw and other Polish democratic leaders from Poland and from abroad.

In the opinion of the United States Government the Crimean decision on Poland can only be carried out if a group of genuinely representative democratic Polish leaders are invited to Moscow for consultation. The United States

1. On his arrival in Washington, Eden had persuaded the Americans that discussion of the Polish question could not be postponed until San Francisco. Accordingly, Eden and Stettinius met Molotov on the evening of 22 April and twice on the 23rd. On these occasions no progress was made. Truman himself decided to intervene and on 23 April saw Molotov and told him 'in words of one syllable' (F.R.U.S. 1945, V, p. 233) of his dissatisfaction with the Soviet position over Poland. It was on this occasion that he presented this note to Molotov (For the meeting, F.R.U.S. 1945, V, pp. 256–8; F.O. 371. N4493/6/55).

268 FROM DECEMBER 1944 TO THE POTSDAM CONFERENCE

Government cannot be party to any method of consultation with Polish leaders which would not result in the establishment of a new Provisional Government of National Unity genuinely representative of the democratic elements of the Polish people. The United States and British Governments have gone as far as they can to meet the situation and carry out the intent of the Crimean decisions in their joint message delivered to Marshal Stalin on April 18th.

The United States Government earnestly requests that the Soviet Government accept the proposals set forth in the joint message of the President and Prime Minister to Marshal Stalin. And that Mr. Molotov continue the conversations with the Secretary of State and Mr. Eden in San Francisco on that basis.

The Soviet Government must realize that the failure to go forward at this time with the implementation of the Crimean decision on Poland would seriously shake confidence in the unity of the three Governments and their determination to continue the collaboration in the future as they have in the past.

No. 140

Marshal Stalin to Winston Churchill: Letter
24 April 1945
Stalin Correspondence, I, No. 439

I received the joint message from you and President Truman on April 18.[1]

It would appear that you still regard the Polish Provisional Government, not as the core of a future Polish Government of National Unity, but merely as a group on a par with any other group of Poles. It would be hard to reconcile this concept of the position of the Provisional Government and this attitude towards it with the Crimea decision on Poland. At the Crimea Conference the three of us, including President Roosevelt, based ourselves on the assumption that the Polish Provisional Government, as the Government now functioning in Poland and enjoying the trust and support of the majority of the Polish people, should be the core, that is, the main part of a new, reconstructed Polish Government of National Unity.

You apparently disagree with this understanding of the issue. By turning down the Yugoslav example as a model for Poland, you confirm that the Polish Provisional Government cannot be regarded as a basis for, and the core of, a future Government of National Unity.

2. Another circumstance that should be borne in mind is that Poland borders on the Soviet Union, which cannot be said about Great Britain or the U.S.A.

1. Stalin sent an almost identical letter to Truman (Stalin Correspondence II, No. 293) in which he also acknowledged receipt of Truman's note to Molotov (see above, No. 139).

Poland is to the security of the Soviet Union what Belgium and Greece are to the security of Great Britain.

You evidently do not agree that the Soviet Union is entitled to seek in Poland a Government that would be friendly to it, that the Soviet Government cannot agree to the existence in Poland of a Government hostile to it. This is rendered imperative, among other things, by the Soviet people's blood freely shed on the fields of Poland for the liberation of that country. I do not know whether a genuinely representative Government has been established in Greece, or whether the Belgian Government is a genuinely democratic one. The Soviet Union was not consulted when those Governments were being formed, nor did it claim the right to interfere in those matters, because it realises how important Belgium and Greece are to the security of Great Britain.

I cannot understand why in discussing Poland no attempt is made to consider the interests of the Soviet Union in terms of security as well.

3. One cannot but recognise as unusual a situation in which two Governments — those of the United States and Great Britain — reach agreement beforehand on Poland, a country in which the U.S.S.R. is interested first of all and most of all, and, placing its representatives in an intolerable position, try to dictate to it.

I say that this situation cannot contribute to agreed settlement of the Polish problem.

4. I am most grateful to you for kindly communicating the text of Mikolajczyk's declaration concerning Poland's eastern frontier. I am prepared to recommend to the Polish Provisional Government that they take note of this declaration and withdraw their objection to inviting Mikolajczyk for consultation on a Polish Government.

The important thing now is to accept the Yugoslav precedent as a model for Poland. I think that if this is done we shall be able to make progress on the Polish question.[2]

2. Churchill replied in a very long letter on 28 April (Stalin Correspondence, I, No. 450, reiterating the British position, rejecting Stalin's advocacy of the 'Yugoslav precedent as a model for Poland' and stating that the British had no way of checking the alarming rumours coming out of Poland. He concluded:—

There is not much comfort in looking into a future where you and the countries you dominate, plus the Communist parties in many other States, are all drawn up on one side, and those who rally to the English-speaking nations and their Associates or Dominions are on the other. It is quite obvious that their quarrel would tear the world to pieces and that all of us leading men on either side who had anything to do with that would be shamed before history.

No. 141

Marshal Stalin to Winston Churchill: Letter
4 May 1945
Stalin Correspondence, I, No. 456

I am in receipt of your message of April 28 on the Polish question.

I must say that I cannot accept the arguments put forward in support of your stand.

You are inclined to regard the proposal that the Yugoslav precedent be accepted as a model for Poland as renunciation of the procedure agreed between us for setting up a Polish Government of National Unity. I cannot agree with you. I think that the Yugoslav precedent is important first of all because it points the way to the most suitable and practical solution of the problem of forming a new United Government based on the governmental agency at present exercising state power in the country.

It is quite obvious that, unless the Provisional Government now functioning in Poland and enjoying the support and trust of a majority of the Polish people is taken as a basis for a future Government of National Unity, it will be impossible to count on successful fulfilment of the task set by the Crimea Conference.

2. I cannot subscribe to that part of your considerations on Greece where you suggest three-Power control over the elections. Such control over the people of an allied country would of necessity be assessed as an affront and gross interference in their internal affairs. Such control is out of place in relation to former satellite countries which subsequently declared war on Germany and ranged themselves with the Allies, as demonstrated by electoral experience, for example, in Finland, where the election was held without outside interference and yielded positive results.

Your comments on Belgium and Poland as war theatres and communication corridors are perfectly justified. As regards Poland, it is her being a neighbour of the Soviet Union that makes it essential for a future Polish Government to seek in practice friendly relations between Poland and the U.S.S.R., which is also in the interests of the other freedom-loving nations. This circumstance, too, speaks for the Yugoslav precedent. The United Nations are interested in constant and durable friendship between the U.S.S.R. and Poland. Hence we cannot acquiesce in the attempts that are being made to involve in the forming of a future Polish Government people who, to quote you, "are not fundamentally anti-Russian", or to bar from participation only those who, in your view, are "extreme people unfriendly to Russia". Neither one nor the other can satisfy us. We insist, and shall continue to insist, that only people who have demonstrated by deeds their friendly attitude to the Soviet Union, who are willing honestly and sincerely to cooperate with the Soviet state, should be consulted on the formation of a future Polish Government.

3. I must deal specially with paragraph 11 of your message concerning

the difficulties arising from rumours about the arrest of 15 Poles, about deportations, etc.

I am able to inform you that the group of Poles mentioned by you comprises 16, not 15, persons. The group is headed by the well-known General Okulicki. The British information services maintain a deliberate silence, in view of his particular odiousness, about this Polish General, who, along with the 15 other Poles, has 'disappeared'. But we have no intention of being silent about the matter. This group of 16, led by General Okulicki, has been arrested by the military authorities of the Soviet front and is undergoing investigation in Moscow. General Okulicki's group, in the first place General Okulicki himself, is charged with preparing and carrying out subversive activities behind the lines of the Red Army, subversion which has taken a toll of over a hundred Red Army soldiers and officers; the group is also charged with keeping illegal radio-transmitters in the rear of our troops, which is prohibited by law. All, or part of them — depending on the outcome of the investigation — will be tried. That is how the Red Army is forced to protect its units and its rear-lines against saboteurs and those who create disorder.[1]

The British information services are spreading rumours about the murder or shooting of Poles in Siedlce. The report is a fabrication from beginning to end and has, apparently, been concocted by Arciszewski's agents.

4. It appears from your message that you are unwilling to consider the Polish Provisional Government as a basis for a future Government of National Unity, or to accord it the place in that Government to which it is entitled. I must say frankly that this attitude precludes the possibility of an agreed decision on the Polish question.[2]

1. See Introduction, p. 42.
2. The Prime Minister on receipt of this letter sent a copy to Truman. He argued that a meeting of the three heads of governments was now essential. In the meantime 'We should hold firmly to the positions obtained or being obtained by our armies in Yugoslavia, in Austria, in Czechoslovakia, in the main central United States front and on the British front reaching up to Lubeck including Denmark' (F.O. 371. N5109/6/55). Truman agreed to the proposal for a tripartite meeting but stated that it could not take place before July (F.O. 371. N5505/6/55). He felt that one should hold firm and told Eden that he did not believe that there would be a solution of the Polish question.

No. 142

Anthony Eden to Winston Churchill: Telegram
SAN FRANCISCO, 9 May 1945
F.O. 371. N5169/6/55

Mr. Stettinius asked me to see him this morning about Poland.[1] He and Mr. Harriman who was present said that they had been thinking over the next move on the Polish question. Mr. Harriman was anxious to adhere to part B of the plan in my telegram No. 85.[2] He thought that it was important to keep this question open and before Marshal Stalin's attention pending another meeting of the Big Three. He therefore felt that he and Sir A. Clark Kerr who are leaving here today should after visiting Washington proceed to London in order to see you and M. Mikolajczyk on their way back to Moscow. They would see whether it were still possible to reach with the latter some understanding as to the type of reorganized Government which we could agree to, and the names and position of the Poles whom M. Mikolajczyk would wish to be included in it. If any progress were made on these lines, and subject to the approval of His Majesty's Government and the United States Government, the two Ambassadors might then be in a position on their return to Moscow to discuss the matter further with Marshal Stalin. Mr. Harriman admitted that the prospects of any agreement being reached by this means were now slender, but he argued that Marshal Stalin was likely to be more open to argument than M. Molotov and that it might at any rate be possible to narrow down our differences to some extent preparatory to a meeting between Marshal Stalin, the President and yourself.

2. I reminded Mr. Stettinius and Mr. Harriman of Marshal Stalin's last unhelpful message to you or May 4th[3] and told them that I understood that you might shortly telegraph to the President suggesting a meeting of the three heads of Governments. I told them that M. Molotov had seemed disposed to accept the idea of such a meeting, and I warned them that I thought you might very likely take the view that it would be better to take no further step in the Polish question until such a meeting had taken place. There was also the consideration that the recent episode of the arrest of the sixteen Poles in Poland might well render any conversations with M. Mikolajczyk unfruitful at present. It was however agreed that Mr. Harriman should discuss his plan with the President on his way through Washington and that I should warn you of what Americans have in mind.

3. I shall be grateful for any comments you may have. It might be useful if you were to repeat to Washington for the information of Clark Kerr any telegram you may send me. I think it would do nothing but good that Harriman and Clark Kerr should come back via London. They could then see you and Mikolajczyk. This would not tie us down to acceptance of any specific procedure for the future.[4]

1. For the U.S. version of this conversation, F.R.U.S. 1945, V, pp. 291–3.
2. This plan had been prepared by Harriman and Stettinius for submission to the President (F.O. 371. N4854/6/55). It involved Eden and Stettinius telling Molotov in San Francisco that their governments would not accept Stalin's position as outlined in the letter of 24 April. Harriman and Clark-Kerr were then to go to London in an attempt to get Mikolajczyk to agree to concrete proposals for the reorganization of the provisional Polish government. The most the non-Warsaw Poles could expect, it was held, was one third to 40% of all cabinet posts. The ambassadors would then return to Moscow and ask Stalin to receive them 'to present the final proposals of the American and British governments on the Polish question.'
On 2 May, Stettinius and Eden had spoken to Molotov and on 3 May Eden saw Molotov alone. Little progress was made and such advances as were achieved as over Mikolajczyk's acceptability, were frustrated by the new crisis created by the Soviet

announcement of the arrest of the sixteen Poles which led the UK and US governments to suspend talks.

2. See above, No. 141.

3. The Foreign Office felt this plan was 'futile if not dangerous' and Eden was asked to inform the State Department that Churchill did not approve (F.O. 371. N5169/6/55). The settlement of the problem was thus to be put off until the proposed meeting of heads of government. Although Truman had agreed with Eden that they were to 'stand pat on our understanding of the Yalta agreement until the trial of the sixteen Poles', (F.O. 371. N5503/6/55) in the event, he sent Harry Hopkins to Moscow on 23 May in a last attempt to reach a negotiated settlement.

No. 143

Sir Archibald Clark-Kerr to Anthony Eden: Telegram
1 June 1945
F.O. 371. N6293/6/55

Mr. Hopkins has had two more talks with Marshal Stalin about Poland.[1] At first Stalin was accommodating but non-committal. At second in which Molotov played a large part he was in 'trading' mood, inclined to drive a bargain. He suggested that Moscow Commission should get to work again on basis of calling the following men for consultation.

(1) From London: Mikolajczyk, Grabski or (repeat or) Stancyck and Kolodzei.[2]

(2) From Poland: Witos or (repeat or) Sapieha Zulawski Kutzreba Krzyzanowski (Rector of Cracow University) and Kolodzeiski (Director of Library of Sejm and now head of Co-operative Union).

2. On balance this list seems to us here and to the Americans to be about as good a one as we could have hoped for. It compares very well with Molotov's last proposal . . .[3] and not unfavourably with that in joint message of April 18th. and I think we would be wise to accept it provided something can be done about the 15 Poles now under arrest.

3. Mr. Hopkins had this matter out with Stalin last night. Stalin was 'tough' but not unresponsive. He said General Okulicki had been undoubtedly guilty of acts of terrorism and must be dealt with accordingly. The 'majority of the others' had been in wireless communication with London and this was a serious offence. On pressure from Mr. Hopkins he seemed ready to admit this was the only charge against them and when Mr. Hopkins said that the

1. Harry Hopkins arrived in Moscow on 25 May and left on 7 June. For the American account of his visit see F.R.U.S. 1945, V, pp. 299–315, 318–320, 326–31; F.R.U.S. Potsdam, I, pp. 24–62. At the first meeting on 26 May, Hopkins had stressed the harmful effects which the disagreement over the Polish question was having on American public opinion. On 27 May, Hopkins assured Stalin that the U.S. had no desire to establish a *cordon sanitaire,* while Stalin made clear his willingness to give the non-Warsaw Poles four of eighteen posts in a reformed cabinet.The meetings described here took place on 30 and 31 May.
2. Kołodziej was the communist secretary of the Polish seaman's union. At his meeting with Hopkins on 6 June, Stalin was prepared to replace him by a non-party but left-leaning engineer, Julian Zakowski.
3. At the meeting of the Polish Commission on 2 April. (See above, No. 135, note 2).

war was over and the whole thing might well now be forgotten Stalin indicated that this would be taken into consideration and that the prisoners would be dealt with leniently. But trial must proceed.

4. We are dining with Stalin tonight when Mr. Hopkins intends to press him very hard and to make it clear that without the release of at least Mikolajczyk's friends among the political party leaders it will be very hard to get things going again.[4]

4. Harriman raised this question both at the dinner and at the talk on 6 June.

No. 144

Winston Churchill to Sir Archibald Clark-Kerr: Telegram (Extracts)
LONDON, 9 June 1945
F.O. 371. N6696/6/55

Position reached as a result of Hopkins' and Harriman's latest conversation with Stalin[1] has been explained to Mikolajczyk, to whom it was made clear that in effect no substantial satisfaction had been obtained on any of his points summarised in my telegram No. 3034 [of 4th June],[2] except for his sole condition that invitation will be issued by the Moscow Commission. Mikolajczyk confirmed that he and Stanczyk were nevertheless still prepared to respond to an invitation from the Commission on the present basis.

2. As regards choice between Kolodzei and Zakowski he prefers latter as being less controversial figure... You may accordingly confirm to Stalin that His Majesty's Government agree to the issue by the Commission of invitations to Mikolajczyk, Stanczyk, Zakowski, Witos, Zulawski, Kutrzeba, Krzyanowski and Kolodzeiski, plus three of four representatives of the Warsaw Provisional Government. I take it that these invitations will reach Mikolajczyk and his travelling companions within the next few days and that arrangements will be made at your end to fly the party direct from London to Moscow. It would be best for him to travel in British or American aircraft.

3. We cannot press the Russians further at this stage to meet us over the special desiderata put forward by Mikolajczyk but we must give him and his friends all the support we properly can in his difficult negotiations in Moscow.

1. On 6 June. Already on June 1 Truman had cabled Churchill describing the results of Hopkins' conversations as 'very encouraging' (F.R.U.S. 1945, V, pp. 314–5). Churchill in his replies of 2 and 4 June, while not disagreeing openly, was markedly less optimistic (F.R.U.S. 1945, V, pp. 317, 321–2).
2. For this see Churchill's telegrams to Truman of 4 June (F.R.U.S. 1945, V, pp. 321–4). Mikołajczyk stated that those participating in the conference should be granted freedom of movement and freedom from arrest during and after the conversations. While he would not insist on the release of the sixteen arrested men, he felt it was absolutely necessary to create the right conditions for an agreement. He also pointed out that Grabski was ill and could not travel and that the absence of any member of the Christian Democratic party among those invited was unfortunate.

We must do our best to keep Stalin up to his promise to take fully into consideration Mr. Hopkins' appeal for the release of the majority of the sixteen
arrested men.[3] We must also be ready to press in the Commission for invitation
of additional representative party leaders, such as Popiel, Piwowarczyk and
Trampczynski if asked for by Mikolajczyk. At present only 2 out of the 4
main political parties will be represented at the meeting.

4. Our agreement to Stalin's list without any further preliminary conditions
represents in fact a marked retreat from the position which we have hitherto
held. By agreeing, for instance, as Mr. Hopkins suggests we must,
additional invitations will require agreement of all members of the
Commission, we shall now be accepting the original Russian claim that the
Warsaw Poles have the right to veto our proposed candidates.

5. Our concessions will be justified only if conversations result in formation of a re-organised provisional government in which elements not included in the present provisional Government enjoy substantial representation and a proportion of key positions. I therefore agree with you that we
must reject any attempt to pin us down in advance of any agreed percentage,
such as the Yugoslav formula which has turned out to be a fraud leading to
what we now see. For the same reason you should avoid committing yourself
before the conversations begin among the Poles themselves to any formula
about the basis of the re-organised Government such as that proposed in
paragraph 4 of your telegram No. 2287.[4] You may, if necessary, point out
that we have never denied [see joint message from President and myself to
Stalin of 18th April] 'that among the three elements from which the new
provisional Government of National Unity is to be formed the representatives
of the present Warsaw Government will play unquestionably a prominent part'.
You may also, if necessary, agree to Warsaw Poles arriving first in Moscow but
you should not easily agree to their being received in advance of the
Commission as such.

6. But the one absolutely essential requirement, if any settlement reached
in Moscow is to be accepted by Parliament and public opinion here, is that
His Majesty's Government should not lay themselves open to the charge of
having followed the Munich pattern and imposed, for the sake of our relations
with the Soviet Government, on an unwilling Polish people a settlement agreed
upon in advance among the Great Powers. We must above all else maintain
the position that the role of the Commission is to act as mediators only,
assisting the Poles to reach among themselves a settlement which can then be
endorsed and approved by the Poles. No doubt this settlement will inevitably

3. The men were not in fact released and on June 21, Okulicki was sentenced to ten years
imprisonment, Jankowski to eight years and Bien and Jasiukowicz to 5 years each. Three
of the others were acquitted and the rest received sentences ranging from 4 to 18 months.
4. In this telegram of 6 June (F.O. 371. N6534/6/55), Clark-Kerr proposed accepting a
statement on the lines that 'the newly reorganized Polish Government which would be
called the Polish Provisional Government of National Unity must be formed on the basis
of the present Provisional Government functioning in Poland.'

be 'based upon' the present Warsaw Government. But, so far as public appearances are concerned, it is one thing for the Poles themselves to reach the conclusion that such is the logical outcome and quite another matter for them to be told before they begin their discussions that this is what they must accept. I rely on you to respect this distinction in your discussions with M. Molotov.

No. 145

Averell Harriman to Acting Secretary of State Grew: Telegram
MOSCOW, 28 June 1945
F.R.U.S. Potsdam, I, No. 492

Following is briefly my reaction to the Polish Agreement. I am somewhat disappointed that the outsiders did not get seven instead of five posts in the new Govt. — one additional Socialist and one from the Christian Labor Party. I believe this could have been done if the outside Socialists had taken a stronger position in the negotiations with the Warsaw reps.[1] Zulawski if his health had permitted would have been accepted. There appears to be a gentlemen's agreement that the Christian Labor leader, Popiel will be admitted to the Govt. on his return from London. The Socialists also hope to consolidate their party and obtain stronger representation in the Govt. at a later date.

I feel that Mikolajczyk is better off not to be Prime Minister under the present difficult situation both economic and political and that he has as strong a position as he could hope for as Deputy Prime Minister and Minister of Agriculture which latter post will necessitate his traveling around the country. With four new members of the Peasant Party in important posts in the Govt. he should be in a position to exercise substantial influence.

The matter which gives all concern is the retention of the independent Ministry of Internal Security under a Communist.[2] This Ministry is developing a secret police on the Russian style. The manner in which this Ministry is administered is the crux of whether Poland will have her independence, whether reasonable personal freedoms will be permitted and whether reasonably free elections can be held.

Mikolajczyk does not expect the full freedoms which he would like for Poland and the Polish people. On the other hand he is hopeful that through the strength of the Peasant Party a reasonable degree of freedom and independence can be preserved now and that in time after conditions in Europe become more stable and Russia turns her attention to her internal development controls will be relaxed and Poland will be able to gain for herself her indepen-

1. This was also Clark-Kerr's view. He felt that the Poles from Poland were so fearful of a breakdown that they pressed Mikołajczyk to accept moderate terms. Stańczyk, too, was unwilling to ask too much (F.O. 371. N7295, 7312/6/55).
2. Stanisław Radkiewicz.

dence of life as a nation even though he freely accepts that Poland's security and foreign policy must follow the lead of Moscow.

During the course of the negotiations I spent a good many hours with the principal Warsaw leaders, Bierut, Morawski and Gomulka. . . . Mikolajczyk recognizes the importance of the Communist Party and of these men particularly the two Communists in the all important relations with Russia and says that he is ready to work closely with them even though they represent only a very small fraction of the Polish people.

I feel that Mikolajczyk and his associates have been wise in accepting the best deal they could make on their own and not coming to Clark Kerr and myself for direct assistance on improving the present agreement since it is the future decisions that are all important. It is impossible to predict the trend of events in Poland but I believe that the stage is set as well as can be done at the present time and that if we continue to take a sympathetic interest in Polish affairs and are reasonably generous in our economic relations there is a fair chance that things will work out satisfactorily from our standpoint.[3]

3. The U.K. Government, while welcoming the settlement, had some reservations. In particular, the Foreign Office informed Clark-Kerr that the British were not obliged to recognize the new government until it had been 'properly formed' and this, in terms of the first two paragraphs of the Yalta agreement on Poland meant a committment to free elections (F.O. 371. N7229/6/55). Churchill was particularly unhappy about the heavy sentences on Okulicki and his associates and argued that an amnesty would be in order. He felt however that ' a complete stop should be put to the activities of the London Poles in dropping peoples and supplies in Poland' (F.O. 371. N7296/6/55).

The Polish Question at the Potsdam Conference

No. 146

Statement on the Polish question as agreed by the Heads of Government at the fifth plenary meeting of the Potsdam Conference[1]
21 July 1945
F.R.U.S. Potsdam, II, No. 1131

1. At the second meeting of the conference, Stalin proposed a Soviet draft to deal with the problems of the liquidation of the London government (U.K. Minutes, F.O. 371. U6197/3628/70, pp. 103–5; U.S. Minutes, F.R.U.S. Potsdam, II, 91–4, 94–8; Soviet Minutes, Soviet protocols pp. 157–161). It was agreed to refer this question to a meeting of the Foreign Ministers. At this meeting on 19 July, (F.O. 371. U6197/3628/70, pp. 108–9; F.R.U.S. Potsdam, II, pp. 103–5) Eden presented a draft which was the basis of this statement. In view of disagreement over the wording, this draft was referred to a drafting committee of the three foreign ministers with one assistant each. This committee which met three times, referred a number of unresolved points to the fourth meeting of Foreign Ministers on 21 July (F.O. 371. U6197/3628/70, pp. 139–142; F.R.U.S. Potsdam, II, pp. 187–94). Two unresolved points (on the responsibility of the new Polish government for the liabilities of the London government and on the holding of free elections and the freedom of the press) were agreed on at the fifth plenary meeting on July 21 (F.O. 371. U6197/3628/70, pp. 145–7; F.R.U.S. Potsdam, II, pp. 203–14; Soviet protocols, pp. 192–7).

1. We have taken note with pleasure of the agreement reached among representative Poles from Poland and abroad which has made possible the formation, in accordance with the decisions reached at the Crimea Conference, of a Polish Provisional Government of National Unity recognised by the Three Powers. The establishment by the British and United States Governments of diplomatic relations with the Polish Provisional Government has resulted in the withdrawal of their recognition from the former Polish Government in London, which no longer exists.

2. The British and United States Governments have taken measures to protect the interests of the Polish Provisional Government, as the recognised Government of the Polish State, in the property belonging to the Polish State located in their territory and under their control whatever the form of this property may be. They have further taken measures to prevent alienation to third parties of such property. All proper facilities will be given to the Polish Provisional Government for the exercise of the ordinary legal remedies for the recovery of any property belonging to the Polish State which may have been wrongfully alienated.

3. The Three Powers are anxious to assist the Polish Provisional Government in facilitating the return to Poland as soon as practicable of all Poles abroad who wish to go, including members of the Polish armed forces and merchant marine. They expect that those Poles who return home shall be accorded personal rights and rights of property on the same basis as all Polish citizens.[2]

4. The Three Powers note that the Polish Provisional Government in accordance with the decisions of the Crimea Conference has agreed[3] to the holding of free and unfettered elections as soon as possible on the basis of universal suffrage and secret ballot in which all democratic and anti-Nazi parties shall have the right to take part and to put forward candidates; and that the representatives of the Allied Press shall enjoy full freedom to report to the world upon developments in Poland before and during the elections.

2. The original British draft read:
> It is their desire that as many of these Poles as possible should return home, and they consider that the Polish Provisional Government could itself greatly assist in this regard by giving specific undertakings that those Poles who return will do so with full assurance of their personal security, freedom and livelihood.

The Soviets objected to this as placing all responsibility for the return of Poles abroad on the Polish government. Molotov also felt no government could be *required* to provide for 'livelihood' without qualification.

3. The British draft wanted 'is pledged'. It also called for an additional sentence before the last reading:
> It is the confident hope of the Three Powers that the elections will be so organised as to enable all sections of Polish opinion to express their views freely, and thus play their full part in the restoration of the country's political life.

No. 147

Meeting between Truman, Byrnes and Molotov (Extracts)
29 July 1945
F.R.U.S. Potsdam, II, pp. 471–2

. . . THE SECRETARY said that there were two principal questions, in his opinion, which remained outstanding and if they could reach a decision on those it would be possible to consider winding up the Conference. These questions were:

1. The Polish western boundary.
2. German reparations.

THE SECRETARY said that if we were able to get an agreement on reparations along the lines of his proposals to Mr. Molotov[1] that the United States was prepared to go further to meet the Soviet wishes in regard to the Polish western frontier and would make the following proposal in that regard. (He handed Mr. Molotov a copy of the proposed United States suggestion with regard to the Polish western frontier, copy attached[2]).

After it had been translated, MR. MOLOTOV said that this would not put under Polish administration the area between the Eastern and Western Neisse. He said the Poles were most insistent upon receiving this and he recalled that Mr. Mikolajczyk had made a most convincing and definite argument before the three Foreign Ministers as to the vital importance of this area for Poland.

THE SECRETARY pointed out that this was true, but that since the final determination of the boundary would await the peace settlement, it did not follow that Poland might not receive this additional area if the peace conference so desired. He then said that as the President had frequently remarked, it had been agreed at Yalta and elsewhere that there would be four occupying powers in Germany, but that we now had a situation when there was in fact a fifth – Poland – which had been assumed without consultation or agreement with the United States, French, or British Governments.

MR. MOLOTOV replied that this was no one's fault; it was an extraordinary condition, since all Germans had fled the region.

THE PRESIDENT then remarked that he had thought that this suggestion would be agreeable to the Soviet Delegation, since in his opinion it represented a very large concession in our part and he hoped Mr. Molotov would submit it to Marshal Stalin. . .

1. This was for a reparations plan in terms of which each power would take reparations from its own zone, but the Soviets would in addition receive 25% of the total equipment available as reparations from the Ruhr. See Introduction, p. 45.
2. This proposed a frontier on the Oder and eastern Neisse.

No. 148

Eleventh plenary meeting of the Potsdam Conference (Extracts)[1]
31 July 1945
F.O. 371. U6197/3628/70

3. Western Frontier of Poland.

MR. BYRNES said that, as part of their attempt to secure agreement on
Reparations and on the proposed statement on the admission of neutral and
ex-enemy States to the United Nations, the United States Delegation had put
forward a proposal which would permit the Polish Provisional Government to
take over, on a provisional basis pending final determination of their western
frontier in the peace settlement, the administration of the territory in the
eastern part of pre-war Germany to which they were laying claim. . .[2]

MR. BEVIN said that he would like to know more precisely what was
involved in this proposal for provisional administration of this territory by
the Polish Provisional Government.[3] Thus, was it proposed that the administration of this territory, which was within the Soviet zone of occupation,
should be handed over entirely to the Polish Provisional Government? Would
all Soviet troops be withdrawn from this area?[4] What assurances could be
given that the Polish Provisional Government would be enabled to bring into
force at an early date the conditions envisaged in paragraph 4 of the agreed
statement on the Polish question (P. (Terminal) 23)?[5]

Mr. Bevin said that he had received representatives of the Polish
Provisional Government that morning and had discussed some of these question
questions with them.[6] All these points were of great importance from his
point of view, as he would have to defend in the British Parliament any change
of responsibility for this territory, and Parliament would be greatly influenced
by the account which he was able to give of what changes were actually going
to take place in this territory as a result of the decision now proposed by the
United States Delegation. The Polish representatives had assured him that it
was their firm intention to hold free and unfettered elections on the basis of

1. For the U.S. minutes, F.R.U.S. Potsdam, II, pp. 518–20; for the Soviet minutes,
Soviet protocols, 275–8.
2. See below, No. 149.
3. According to the U.S. and Soviet minutes, Bevin also stated that his instructions were
to stand for the Eastern Neisse.
4. Stalin replied in discussion that all Soviet troops would have been withdrawn already,
if the area had not lain on Soviet lines of communication to Germany.
5. The promise to hold free elections.
6. For these conversations F.O. 371. U6197/3128/70, pp. 307–15. In a private conversation with Bevin on 31 July, Mikołajczyk had outlined his plans for the future and had
stated that 'the real fight for the independence of Poland was now taking place in
Poland itself' (p. 311). He argued that the departure of the Red Army and the N.K.V.D.
was essential and that free elections could only take place if there was unrestricted
expression of opinion by all political parties. The satisfaction of Poland's territorial
aspirations in the west was essential both for economic reasons and to deprive the
communists of the argument that the west was hostile to Poland. Mikołajczyk expressed
similar views in two memoranda to Harriman (F.R.U.S. Potsdam, II, No. 1136, 7).

universal suffrage and secret ballot, under the 1921 Constitution, and that it was their aim to do so not later than the early part of 1946, provided that conditions were established which made it possible to hold such elections. They had assured him that they intended to give full facilities to the press. They would also ensure freedom of religion throughout their country. A further point in which the British Government were deeply concerned was the repatriation of Poles from abroad, not only civilians but also members of the Polish forces; and he had asked the Polish representatives for an undertaking that Poles returning to Poland would receive exactly the same treatment as Poles already resident in Poland.

Mr. Bevin said that he observed from the memorandum by the United States Delegation that it was proposed that the area under discussion should not be considered part of the Soviet zone of occupation. He understood that, although this area would come under Polish administration, it would remain under the jurisdiction of the Control Council for Germany. If it were proposed to exclude the area from this jurisdiction, it would presumably be necessary to obtain the agreement of the French, who were members of the Control Council. . .[7]

7. When agreement on the U.S. proposal was reached, it was also resolved that each of the three governments should at once inform the French.

No. 149

Communiqué of the Potsdam Conference (Extracts)
2 August 1945
F.R.U.S. Potsdam, II, pp. 1579–80

The Conference considered questions relating to the Polish Provisional Government and the western boundary of Poland.

On the Polish Provisional Government of National Unity they defined their attitude in the following statement:

A. (As in No. 146).

B. The following agreement was reached on the western frontier of Poland:

In conformity with the agreement on Poland reached at the Crimea Conference the three Heads of Government have sought the opinion of the Polish Provisional Government of National Unity in regard to the accession of territory in the north and west which Poland should receive. The President of the National Council of Poland and members of the Polish Provisional Government of National Unity have been received at the Conference and have fully presented their views. The three Heads of Government reaffirm their opinion that the final delimitation of the western frontier of Poland should await the peace settlement.

The three Heads of Government agree that, pending the final determination of Poland's western frontier, the former German territories east of a line running from the Baltic Sea immediately west of Swinemunde, and thence along the Oder River to the confluence of the western Neisse River and along the western Neisse to the Czechoslovak frontier, including that portion of East Prussia not placed under the administration of the Union of Soviet Socialist Republics in accordance with the understanding reached at this conference and including the area of the former free city of Danzig, shall be under the administration of the Polish State and for such purposes should not be considered as part of the Soviet zone of occupation in Germany.